WORKS ISSUED BY

THE HAKLUYT SOCIETY

A REGIMENT FOR THE SEA
BY
WILLIAM BOURNE

SECOND SERIES
No. CXXI

ISSUED FOR 1961

HAKLUYT SOCIETY

PATRON:
H.R.H. THE DUKE OF GLOUCESTER, K.G., P.C., K.T., K.P.

COUNCIL AND OFFICERS, 1962

PRESIDENT
Sir ALAN BURNS, G.C.M.G.

VICE-PRESIDENTS
J. N. L. BAKER, Esq., M.A., B.Litt.   Professor E. G. R. TAYLOR, D.Sc.
JAMES A. WILLIAMSON, Esq., D.Lit.   Professor D. B. QUINN

COUNCIL (WITH DATE OF ELECTION)

W. E. D. ALLEN, Esq., F.S.A. (1961)
Professor C. F. BECKINGHAM (1958)
Professor C. R. BOXER, F.B.A. (1960)
G. R. CRONE, Esq., M.A. (1961)
E. S. DE BEER, Esq., D.Litt. (1961)
Professor G. S. GRAHAM (1960)
Sir HARRY LUKE, K.C.M.G., D.Litt. (1961)
F. B. MAGGS, Esq., F.S.A. (1962)
J. W. S. MARR, Esq. (1960)

G. P. B. NAISH, Esq. (1960)
J. H. PARRY, Esq., Ph.D. (1962)
Royal Geographical Society (General Sir JAMES MARSHALL-CORNWALL)
Miss ALWYN RUDDOCK, Ph.D., F.S.A. (1962)
Lieut.-Cdr. D.W. WATERS, R.N. (1959)
Sir RICHARD WINSTEDT, K.B.E., C.M.G., F.B.A. (1959)
D. P. J. WOOD, Esq., Ph.D. (1959)

TRUSTEES
J. N. L. BAKER, Esq., M.A., B.Litt.   E. W. BOVILL, Esq., F.S.A.
Sir GILBERT LAITHWAITE, G.C.M.G., K.C.B., K.C.I.E., C.S.I., Hon. LL.D.

TREASURER
J. N. L. BAKER, Esq., M.A., B.Litt.

HON. SECRETARIES
R. A. SKELTON, Esq., B.A., F.S.A., F.R.Hist.S., British Museum, London, W.C.1
Miss EILA M. J. CAMPBELL, M.A., F.S.A., Birkbeck College, London, W.C.1

HON. SECRETARIES FOR OVERSEAS

Australia: G. D. RICHARDSON, Esq.
Canada: Professor J. B. BIRD
New Zealand: C. R. H. TAYLOR, Esq., M.A.
South Africa: DOUGLAS VARLEY, Esq.
U.S.A.: W. M. WHITEHILL, Esq., Ph.D., F.S.A.

PUBLISHER AND AGENT FOR SALE AND DISTRIBUTION OF VOLUMES
CAMBRIDGE UNIVERSITY PRESS, Bentley House, 200 Euston Road, London, N.W. 1.

The annual subscription to the Society is £2 2s. sterling ($6 U.S. currency) payable on 1st January. There is no entrance fee.

Members are entitled to all volumes issued by the Society (other than those of the Extra Series) during the period of their membership. As a rule, two volumes are produced each year.

Applications for membership may be addressed to any of the Honorary Secretaries. No proposer is necessary.

¶ A REGIMENT
for the Sea:
Conteyning moſt profitable Rules, *Mathematical experiences, and perfect* knovvledge of Nauigation, for all Coaſtes and *Countreys: moſt needefull and neceſſarie for all Seafaring* men and Trauellers, as Pilotes, Mariners, Marchants. &c. Exactly deuiſed and made by VVilliam Bourne.

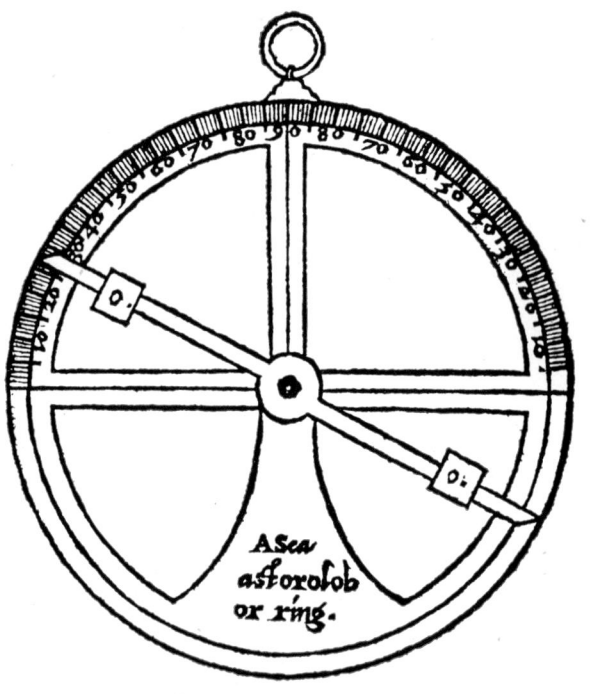

A Sea aſtorolob or ring.

¶ Imprinted at London by Thomas Hacket, and are to be ſolde at his ſhop in the Royall Exchaunge, at the Signe of the Greene Dragon.

Fig. 1. Title-page of *A Regiment for the Sea*, by William Bourne, 1574

A REGIMENT FOR THE SEA

and other writings on navigation

by

WILLIAM BOURNE

of Gravesend, a gunner

(c. 1535–1582)

Edited by

E. G. R. TAYLOR

*Emeritus Professor of Geography in the
University of London*

CAMBRIDGE
Published for the Hakluyt Society
AT THE UNIVERSITY PRESS
1963

PUBLISHED BY
THE SYNDICS OF THE CAMBRIDGE UNIVERSITY PRESS

Bentley House, 200 Euston Road, London N.W. 1
American Branch: 32 East 57th Street, New York 22, N.Y.

©

THE HAKLUYT SOCIETY
1963

*Printed in Great Britain
by Robert MacLehose & Company Limited
at the University Press, Glasgow*

PREFACE

THE interest taken today by so many people in the early history of science and technology suggested to the present editor that it would be an appropriate moment to publish among the Hakluyt Society's volumes what is perhaps the earliest technical manual written by an Englishman. The Council of the Society agreed, for it was a Seaman's Manual, fitted therefore to accompany and illuminate the histories of great sea-voyages with which the name of the Society is associated. Moreover the writer of the Manual was a contemporary of Richard Hakluyt himself, and although there is no evidence that they ever met, the great historiographer shared with William Bourne a strong and constant urge to see England great upon the sea.

As quite a young man Bourne, 'student in the mathematics', attracted the attention of Sir William Cecil, a statesman whose eagerness to encourage technical advance in this country his biographers unfortunately ignore or brush aside. And of course our author met Dr Dee, not indeed as an astrologer, but as a fellow enthusiast for trained seamanship, and the first to forecast a British overseas empire.

The book which forms the core of this volume, the *Regiment for the Sea*, is not without its romantic fringes. Bourne wrote as he spoke, so that out of his instruction book for sailors emerges a picture of the man himself, serious, reliable, patriotic, and with an inborn impulse to teach. A middle-class Elizabethan, of whom we meet too few, he also found time to serve on the town council, to keep an inn, and be a careful father to seven boys.

The editor wishes to express her deep gratitude to Mr R. A. Skelton, Honorary Secretary of the Society, for his unsparing help in preparing this book for the Press. Sincere thanks are also due to many others who have answered inquiries or supplied material, among them Lieut-Commander D. W. Waters, Mr

PREFACE

G. R. Crone, Dr Helen Wallis, Miss E. M. J. Campbell, Brigadier O. F. G. Hogg, O.B.E., the Borough Librarian of Gravesend (Mr E. N. Moore), and Lieut-Commander Michael Godfrey.

She is also indebted to Lord Salisbury, who courteously allowed the reproduction of two maps from the archives at Hatfield House (Figs. 3 and 15); to Messrs Methuen & Co. and Messrs Hollis & Carter, who kindly lent blocks; and to the owners of originals whose permission to reproduce is acknowledged in the list of illustrations.

Finally, mention must be made of Mrs S. J. Arthur, Mrs M. Ibbett and Mrs A. May, who expended so much care on the excellent typing of three difficult texts and miscellaneous manuscript material.

E. G. R. Taylor

RALPHS RIDE,
BRACKNELL

Easter 1961

CONTENTS

PREFACE	page v
LIST OF ILLUSTRATIONS	ix
ACKNOWLEDGMENTS	x
BIBLIOGRAPHY	xi
GENERAL INTRODUCTION	xiii

★ ★ ★

I *An Almanacke and Prognostication for three yeares ... nowe newlye added vnto my late Rulles of Nauigation*, 1571

Editor's Note	1
Text (edition of 1571)	23

II *A Regiment for the Sea*, 1574

Editor's Note	115
Text	135

III *A Regiment for the Sea*, 1580

Editor's Note	283
Texts: (i) The second Address 'To the Reader'	292
(ii) The textual additions	296
(iii) 'Hydrographicall Discourse' of the Passage to Cathay	301

IV *An almanacke & prognostication for x. yeeres*, 1581

Editor's Note	315
Text	321

★ ★ ★

APPENDIXES:

A. 'Canon Gubernauticus' by John Dee, 1558	415
B. The Wills of William Bourne (1573), and Dorothy Bourne (1582)	434
C. The Writings of William Bourne, c. 1565–1581: a Bibliography	439
INDEX	461

LIST OF ILLUSTRATIONS

1. Title-page of *A Regiment for the Sea*, by William Bourne, 1574   *frontispiece*

2. From London to the Medway: detail of Symonson's map of Kent, 1596   *facing page* xiii

3. Gravesend and Tilbury Bulwark: inset of William Borough's MS chart of the Thames, 1596   *facing page* xviii
   Hatfield House maps, I. 56.

4. William Bourne's surveying instrument   *page* xxx
   B.M., Sloane MS 3651, fol. 65.

5. Bourne's triangulation round Gravesend and Tilbury   *page* xxxi
   B.M., Sloane MS 3651, fol. 68v.

6. 'The plat off ye Ryuer of Tames', by William Bourne   *facing page* xxxii
   B.M., Sloane MS 3651, fol. 74v.

7. Tail-piece of *An Almanacke and Prognostication for three yeares*, by William Bourne, 1571   *page* 114
   The tail-piece is the printer's device of Thomas Purfoot.

8. Edward Fiennes, Lord Clinton and Saye, Lord High Admiral, 1562   *facing page* 115
   Oil-painting in the Ashmolean Museum, Oxford. Lord Clinton, created Earl of Lincoln in 1572, was Lord High Admiral 1558–85.

9. The Lord High Admiral's flagship   *page* 116
   Woodcut on verso of title-page of *A Regiment for the Sea* 1574; reprinted on title-page of subsequent editions. The galleon is perhaps the *Foresight*; see p. 115, n. 2.

10. The seaman's instruments   *facing page* 119
    Title-page of *The Mariners Mirrour* (London, 1588), engraved by T. de Bry.

LIST OF ILLUSTRATIONS

11. Log and log-line, and sand-glass *page* 127
    From Samuel de Champlain, *Voyages* (Paris, 1632).

12. Chart of the north-east Atlantic by Thomas Hood, engraved by Augustine Ryther, 1592 *facing page* 130
    Accompanying *The Mariners guide*, added by Hood to his edition (1592) of Bourne's *A Regiment for the Sea*.

13. 'Sir Humfray Gylbert knight his chart', drawn *c.* 1582, perhaps by Dr John Dee *facing page* 286
    Original in the Free Library of Philadelphia. The polar projection illustrates Bourne's contention that the shortest way to Cathay lay across the Pole.

14. George Best's chart of the North-west, with Frobisher's Straits *facing page* 289
    From G. Best, *A True Discourse of the late Voyage of Discovery* (1578).

15. Upnor Castle and the Medway: detail from an anonymous MS chart, *c.* 1580 *facing page* 315
    Hatfield House maps, I. 47.

16. Tail-piece from John Wight's edition of *A Regiment for the Sea* (1580) *facing page* 458

ACKNOWLEDGMENTS

Reproductions have been made by courteous permission of the owners of originals, as follows: the Royal Institution of Naval Architects (1, 9); the Trustees of the British Museum (2, 4-6, 14); the Most Honourable the Marquess of Salisbury (3, 15); the Master and Fellows of Magdalene College, Cambridge (12); the Director of the Ashmolean Museum, Oxford (7); the Trustees of the Free Library of Philadelphia (13).

Blocks were kindly lent by Messrs Methuen & Co. (Figs. 4, 5, from E. G. R. Taylor, *Tudor Geography 1485-1583*, London 1930) and by Messrs Hollis & Carter (Figs. 7, 12, from D. W. Waters, *The Art of Navigation in England in Elizabethan and Early Stuart Times*, London 1958; and Figs. 10, 11, from E. G. R. Taylor, *The Haven-finding Art*, London 1956).

BIBLIOGRAPHY

AVERALL, William. *A wonderful and strange news which happened in Suffolk and Essex*. London, 1583.
BARLOW, William. *The Nauigator's Supply*. London, 1597.
BEST, George. *A true Discourse of the late Voyage of Discovery*. London, 1578.
CHENEY, C. R. (ed.) *Handbook of Dates for Students of English History*. London, Royal Historical Society, 1955.
CHUMOLSKY, T. A. (ed.) *Tres roteiros desconhecidos de Ahmad ibn-Mādjid*. Lisboa, 1960.
CRUDEN, R. P. *The History of Gravesend and of the Port of London*. London, 1843.
CUNINGHAM, William. *The Cosmographical Glasse*. London, 1559.
DEE, John. [Preface to the English Euclid.] London, 1570.
DIGGES, Leonard. *A Generall Prognostication*. London, 1553.
— —. *A Boke named Tectonicon*. London, 1556.
DIGGES, Leonard and Thomas. *Pantometria*. London, 1571.
DIGGES, Thomas. *Alae seu Scalae Mathematicae*. London, 1573.
— —. *Stratioticos*. London, 1590. (Second edition.)
EDEN, Richard. *The Arte of Nauigation ... Written in the Spanysh Tongue by Marten Curtes*. London, 1561.
— —. *A very Necessarie Booke concerning Nauigation*. London, 1578.
GILBERT, Humfrey. *A Discourse for a new Passage to Cataia*. London, 1576.
GREG, Sir W. W., and BOSWELL, E. (ed.) *Records of the Court of the Stationers' Company, 1576–1602*. London, Bibliographical Society, 1930.
HAKLUYT, Richard. *The Principal Nauigations ... of the English Nation*. London, 1598–1600.
HALLIWELL, J. O. *Rara Mathematica*. London, 1839.
HARVEY, Gabriel. *Pierces Supererogation*. London, 1593.
LEVITIUS, Cyprianus. *Ephemerides, 1556–1606*. Augsburg, 1557.
NORMAN, Robert. *The Safeguard of Saylers, or Great Rutter*. London, 1584.

BIBLIOGRAPHY

NUNES, Pedro. *Tratado em defensam da carta de marear*. Lisboa, 1537.
PECK, Francis. *Desiderata Curiosa . . . A new edition*. London, 1779.
PEELE, James. *Maner and fourme how to kepe a perfecte reconynge*. London, 1553.
RASTELL, John. *A new interlude and a mery of the nature of the iiij. elements*. London, 1519.
RATHBORNE, Aaron. *The Surveyor*. London, 1616.
SHEPHERD'S KALENDAR. *Heere Beginneth the Kalender of Sheepehards*. London, 1560.
TAYLOR, E. G. R. *Tudor Geography 1485-1583*. London, 1930.
——. 'Master Hore's voyage of 1536'. *Geogr. Journal*, LXXVII (1931), 469-70.
——. 'Jean Rotz and the variation of the Compass, 1542' [and] 'Jean Rotz and the marine chart, 1542'. *Journal of the Inst. of Navigation*, VII (1954), 9-15, 136-143.
——. *The Mathematical Practitioners of Tudor and Stuart England*. London, 1954.
——. *The Haven-finding Art*. London, 1956.
——, (ed.) *A Brief Summe of Geography, by Roger Barlow*. London, Hakluyt Society, 1932.
—— (ed.) *The Troublesome Voyage of Captain Edward Fenton, 1582-3*. London, Hakluyt Society, 1959.
WATERS, D. W. *The Art of Navigation in England in Elizabethan and Early Stuart Times*. London, 1958.

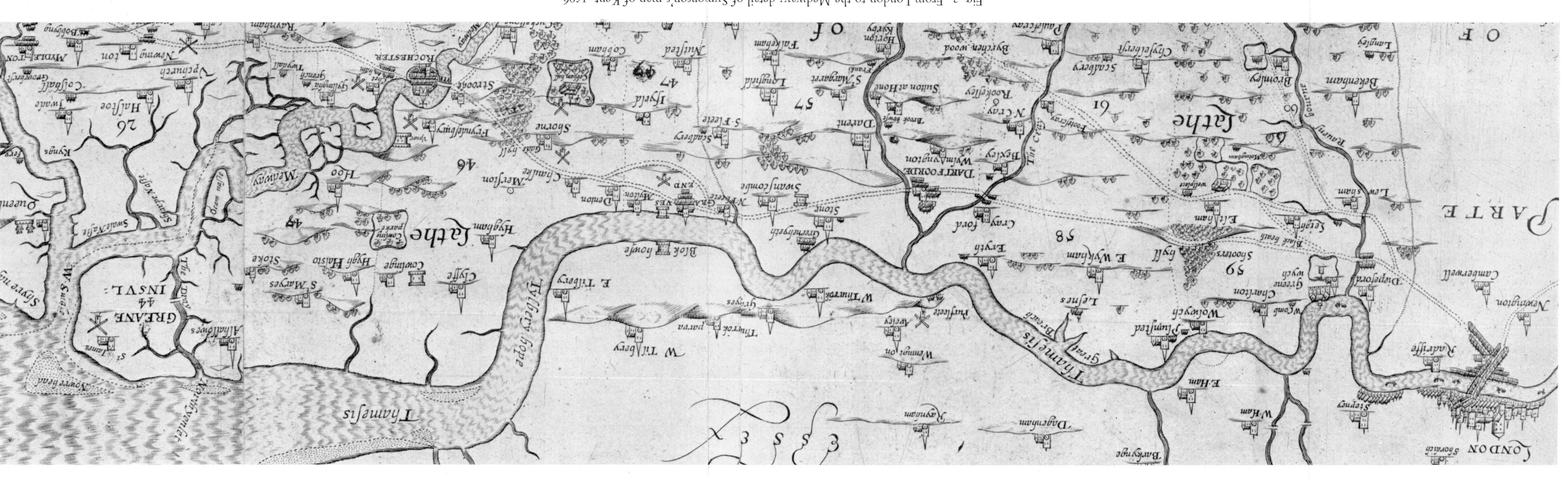

Fig. 2. From London to the Medway: detail of Symonson's map of Kent, 1596

GENERAL INTRODUCTION

WILLIAM BOURNE was a remarkable man. Born during the latter half of the reign of Henry VIII, he was to emerge during that of the first Elizabeth as the successful writer of a new type of text-book, one intended for a new type of reader. Neither a scholar nor of gentle birth, he intruded into the field of authorship which was still generally regarded as the preserve of the scholar and the gentleman. Scientific books in particular, based as they still were on ancient learning, were expected to appear only from the university, and to be read only by those who were proficient in Latin. Yet here was a Gravesend inn-keeper (for such was Bourne's status) who produced, and dedicated to various noblemen,[1] a whole series of technical manuals written in English. This daring behaviour naturally exposed him to much unkindly and scornful criticism from gentlemanly and scholarly authors. He was hurt by this, but eagerly excused himself. He was only a 'simple man', he declared, and his books were not intended for the 'learned sort'. They were meant only for 'meaner men' to read, men who at present were utterly ignorant.[2]

Bourne addressed himself, in fact, in the first instance to the skilled artisans and master-craftsmen who were his own friends and neighbours. These were the men whom, because of his own mathematical bent, because, too, of a strong personal impulse, he was so eager to instruct. And he justified himself by recalling 'the opinion and sayings of the sage and aunoient Writers, that one man should be an instructer to another'; a tag he had possibly picked up at school.

[1] His principal patron was Edward Fiennes, Lord Clinton (1512–85), who was first appointed Lord Admiral in 1550-1554, and created Earl of Lincoln in 1572 (Fig. 7).

[2] In a manuscript c. 1573 (see below, p. xxvi), he wrote: 'To ye gentell reder: I praye you hold me excused, I being alltogether ignorante, lacking the capacitye bothe of knowledge and experience have taken upon me . . . to open any scyence.'

The social changes, particularly the increase of literacy (fostered by the grammar schools) and the many advances in technology, which characterized Tudor England, had created the need for a new class of mathematical books. These had to be simply written, knowledgeable, and above all practical. Yet in this country books of such a character were up till then wanting. They were of a kind that neither the scholar, isolated in the narrow circle of the university, nor the cultured gentleman, secluded in his library, had the necessary gifts and experience to write. Their potential readers, the master shipwright, the ship-master, the master-gunner, for example, were on the other hand the very people whom Bourne met, and knew, and saw at work, every day. Such men were remote indeed from the literary world, but here was an individual who believed that he could give them the particular knowledge that they needed — mathematical rules instead of the customary rule of thumb, academic learning couched in homely style to correct or supplement their traditional lore.

A demand for new writing in the vernacular had already been voiced in England quite early in the sixteenth century. It came from the humanist circle gathered round Sir Thomas More. His brother-in-law John Rastell had expressed it pungently in his *New Interlude*:

> ... divers pregnant wits be in this land
> As well of noblemen as of mean estate
> Which nothing but English can understand
> Then if cunning Latin books were translate
> Into English, well correct and approbate,
> All subtle science in English might be learned.

Whether in direct response to this appeal or no, Dr Recorde, the Welsh scholar and university teacher from Tenby, did publish a valuable set of text-books in English between 1542 and 1557. These works made it possible for any intelligent man with the ability to apply himself to master a group of subjects which are basic to all science: arithmetic, plane geometry, and the geometry of the sphere. The books appeared during the years in which Bourne was growing up to manhood, and he undoubtedly read and mastered them. And in addition, like many other middle-class youths, he was powerfully influenced by the first English writer to attack the problem of mathematics for the artisan — Leonard Digges.

Digges was a gentleman of East Kent and a university man. He is first heard of expounding geometrical principles (with practical demonstrations drawn from gunnery), among a group of friends on the bulwarks of Calais in 1542. Many people must already have begun asking the question: why should we English have to employ an Italian engineer to build our fortresses? Or, why must we engage a Spanish, or a Portuguese, or a French pilot to take our ships across the ocean? Or again, why should we have to buy our marine charts in Lisbon, our globes and maps in the Low Countries? Digges had realized that the answer was the same in every case. These foreigners knew how to apply geometry to mensuration, they could read mathematical tables, they could construct and handle mathematical instruments. But our people knew nothing of such things. The instructions for carrying out mathematical practices, the methods of computing mathematical tables, the designs for making mathematical instruments, all were as Digges phrased it, 'locked up in strange tongues'.[1] This had, of course, been no hindrance to Leonard himself. As a scholar, he could read the books of the German Peter Apian, of the Italian Nicholas Tartaglia, of the Fleming Gemma Frisius, and of the Frenchman Orontius Finaeus. And that whether they wrote in Latin or each in his native tongue. All these men were already teach-

[1] William Cuningham was to write his *Cosmographical Glasse* (1559) in English, and he dedicated it to the Earl of Leicester. Robert Dudley very probably was not at home in Latin, but as a young man he had shown himself very interested in applied mathematics. Cuningham's style, however, was unsuited to the artisan reader, who could hardly see himself as Spondaeus conversing learnedly with Philonicus, although there was much that was relevant to Navigation in the book.

ing their compatriots ways of applying mathematics to gunnery, to navigation, to surveying, to cartography and cosmography, to horology. Furthermore they all concerned themselves directly with the design and construction of mathematical instruments. It was ironical that when Leonard Digges had succeeded in putting some of the more elementary parts of their teaching into two small English books — called respectively *A Prognostication* (1553) and *Tectonicon* (1556) — he had to employ a Flemish immigrant to print them, as well as to make the instruments he there described. This man was Thomas Gemini,[1] best known perhaps as a fine engraver, but also practising as an instrument-maker and cartographer. Digges's career, unfortunately, was brought to a close in 1554, when he joined in Wyatt's rebellion. He was attainted, deprived of his estates, and exiled. But his *Prognostication* (which included a Kalendar) continued to be reprinted through the century. William Bourne studied *Tectonicon* carefully, and concluded that he had something to add to it. But as everything that he wrote was closely bound up with his personal circumstances, these must first be examined.

Gravesend, where William was born, lived and died, had long been an active and important port both for river and sea traffic as it still is today.[2] Situated on the southern or Kentish bank of the river Thames, it lies 26 miles below London Bridge and 21 miles above the Nore Lightship where the wide estuary begins. Not very far up-river there then stood Greenwich Palace, where Queen Elizabeth held Court, while about ten miles downstream was the mouth of the river Medway, within which the Royal Navy lay at anchor, guarded by Upnor Castle. Much of the lower Thames is bordered by marshes which until reclaimed were liable to flood, but here and there the compact, porous chalk, of which the Kentish Downs are built, comes down to

---

[1] E. G. R. Taylor, *Mathematical Practitioners*, p. 165.
[2] R. P. Cruden, *The History of the Town of Gravesend* (1843). The author reproduces all the surviving documents in which William Bourne's name is mentioned, and his book is a main source for the activities of Gravesend described below.

the water's edge, and even reappears on the opposite Essex bank of the river. At such points, there is well-drained land rising above flood-level, and since earliest times this firm ground has provided convenient sites for settlement. It is on one of these 'rises' that Gravesend was built, just below Erith marshes, with the two Tilbury villages facing it across the river, also built on the chalk outcrop.[1] Behind Gravesend the old Roman road between Dover and London passes within a mile or two, and as, prior to the making of the toll-roads, the safest and most comfortable way of travel was by water, much incoming traffic was transferred to the river at this point. Similarly, outgoing traffic from London only left the Thames at Gravesend where it took the road. The much-frequented stretch of water between Gravesend and Billingsgate Stairs in the City of London was known as the Long Ferry. Ever since mediaeval days traffic over it had been provided by a carefully organized service of barges or wherries. These vessels went up on the flood-tide and came down on the ebb, and were consequently known as Tide Barges. The daily tidal time-lag meant a daily change of time-table, and departures were cried in the streets. The people of Gravesend must have been sharply aware of the 'age of the moon', which governs the hour of the tides. This was certainly the case with William Bourne, as his books demonstrate.

The running of the public barges was reserved to the citizens of Gravesend, and the ownership of a 'Tide', or place in the rota of sailings was a valuable property which was passed on from father to son, as in Bourne's case. While no poaching was allowed on the general traffic in passengers and goods to which the tide-barge owners had the first right, there were also wherries and tilt-boats for private hire. The latter provided luxury transport for the nobility and gentry when they used the Long Ferry.

But river traffic was not the only business centred on

[1] See Symonson's map of 1596 (Fig. 2).

Gravesend. The port was reckoned the last 'creek' of the Port of London, and here all the customs formalities had to be gone through by the masters of ships putting out to sea. The 'searchers' came aboard to examine the holds, and the 'cockets' of relevant ship's papers were handed over to them for inspection. At Gravesend, besides, the master had to send to Dover or Harwich for the Trinity House pilot whom he was obliged to employ to take him out of the estuary — a stretch of water remarkable for its intricate channels and shifting sandbanks. Since it might also be necessary to wait on wind and weather, it can be well understood that ships outward bound were anchored before Gravesend for periods from at least a couple of days up to several weeks. As a consequence the town was full of ale-houses and inns where the sailors spent their waiting time, while the ship's officers and petty officers would bring their women-folk so far before they said goodbye.

A famous occasion (described by Richard Hakluyt[1]) which William Bourne must have witnessed as a young man, was the departure of the third Muscovy expedition in 1556. Sebastian Cabot, then Governor of the Muscovy Company, brought a party of ladies and gentlemen down to Gravesend to look over the *Searchthrift*, a pinnace that was being taken to explore the Arctic shore of Russia that summer. Stephen Borough was her master designate, while his brother William was to serve as mate. Richard Chancellor, discoverer of the White Sea route, was Captain and Chief Pilot of the four 'great ships' of the fleet. It was to prove his last voyage. The Boroughs entertained the party on the pinnace, and afterwards Cabot gave them all a return banquet ashore at the Christopher Inn. This was the occasion when Sebastian astonished everybody by joining in the dancing, for he was a very old man. And like Chancellor he was soon to die.

It can hardly be doubted that William Bourne had also been among the spectators, three years earlier, at the setting out of

---

[1] Richard Hakluyt, *Principall Navigations* (1589), p. 311.

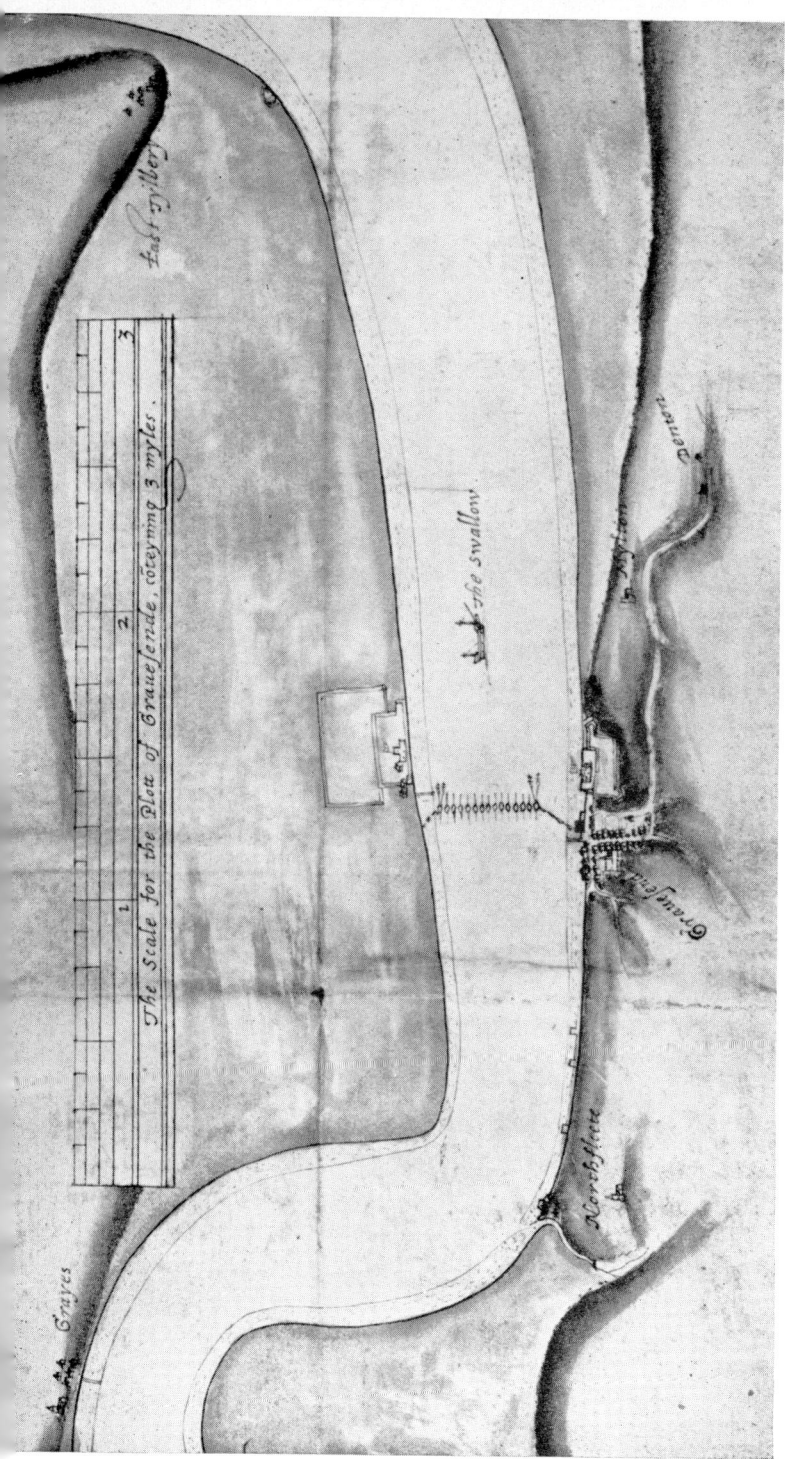

Fig. 3. Gravesend and Tilbury Bulwark: inset of William Borough's MS chart of the Thames, 1596

Hatfield House maps, I, 56

the very first fleet bound for the North-east Passage. The ships had anchored before Gravesend after being towed in state past Greenwich Palace, where the young King Edward, for whom the spectacle had been arranged, actually lay dying. Chancellor and the two Boroughs were all serving in the *Edward Bonaventure*, but the younger brother was then still an apprentice before the mast. Some twenty-odd years later Bourne's own step-son was to leave Gravesend to sail for the North-west Passage with Frobisher. If William himself never went to sea there was yet little he did not know about the ways and needs of sailors.

But ships and sailors, customs officers and pilots, shipwrights and ship-chandlers — the whole business of the river and the sea — still did not add up to the whole sum of influences brought to bear on a young man growing up at Gravesend. Where the town stood the Thames was barely eight hundred yards wide, with a firm footing on either bank. Henry VIII chose it as the site for the fortifications designed to defend London against attack from the sea. Bulwarks, i.e. small forts and ramparts, were built in 1539 in Tilbury parish in Essex and also at Gravesend. The small permanent garrisons attached to them[1] required to be supplemented by the citizen soldiery in times of emergency.[2] The bulwarks were mounted with cannon, and William Bourne had trained and prepared himself to do service as a gunner — 'your poore gunner' as he describes himself to Sir William Winter, the Queen's Master of Ordnance.[3] He lived, in fact, in the immediate company of

---

[1] According to an early (undated) document of Queen Elizabeth's reign setting out the Queen's *Annual Expence*, the establishment at the two Tilbury forts was two captains, two porters, six soldiers, five grooms and an unspecified number of gunners. At Gravesend there were a captain and porter, two soldiers and five grooms. A gunner's pay was sixpence a day. A captain had one shilling. The document is printed in Francis Peck's *Desiderata Curiosa* (1779).

[2] In the Gravesend Register of Deaths a Mr Jasper May is described as a shipwright and 'one of the Gunners of Gravesend Bulwark' (Cruden, p. 211).

[3] William Winter (1525?–1589), Master of Ordnance of the Navy 1557, knighted 1573.

soldiers as well as of sailors, and both groups, to his mind, were urgently in need of professional instruction. Such instruction he himself, as a 'Student of the Mathematicks', was able to provide, and indeed had a duty to provide, so he believed.

Of Bourne's early life little is known, save for the cardinal fact that he was born into the small group (comprising little more than fifty individuals) who were reckoned the 'capital inhabitants' of Gravesend. His father, John Bourne, was the owner of house-property which he remaindered to his unborn grandsons. He died in 1560, and two years later, when Gravesend received its first Charter of incorporation, William was appointed one of the jurats, or town councillors. His name appears in several later lists of jurats (e.g. in 1568 and 1573), while in 1571–2 he served a term as port-reeve, the equivalent of mayor. His mother was still living in 1573, and it appears probable that he was an only son, born about 1535. He died early in 1582,[1] but the fact that his very brief Will[2] was drawn up in 1573 suggests that he suffered a serious illness at that time, since a Will was usually made only in immediate expectation of death or before some dangerous journey.

As his Will indicates, Bourne was by that date a married man, the father of four little boys, about whose schooling he was concerned. He had chosen as his wife a Mistress Dorothy Beare, a local widow, who was apparently also well-to-do. She was already the mother of three well-grown sons, whose names later appear among the 'capital inhabitants' of Gravesend. The two elder, Samuel and John Beare, were each in turn to serve terms as port-reeve, as did Bourne's own son Richard when he came to manhood. Like Bourne himself the Beares had an interest in the Long Ferry, while the youngest brother, James, was apprenticed to the sea, where he had a long and

---

[1] The Gravesend Register has the entries: '1582 March 22nd was William Bourne a householder buried,' and 'Dec. 13th was Dorothie Bourne, widow, buried' (Cruden, p. 212).
[2] See below, p. 435.

distinguished career.¹ Since he was old enough to hold the office of Master of a ship in 1577, while his brother John had been made a freeman of Gravesend in 1572, it is reasonable to conclude that Mistress Beare's first family were born not much before or after 1550. Her marriage to Bourne can hardly have been before 1565, for none of the younger children had come of age before they lost both parents at a few month's interval in 1582. The only daughter, Marie, had not been born in 1573 when William made his Will, and this little girl was her mother's first concern when on her death-bed she dictated her own Will to the curate of Gravesend.

It is from Dorothy Bourne's Will² that we learn something of the style and comfort in which the family lived. They kept several servants. The best bed was hung with silk curtains, there was silver plate for the table; besides a housewifely store of linen, and some good pieces of furniture. A number of handsome garments of her late husband's, besides her own rings, went to Dorothy's grown sons, while her personal clothing was to be divided among her three daughters-in-law. Little Marie was placed in the custody of John Beare, who was appointed executor of the Will. The overseer was Edward Darbyshire. This man must have been the most prominent of Gravesend's citizens. He was three times port-reeve and lived in what was described as a 'mansion-house'. No doubt he was a family friend. The 'capital inhabitants' of the port formed a close-knit intermarrying group. Bourne's share in the Long Ferry took the form of two 'half-Tides' in which his partners (owning the

---

¹ James Beare died in 1609. His monument (now destroyed) in Gravesend Church showed five sons and five daughters, and his epitaph (Cruden, p. 221) ran:

> 'After much wery sayling, worthie Bere
> Arryved this quiet port, and harbers here.
> As skilfully in honestie he brought
> His humaine Vessel home, as he was thought
> Equall with any that by Card or Starr,
> Took out and brought again his Barke from far.
> So let him rest in quiet. . . .'

² See below, p. 436.

other 'half-Tides') were two cousins, Clegant and Warde, whose family names appear several times in contemporary Gravesend records. Since the Tides were passed from parent to child, there is a suggestion here of a common grandparent.

That William Bourne was an inn-keeper we learn from the appearance of his name in a list of persons fined for small breaches of the regulations under which beer was sold. It was during his year of office as port-reeve. The same list contains the name of William Morris, at whose inn the farewell party took place in 1582 when Captain Luke Ward sailed from Gravesend to join Captain Edward Fenton on the voyage intended for Cathay by the Cape Route.[1] The date was only two months after Bourne's death, and the chaplain of the fleet, Richard Madox, carried a copy of his *Regiment*, the book that is printed here.

How and when William Bourne began his career as a mathematical instructor and writer (a 'practitioner' as they called themselves), must be largely a matter of inference. There was rarely any mathematical teaching in the grammar schools. Boys intended for business were sent to the writing-master, from whom, in addition to acquiring a clerkly hand they learnt simple arithmetic and the keeping of accounts. Such was the training which the Muscovy Company provided for little Nicholas Chancellor after his father, Richard, was drowned in 1556. A successful master often put his teaching notes together into a published book, although some went no farther than selling hand-copied sets to their pupils. It was for long the custom for them to refer to these pupils as their 'friends', so that it was not unusual for an author to say that his book appeared owing to the persuasion of his friends.[2] The artifice

---

[1] See E. G. R. Taylor (ed.), *The Troublesome Voyage of Captain Edward Fenton* (Hakluyt Society, 1959).

[2] In the preface to his *Maner and fourme how to kepe a perfecte reconyng* (1553), James Peele writes: '... many which have liked this my peines and diligence herein, have required me, that every good thyng, the further it goeth, the better ... I therefore ... have endevoured (to my small powers) not only to satisfie the request of my said

GENERAL INTRODUCTION

was exposed by a blunt Scottish teacher, John Wilson, in 1714, who openly said that he produced his text-book 'for the genetlemen who attended my lessons'.

A writing master, of course, did not go far enough into mathematics to satisfy gentlemen who wanted to understand the military art — range-finding, tunnelling, or the use of siege-engines — nor could he serve the purposes of the country gentleman who desired an elaborate sun-dial or a scale-plan of his estates. Such a client called a 'mathematical practitioner' into his chamber, or even made one a member of his household, where he might also act as tutor. Thomas Digges publishing his late father's manuscript teaching manual under the title of *Pantometria*, recalled the 'conferences' on the subject matter which Leonard had held with Sir Nicholas Bacon to whom the printed book was now dedicated. John Dee, the intimate friend of Leonard Digges, was at about the same time teaching military mathematics to John Dudley, one of the Earl of Northumberland's sons, a young man whose early death in 1554 he was soon to deplore.[1]

The custom arose for such a mathematical practitioner to advertise his skill indirectly by publishing an '*Almanack and Prognostication*', as Leonard Digges did in 1553. Indeed by the early seventeenth century such Almanacs often contained advertisements openly soliciting pupils, and giving a résumé of the author's teaching syllabus. But in the sixteenth century, at least in Bourne's lifetime, this was not so. There was greater reticence. The ordinary public thought of the Almanac maker chiefly as an astrologer, a man who could be asked to name fortunate and unfortunate days for domestic and business

frendes, but also the greate lacke and nedefull instruction, whiche many have wanted in their accomptes'. Another well-known writing-master of the day was John Mellis, who lived 'at Mayes Gate, nie to Battle Bridge in the parish of Southwark', and was the author of *A Shorte & plaine Treatise of Arithmeticke in whole numbers*. A third was Humfrey Baker, who in 1558 translated *Les Canons et documens tresamples, touchant l'usage et practique des communs Almanacks* written by Oronce Finé for the instruction of the unlearned.

[1] E. G. R. Taylor, *Tudor Geography*, pp. 89, 191.

transactions, or could cast the horoscope of a child. Digges, however, although he defended astrology, took a step forward when he added to his *Prognostication* a number of Tables, notes, and diagrams likely to prove of special interest to seamen and artisans. Bourne followed this example when he published his first *Almanack and Prognostication* in 1567. He deprecated astrology but offered to the reader an addendum in the shape of *Serten Rules of Navigation* which in effect comprised a little Sea Manual. It is likely that he had begun to teach applied mathematics some years earlier, for the monthly Kalendar which he now printed was one which contained the movable feasts for 1564. The Almanac (as distinct from the Kalendar) gave the dates of the phases of the Moon through the months and was correct for the years 1571-3 (found in the second edition, of which alone complete copies have survived) and was presumably correct also for the years 1567-9 in the first of the two editions. In 1574 William 'put to print' (as it was expressed) his principal work, the *Regiment for the Sea*, which contained a new Kalendar, besides a number of Tables, for the years 1574-7. Subsequent editions carried the Tables on until 1580, when he prepared his second *Almanack and Prognostication*, which was for the ten years 1581-90. These three works — the two *Almanacks* and the *Regiment* — are here printed in full, and will presently be discussed in more detail.[1] Meanwhile a return will be made to a consideration of such biographical facts as can be learned from Bourne's other writings.

A manuscript pamphlet of his survives[2] which was written at the request of Lord Burghley, whom he there addresses under a title (Lord Treasurer) which was not appropriate until September 1572. Its subject was Optics, and in particular the properties and capacities of mirrors and lenses. In it the writer states as his final conclusion that what Thomas Digges had claimed with regard to his father's experiments with perspec-

[1] Pp. 1, 135, and 321.
[2] British Museum, Lansdowne MS 121. Printed in J. O. Halliwell, *Rara Mathematica* (1839).

tive glasses was probably correct. Now the description which the younger Digges had given of Leonard's 'seeing at a distance' was to be found in the book called *Pantometria* which was published in 1571.[1] It seems likely, therefore, that Burghley's conference (his second one) with Bourne and his request for written information about reflecting glasses and lenses were the result of his reading this book. In his opening paragraphs Bourne declares that he had been unable to pay as much attention to optical experiments as Dr Dee and Thomas Digges had done partly because of his 'great charge of children'. This was a favourite excuse of the day for any remissness, but it adds weight to the suggested date 1572, since the writer then had his own four little boys to care for, while his three step-sons were just emerging into the adult world.

If this date is accepted, then an earlier conference with Lord Burghley, which is mentioned as having taken place seven years ago, can be put at about 1565. This had been the outcome (so Bourne says) of the great statesman's perusal of a little manuscript which the Gravesend inn-keeper had sent him. This paper (now lost) dealt with the buoyancy of water, for the fact that a ship lay a few inches higher in salt water than in fresh was one of great importance to seamen when (say) crossing a bar. It would naturally be observable when ships came into the Thames, since a ship was marked with a load-line. After this conference Bourne wrote what he called a 'little book of Static' (also lost), which dealt more widely with the measurement of a ship's capacity and displacement. This, he now said, had proved very useful to local shipwrights, which suggests that he had circulated written copies of it to 'friends'.

The book of static, further enlarged and improved, is next to be found as part of a comprehensive manuscript which Bourne prepared and dedicated to Lord Burghley at a date which

---

[1] 'My father ... hath by proportionall Glasses duely situate, in convenient angles not onely discovered things farre off....' The claim is repeated in much the same terms in the same writer's *Stratioticos* (1579).

cannot be later than 1573.[1] The formal Dedication to the Lord Treasurer under his full titles, the Preface to the Reader, the many illustrations, and the inclusion even of a rhymed head-piece and tail-piece,[2] all point to this manuscript having been prepared with an eye to the press. It was customary to offer a manuscript first of all to a patron, but in this case patronage (usually in the form of a monetary gift) was apparently not secured. The material of the work was therefore reorganized and divided into two separate books which the author in 1574 promised his readers they should have if they showed appreciation of the *Regiment for the Sea*. This proved to be forthcoming, for the *Regiment* [i.e. Rule] *for the Sea* was indeed welcome as providing a complete English seaman's manual. It embodied and improved upon the 'Rules' that had been attached to the *Almanack* of 1567 and that of 1571. As will presently appear, both *Rules* and *Regiment* sprang in part from Bourne's critical attitude towards an English translation of a Spanish sea-manual which had been published in 1561. For the moment, however, it may merely be noted that he must have been playing the role of instructor to navigators as well as instructor to the ships' carpenters and 'naupagers' (as he called the shipwrights) during the mid-sixties. The first part of the manuscript unsuccessfully offered to Lord Burghley about 1573 was, however, mainly concerned not with ships but with gunnery and the associated military arts. Besides the actual handling of ordnance, the soldier, if an officer, had to master the geometrical determination of heights and distances, the scale survey of the terrain and so forth. Bourne was clearly prepared to instruct

[1] British Museum, Sloane MS 3651.
[2] Head-piece: Nothing so base boot vantage you may wyn,
Nothing so smalle boot som gayn ys ther in
Then rise you all and tacke of ye beste
Excepte my good wyll though you lyck not ye rest.

Tail-piece: Yt hath bynne seene and knowne yt knolledge dyd availle
boot now in these dayes money doth prevaylle
Yet on ye eand yf you marck yt well ye worlld is so frayll
that knoledge shall prosper when yt money shall faylle.

the soldier equally with the sailor, the land-surveyor as well as the carpenter.¹ He covered, in fact, what came to be the standard range of the so-called 'mathematical practitioner' with the exception (curiously enough) of horology, which at that time meant the geometry of sun-dials.

A very few years showed the *Regiment* to be an assured success, and by 1578 Bourne had found important patrons for the manuscript material which he still had in hand. The first part, entitled *The Art of Shooting in Great Ordnance*, which was almost directly borrowed from the Italian work of Nicholas Tartaglia, he dedicated to the Master of the Queen's Ordnance, Sir William Winter. The second part, *The Treasure for Travellers*, which dealt with mensuration, mathematical instruments, survey, and kindred matters had as patron Ambrose Dudley, Earl of Warwick, who was General of Ordnance.² To both these high artillery officers Bourne described himself as a gunner. In the same year he published a miscellany of notes which he entitled *Inventions and Devices*.³ This contained various suggestions for military and nautical strategic and tactical tricks, improvements, and novelties. Again it was largely derivative. There can be no doubt that Bourne had read Tartaglia's *Quesiti é Inventioni* and Jacques Besson's *Théâtre des Instruments*, but his was the first of such books to appear in English. An interesting point for sailors was the mention of a mechanical (geared) log for measuring a ship's way, which Bourne said Humfrey Cole had made.⁴ Cole was the successor to Gemini as the leading instrument-maker in England, but the device was one that Besson had already pictured in his book.⁵

¹ See Fig. 6, Bourne's survey of part of the Thames.
² For illustrations of Bourne's survey methods, see Figs. 5, 6.
³ This work was dedicated to Lord Charles Howard, later to become Lord High Admiral, but it had evidently been originally offered in manuscript to Lord Clinton. 'The thing is such as you have already seen the written copy at my good Lord and Masters hande, the Earle of Lincolne,' wrote Bourne.
⁴ Taylor, *Tudor Geography*, p. 171. Bourne says: 'The deviser of this Engine or instrument [No. 21] was Humfrey Cole.'
⁵ Richard Eden who was a personal friend of Besson comments on this device as follows: 'By whiche description, some do understand that the knowledge of the

The Frenchman had also shown a geared carriage in which a land surveyor could ride while he read from a dial the distances that he had covered in each direction. But, in fact, the mechanical difficulties involved in making self-registering instruments of this kind either accurate or reliable were still insuperable. Bourne nowhere suggests that they were really in use.

The conclusion cannot be escaped (since so large a part of his writing was derivative) that this Gravesend burgess could read and understand the works of Italian and French authors. But there is no information available as to when or how he mastered foreign languages, nor is it known what general schooling he had had when a boy. He clearly had access to many books, and in the Preface to his *Almanack* of 1581 (written in 1580) he is able to quote from North's translation of Plutarch's *Lives* published only the year before. But there is nothing either in his own Will or that of his widow to suggest that he had formed a library. It is possible that (like Hakluyt) he was allowed the run of some gentleman's library. However that may be, it is clear that between the dates of publication of his first *Almanack* (1567) and his *Regiment for the Sea* (1574) he had studied to some purpose two important English books. The first was Sir Henry Billingsley's English translation of Euclid's *Elements*, to which Dr John Dee had written a lengthy *Preface* (1570). This *Preface* profoundly influenced several generations of 'mathematical practitioners'. It set out in clear and persuasive language the

---

longitude might so be founde, a thynge doubtlesse greatly to be desyred, and hytherto not certaynly knowen, although *Sebastian Cabot* on his death bed tolde me that he had the knowledge thereof by divine revelation, yet so, that he myght not teach any man. But I thinke that the good olde man, in that extreme age, somewhat doted, and had not yet, even in the article of death, utterly shaken off all worldlye vayne glorie. As touchyng whiche knowledge of the longitude, to speake a little more by occasion now given, it shal not be from the purpose, to rehearse the saying of that excellent learned man Johannes Fernelius, in his incomparable booke *De abditis rerum causis*.... "We have put our helping hands to the Art of Navigation & Geography, for by observation of the houres of the Equinoctial, we have invented how, in whatsoever region or place of the worlde a man shalbe, he may know in what longitude he is." ' R. Eden, *A very necessarie . . . Booke concerning Nauigation* (1578), Epistle Dedicatorie The principle that longitude difference was to be measured by time difference was familiar to astronomers. It was the means of application that was lacking.

basic relationship which arithmetic and geometry bore to each and all of the Arts, Crafts and Sciences. These in their turn were the basis of the country's prosperity. The whole argument was then summarized in tabular form so that the navigator, the land-surveyor, the horologist and other technicians could see their place in the whole scheme of applied mathematical knowledge.[1]

Dee was to become personally known to William Bourne. Esteemed the greatest English mathematician of his day, he had been adviser to the Muscovy Company on matters of navigation since it was first founded. In this very Preface he recalls that he had instructed its chief pilots, Stephen and William Borough.

The second book that Bourne studied with as much care, although with less enthusiasm than the first, was Thomas Digges's edition of his father's *Pantometria* (1571), to which reference has already been made. Although the book deals in the main with such military matters as ground-survey and range-finding, it is best known to-day for its description of a simple instrument for taking a simultaneous observation of the bearing and elevation (i.e. the azimuth and altitude) of a distant object. The instrument became known as a theodolite (at first spelt theodelite), and was immediately popular among land-surveyors. Bourne had used the old-fashioned circular plate,[2] a simplification of the back-plate of the astrolabe, into which a little magnetic needle was inserted. He gives a specimen of a survey which he had made from a base line near Gravesend — the earliest known example of an actual piece of what is termed triangulation.[3] It appeared in the manuscript already referred to as offered to Lord Burghley in 1573, and was printed in 1578 in the *Treasure for Travellers*. It is a very crude piece of work — there was no careful ground measurement of the base-line for

[1] The scheme culminated in 'Archemastrie': 'This Arte tendeth to bryng to actual experience sensible, all worthy conclusions by all the Artes Mathematicall purposed.' See Taylor, *Mathematical Practitioners*, facing p. 432.
[2] See Fig. 4.   [3] See Fig. 5.

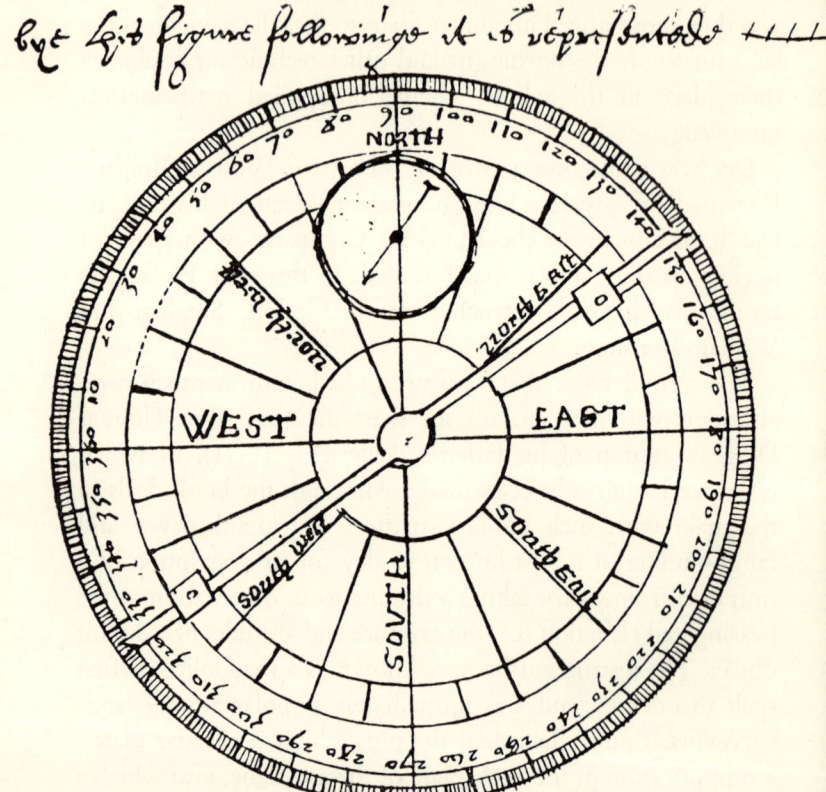

Fig. 4. William Bourne's surveying instrument
B.M., Sloane MS 3651, fol. 65

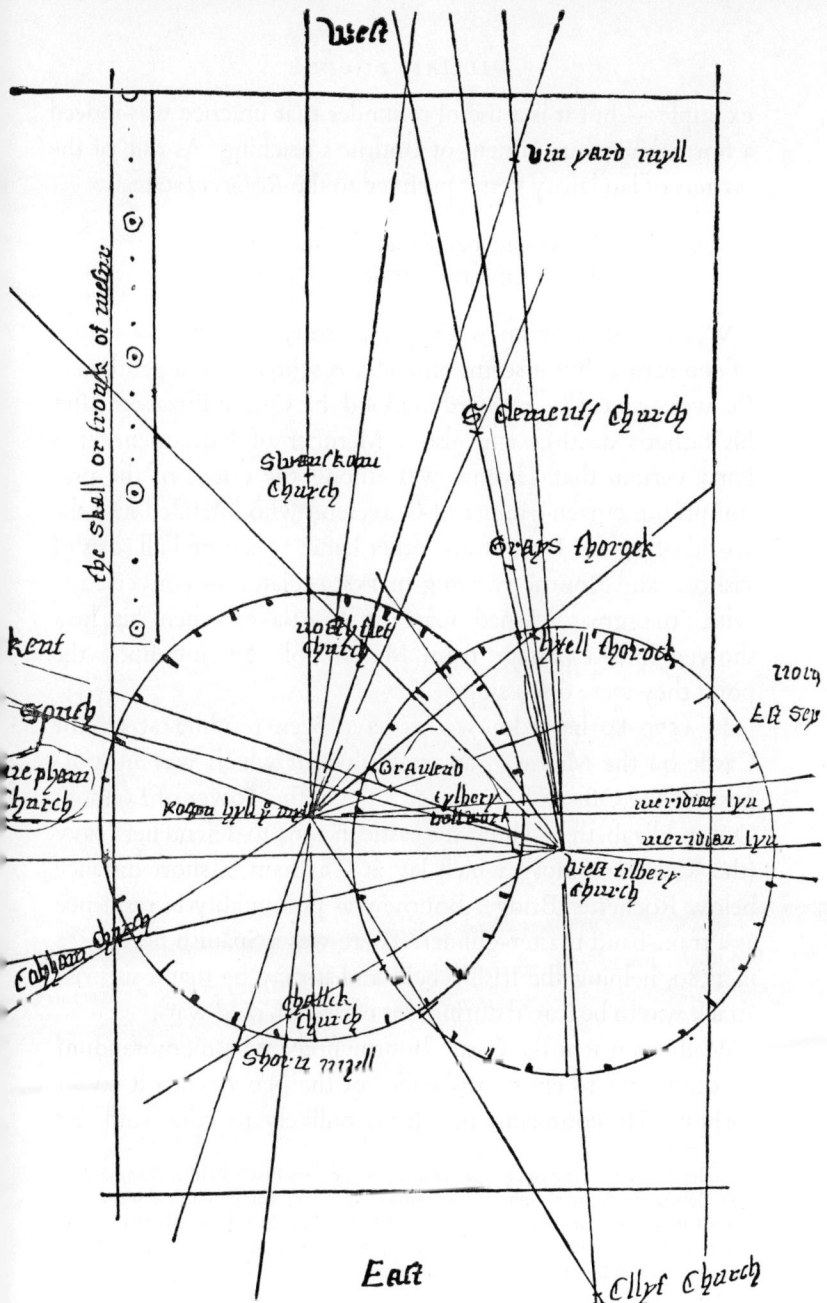

Fig. 5. Bourne's triangulation round Gravesend and Tilbury
B.M., Sloane MS 3651, fol. 68v

example — but it is a useful reminder that practice was indeed a normal accompaniment of Bourne's teaching. As one of the writers of laudatory verses prefixed to the *Regiment* states:

> Thou hast besides all this the truth
> By practise truly tride . . . [p. 145].

Whether Bourne knew Digges personally must be a matter of conjecture, but it seems unlikely. A scholar and a gentleman (he was eventually 'restored in blood' by Queen Elizabeth after his father's death),[1] and also a Member of Parliament, it is fairly certain that Thomas was among the critics of the presumptuous citizen-gunner of Gravesend who intruded into the world of books. Dee, on the other hand, welcomed all sorts of visitors, and Bourne (writing in 1580) relates his conversation with 'the great learned man' at Mortlake, when his host showed him a passage from Marco Polo bearing upon the point they were discussing.[2]

In 1579–80 he is known to have been residing at Upnor Castle on the Medway, an establishment which was an 'outpost' of the Office of Ordnance, then in the Tower of London. Queen Elizabeth had built the castle in 1564 to defend her Navy (the 'Queen's Ships') which lay at Chatham, a short distance below Rochester Bridge. Bourne was presumably in residence as a train-band master-gunner. There was a Spanish fleet at sea in 1580, helping the Irish rebels, and it may be that a surprise attack was to be feared during this period of 'cold war'.

While he was at the Castle Bourne prepared a memorandum on the means to ensure the safety of the Navy when it lay in harbour. He complains that he is unlikely to command the

---

[1] In his *Stratioticos* (2nd ed., p. 359) Thomas Digges says that his father 'having bene long debarred his owne inheritance and native Soile, being restored ment then immediately to return to his wonted places of Exercise . . . So sithence his death . . . by continuall Law Brables . . . I have for many yeares been so vexed and turmoiled . . .'. This suggests that Leonard died before his return to England, or immediately after it.

[2] See p. 313

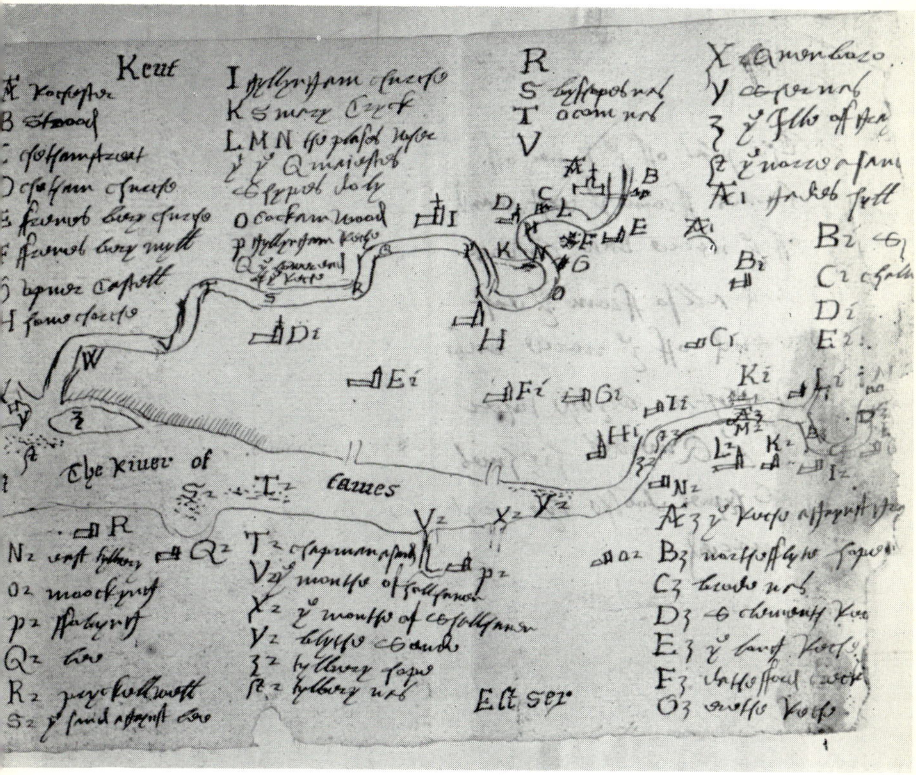

Fig. 6. 'The plat off yᵉ Ryuer of Tames', by William Bourne
B.M., Sloane MS 3651, fol. 74v

attention of the authorities, since he has no status,[1] and it is worth notice that Thomas Digges had written an essay about the same time (but a very poor one) on the same theme of the possible invasion of Kent and elsewhere.[2] This was appended in 1590 to his *Stratioticos*. Digges's patron was Leicester, whose attention he could command as well as that of Lord Burghley. Bourne's special point was that it was fallacious to trust to heavy ordnance to repel invading ships. Their sails and rigging could be damaged by the cannon-balls, but they would not be sunk. A chain across the river would be a greater safeguard, and he quotes from his *Inventions and Devices* (1578) the stratagems that could be employed once the enemy was checked by the chain.[3] From the same book he cites the means by which the enemy might shield his ships from gunfire off Portsmouth, which others had suggested was a suitable port for laying up the Queen's Ships. The new fortifications (on which Richard Popinjay, Master of Works, was now engaged there) would, he said, provide no safety.

The *Inventions and Devices* was the third of his books to be published in 1578, and the manuscript had originally been offered to the Lord High Admiral, Clinton, who had earlier accepted the dedication of the *Regiment*. The Earl of Lincoln had, however, merely shown it to Lord Charles Howard, and it was the latter who accepted the Dedication. Clinton, however, lent his name to what was to prove Bourne's last book, the *Almanack and Prognostication for Ten Years* which was completed at Upnor Castle in December 1580. The fact that, in the

[1] 'All thogh y^t I have not to doe, nether no person doothe aseke me y^t questione, thynkynge me to symple in soche waytie affaires, y^t ys to say in those Corses y^t doothe Concerne ye statte & preservation of ... ye holle navie....' *A Dyscourse as tochynge ye Q. magisties Shyppes*, 2 March 1579, B.M., Lansdowne MS 20.

[2] This essay lacks the professional knowledge displayed by Bourne, who gives details e.g. for the placing of a cable strengthened by chains across the Medway at Upnor Castle to 'stay' the Queen's enemies.

[3] Whether as a result of Bourne's representations or no, within three years of his death a heavy iron chain, raised and lowered by a windlass, had been placed across the Medway at Upnor. The cost was £600. See J. A. Williamson, *Hawkins of Plymouth* 1949), p. 264.

dedications of 1574 and 1580 alike, William Bourne terms the Lord Admiral his 'good lord and master', and one to whom he is indebted for favours, makes it reasonable to suggest that he was in some way attached to Lord Clinton's household, but there is no record of any definite appointment.

In the annals of Gravesend Bourne's death is recorded simply as that of 'a householder'.[1] Nevertheless, that he had achieved more than a local reputation is witnessed by an appreciative reference to him by a distinguished contemporary, Gabriel Harvey. This well-known critic and controversialist was a great admirer of the newly appearing 'mathematical practitioners', as appears from his marginal notes on some of their books. What he wrote in 1593 of William Bourne may therefore serve well as the inn-keeper's epitaph:

> He that remembereth Humphrey Cole a Mathematicall Mechanician, Matthew Baker a shipwright, John Shute an architect, Robert Norman a Navigatour, WILLIAM BOURNE a Gunner, John Hester a Chymist, or any like cunning, and subtile Empirique, (Cole, Baker, Shute, Norman, Bourne, Hester, will be remembered, when greater Clarkes shalbe forgotten) is a prowd man, if he contemne expert artisans, or any sensible industrious Practitioner, howsoever Unlectured in Schooles or Unlettered in Bookes.[2]

These self-educated men had, indeed, an advantage over those schooled in the classics in that they enjoyed a freshness of outlook and a readiness to speculate unchecked by an inculcated reverence for authority. Bourne, for example, had not been taught to look into the pages of Aristotle or Pliny for answers to questions on natural history. He could add to his *Treasure for Travellers* a fifth book in which he offers commonsense explanations of the origin of coastal land forms by erosion and deposition, of the saltness of the sea as derived from such veins of salt as are found in the rocks, of earthquakes, tides and currents and so on. Here a comparison may be made with

[1] See p. xx, n. 1. [2] Gabriel Harvey, *Pierces Supererogation* (1593).

another 'unlearned' contemporary, Bernard Palissy, the potter. Palissy drew large audiences in Paris to his lectures — based on observation — concerning the surface features of the Earth. It was no great disadvantage to William Bourne that he was, as he termed himself, a 'simple' man. He was also an intelligent one, a man who reflected on what he saw. And his books were read.

I

An Almanacke and Prognostication for three yeares . . . nowe newlye added vnto my late Rulles of Nauigation[1]

EDITOR'S NOTE

During the reign of Henry VIII there was scarcely an Englishman to be found who was skilled in 'the New Navigation', new because it made use of mathematics and astronomy. Spanish pilots were employing it for their regular sailings to the New World, Portuguese pilots for reaching Brazil, India and the Far East, but in England it was still chiefly the military engineers who were interested in mathematical instruments, and in maps or plans. The English sailor found no use for the chart, nor for any instrument designed to measure the height of sun and star. He was satisfied to feel his way about the sea with lead and line, and to store his memory with land-marks and leading marks.

The reason for this contrast was simple. Our islands stand upon a broad platform, termed the Continental Shelf, over which the sea is less than a hundred fathoms deep. This shelf or platform stretches well out into the western ocean, and as it has a steep, almost cliff-like, outer edge the navigator approaching it from deep water, whether from the Atlantic or across the Bay of Biscay, is quickly aware that he has reached it. He is 'in soundings'. Although still far out of sight of land he early learned to judge his position merely by the minor changes of bottom contour and by the nature of the 'ground' brought up in the lump of tallow with which he armed his lead.

The Shelf, of course, has its special dangers. The range of the tides over it, that is to say the twice daily change of the depth of water, can be phenomenal at its inner limit. Moreover the tides generate powerful streams, cross-streams, 'rips', overfalls, and

---
[1] The title of the surviving edition of 1571.

even whirlpools as they ebb and flow. Such 'dangers' were all memorized by the sailor, and were written into his rutter or sailing directions. The 'good' pilot had first and foremost to know his tides, and this meant familiarity with the Lunar Kalendar, or 'Almanacke', in other words the changing phases of the moon. It is these that govern the monthly occurrence of spring tides and neaps, and their seasonal augmentations and diminutions. Fortunately the hour to hour positions of the moon during her monthly cycle had always been of first importance to the astronomer-astrologer, and by his rules the hour and date of each new moon could be predicted for centuries ahead. When printed Almanacs appeared in England at the beginning of the sixteenth century, they were obviously of special value to seamen, who could at once obtain from them the 'age of the moon' which governed the hour of each day's tides. Theoretically high tide should occur at any seaport when the moon crosses the local meridian, but in fact the arrival of high water may be delayed. The interval of time between the theoretical and the actual tide is termed 'the establishment of the port', which of course the local sailor learnt by observation from childhood. Like everyone else, he knew, besides, how to judge the time roughly by the position of the sun and stars, while as an apprentice to the sea he also had to learn to 'box the compass' (i.e. name its thirty-two points). He was further advised to practise with his pen the drawing of shore profiles and port entries, with their landmarks.

The simple navigating methods of the English sailor were also those of the sailors of Brittany and Normandy, and the first English sea-manual was taken from the French. Translated and edited by the printer, Robert Copland, it first appeared in 1528 under the title of *The Rutter*[1] *of the Sea*. It is, perhaps, a commentary on the backward state of English printing in that it does not contain the woodcuts of shore-profiles and harbour entries that were already to be found in its French counterpart.

[1] A word derived from the French *routier*.

By an accident of geography the method of navigation by lead and line sufficed also to carry the English West Country fishermen as far as the cod-banks of Newfoundland, where with their Norman and Breton neighbours they joined the Portuguese and Galicians. The Grand Banks are in fact just such an immense ocean-jutting platform as that on which the British Isles stand, and they have just such a steep edge towards the ocean basin. Long before he reached the American continent itself, the fisherman, dropping his 'dipsie' lead, found himself in soundings, and soon learned to move confidently about the Banks. These early American voyages (termed colloquially voyages to the Utter or Outer Parts) went practically unrecorded at home. They are only heard of when some dispute brought the participants into the High Court of Admiralty or when a Richard Hore took a few inquisitive gentleman passengers aboard as in 1536.[1]

The simplicity of the early navigation methods has its silent witness in the shape of the provision which the shipowner was expected to make for them. A study of ships' inventories shows almost invariably a mariners' or magnetic compass, a heavier (deep-sea) and a lighter (inshore) lead and line, with a dial or sandglass for measuring the two-hour half-watches. A pilot of the fifteenth or sixteenth century who wished to practise the 'new navigation' had himself to supply the instruments, tables and charts that were necessary for it. These were costly and so became his most precious possession. It was Francis Drake's habit, when he seized a ship, to throw the pilot's equipment overboard, leaving him bereft indeed.

The essence of the 'new navigation' is conveyed by the phrase 'running down the latitude'. The recovery of Ptolemy's maps at the beginning of the fifteenth century had reintroduced the method of defining geographical position in terms of co-

[1] The company mustered at Gravesend in April 1536. The lurid report of their adventures obtained many years later by the younger Hakluyt is not borne out by certain legal proceedings which followed the voyage. See E. G. R. Taylor, 'Master Hore's voyage of 1536', *Geogr. Journal*, LXXVII (1931), 469-70.

ordinates, that is to say, by the circles of latitude and the meridians of longitude on the globe. Once the latitude of a port is known, and its general position—either to the east or to the west of the observer—it can be found by the pilot of a ship despite the featureless, pathless waters around him. He seeks that latitude and follows it until the port is reached. The early Portuguese sailing manuals contained lengthening lists of key latitudes, and during the first years of the sixteenth century chart-makers added a meridian divided into degrees of latitude along the margin or down the centre of the chart. They still, however, drew the customary pattern of rhumb-lines (corresponding to compass directions) radiating from a formal arrangement of wind-roses, a pattern which had not been altered for centuries.

To navigate by the latitude, however, made much greater demands upon a pilot than navigating by lead and line. It involved an elementary knowledge of the sphere and its circles, the use of mathematical instruments and tables, besides the working out of a simple mathematical calculation. It involved, too, the appreciation of the properties of chart and scale, while the navigator had to know how to use a pair of dividers to take measurements and plot a course. The pilot, in fact, had to be a man of some education and must be carefully trained for his task, which explains why chief pilots in Portugal and Spain were men of standing, and might even be men of birth. In England it was an unusual thing for a gentleman to apprentice his son to the sea. The captain and chief officer of a ship, even the admiral of a fleet, were normally military men, and landsmen. The ship-master (who here was also the pilot) learned his craft by apprenticeship, and served under the captain's orders. Local pilots were taken aboard when a ship approached harbour, but in England there was no separate category of ocean pilots, although Bourne was to see in the course of twenty years the general acceptance of the 'new navigation' methods which he taught.

The exclusive rights of possession and exploitation in newly discovered territories which in 1493 the Pope had granted to Portugal and Spain were, as might be expected, early challenged by other sea-board countries, and particularly by France. French pirates and French 'illegal' traders (usually Huguenots) were soon frequenting the shores of West Africa, Brazil and the West Indies. To meet their needs a flourishing school of chartmakers sprang up at Dieppe and a number of outstanding French mariners mastered the new navigation. By 1535, despite the protests of the Emperor Charles V, exploration of the mainland behind the Grand Banks was planned and begun. The Master-pilot of this first adventure was Jacques Cartier of St Malo.

Within a very few years of Cartier's voyages, which centred on the St Lawrence River, two attempts were made to stir the English King Henry VIII to some similar action. A member of the English merchant-colony in Spain, Roger Barlow, presented the sovereign with a manuscript entitled *A Briefe Summe of Geographia* to which he prefaced a summary of the Spanish sea-manual.[1] This included all the most essential instructions for navigation by the latitude, particularly a four-year table of the sun's declination day by day. Towards the close of the text Barlow urged once again a proposal that his dead friend Robert Thorne had made long since, namely that the English should seek the Spiceries northwards by a trans-Polar route. Barlow wrote in 1541, and at about the same time one of the small band of highly skilled and already well-known French pilots, Jean Rotz, offered his services to the English King.[2] He too accompanied his offer with a manuscript of value to seamen. It included a set of working drawings for making an elaborate instrument by which the variation of the magnetic compass could be determined, and an actual instrument was presented with it.

[1] Edited by E. G. R. Taylor for the Hakluyt Society, 1932.
[2] E. G. R. Taylor, *Tudor Geography*, ch. IV. See also two papers on Rotz in *Journal of the Institute of Navigation*, VII (1954).

Henry VIII rewarded Rotz with a salaried post as Hydrographer (i.e. chart-maker), and the Frenchman (actually he was of Scots descent) prepared for him an elaborate atlas of charts in the style of the Dieppe school. To this he prefaced a sailing manual.[1] Yet, although there were subsequent rumours that a voyage was intended by the north, all this came to nothing.

Nevertheless, the Lord Admiral, Viscount Lisle (later Earl of Warwick and Duke of Northumberland), who took office in 1543, included overseas enterprise and conquest among his many ambitions. Among other foreign pilots he had taken yet another Dieppe mariner, Jean Ribault (later to become well-known) into his service. There had been, besides, for ten years or more, an English sea captain who had equipped himself for the new navigation. This was John a Borough, a Devonshire man, who sailed in the service of the Plantagenet Lord Lisle. He furnished himself with Spanish and Portuguese instruments, sea-books and charts, and could also himself draw a chart. His master was Deputy for Calais for several years before his death, and it seems likely that this continental outpost of England provided a useful intermediary for the transmission of Continental learning and techniques across the Channel.

When Edward VI came to the throne, Sebastian Cabot was sent for and was set to work with Jean Ribault to draw up plans and prepare charts for a voyage to Cathay. It seems odd that in spite of the fact that Sebastian, about forty years earlier, had sailed north-west and entered Hudson's Strait, the decision now was to go by the north-east. A young Bristol man, Richard Chancellor, was given some years' training at Sir Henry Sidney's expense to act as chief pilot after the Spanish style, and although John a Borough is no longer heard of, there now appears a Stephen a Borough (probably a son) who is competent to serve under Chancellor as Master. That he was familiar with the 'new' navigational methods his Journal for the 1556 voyage clearly shows. His younger brother William, also ap-

[1] B.M., Royal MS. 20. B. vii.

prenticed to the sea, was in the same ship, the *Edward Bonaventure*, although still before the mast in 1553.

Towards the end of Mary's reign, Stephen Borough (as he was now called) paid a visit to Spain, and was invited to witness the methods employed for training the Spanish pilots. He and his brother, now Chief Pilots of the Muscovy Company, had received advanced instruction from Dr Dee, but Dee never published his nautical manuscripts and tables,[1] and there was still a great shortage of skilled English mariners. Stephen thereupon persuaded a small group of the governing body of the Muscovy Company to provide the money for a translation of the leading Spanish sea-manual, a copy of which he had doubtless brought back with him. The book was Martin Cortes's *La Arte de Navegar* (1551) and the translator chosen was Richard Eden, historiographer of the early north-eastern and African voyages. Eden knew personally all the parties concerned, and had sat beside old Cabot on his death-bed. Himself a Cambridge man, his English version of the *Arte of Navigation*[2] was written in formal scholarly style, with a long and learned Introduction matching that of the original. And it is here that William Bourne comes into the picture.

Bourne studied the English *Arte of Navigation* very minutely, and came to the conclusion that whatever might be the case in Spain, where would-be pilots had to attend courses of instruction and submit to public examination at the Casa de Contratación, it was too difficult a book for the English apprentice to the sea. These youths needed something very plain and straightforward. They were likely to have a limited vocabulary and only a very elementary knowledge of arithmetic. Even the older men could not handle an astronomer's *Ephemerides* or

---

[1] In 1576 he put them together under the title of *Queen Elizabeth her Tables Gubernatick*, to form Volume II of *The British Complement of the Perfect Art of Navigation*, a four-volume work of which only Vol. I was ever printed. See Taylor, *Tudor Geography*, ch. VI; and Appendix A below.

[2] *The Arte of Nauigation . . . Written in the Spanysh tongue by Marten Curtes* (London, 1561).

work out the sun's declination from his place in the zodiac as Cortes apparently expected pilots to do. Bourne was speaking from experience. His own young stepson, James Beare, was a mariner's apprentice, as no doubt were others in his circle of acquaintance. He prepared a simpler version of the book for his pupils or 'friends', and then decided (or was persuaded) to publish this as an Addendum to his first *Almanacke and Prognostication*.

The printer who undertook publication was Thomas Purfoote, and he would necessarily need to obtain a 'license to print' from the Stationers' Company. But it seems that the printer of the English *Cortes* (who held what today would be called the copyright) was immediately up in arms, and Bourne had to cut his 'copy' where it appeared to duplicate Eden's translation. This translation had been printed by Richard Jugge, the Queen's printer. But what is known about the matter is only by inference from the remarks (with their undertones of petulance and protest) which Bourne interjected into his printed text. When, for example, he is explaining how to allow for the small angular distance which separates the Pole Star from the true Celestial Pole, he is obliged to substitute a new Rule, which he formulates in terms of the 'Pointers', two stars in the Great Bear. Yet, 'I would have pointed thee to Guard-Stars [he writes] but I could not be suffered.'

The Guard Stars, or Two Brothers in the Lesser Bear were those used for finding the height of the Pole by the Portuguese, Spaniards and French, and were essential adjuncts to the standard diagram that had appeared in all sea-manuals for eighty years or more. This diagram Bourne had perforce to omit. He was obliged also to say to the reader that if he wanted to know how much easting or westing he had made when sailing a certain distance on his course 'then read the *Arte of Navigation*'. And he must do the same to learn how to make and use his cross-staff or *balestilha*, 'for I must meddle with nothing contained in that book.' Finally and more specifically, when the English author came to the subject of navigating instruments in general, he had to write: 'Now for to make your instruments for the Sea with their uses, you shall repayre to the booke of Navigation, made by Martine Curtis a Spaniarde, imprinted by master Jugge printer to the Queenes majestie, which booke hath been very chargeable to him, therefore it is not for me to meddle with nothing contained in that booke, or else I would have shewed you the makinge of an Equinoctiall diall, with his use, which is very profitable.'

In the absence of any record in the Stationers' Register it must be assumed that an agreement had been reached between the two printers, Purfoote and Jugge, to which the author himself only gave reluctant consent. In Elizabethan days, the ownership of a book rested in perpetuity with the printer, but there is no clear indication of what, apart from pirating the whole text, was considered an infringement of his copyright.

This first printed book of William Bourne's was typically an *Almanacke and Prognostication*, which he compiled for 1567–9. It enabled the author to advertise himself as a 'Student of the Mathematicall Science', and by implication as an instructor therein. It is therefore surprising to find that the monthly Kalendar with which this book begins is marred by errors and confusion to a quite extraordinary degree. Nor was there any revision of this for the second edition (of which alone a copy survives), which covered the years 1571, 1572 and 1573. The fundamental mistake was to include in the Kalendar the dates of the moveable Feasts and those of the Law Terms which depend upon them: all these, of course, alter yearly with the date of Easter Sunday, which in turn depends upon the cycle of the moon. And in fact the basic Kalendar used was one for 1564, already three years out-of-date in 1567. Bourne had also tried to fit into it all the dates of the principal English fairs. These, of course, required a separate table, for not only do their dates alter, since they cannot fall on a Sunday, but half a dozen or so may possibly be held on the same date in different parts of the country. This put the printer in a quandary, as the columns of a Kalendar are so narrow that he was obliged to encroach on the space allotted to two or three days. As a result the saint's name for any one of those days had either to be omitted or was pushed forward incorrectly.

It might be imagined that all the so-called 'black-letter' saints' names would have been removed from the yearly Kalendars after the Reformation, as they were from the Prayer Book. This was not so since it was customary to use them for dating purposes. The numerical date itself might well be unknown to the user. A countryman would be aware, for example, that the common fields were thrown open for grazing on Lammas Day, without knowing that this was August 1. Even today a Spanish tradesman will say that he has no fresh stocks coming in 'until Three Kings', when he means until January 6. Many minor saints' names, however, differed widely from one Kalendar to another even in the same country. While Bourne's list often coincides with that found in the popular *Shepheard's Kalendar* (a translation from the French), the coincidence is not complete.[1] A few days are here and there left blank, apparently at random, while in others some piece of secular information is inserted. Among these latter are the deaths of Henry VIII and Edward VI, and the dates of the birth and accession of Queen Elizabeth. The last is incorrectly given, November 19 instead of November 17. There are other minor errors, too, such as the duplication of the date of the Spring Equinox (*Equinoctium*) and a second ending to the Dog Days on September 6. It is possible that Bourne had handed over an old and much annotated Kalendar to the printer, who made what he could of it.

There was no such carelessness over the 'Almanacke'. Here, given monthly for the years that each edition covered, were the predicted dates of the phases of the moon, essential for the seafarer. And for each year the prime, epact and Sunday letter were provided, from which calculation of the age of the moon

---

[1] The *Kalendrier de Bergers* was first translated in 1503 as *The Kalendayr of the shyppars*. Editions continued to appear until 1656.

could be made, and there were notes on forthcoming eclipses.

The modern reader may have been puzzled by a seemingly irregular series of figures which forms the first column of the Kalendar. Bourne does not mention or use these, but they are explained in the *Shepheard's Kalendar*. The two points (termed the Dragon's Head and the Dragon's Tail) at which the moon's orbit intersects the ecliptic move slowly round through the signs of the Zodiac, and return on themselves every nineteen years. The year number in this cycle which corresponds to a particular Kalendar year is termed the Golden Number or Prime of that year. It decides not only the date of Easter but the day and hour of the monthly new moon, and hence the seaman's tide-table. If, for example, the Prime for a certain year is 12, the Kalendar-maker puts the figure 12 against the date in each month when the new moon will appear, and by putting each of the nineteen figures against the appropriate date he can thus provide a perpetual lunar Kalendar or Almanac. That Bourne did not in fact make any use of these figures can soon be discovered. The Golden Number or Prime which he gives for the year 1573 is 16, and in the Almanac he predicts new moons for March 3 and December 24. But the number 16 appears in the margin against March 8 and December 28 in the Kalendar. Secular astronomical change and slow cumulative error may account in part for the discrepancy, but Bourne's source has not been traced. His figures do not tally with those in the only *Ephemerides* he mentions. This was the huge and costly volume by Cyprianus Levitius of which there was a copy in Lord Lumley's library. It was compiled for the meridian of Augsburg, which the author considered to be forty-three minutes of time east of London, i.e. the time there was forty-three minutes later than in England. Bourne was of course aware of the correction necessary to be made for a difference of meridian in astronomical tables. He possibly possessed a copy of John Feild's *Ephemeris Anni 1557* (1556) computed for the meridian of London and based on the recent Tables of Copernicus and

Erasmus Reinhold. There was also in print *An Almanack and Kalendar containing the Day, Hour and Minute of the Change of the Moon for Ever*, computed by the physician Humfrey Lloyd who married Lord Lumley's sister. No copy is known today, but it may be dated about 1563.

The word FINIS is found on folio B vii v (p. 49) and closes the section of the book devoted to the Kalendar and Almanac. This was in accordance with current English law which ordered the separate printing, under a fresh title, of any prognostication or astrological matter following the Almanac. While Bourne rejected astrology, unlike many contemporary practitioners, and therefore refused to predict coming events from the conjunctions of planets and stars, he found himself obliged to satisfy the popular demand for certain prognostications. He gave, for example, the standard rules governing days for bathing, purging and letting blood, as well as those for sowing, planting and grafting. He also added the age-old general descriptions of the natures and influence of the planets and the Signs of the Zodiac.

The Rules of Navigation, which give the book its value to-day, follow this meagre section of prognostication, and occupy about two-thirds of the whole. Each Rule is in fact a chapter, sometimes a long one, which may touch on several subjects. The first gives a portrait of the good mariner, and here Bourne sensibly advises any man who goes to sea to train for one of the skilled technical posts, that of gunner, ship's-carpenter or navigator. The master-gunner, like the master and pilot, messed in the Great Cabin, and the carpenter was a key man, responsible for the fabric of the ship. As to the master, his knowledge of moons and tides is put down as his first qualification, just as Chaucer placed it in his description of the Shipman, and as, too, it is placed in a near-contemporary description of the skills required of an Arab pilot.[1] Nor is it until all the essential features of the traditional method of navigation (i.e.

---

[1] By Aḥmad ibn-Majīd, the pilot who took Vasco da Gama to India.

as used when in soundings) have been detailed that the author turns to sailing by the latitude. When he does so, his preoccupation with far northern waters reveals itself. Once north of England, he states, observation of the Pole Star, which is comparatively simple, becomes unsatisfactory because the luminary is so high in the sky. The sun should be used, or at night one of the fixed stars nearer the equinoctial. This involves the use of astronomical tables besides requiring a capacity for arithmetical computation.

The man of the 'meanest sort', that is to say the actual beginner in sail, is now taken through the rhumbs of the compass and the tide-table. But he is likely to have become greatly confused by the subsequent difficult astronomical chapters which explain the meaning of Prime and Epact and how to calculate the age of the moon. He would obviously prefer to take the latter on trust from the Almanac. In the fifth Rule, however, Bourne comes to a more practical subject which had caused him concern. It was the custom among sailors to use the compass-fly or card as though it were the face of a twenty-four-hour clock. Each of the 32 points or rhumbs marked an interval of 45 minutes in time from its neighbour. The north point represented midnight and the south point noon. Thus they would say 'moon north-east, full sea', to describe an 'establishment of the port' that was three hours after the moon crossed the meridian. North-east was the equivalent of 3 a.m. If the establishment was $1\frac{1}{2}$ hours, they would say 'moon NNE, full sea' and so on. But as Bourne pointed out, the moon travels round an orbit that is oblique to the observer's horizon, so that the shadows that the planet casts do not mark out equal hourly distances round a circle any more than do the sun's shadows on a sun-dial. If the compass-card is to be used as a clock, then it ought to be held parallel to the plane of the moon's orbit. In fact it should be transformed into what was called an equinoctial dial.

In the course of the same Rule or chapter numbered five Bourne inserts a woodcut (p. 68) of a well-drawn volvelle, although he does not explain it. It enables the age of the moon throughout a monthly cycle to be obtained by the moveable Moon pointer, as also the relation of moon and sun. The presence of symbols indicative of the possible conjunctions of sun and moon (in trine, in sextile or in opposition) suggests that the woodcut is taken from an astrological instrument.[1]

In the sixth Rule Bourne turns to what is really the crux of the whole work—the determination of latitude by means of a noon observation of the sun. This requires the use of the Table of Solar Declinations. He gives the warning, which very few appreciated, that the declination was strictly correct only for noon-tide at the place of observation, i.e. for local time there. As the sun takes his apparent daily journey round the earth his declination is continuously changing. However, only at or near the equinoxes (as the Table shows) was there a significant change within the course of the interval of twenty-four hours between noon and noon. Consequently the Table actually held good over a wide range of longitudes during the summer and midwinter months. The author claims that he had computed the tables himself from the *Ephemerides*, presumably by making a correction for local time at London. He prints this Table unchanged in all his books, but in the *Regiment for the Sea* (pp. 190-205) a fourth year is added, completing the Leap Year cycle. This was a very necessary improvement.

Since the observations of heavenly bodies must be made at the moment they cross the north-south meridian (i.e. at their moment of transit), a method for finding the meridian line is given, and the fact that a magnetic needle may vary from pointing due north is touched upon. Here Bourne shows his personal knowledge of sailors' private practices, for he warns them not to try to make a needle point 'true' by shaving it so as to make it 'balance': Robert Norman the compass-maker had used some

---

[1] A tide-computer made by Humfrey Cole about this time is shown in D. W. Waters, *Art of Navigation*, Pls. XLIII and XLIV, but Bourne's woodcut more closely resembles the undated Pl. LII in the same book.

such practice to remedy the dip of the needle from the horizontal, which he thought was an accidental defect. Only after spoiling a specially fine needle did it occur to him that 'dip' was an intrinsic magnetic property, which he then measured.

In the eighth Rule the method of using the North or Pole Star to determine latitude is described, but as has already been mentioned, this was done under the hampering restrictions imposed by Richard Jugge. Bourne was also constrained against his will by sailors' custom. He found the seaman's conviction that the distance between Pole and Star was $3°\frac{1}{2}$ too strong for him, and felt obliged to use this figure although he believed that the correct distance was over $4°$. Here he was perhaps relying on the opinion of the Portuguese authority Dr Pedro Nunes, who put it at $4° \ 10'$, but in fact this was even more inaccurate than $3°\frac{1}{2}$. Owing to the precession of the equinoxes the Star was slowly approaching the celestial Pole, and the English mathematicians Thomas Digges and Thomas Hariot were shortly to put the figure at only $2° \ 55'$. To-day it is a mere few minutes of arc.[1]

The height of the Star, Bourne says, can be most conveniently found with the cross-staff or *balestilha*, but the observation becomes difficult in high latitudes because with this instrument the observer has to sight star and horizon simultaneously at either end of the transitory or cross-piece of the staff. The seaman's astrolabe should therefore be substituted or reliance placed on the noon observation of the sun taken with the staff.

The next Rule was one that was normally set out in the form of a diagram, as in Cortes's book, but Bourne had to express it in writing. It answered the question: How far must a ship sail along a certain course or rhumb in order to raise the Pole (i.e.

---

[1] The higher figure was accepted by many scholars on the authority of the renowned astronomer Johann Werner who had computed it from a re-examination of the Alfonsine Tables. It is typical of the mental attitude of the age that Werner's figure was not checked or challenged by scholars until the latter part of the century, when the new spirit of enquiry began to gain ground, and the 'word of the master' could be questioned.

alter the latitude) by 1°? The answer is obtained by the solution of a triangle of which two angles and the included side are known. And the sailor had not to work this out, he merely read the diagram. The actual figures are found on it for each of the seven rhumbs within a quadrant, but they depended upon the unit which was taken as the measure of one degree of latitude. The Portuguese navigators accepted a degree of $17\frac{1}{2}$ leagues, each league containing four sea-miles. Bourne replaced this by the English sailor's measure—a degree of latitude contained 60 miles each of 1,000 geometrical paces or 5,000 feet. Thus the sea-mile was shorter than the Statute Mile which measured 5,280 feet, reducing the degree to something like $\frac{4}{5}$ of its true length. For each rhumb he also gave the ship's departure from her meridian (east or west) when she had raised or laid a degree, a figure also obtainable from the solution of the so-called 'nautical triangle'. But if (as was then probable) the seaman was using a chart made in Lisbon, which would be based on the measure of $17\frac{1}{2}$ leagues to a degree, he was told to turn to Cortes's book. There, however, so Bourne said, he would only find the meridian change appropriate when a ship was at the equator. But this was not so, Cortes expressed the easting or westing made good in terms of the 'great degree', i.e. the degree of longitude at the equator, and then gave a second table showing the proportion that the shorter degrees of longitude bore to this 'great degree', latitude for latitude. For example at latitude 60° N. or S. the degree of longitude measures just half the 'great degree'. Bourne comes back to this question of the length of a degree of longitude at various latitudes in the twelfth Rule.

In his tenth Rule he suddenly reverts to the question of 'soundings', i.e. the use of lead and line when entering the Channel (La Manche or the Slieve). But it is worth noticing that he does not attempt to describe the navigation of the pilotage waters of East Kent and the Thames Estuary. He wisely leaves this to men of 'more cunning and experience' than himself—that is to say to his friends the Trinity pilots whom he met and knew at Gravesend. The eleventh Rule deals with the direct determination of longitude at sea, which Bourne considers (and rightly) to be so difficult that seamen should leave it alone and rely for their position on their dead reckoning, i.e. on the east or west distance they estimate to have covered along their course. But he points out (as Ptolemy had indicated fourteen centuries earlier) that theoretically a sailor possessing a book of *Ephemerides* can find his longitude without any apparent difficulty. The daily position of the moon in the Signs of the Zodiac is tabulated in terms of her latitude and longitude so that her distance from any particular bright fixed star at any hour can be ascertained. An observer finding her at a greater or less distance from that star, and knowing her rate of motion, can calculate the time difference between his position and that at the meridian for which his *Ephemerides* were calculated. The time difference is equivalent to a degree of longitude for every four minutes of the clock. Jean Rotz gave two examples of finding longitude by lunar distance, one by her distance from the sun, a second by her distance from the star Aldebaran. This was in the manuscript which he presented to Henry VIII.[1] Richard Madox, who sailed with Edward Fenton in 1582, described the principle of the method, believing that he was the first to do so. But Amerigo Vespucci had attempted it in 1498. Success was impossible, not least because of the irregularity of the motions of the Moon, in addition to the lack of a 'precise instrument' such as Bourne pointed out was necessary for the observation. And any such instrument would be rendered useless by the motion of the ship.

In his fourteenth Rule the writer is back on firmer ground. He gives an extra method of finding latitude for those who travel to the northwards—the servants of the Muscovy Company, sailors going to Iceland and the Grand Banks—a method serving also as far south as the Canary Islands. This was to take the

[1] Taylor, *Tudor Geography*, 63–70.

altitude of one or other of a group of twelve bright stars as it crossed the meridian. The distance of each star from the equinoctial, i.e. its declination, is tabulated in degrees and minutes, so that a simple addition or subtraction sum gives the height of the equinoctial above the horizon. As he had already explained, the equinoctial is by definition 90° from the Pole, while the height of the Pole is equal to the observer's latitude.

The stars selected are well distributed round the Zodiac, so that two or three will always be in the night sky. A second set of tables gives the times at which they cross the London meridian, for fortnightly intervals. The user must add proportionally the daily four minutes gain of star time on sun time if he uses intermediate dates. The tables cannot really be called clear or well arranged, and the use of any table presents a real difficulty to a person with little education. Teaching the 'new navigation' must have been a truly formidable task. The contemporary Dutch sea-manual when it reached England also included a short table of bright fixed stars, and Arab seamen always used them, particularly Canopus and Arcturus, in preference to the sun. Bourne's remark that the tables would serve for a hundred years was the stock comment, since for such a period the precession of the equinoxes could be ignored. It is less than a minute every year.

How to find the time by star-rise and star-set is explained. The 'two-hour watch' glass, re-set by the sun at noon whenever it was possible, must, however, have been a very rough and ready time-piece. It is noteworthy that Bourne makes no mention of the nocturnal, which was already in use in his day for telling the time. Perhaps it was then too costly for sailors. Writing in 1584 Robert Norman describes a very simple form of the instrument which could have been made aboard.[1]

The Gravesend inn-keeper was obviously fascinated by astronomy and would have written at much greater length on the subject, but (he says), 'I am not worthy to make any

---

[1] Robert Norman, *The Safeguard of Saylers* (London, 1584).

rehearsal of it.... For there be a number of most prudent and famous Autours' who had already dealt with it. He goes on to name some of these, among whom may be recognized Sacrobosco (whose *Treatise on the Sphere* was attached to the Portuguese Seaman's Manual), Orontius (Finaeus), and of course Dr Recorde.

In the fifteenth Rule Bourne comes face to face with wha was long a great subject of contention between the sailor and the mathematician. 'The moste part of seamen make their accompt as though that the earth were a platte-form.' This was not because they thought the earth was flat, but because 'It is impossible to drawe ye face of the earth and the sea true upon a platteforme' i.e. upon a plain sheet of parchment, for 'the meridianes growe together [i.e. converge] and [so] shall not your lynes and pointes be accordinge to the Arte of Hydrographie'. The Art of Hydrography, or chart-making, had been established in the thirteenth century for ships of the Mediterranean world, which sailed not by latitude and longitude but solely by compass direction and distance. A fixed geometrical pattern of wind-roses and rhumb-lines (explained in Cortes's book) was first drawn on the parchment, and the map outline was then added. All the north-south rhumbs were parallel, and when the chart was of a small area, or covered an area within twenty degrees of the equator, the distortion was not great. However, it increased rapidly polewards, and since while north-south distances remained correct, east-west distances were increasingly falsified, directions were also rendered incorrect. A straight line drawn between two sea-ports did not represent the true course between them. It was only a year or two after Bourne wrote (1569) that Mercator published a world map showing how this defect could be remedied by increasing all north-south distances *pari passu* with the increases east-west due to the parallel meridians. The map then became direction-true, but the scale now altered from one latitude to the next, a seemingly insuperable difficulty for the sailor.

John Dee tackled the problem for the Muscovy Company's chief pilots by drawing up a table of the successive points actually reached when a ship sailed from one latitude to the next (0° to 80°) on each of the seven rhumbs.[1] These positions, when plotted on a globe, or on a polar projection of a hemisphere, showed that rhumbs were in fact spiral lines—another anomaly that the ordinary sailor could hardly be expected to understand! Bourne's proposal was that when he was in high latitudes the master should prick his position not on the chart but on a globe, and then divide the quadrant in which he found himself into its seven rhumbs, when he would see the point on the next meridian to which each course would lead him. This operation he was to repeat as often as possible, but in view of the fact that coastal outlines in high latitudes as found in contemporary maps and globes were largely guess-work, the method could have helped the navigator but little.

In the sixteenth and final Rule the author returns once more to the matter about which he had already expressed concern, namely the sailor's use of the horizontal fly of the compass as a time-piece. And despite the fact that he had agreed to meddle with nothing that Martin Cortes had dealt with, he now feels impelled to describe a crude form of equinoctial dial such as the master or the ship's carpenter could make from material lying to hand (p. 109).

In conclusion, and without explanation he adds a Kalendar of the Seven Stars or Pleiades (p. 110). This pale cluster in the sky had been the countryman's guide to time and the seasons since remote antiquity. To the Greeks the rising of the Pleiades with the sun marked the arrival of Summer, while when they rose at sunset and shone through the night, the winter had certainly begun. In London they are above the horizon for more than sixteen hours, but the long daylight obscures them entirely throughout the month of May.

It was a fact familiar to everyone in Elizabethan days that

[1] See Appendix A, below.

star-time daily gained four minutes on sun-time, but the seaman who made long voyages still needed to be reminded that tables, which were computed for a particular meridian, in Bourne's case for London, ought to be corrected for local time when used far from home. In Frobisher's Bay it was only 7 a.m. when it was noon in the capital city, and when local noon came round the planets had moved along their orbits and so changed their positions, however slightly, against the background of the fixed stars. The moon, indeed, moves swiftly, but it must have been poor comfort to the seaman to learn that if he knew his longitude to the minute he could time the phases of the moon from his London Almanac. For it was from the moon, the astronomers said, that he must find his longitude! There were still two centuries to wait for the perfect clock and the correct table of the moon's motions which gave the answer, and a further two centuries before the radio Time Signal ended the problem once and for all.

An Almanacke and Prognostication

for three yeares that is to saye for the yeare of oure Lord. 1571. and 1572. & 1573. nowe newlye added vnto my late Rules of Nauigation, I was printed iiij. yeres past.

¶ Practised at Grausend for the Meridian of London by William Bourne student of the Mathematicall science.
(.∴.)

¶ Imprinted at London in Paules Churchyarde, at the signe of the *Lucrece*, by Thomas Purfoote.
(.∴.)

❡ January hath xxxi. dayes.

iij	A	*Newe yeeres daye.*	1
	b	❡ Fayres.	2
xi	c	Octau. saint Stephen.	3
	d	Octa. Saint John.	4
xii	e	Octaue Innocent.	5
viij	f	*Twelfe daye.*	6
	g	Felix and January.	7
xvi	A	Luciani Priest.	8
v	b	Lewes confessor.	9
	c	Paule the firste heremite.	10
xiij	d	*Sol in Aquario.*	11
xj	e	Archadius martyr.	12
	f	Hylary martyr.	13
x	g	Felix priest.	14
	A	Maurice abbot.	15
xviij	b	Marcelli martyr.	16
vij	c	Saint Anthony martyr.	17
	d	The deathe of Kinge Henry.	18
xv	e	Fabian and Sebastian.	19
iiij	f	Agnes virgin.	20
	g	Vincent abbot.	21
xij	A	Maurice abbot.	22
i	b	Emerentianus.	23
	c	❡ *Terme beginneth.*	24
ix	d	Conuersa. of Saint. Paule.	25
	e	*Septuagesi.*	26
xvij	f	Faires at Bristowe.	27
vi	g	Julian bishop.	28
	A	Policarpe bishop.	29
xiiij	b	Agnes the seconde.	30
iij	c	King. Edward began his raign.	31

¶ February hath xxviij. dayes.

	d	his raigne Fast ¶ Faires.	1
xi	e	Purification of Mary,	2
xix	f	at Bathe and Maidstone,	3
viij	g	Gilbert,	4
	A	Agnes virgin.	5
xvi	b	Vedastus and Amandus,	6
v	c	Angule byshop,	7
	d	Paule byshop	8
xiij	e	¶ Sonne in Pisces,	9
ij	f	Arelonie virgin,	10
	g	Scolastica virgin,	11
x	A	Terme endeth,	12
	b	Eufraste virgin.	13
xviij	c	Valentine, at Feuersam,	14
vij	d	Aishewenesday, at Lychefied,	15
	e	Raiston and Tamworth,	16
xv	f	the next daye after,	17
iiij	g	Symon byshop,	18
	A	Sabin and Julian martyr,	19
xij	b	The first monday in Lent, at	20
i	c	Ciceter and Abington,	21
	d	Embring dayes.	22
ix	e	¶ Fast.	23
	f	Mathie Apostle. The	24
xvij	g	place of leape yeare,	25
vi	A	Henley vpon Thames.	26
	b	and Teukesbury,	27
xiiij	c	Oswalde byshop.	28

ALMANACKE FOR THREE YEARES, 1571

iij	d	¶ Marche hath .xxxi.	1
	e	Dauid byshop. Faires.	2
xi	f	Translati. of. S. Mar.	3
	g	Saint Adriane.	4
xix	A	Focas.	5
viij	b	Victor and Victorine.	6
	c	Perpetue and Felix,	7
xvi	d	Deposi. of saint Felix,	8
v	e	Agapite virgin.	9
	f	Querrion and Candi	10
xiij	g	¶ Sonne in *Aries*.	11
ij	A	The .4. Sondaye in Lent,	12
	b	at Stamforde	13
x	c	at Sudbery.	14
	d		15
xviij	e	*Equinoctium*.	16
vij	f	Patrike byshop,	17
	g	Edward king.	18
xv	A	The .v. Sondaye, at Grantam,	19
iiij	b	at Salisbury the mondaye.	20
	c	before our Lady daye.	21
xij	d	Cutberth abbot,	22
i	e	Theodore priest, at Wisbich	23
	f	Palmsondaye euen.	24
ix	g	*Annunciation of mary*.	25
	A	at Northampton,	26
xvij	b	at Walden,	27
vi	c	Dorothe virgin,	28
	d	*Victorine*.	29
xiiij	e	Quirine martyr	30
	f	Adelmus byshop.	31

¶ Aprill hath xxx. dayes.

	g	¶ Fayres.	1
xi	A	*Easter daye.*	2
	b	Richard byshop.	3
xix	c	Ambrose byshop,	4
viij	d	at Wallingforth,	5
xvi	e	Dixtus bishop,	6
v	f	at Darby	7
	g	Egesippi and sociorum.	8
xiij	A	at Bickelsworth and at	9
ij	b	Byllingworth	10
	c	at Casam the monday after	11
x	d	Fabian martyr, ¶ *Sol in Taur.*	12
	e	Tilburti, and Valeria.	13
xvij	f	*Valerianus.*	14
vij	g	Oswalde byshop.	15
	A	Isidore byshop.	16
xv	b	Aniceti byshop,	17
iiij	c	Eluthery byshop,	18
	d	*Terme beginneth*	19
xij	e	Victor byshop.	20
i	f	The. iiij. sunday after Easter	21
	g	Faire at Louth	22
ix	A	George at chairing and	23
	b	Ipswiche, amtill and	24
xvij	c	Hiningam, Gilford *marke*	25
vi	d	*Euangelist*, at Duttly.	26
	e	Anastasius,	27
xiiij	f	Vitalis martyr,	28
iij	g	Petrus martir,	29
	A	S. Erkenwalde, ¶ Fast.	30

ALMANACKE FOR THREE YEARES, 1571

¶ Maye hath .xxxi. dayes

xi	b	Phillip and Jacob. ¶ Faires,	1
	c	at Stow the olde, at Rea-	2
xix	d	ding, at Maidstone,	3
viij	e	at Lecester,	4
	f	and Chenceford.	5
xvi	g		6
v	A		7
	b	Jhon Beuerley.	8
xiij	c	at Beuerley.	9
ij	d		10
	e	Ascention day. Sol in Gemi.	11
x	f	Brimincham and saint	12
	g	Edes and at Bishop statford,	13
xviii	A	Terme endeth.	14
vii	b	Boneface byshop,	15
	c	Brandine byshop.	16
xv	d		17
iiij	e		18
	f	Dunstone bywop.	19
xii	g	Barnardine.	20
i	A	Whitsonday.	21
	b		22
ix	c	Cauntebury,	23
	d	Qoiston and Stow the olde.	24
xvij	e	Kingston vpon Thames.	25
vj	f		26
	g	Beda priest,	27
xiiij	A	Trinitie Sonday, at	28
iij	b	Rowell.	29
	c		30
xi	d		31

❡ June hath. xxx. dayes.

	e	*Corpus Christi.* ❡ Faires.	1
xix	f	at Couentree S. Edes.	2
viij	g	at bishop Stratforth and	3
xvi	A	at Rosse.	4
v	b		5
	c		6
xiij	d	Transla. of Wolstan.	7
ij	e		8
	f	Transla. of Edward,	9
x	g	Jue confessor	10
	A	vpon Barnabas day, at Okingham.	11
xviij	b	*Sol in Cancer.*	12
vij	c		13
	d	Basill bishop,	14
xv	e		15
iiij	f	S. Richarde.	16
	g		17
xij	A		18
i	b		19
	c		20
ix	d	at Sherewesbury, and at	21
	e	S. Albon S. Jhons	22
xvij	f	Euens euen,	23
vi	g	Nat. of Jhon Bap. at	24
	A	Cambridge, Glocester,	25
xiiij	b	Lincolne, Winsor Caun-	26
iii	c	terbury, Colchester,	27
	d	Peter Apostle & Paul	28
xi	e	at Wol-lerhamton, at Peter-	29
	f	borowe.	30

30

(July hath xxxi. dayes

xix	g	(Faires,	1
viij	A	Visitation of mary,	2
	b		3
xvi	c	Transla. of saint marke,	4
viii	d		5
	e	Jhon Beuerley.	6
xiij	f	Dogge dayes beginneeth,	7
ij	g	Grimbald,	8
	A	Cyrillus byshoppe.	9
x	b		10
	c	at Partney fathorsefaire.	11
xviij	d	Nabor and Felix.	12
vij	e		13
	f	(*Sol in Leo.*	14
xv	g	Transl. of s. Swithin.	15
iiij	A	at Pinchebacke	16
	b	saint Kelems daye at	17
xii	c	Winchcome.	18
i	d		19
	e	saint Margaret at Ux-	20
ix	f	bridge and Catesby,	21
	g	Mary Mag. at Marlebo-	22
xvij	A	row Winchester, Colches-	23
vi	h	ter, Tethe and thetford	24
	c	James apostle at	25
xiiij	d	Bristow, Ipswiche	26
iij	e	Northampton Darby	27
	f	saint James beside	28
xi	g	London, Reading,	29
	A	Louth and Maulsbery,	30
xix	b		31

(August hath. xxxi. dayes.

viij	c	Lammas day.	1
xvi	d	Feuersam, Dunstable. S. Edes,	2
v	e	Budforth, marram	3
	f	Church, Wisbich.	4
xiij	g	Esay the Prophete,	5
ij	A	*Transfiguratio domini.*	6
	b	Feast of Jesu.	7
x	c		8
	d	Romayne martyr.	9
xviij	e	s. Laurence daye at Bedforth	10
vij	f	Fernam, Stodes, blake	11
	g	amoore, saint Laurence.	12
xv	A	at Waltam:	13
iiij	b	(*Sol in Virgo.*	14
	c	*Assumption of mary,*	15
xij	d	Rochus.	16
i	e	*Dogge dayes ende.*	17
	f	Agapite martyr.	18
ix	g		19
	A	Lewes byshop.	20
xvij	b	Saint Barnard.	21
vi	c		22
	d	Fast.	23
xiiij	e	at London, Tewkesbury,	25
iij	f	*Bartholomew apostle*	24
	g	at Nantwiche	26
xi	A	Northalerton	27
	b	Sudbery,	28
xix	c	Decola. of saint Jhon.	29
viij	d		30
	e	Cutbert virgin.	31

32

❡ September hath .xxx. dayes.

xvi	f	❡ Fayres.	1
v	g	Anthony martyr,	2
	A	Prothus.	3
xiij	b	Transl. Cutbert,	4
ij	c	Eugedij confessor,	5
	d	Dogge dayes ende.	6
x	e	Natiuitie of mary, at	7
	f	Cambridge Sturbridge,	8
xviij	g	at London in Southwarke,	9
vij	A	at Partney three Lady	10
	b	dayes fayre,	11
xv	c	Martine Bishop,	12
iiij	d	*Sol in Libro.* Amantij martir.	13
	e	Holy Rodde daye, at	14
xij	f	Waltam abbey, and at	15
i	g	Wotten vnder hedge,	16
	A	and at Spalding,	17
ix	b	Uxbridge and Catesby	18
	c	S, Laurence.	19
xvij	d	❡ *Ember daye*,	20
vi	e	Mathew apostle at Croyden,	21
	f	Holden in Holdernes.	22
xiiij	g	Saint Edmondes bury,	23
iij	A	Firmin byshop,	24
	b	Cypriane and Justiniane,	25
xi	c	Cosme Damiane.	26
	d	Exuperty byshop,	27
xix	e	Michael Archaun. at maulton	28
viij	f	S. Jues, Hadley, Latham,	29
	g	Milnall, and Sittingborne,	30

(October hath .xxxi. dayes.

xvi	A		1
v	b	Leodegarius martir.	2
xiij	c	Candidi martir.	3
ij	d	Frauncis Confessor.	4
	e	Appolin martir.	5
x	f	Sainct Faithes adye	6
	g	Saint Sithes besyde	7
xviij	A	Norwiche.	8
vii	b	Mercell & Mercelliani,	9
	c	¶ Terme beginneth	10
xv	d	Nicase byshop.	11
iiij	e	The birth of king Edward	12
	f	Saint Edwardes daye at	13
xij	g	Grauesen, at Win- Sol in Scor.	14
i	A	sor and Marfield.	15
	b	S. Wulfrane byshop.	16
ix	c	Etheldrede virgin.	17
	d	Luke Euangelist, at	18
xvii	e	Ely and Stainton.	19
vi	f		20
	g	X. Thousand virgins.	21
xiiij	A	Mary Salome.	22
iij	b		23
	c	Maglory byshop.	24
xi	d	Crispin and Crispiniani	25
	e		26
xix	f	¶ Fast.	27
viij	g	Symon and Jude, at	28
	A	Harford, Ciceter and	29
xvi	b	Newmarket.	30
v	c	Quintine ¶ Fast.	31

❡ Nouember hath xxx. dayes.

	d	All saintes day. ❡ Faires.	1
xiij	e	All soules day at	2
ij	f	Kingston and Blechingly,	3
	g		4
x	A		5
	b	Saint Leonardus day,	6
xviij	c	at Neweportponde,	7
vij	d	and at Standley,	8
	e	*Theodoretus.*	9
xv	f	Martine byshop,	10
iiij	g	Amantij martyr	11
	A		12
xij	b	s. Edmonde kinge at ❡ *Sol in Sagi.*	13
i	c	Saint Edmondes bury.	14
	d		15
ix	e	Edmond archbishop	16
	f	Hewe byshop,	17
xvij	g	at Lincolne,	18
vi	A	Q. Elizabeth began.	19
	b		20
xiiij	c		21
iii	d		22
	e	Clement byshop.	23
xi	f		24
	g	Katherine virgin.	25
xix	A		26
viij	b		27
	c	Terme endeth ✠ Faires.	28
xvi	d	Rochester & Maidenhead.	29
v	e	Andrewe Apostle at	30

			❡ December hath xxxi. dayes.	1
	f			1
xiij	g		❡ Faires	2
ij	A		Advent Sundaye,	3
x	b		Barbara virgin.	4
	c		Saba abbot,	5
xviij	d		saint Nicolas Bishop.	6
vij	e		at Spaldinge,	7
	f		*Conception of mary.*	8
xv	g		Cipriani abbot.	9
iiij	A		Eulalie virgin.	10
	b		Damasius,	11
xij	c			12
i	d		Saint Lucie virgi. ❡ *Sol in Cap.*	13
	e		Nicasius byshop.	14
ix	f		Valerian byshop.	15
	g		Lazary byshop,	16
xvii	A			17
vi	b		Gracian byshop.	18
	c		Ignatius byshop.	19
xiiij	d		*Embring dayes:*	20
iij	e		*Thomas apostle.*	21
	f		XXX. martirs,	22
xi	g		Victor Virgin.	23
	A		❡ Fast.	24
xix	b		*Natiuitie of Christ,*	25
viij	c		*Steuen martir.*	26
	d		*Jhon Euangelist,*	27
xvi	e		*Innocentes daye,*	28
v	f		Thomas Becket, at	29
	g		Caunterbury	30
xiii	A		Syluester Byshop.	31

⁋ *The Declaracion of this*
Allmanacke for the
yeare of our Lord.
1571.

T H E Gold n nomber.   14.
The Circle of the Sunne.   12
The Epacke.   4.
The Dominicall letter.   G.

Betwene Christmas & shroftyde viij. wekes and vi. dayes.
Ashe wendsdaye the xxviij. daye of February.
Esterdaye the xv. daye of Aprill.
Rogacion sondaye the xx. daye of Maye.
Whyt Sondaye the iij. daye of June.
This yere 1571. is no Eclypes of the Soune nor of the mone.

⁋ *Ianuarye hath xxxi. dayes.*

T H E firste quarter the .3. daye at 3. of the clocke 5. minutes in the morninge coulde.

The full Mone the 11. day at 7. of the clocke 18. minutes in the Morninge temperat could.

The last quarter the 19. daye at one of the clocke in the Morninge raine and coulde.

The new Moone the 25. daye at 2. of the clocke 56. minutes in ye after none could wind.

⁋ *Februarye hath xxviij. dayes.*

The first quarter the firste daye at 12. of the clocke 4. minutes at midnighte could the winde North.

The full Mone the 9. daye at 12. of the clocke 42 minutes at midnight great and most vement winde.

The last quarter the 17. day at 10. of the clocke in the morninge temperat.

The newe Mone the 24. daye at 2. of the clock 28. minutes in the morninge moyst.

¶ *Marche hath xxxi. dayes.*

The first quarter the 3. daye at 4. of the clocke in the after none moist.

The full Mone the 11. daye at 3. of the clocke 48. minutes in the after none temperat.

The last quarter the 18. day at 4. of the clocke 48. minutes in the after none could.

The new Mone the 25. day at 4. of the clocke 46. minutes in the after none very hoot & drye for that season of the yere.

¶ *Aprill hath xxx. dayes.*

The first quarter the 2. day at one of the clocke at none moist.

The full Mone the 10. day at one of the clocke 42. minutes in the morning darcke cloudy wether for to Folow.

The last quarter the 16. day at 9. of the clocke 50. minuts in the after none tempestrus wether.

The newe Mone the 24. daye at 6. of of the 13. minutes in the morninge temperat.

¶ *May hath xxxi. dayes.*

The first quarter the 2. daye at 6. of the clocke in the morninge temperat and windy.

The full Mone the 9. daye at 11. of the clocke 56. minutes at none moist.

The last quarter the 16. day at 3. of the clocke 50. minuts in the morninge temperat.

The new Mone the 23. daye at 6. of the clocke 24. minutes in the after none windy

The first quarter the last daye at 9. of ye clocke 40. minutes at nighte temperat but after 2. or 3. dayes great windes.

ALMANACKE FOR THREE YEARES, 1571

⁋ *Iune hath xxx. dayes.*

The full Mone the 7. daye at 8. of the clocke. 40. minutes at nighte temperat.

The last quarter the 14. daye at 12. of the clocke at none warme.

The newe Moone the 22. daye at 9. of the clocke 17. minutes in the morninge moyste.

The firste quarter the laste daye at 10. of the clocke in the morninge winde and tempestes.

⁋ *Iulye hathe. xxxi. dayes.*

The full Mone the 7. daye at 3. of the clocke 11. minutes in the morninge windy.

The last quarter the 13. day at 11. of yͤ clocke 20. minutes at nighte temperat.

The newe Moone the 21. daye at 12. of the clocke .33. minutes at midnighte thonder and lightninge.

The first quarter the 29. daye at 9. of the clocke at nighte moyste.

⁋ *August hathe xxxi. dayes*

The full Mone the 5. daye at 11. of the clocke 14. minutes in the morninge, raine and tempestes.

The last quarter the 12. daye at oue a clocke at none raine and tempestes.

The newe Mone the 20. day at 3. of the clocke 53. minutes in the after none temperat.

The first quarter the 28. day at 3. of the clocke in the morninge, warme.

⁋ *September. hath xxxi. dayes.*

The full Moone. the 3. daye at 4. of the clocke 52. minutes at nighte greate and most terrible windes.

The last quarter the 11. day at 6. of the clocke 2. minutes in the morninge cloudye wether and windye.

The newe Moone the 19. daye at 6. of the clocke 54. minutes in the morninge temperat & coulde.

The first quarter the 26. day at 10. of the clock 48. minutes in the morninge temperat.

¶ *October hath xxxi. dayes.*

The full Moone the 3. daye at 6. of the clocke 24. minutes in the morninge temperat.

The last quarter the 10. daye at 12. of the clocke at midnighte moyste.

The newe Moone the 18. daye at 8. of the clocke 41. minutes at nighte, lyke to be foulle wether.

The firste quarter the 25. day at 6. of the clocke 30. minutes at nighte lyke to be no good wether.

¶ *Nouember hath xxx. dayes.*

The full Mone the firste daye at 8. of the clocke 20. minutes at nighte temperat.

The last quarter the 9. daye at 9. of the clocke at night raine.

The newe mone the 17. daye at 9. of the clocke 14. minutes in the morninge coulde & moist.

The first quarter the 24. day at 2. of the clocke 3. minutes in the morninge moist.

¶ *December. 1571.*

The full Moone the firste daye at 12. of the clocke 40. minutes at hye none coulde miste wether.

The last quarter the 9. daye at 3. of the clocke 40. minutes at after none coulde.

The newe Moone the .16. daye at eighte of the clocke .17. minutes at nighte raine, winde and sleete.

The firste quarter the .23. daye at .11. of the clocke in the morninge. moiste.

The full Moone the laste daye at seuen of the clocke sixe minutes in the morninge moiste lyke to snowe.

*The Declaracion of the All-
manacke for the yeare of
our Lorde God .1572. be-
inge Lepe yeare.*

THE Golden nomber.   15.
The Circle of the Sunne.   13.
The Epacte.   15.
The Sondaye letter.   F. and E.
Betwene Christmas and shroftyde 7. wekes and 5. dayes.
Ashewenesdaye the 20. daye of Februarye.
Ester daye the 6. daye of Aprill.
Rogacion Sondaye the xi. daye of Maye.
Whyt sondaye the 25. of Maye.

¶ This yeare of oure Lorde 1572. there shalbe an Eclipes of the moone the 25. daye of June at 11. of the clocke 18. minutes in the eueninge and shalbe darckened 7. pointes 12 minutes in the signe of Capricorne 13. degres and 30. minutes within 9. degres and 46. minutes of the Dragōs tayle, and shall beginne for to come vndernethe the shadow of the earth with vs at London at 8. of the clocke 53. minutes, and shalbe at the greatest darckenes at 10. of the clocke 18. minutes & shal end here Eclipes at 11. of ye clocke 43. minutes so that it shall contenuwe frō the beginning vnto the ende 2. oures 50. minutes and the princepall of the Eclipes shallbe sene in the Southe Southe Est.

¶ *Ianuarye 1572.*

The last quarter the 8. daye at 11. of the clocke in the forenone temperat coulde.

The newe Mone the 15. daye at 6. of the clocke 38. minutes in the after none inclyned to bee winde and moiste.

The first quarter the .21. daye at 12. of the clocke at midnighte coulde lyke to be snowe.

The full Moone the 30. daye at one of the clocke 58. minutes in the morninge froste.

WILLIAM BOURNE

¶ *Februarye 29. dayes.*

The laste quarter the 7. daye at 2. of the clocke in the morninge coulde rayne and cloudy.

The newe Mone the 23. daye at 4. of the clocke 38. minutes in the after none moyst.

The first quarter the 20. daye at 4. of the clocke 5. minutes in the after none temperat.

The full Moone the 28. daye at 6. of the clocke .40. minutes in the after none darcke raine wether.

¶ *Marche 1572.*

The last quater the 7. daye at hye none 50. minutes temperat.

The newe Moone the 14. daye at 7. of a clocke 26. minutes in the morninge temperat, but after 3. dayes great windes.

The first quarter the 21. daye at 9. of the clocke 50. minutes in the forenone warme.

The full Moone the 29. day at 12. of the clocke 13. minutes at hye none coulde and raine.

¶ *Aprill 1572.*

The laste quater the 5. daye at 7. of the clocke 52. minutes in the eueninge hotte with thonder and lighteninges.

The newe Moone the 12. daye at 12. of the clocke 43. minutes at hyghe none winde but after that fayre and temperate.

The firste quarter the 20. daye at 4. of the clocke in the morninge temperat warme.

The full Moone the 28. day at one of the clocke 28. minutes in the morning thonder and tempestes.

¶ *Maye 1572.*

The last quarter the 5. daye at one of the clocke in the morninge temperat and windy.

The newe Moone the 11. daye at 11. of the clocke 43. minutes at hyghe midnighte temperat.

The first quarter the 19. daye at 7. of the clocke 49. minutes in the after none temperat.

The full Moone the 27. daye at 11. of the clocke .56. minutes at hyghe none fayre wether.

⁌ Iune 1572.

The last quarter the 3. daye at 5. of the clocke in the morninge temperat.

The newe Moone the 10. daye at 11. of the clocke 56. minutes at hyghe none temperat.

The firste quarter the 18. daye at one of the clocke 40. minutes at none temperat.

The full Mone the 25. daye at 10. of the clocke 18. minutes at nighte temperat.

⁌ Iuly 1572.

The laste quarter the seconde daye at .10. of the clocke 40. minutes before none raine & thonder.

The newe Moone the 20. daye at one of the clocke. 40. minutes in the morninge, raine & tempestes.

The first quarter the 18 daye at 6. of the clocke in the forenonne hoate wether lyke to thonder and lighteninge.

The full Moone the 25. daye at 4. of the clocke 10. minutes in the morning close wether and altration of wether.

The last quarter the laste daye at 8. of the clocke at nighte temperat.

⁌ August .1572.

The newe Moone the eighte daye at .5. of the clocke in the after none raine hayle thonder and tempestes.

The firste quarter the 15. daye at 7. of the clocke at nighte winde and altration of wether.

The full moone. the 23. daye at .12. of the clocke at hyghe none rayne and tempestes.

The laste quarter the .30. daye at sixe of the clocke 40. minutes in the morninge temperat.

❧ September 1572.

The newe Moone the seuenth daye at 9. of the clocke 28. minutes in the forenone temperat coulde.

The fyrste quarter the .15. daye at 5. of the clocke in the morning temperat, & moyst wether.

The full Moone the 21. daye at eighte of the clocke .34. minutes at nighte, warme.

The laste quarter the .28. daye at .11. of the clocke at nighte temperat and moiste.

❧ October .1572.

The newe moone the seuenthe daye at 2. of the clocke 47. minutes in the morninge greate windes.

The first quarter the 14. daye at 2. of the clocke at night raine.

The full Moone the 21. day at sixe of the clocke 30. minutes in the morninge raine.

The last quarter the 28. daye at 5. of the clocke 47. minutes at night, temperat according vnto the tyme of the yeare.

❧ Nouember .1572.

The newe moone the 5. daye at 6. of the clocke 35. minutes at night raine.

The first quarter the 12. day at 9. of the clocke 5. minutes at night temperat and after altration of wether.

The full mone the 19. day at 6. of the clocke 29. minutes at nighte, raine.

The last quarter the 27. daye at one of the clocke 45. minutes at none temperat.

❧ December .1572.

The newe mone the 5. daye at 8. of the clocke 53. minutes in the morninge temperat.

The first quarter the 12. daye at 5. of the clocke in the morninge frost.

The full Moone the 19. daye at 9. of the clocke 24. minutes in the forenone coulde lyke to snowe.

The laste quarter the 27. daye at 11. of the clocke 10. minutes before none temperat, but after wardes winde and alltration of wether.

The Declaration of the All-manacke for the yeare of oure Lorde .1573.

THE golden nomber.	16.
The Cirkell of the sonne.	14.
The Epacte.	26.
The Sondayes letter.	D.

Between Christmas and shroftyde 5. wekes and 5. dayes.
Ashe wenesdaye the 4. daye of February.
Ester daye the 22. of Marche.
Rogacion sondaye the 26. daye of Aprill.
Assension daye the 30. daye of Aprill.
Whitsondaye the 10. daye of Maye.
⁋ This yeare of oure Lorde .1573. there shalbe an Eclipse of the mone the 8. daye of December at eighte of the clocke .42. minutes at night & shalbe darckened 19. pointes .38. minutes yᵉ

mone being in yͤ signe of Gemi .26. degres 34 minutes with in one degree and 31. minutes of the Dragons hed and the mone shall beginne for to come vndernethe the shadowe of the earthe with vs at London at 7. of the clocke 36. minutes and shalbe at the greatest darknes at 8. of the clocke 42. minutes and shall ende hyre Eclipes at 9. of the clocke 46. minutes. So that it shall continewe from the beginninge vnto the eande .2. ours 8. minuts and the principall of the darcknes of the Mone shalbe sene nere the southe est.

Ianuary .1573.

The newe moone the 3. daye at 9. of the clocke 56. minutes at night could froste and 3. dayes after coulde stormes.

The firste quarter the 10. daye at one of the clocke at none temperate for that tyme of the yeare.

The full mone the 18. daye at 2. of the clocke 14. minutes in the morninge raynne.

The laste quarter the .26. daye at .6. of the clocke in the morninge temperat and moiste accordinge vnto the tyme.

Februarye .1573.

The newe Moone the seconde daye at eight of the clocke 41. minutes in the morninge temperat.

The firste quarter the 9. daye at one of the clocke in the morninge windy.

The full moone the 16. daye at 7. of the clocke 44. minutes at nighte reasonable wether.

The last quarter the .24. daye at .11. of the clocke 20. minutes at nighte temperat.

Marche 1573.

The newe Moone the thyrde daye, at sixe of the clocke 24. minutes at after none moyste wether.

The firste quarter the 10. daye at 11. of the clocke 50. minutes at hye none raynne and tempestes.

ALMANACKE FOR THREE YEARES, 1571

The full moone the 18. day at   . of the clocke 6. minutes at none temperat warme.

The last quarter the 26. daye at 8. of the clocke 40. minutes at none raine.

❧ Aprill 1573.

The newe Moone the seconde daye at .3. of the clocke 13. minutes in the morninge, warme wether.

The firste quarter the 9. daye at 2. of the clocke in the morninge temperat.

The full Moone the 17. daye at 6. of the clocke 44. minutes in the morninge temperat.

The laste quarter the 25. daye at one of the clocke in the morninge muche winde.

❧ Maye 1573.

The newe Moone the firste daye at .11. of the clocke 49. minutes at none temperat and fayre.

The firste quarter the 8. daye at 9. of the clocke in the after none temperat.

The full Moone the .16. daye at neyne of the clocke 11. minutes at nighte fayre and drye wether.

The laste quarter the .24. daye at three of the clocke 40. minutes in the morninge temperat and moiste.

The newe Mone the 30. daye at 9. of the clocke at nighte tempesteous wether.

❧ Iune 1573.

The firste quarter the seuenthe daye at none stormye wether longe together.

The full Moone the 15. daye at 9. of the clocke 6. minutes in the morning tempestes wether.

The laste quarter the 22. daye at 7. of the clocke 34. minutes in the morninge rayne and tempestes.

The newe Moone the 29. daye at 7. of the clocke .4. minutes in the morninge moiste wether.

(July 1573.

The firste quarter the .7. daye at .5. of the clocke 34. minutes in the morning temperat and moiste.

The full Moone the 14. daye at 7. of the clocke 22. minutes at after none windye.

The laste quarter the 21. daye at one of the clocke 5. minutes at none fayre and warme.

The newe Moone the 28. daye at 6. of the clocke .54. minutes at after none fayre and warme.

(August 1573.

The firste quarter the 5. daye at 10. of the clocke at nighte darcke cloudy wether.

The full Moone the 13. daye at .4. of the clocke 31. minutes in the morninge temperat.

The laste quarter the 19. daye at eighte of the clocke 31. at nighte tempestes wether.

The newe Moone the 27. daye at .9. of the clocke 54. minutes in the morning temperat and windye.

(September .1573.

The firste quarter the 4. daye at one of the clocke .40. minutes at none raine and greate tempeste.

The full Moone the 11. daye at one of the clocke 11 minutes at none temperat and moyst.

The laste quarter the 18. daye at 4. of the clocke in the morninge moiste.

The newe Moone the 26. daye at twoo of the clocke 36. minutes in the morninge temperat.

(October .1573.

The firste quarter the 4. daye at 4. of the clocke 30. minutes in the morninge windy.

The full Moone the 10. daye at 10. of the clocke 4. minutes at nighte temperat.

ALMANACKE FOR THREE YEARES, 1571

The last quarter the 17. daye at 6. of the clocke at nighte ranye wether.

The newe Moone the 25. daye at 8. of the clocke 40. minutes at nighte raine.

❡ Nouember .1573.

The firste quarter the .2. day at 5. of the clocke at nighte coulde and moiste.

The full Moone the 9. daye at 7. of the clocke 42. minutes in the morninge tempeste wether.

The laste quarter the 16. daye at 9. of the clocke 50. minutes in the morninge stormye wether a longe time together.

The newe Moone the 24. daye at .2. of the clocke 35. minutes in the after none temperat for the time of the yeare.

❡ December .1573.

The firste quarter the seconde daye at three of the clocke twentye minutes in the morninge moiste.

The full Moone the .8. daye at eighte of the clocke 42 minutes at nighte mystinge wether.

The last quarter the 16. daye at 7. of the clocke in the morninge temperat coulde.

The newe Moone the .24. daye at .7. of the clocke 22. minutes in the morninge windye.

The firste quarter the laste daye at 10. of the clocke 40. minutes before none some what temperat wether.

FINIS.

A rule for letting of bloude,
Purginge, Bathinge,
Settinge, Sowinge
and Plantinge.
(.:.)

First, lette no bloude at anye tyme withoute greate cause, for it bringethe weakenes and manye infirmities: If you doe yet see that it be after good disgestion, & fastinge in a fayre temperat daye, and beware of all manner of excesse, as labouringe watchinge, and carnall copulation, and so forth: And after that use fyne meates of lighte disgestion, and abstayne from all the aforesayde vnto the fourthe daye. And these signes be moste vnmete for lettinge of bloud, yͤ Mone beinge in Taurus, Gemini, Leo, Virgo, and Capricornus, the last halfe of Libra, and the firste halfe of Scorpio, the reste all good, so that the Mone be not in the signe that gouerneth the mēber. Furthermore, let the Flegmatike bloude in the signe of Aries, and Sagittarius, the Melancholike persones, in Libra and Aquarius: And for the Cholerike persones, Cancer, Scorpio, and Pisces, and the Sanguine people, Aries, Cancer, Libra, Scorpio, Sagittarius, Aquarius & Pisces: Furthermore, from the new Moone to the firste quarter, a mete tyme for to lette yonge men bloud: And from the firste quarter to the full moone, good for middle age. And from the full to the last quarter, mete for aged folkes. And from the last quarter to the chaunge, beste for old men.

Furthermore, there is to be noted this, that you lett no bloude when that Mars and Saturne have anye aspect the one to the other, neither the moone to Saturne or Mars, neither anye aspect of the Mone to yͤ Sonne, nor the Mone to yͤ tayle of the Dragon, and in the spring time lett bloud at the right side, haruest time at the left side.

¶ Of purginge.

THE best time to take purgations, is neither when the time is to hoate nor to colde: For by the rules Astronomicall, the best time is when the Mone is in coulde and moist signes, as in Cancer Scorpio, Pisces, and Gemini, beinge comforted by anye aspecte of the good planetes: And the Mone in Aries, Taurus, Leo, Virgo, & Capricornus, be naughte to purge, and the cause of the vomitinge of the purgation is, if the mone haue aspect to anye planete retrograte.

¶ To Bathe.

THE mone in Aries, Leo, Sagittarius, Cancer, Scorpio, and Pisces, bee very good to bathe and these folowinge be euill to bathe, as Taurus, Virgo, and Capricornus.

Good to stoppe Fluxes, Rewmes, and Laxes the mone in Taurus, Virgo, and Capricornus.

Good to cōfort the vertue atractiue, the moone in Aries, Leo and Sagittarius.

The powers retentiue, the moone in Taurus, Virgo, and Capricornus.

For the disgestiue, the moone in Gemini, Libra and Aquarius.

For the expulsiue vertue, the moone in Gemini, Cancer, Scorpio, and Pisces.

¶ For setting, sowynge, and Planting.

Good to sowe seades, the moone in Taurus, Cancer, Virgo, Libra, and Capricornus, in the increase of the moone, and to plante and graft, the moone in Taurus and Aquarius, in the increase of the moone, being fixed signes, and being muche the better for planting, sowing, and grafting, the moone hauinge sixtile or trine aspecte with Saturne, it is good to doe any thing about digginge or earing of the grounde.

⁌ Now foloweth the nature of the .xii.
signes with their properties.

Aries is hoate and drie, of the nature of the fier, Collerick, masculine, of the daye orientals of the house of Mars, & the exaltation of the sunne, and a mouable signe, and of a bitter sauour, and of the humaine member, kepeth the head and the face.

Taurus is colde and drie, of the nature of the earth, melancholike, femenine, of the night meridionall, a fixed signe, the house of Venus, the exaltation of the Moone, and of a sower sauour, and keepeth of man the necke and gorge.

Gemini is hoate and moist, of the nature of the ayre, sanguine, masculyne of the daye occidentall and commonly the house of Mercurye, of a sweet sauour, and keepeth of man the shoulders, armes and handes.

Cancer is colde and moist, of the nature of water, flegmatike feminine, of the night septentrionalles, a mouable signe, the house of Luna, the exaltatiō of Jupiter, of a salte sauour, and kepeth of man the breast, stomake, and long.

Leo is hoate and drie, of the nature of fyre, collericke, masculine, of the daie Orientalles, and fixed the house of the Sunne, of a bitter sauour, & kepeth of man the harte, backe and sides.

Virgo is colde and drie, the nature of the earth, melancholike, feminine, of the night meridionals and common the house of Mercury, and of a sower sauour, and keepeth of man the belly, bowelles, and inward partes.

Libra is hoate and moist, the nature of the air sanguyne, and masculine, of the daie Occidentals, and mouable, the house of Venus, the exaltation of Saturne, of a sweate sauoure, and kepeth of man the nauel, and the lower partes of the belly with the loynes.

Scorpio is cold and moist, of the nature of the water, flegmatike, feminine, of the night Septentrionalles, & fixed the house of Mars, of a salt sauour, & kepeth of mā y[e] preuy parts & the blader.

Sagittarius is hoate and drie, of the nature of ayre, colerike and masculine, of the daie Orientals and common the house of Jupiter, of a bitter sauour, and kepeth of man the thighes.

Capricornus is colde and drie, of the nature of the earth, melancholike feminine of the night meridionals, and mouable, the house of Saturne, the exaltatiō of Mars, and a sower sauour, and kepeth of man the knees.

Aquarius is hoate and moiste, of the nature of the ayre, sanguyne masculine, of the daie Occidentals, and fixed the house of Saturne, and of a sweete sauour, and kepeth of man the shinnes and legges,

Pisces is colde and moist, of the nature of the water, flegmatike feminine, of the night Septentrionalles, and common the house of Jupiter, and the exaltation of Venus, of a salte sauour, and kepeth of man the feete.

¶ The nature, course and qualitie of the .vii. lightes or Planetes.

SAturne is hiest of the .vii. Planetes, and slowest of his proper mocion, being colde and drie of nature, malicious, and enemy to nature, a distroier of life, and of the body he gouerneth the right ear, the milt, the bladder, and of humors the melancholike, and part of fleume, his colour is like vnto lead colour, requiring neare .30. yeares to fulfill his course, his metall is lead.

Jupiter is next to Saturne, temperat, faire, and bright, being hoate and moyste, sanguine, louing, hauing regarde ouer the lunges, the sides, the gristels, and of the seade or naturall humor of man, his mettall is tinne, requiring .xii. yeares to finish his course.

Mars is hoate and drie, of nature cruell, and of the body is attributed to him the lefte eare, the vaynes, the genitories, and of humors the cholor: And as some saie, he gouerneth the lyuer, beinge of a read colour, euill of nature, his metall is Iron and steele, and in two yeares he endeth his course through the .xii. signes in the zodiake.

The sunne is placed in the middle of al the planettes most cleare and brighte, the well of pure light, he is the principal planet in the firmament, he is the cause of wynter and sommer, of the daye and the night, being hoate and drie, louinge, giuing life and light to all thinges, hauing natural vertue, and of the members he ruleth the brayne, the marowe, the sight, the senues, and generally all the members of the right part of the bodie, his metal is pure golde, going through the .xii. signes in .365. daies .5. houres .55. minutes .13. secondes.

Venus is colde and moist, louinge, flegmatike, and of the body she gouerneth the backbone, the buttockes, the lower part of the belly, and the matrix, with the moneth fat, her colour is bright, yea brighter then Jupiters, her metall is copper, her course is like the Sunnes course, neuer aboue .48. degrees frō the Sunne, called the morning starre or vesper.

Mercury is next vnto Venus, somwhat shining but not very bright, he is good with the good planetes, and euell with the euill, when he is ioyned with thē, his metall is quicke siluer, his course is like to the Sunnes course, neuer aboue .29. degrees from the Sunne.

The Moone is lowest of all the Planetes, being colde and moyst, of nature louing, hauing domination ouer the stomake & belly, and of the mother of women, and generally ouer the members of the lefte syde of the body, her metall is siluer, running ouer the whole zodiake in .27. days and .8. hours.

Furthermore, you must note that Jupiter and Venus, be called good and fortunate, but Jupiter is called the greater good fortune, and Venus the lesse: Nowe Saturne and Mars, bee called euill fortune, but Saturne is called the greatest vnfortunate, and Mars the lesse. The Sunne or Moone are called meane or betwene both, that is to saye: neither fortunate nor vnfortunate, but indifferēt.

⁋ The table of the contentes
of these Rules folowing.

1 The first Rule is of a good Nauigator.
2 The seconde Rule treateth of the .32. wyndes, belonging to a Nauigator, otherwyse called the 32. pointes of the Compas.
3 The thirde Rule treateth of the golden number or Prime, shewing the Epact, & by the Epact to knowe the age of the Moone.
4 The fourth Rule teacheth you to know by the age of the moone whan it doth flowe at any place where you doe knowe what moone maketh a full Sea, with a tabell of tides ioyned therto.
5 The fifth rule treateth of ye Sunnes & Moones course in the zodiake, and how that you shal know at what houre that the moone shall ryse and set, & at what point, and wynde, with other necessarye thinges.
6 The sixt rule is of a table of declination for .3 yeares, exactly calculated for euery day af ye mōth.
7 The seuenth rule sheweth you how to take the altitude of the Sūne, and by the height of ye Sun to knowe the Equinoctiall, and by the altitude of the Equinoctiall, to know the eleuatiō of the pole artike, and howe that you shall behaue yourselfe with your Astralabe, with an ensample of grauesende, and also howe to gette the true meridia, and also of the Northeasting and Noothweastinge of the compas, necessary for nauigation, otherwise called the variation of the compas.
8 The eigh rule of the north starre, & howe that he should be taken vpon any of the eight principal wyndes or pointes of the compas with an obseruation of the balastela or crosestaffe.
9 The ninth rule is of the sayling of vpon one of the quarters of the compas in howe farre sayling you doe rayse or laye a degree, and what you doe departe from your meridian.

10   The .x. rule treateth of the soūdinges, coming from any place out of the Occidentall Sea.

For to seke vshant or the lezarde, and also all a longest till you doe come to the coast of Flaūders.

11   The .xi. rule treateth of the logitude, although that it be very tedious.

12   The .xii. rule sheweth howe many myles wyll in square to one degree of longitude in euery seuerall latitude betwene the Equinoctiall and any of the twoo poles.

13   The .xiii. rule teacheth of the longitude & the latitude of certaine of the moste notable townes in Englande, and also how lōg that the moone doth chaunge at the one towne before the other, and also the diuersitie of the longest date in Sommer from Southhampton to the North or moste place in Scotlande.

14   The .xiiii. rule is of the longitude and declination of .12. notable fixed starres for nauigation with tables of their shining, and at what point of your compas that they doe both rise and sette, and also tables for euery moneth in ye yeare, declaring at what houre and minute that thei be south running from the first daye of euery moneth to the .15. and from the .15. daye to the last day, and will continue this .100. yeare without much error.

15   The .xv. rule, how to sayle by the Globe.

16   The .xvi. how to know the houre of the day by the Compas.

⁋ The first Rule is of a good
Nauigator.

OF all sciences that is vsed with us in Englād, Nauigation is one of the principall & most necessary for the benefite of our Realme and natiue countrey, and also most defencible against our enemies, because we bee enuironed rounde aboute with the sea, and there be a great number of good and wittie Nauigators, but notwithstāding some simple, and therefore I would wishe those that be Sea men of the meanest sorte (I meane those that sayle for single hires) to practise one of these three faculties, that is to saie: either to be a Gonner, a Carpenter or els to be a Nauigator. For I do see a great nomber that do occupie the Sea, that haue no sight almoste at all in their science, although they have occupied the Sea a long time, whiche is a straunge case, that those men that haue had the dealing therewith to be vtterly voide of knoweledge, their maisters to haue both knowledge and conning, and they to bee altogether ignoraunt, which is occasion that I do thinke that the expert maisters in deede, doe seldome instruct their companie: For if they did, there is no doubte but the multitude would haue more vnderstanding. But wherefore should I waste time in wryting hereof, seing it is instructions that must amend this fault: Wherefore that you may the better vnderstande or knowe my purpose, you shall vnderstande that the good and wittie Nauigator, doth consider and knowe by experience, that the moone doth rule the flouddes, or els he knoweth that in one Moone there is two springes, & two nepes, the one spring to be at the full moone or three daies after, the other at the chaunge, or within twoo or three daies after, and at both the quarters the nepe streames. He doth knowe by experience, that the moone in suche a quarter of the skie maketh a full Sea, so that the raging wyndes doth neither hinder the same, nor cause it to be altered. He dothe knowe how that the streame or floudes or ebbes, doth set from place to place, from nas to nas, from poynt to poynt, in euery place about the Coaste that he hath occupied. And the chiefest thinge that belongeth to a Sea faring man, is to knowe the place that he shall happen to fall with, whiche thing he must knowe by the beholding of the countrey, by taking some principall marke thereof, & the chiefest thing is, to beholde the hilles and vales of the lande, that he may knowe them when he shall happen to see them againe, vpon euery side he must take heade. And as for wooddes and hedges with suche like, are not to be marked, because suche thinges may be cut or felled downe, and so youre marke is lost: Wherfore hylles, vales, cliftes, and Castels, with stepels and Churches, are the beste and most surest markes, that may or can be taken, and are better than hedgrowes, wooddes or trees. Furthermore, the good and wittie Nauigator, by the marke of the shore doth knowe whether there doth lie any daungers, as sandes, rockes, bankes, or shelffes: he knoweth by their soundinge howe neare that he is vnto them, he doth knowe when he hath any occasion to put into any herborowe, whether he haue water enough, yea or nay. Furthermore, he doth knowe by his soundinge, of the depth, and by the grounde that sticketh vpon the tallowe of the lead howe farre that he is shott, although he may see no lāde. Furthermore, he doth knowe when he is in the Occident Sea, by keeping of his course, with what place he shall fall or come to first, he knoweth howe farre that the ship shippe hath ronne or gone, and howe farre that she hath to goe, by keping of accompt or pricking of his carde: he knoweth whether that the shippe goeth to leewardes, or maketh hir waye good: he knoweth whether about the head of the land there runneth any curraunt or not: He knoweth that the indraftes of the lande, causeth the tydes for to runne: he knoweth that the whyte waters or land waters, causeth the ebbes to runne swifter then the flouddes: he knoweth that in runninge up in to a Ryuer, the further he runneth in a floudde, the longer tyde or flowing with him: he knoweth that the salt water or sea water, is more stronger to beare a shippe then the freshe waters or ryuer waters be. Furthermore, he knoweth by the taking of the altitude or height of the Sunne, in what Parrell or Latitude he is in, considering the Sunnes declination, howe farre that he is aboue or beneath the Equinoctial lyne. And furthermore they doe knowe their Latitude or parrel by diuers starres fixed in the firmamēt, as by Oculus tauri, as Orione, his girdell, his shoulders, his feete, and also Alober, or otherwyse called the great Dogge and little dogge, with diuers other starres whiche I passe ouer. And some doe obserue the North star being the tippe of the tayle of Ursa minor, or little beare, but many mē be deceiued in taking of him. But for them whiche doe occupie the South, he is very good, so that they doe knowe the whole compasse of remouing. And for them that doe occupie the North, he will not serue their tournes, because his altitude is so great that your balastela wyll not take him perfecte.

⁋ The second chapiter or Rule, teacheth the .32. wyndes belonging to Nauigation, otherwyse called the .32. pointes of the Compas.

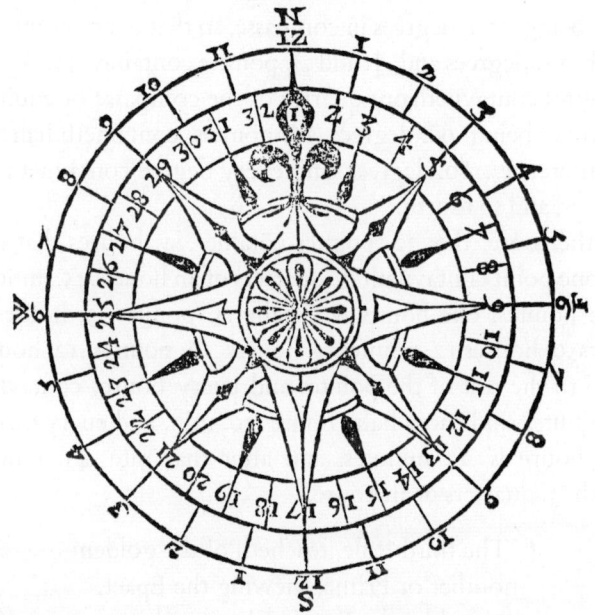

As touching Nauigation, for the instruction of the meanest sort, I haue set this figure or cōpas wher first is to be noted y^e .32. windes or points of y^e compas aboue made. The flower deluce is the first poynt, and these be the names begininge at the North, and so with the course of the Sūne, to say North .1. North and by East .2. North north east .3. North east & by north .4. North east .5. Northeast & by east .6. East northeast .7. East and by north .8. East .9. East and by south .10. East southeast .11. Southeast and by east .12. Southeast .13. Southeast and by south .14. South south east .15. South & by east

.16. South .17. South and by weast .18. South south weast .19. Southweast & by south .20. South weast .21. Southweast and by weast .22. Weast south weast .23. Weast and by south .24. West .25. Weast and by north .26. Weast northweast .27. North weast and by weast .28. Northweast .29. North weast and north .30. North north weast .31. North and by weast .32. This is the whole contentes of the .32 wyndes: And there is in the compasse the contentes of the great circle or equinoctiall circle, being .360. degrees in compasse, so that euery point containeth .11. degrees and .$\frac{1}{4}$. and .4. pointes containe .45. degrees .8. pointes contayneth one quarter of the compasse or equinoctiall circle, being .90. degrees .16. pointes, containeth halfe the circumference .180. degrees, and euery degree contayneth .60. secondes, and so foorth.

Furthermore, the .32. pointes cōtaine .24. houres that is to saye, one point contayneth .3. quarters of an houre .45. minutes, and .2 pointes, one houre & a halfe .4. pointes .3. houres .8. pointes .6. houres 12. pointes .9. houres .16. pointes .12. houres: and so to the rest of the pointes and euery houre, contayneth .60. minutes, and euery halfe houre .30. min. and euery quarter of an houre is .15 minutes, and after that rate .45. minutes maketh .3. quarters of an houre.

⁋ The third Rule, teacheth of the golden
nomber or Prime, shewing the Epact,
and by the Epact to knowe the
age of the Moone.

IT is necessary and cōuenient for the Seafaring men, to knowe the Prime or golden nomber, & by the golden nomber is knowen the Epact, and the Epact sheweth the age of the moone or chaūge daye, within .12. daies vnder or ouer, and by the age of the moone, you may knowe what a clock it doth flowe in any place that you do knowe, what moone doth make a full sea. Therefore it is meete to knowe the Epact, and that is knowne by the Prime or golden nomber. (The cause why it was called the goldē nomber, was because it was sent out of Egipt in letters of golde to the Romaines or citie of Rome.) And it is thus knowen, adde one to the yeare of our Lorde that yeare that you would know the golden nomber or Prime, then deuide the number by .19. the remayner is the Prime, then take the prime and multiplie that by 11. and looke what the nomber commeth vnto, deuide that by .30. the remainder is the Epact, then when ye haue once the Epact, put .11. for euery yeare more then your Epact, and looke what that commeth to, that is your Epact, and if it doe passe 30. put that away and kepe the remainer for your Epact, atd thus this Rule will serue for euer, sauing when the Prime beginneth at one, and then the Epact is .11. and then doing as aforesaide, as you may perceiue by this table hereunder made.

⁋ The tabel of the Prime Epact for .19. yeares, and when those 19. yeares are finished or ended, thē beginne againe, and so it will serue for euer. The first rowe is the yeare of our Lord, the second is the Prime, the third rowe is the Epact.

Yeere of our lord	Prime.	Epact.	yeere of our lord	Prime.	Epact.
1566	9	9	1576	19	29
1567	10	20	1577	1	11
1568	11	1	1578	2	22
1569	12	12	1579	3	3
1570	13	23	1580	4	14
1571	14	4	1581	5	25
1572	15	15	1582	6	6
1573	16	26	1583	7	17
1574	17	7	1584	8	28
1575	18	18			

THe Prime or golden nomber, is the time of .19. yeares, in

the whiche time the moone maketh all her changes of coniunctions with the Sunne, and when all these .19. yeares be expired, then she beginneth againe, as in example, this yeare being the yeare of our Lorde .1556. she chaūged the .21. daie of Marche, and euery yeare doth alter .11. days of her chaunge till the yeare .1585. & then she chaūgeth the said .21. daye of Marche againe, as I shewed you before, the Epact is the putting to .11. for euery yeare. Nowe furthermore, to knowe the age of the moone, do this take your nōber of the Epact for your yeare, then beginne in March alwaies, & then reken how many monethes it is from March reken Marche for one, & then rekē how many days of the moneth it is that you would knowe the age of the moone, then put all your nōbers together, that is to saye: your Epact, your monethes from Marche, your daies of the moneth, then looke how many that cometh vnto that, is the age of ye moone and if it do passe .30. throw all the .30. away & kepe that that will not be .30. for the age of the moone: if iust .30. then it is the chaunge daie, and if it be ye 15 daie of the age of the moone, then the moone is at the full, then betwene .7. daies and .8. of the first quarter: and if .22. daies olde, then the moone is at the last quarter, as for an example, this yeare .1567 and I finde the Epact .20. for the yeare, nowe I would know the age of the moone the .13. daye of June, now I reken how meny monthes it is frō Marche, rekening March for one, & I find it is .4. monthes, then I take & adde al these together, that is to say .20. for the Epact .4. for the monethes, that is to say, March, Aprill, May, & June, & the .13. for the daies of the month, & al cōmeth to .37. the I put away the .30. & there remaineth .7. y^t is the age of ye moone, & shalbe at the first quarter the same night.

⁌ The fourth Rule teacheth howe to knowe by
the age of the moone when it doth flowe at
any place, where you doe knowe
what moone maketh a ful sea.

ALMANACKE FOR THREE YEARES, 1571

Nowe by the age of the moone you may know what a clock that floweth in any place where you doe knowe what moone maketh a full Sea, whiche rule commonly the sea men call the shifting, there Sunne and Moone and many wayes there be to doe, that for this they may doe it, lette them put one ouer into .5. partes, and then take .4 of those partes and put the one fifth part awaye, that serueth for the alteration of .24. houres, and the foure fiue part of an hadoure is .48. minutes, and the fift part of one houre, is .12. minutes. And a floudde and an ebbe, dothe alter .24. minutes forwardes, as this for example: It floweth at .12. of the clocke at the landes ende vppon the chaunge daye, the moone being in the South at all tymes a full Sea, the moone being one daye old, it floweth at .12. of the clocke .48. minutes: Twoo dayes olde, it floweth at one of the clocke .36. minutes: Three daies olde, it floweth at twoo of the clocke 24. minutes. Four daies olde, it floweth at three of the clocke .12. minutes. Fiue daies olde, it floweth at .4. of the clock iust. Sixe daies old, it floweth at foure of the clocke .48. minutes. Seuen dayes olde, at .5. of the clocke .36. minutes. Eight dayes olde, at .6. of the clocke .24. minutes. Nine dayes olde. at .7. of the clocke .12. minutes. Tenne dayes olde, it floweth at .8. of the clocke iust. Eleuē daies olde, at .8. of the clock .48. minutes .12. daies at .9. of the clocke .36. minutes .13. daies olde. at .10. of the clock .24. minutes .14. daies olde, it floweth at .11. of the clock .12. minutes .15. daies olde, it floweth at 12. of the clocke iust, then being the ful moone: and then beginne againe as you did before at one daye olde, and so foorth. For the course of the tydes is nothinge els, but to put for euery daye of the age of the moone one hour, pulling backe the fifthe part of an houre, being .12. minutes, and by this accoumpt you may at all times knowe whan that it doth flowe, by putting to euery floud and ebbe 24. minutes, and two flouddes and two ebbes, putting to .48. minutes. Nowe furthermore, the Sea men vse to make their accompt by this meanes, & it is all one matter, they doe alowe for euery daie of

63

the age of the moone one point and three minutes: for a point of the compas containeth .45 minutes, that is three quarters of one houre, then put .3. minutes to .45. minutes, it maketh .48. minutes and the saide .3. minutes, be the .15. part of a point, and from the chaunge to the full is .15. dayes, then the halfe compas beinge .16. pointes, breake the odde point into .15. partes, and that cometh to .3. minutes, so that the alteration of the tydes for euery .24. houres to be .48. minutes, the 4. fiue partes of an houre, therefore shall folowe a table of tydes, about certain places of this Realme For euery moone containeth .29. daies, 12. houres, 44. minutes, from chaunge to chaunge, and the whole content of the houres of the moone is .708. houres 44. minutes, and there is in euery yeare. 12 chaunges of the moone, and the yeare conteineth 365. daies .v. houres .55. minutes .13. secondes, yet some doe affirme to be odde .6. houres, but there lacketh .4. minutes .47. secondes in the tropicall yeare, and in the yeare is .12. monethes agreable to the .12. moones. The .12. moones containeth .354. daies, so there be .11. daies more in the yrare then there be in the .12. moones, and the yeare is deuided into .12. monethes, whiche monethes hath taken their names at the will and pleasure of men, as January was so called of Janus, because of .2. heades. For that the mouth of January beholdeth the ende of the yeare past, and the beginninge of the yeare to come. February toke his name of certaine Romaines sacrifices called Februa. Marche is socalled of Mars, for Romulus so named it after his father. Aprill comes of Apirio, because that then the earth is opened. May of Maia, the mother of Mercury. June so called by preparinge to the warre. July of Julius Caesar. And August of Augustus Caesar, for in that moneth he entred the counsullship. Then the rest of the monethes tooke their names of their nombre from Marche. Nowe these .12. monethes whiche maketh the yeare, the Sunne doth passe or go through the zodiake, called the .12. signes, which is the occasiō of the yeare. For this is to be noted, that the Sunne as I saide before, doe goe by his naturall mouinge in .365. daies. v houres .55.

ALMANACKE FOR THREE YEARES, 1571

minutes .13. secondes, through the zodiake, contayning .360. degrees, his course being against the .24. houres going from the weast into the East, against the course of primum mobule or first mouer, beinge moued by the mightie prouidēce of God which maketh the .xxiiii. houres and so doth all the seuen lightes or Planetes, except that it be in their retrogatiō, but the Sunne and the moone be neuer retrograte as the other fiue Planetes or lightes be. And this is to be noted, that the moone goeth farther then the Sunne for she goeth through the whole zodiack in .xxvii. daies and eight houres. Nowe in that same tyme the Sunne is remoued by his naturall mouynge from that place of the zodiack, neare seuen and twenty degrees, and then because that the moone hath not founde the Sunne there, it is two daies foure houres foure and fourty minutes more before that the moon ouertaketh the Sunne again. So by that meanes, it is .xxix. dayes .xii. houres, and .44. minutes betweene the chaunge of the moone and the next chaunge, and sometyme in the yeare you shall see the moone rather then at some, as this from January to June, you shall see the moone in fowre and twenty houres after the chaunge, because she hath North declination of the Sunne, and maketh a bygger arche then the Sunne.

From July to December, you shall not see the moone three dayes after, because her Latitude is to the southe part of the Sunne, but you maye see her in .xxiiii. houres before her chaunge. Nowe the Sea men doe Imagyne a Prime daye, whiche is the half quarter of yᵉ moone, that is, when yᵗ the moone is three daies and .18. houres olde, then the moone being .4 pointes to the Eastwardes of the Sunne, whiche is three houres: Nowe they maye in like case obserue that same rule when that the moone is past the full thre daies and .18. houres, & also in the middes of the quarters.

Nowe shall folowe a table of Tydes, and first the moone South or North, on landes ende full Sea.

The moone South and by East, at the Gorre end full Sea.

The moone South south weast, betwene holy Ilande and Tynemouth full sea.

It floweth betwene Tynmouth and Flamborowe head, South weast and northeast moone.

It floweth betwene Flamborowe head & Borlyng towne in the Baye, a South weast and by weast moone.

The moone in the weast southweast, betwene Borlyng towne and Laurenas, full sea.

It floweth betwene Laurenas and Cromer, all alongest the welle, an east and weast moone.

It floweth betwene Cromer and Yarmouthe Rode to Laystowe north Rode, a South east moone.

It floweth betwene Laystowe Rode and Orfordenas, a south east and by south moone.

It floweth betwene Orforde & Orewell wādes a south south east moone.

It floweth betwene the Nasse and the Ware head of Colne, a south and by east moone.

It floweth at the Spyttes and at the Sheue, & all alongest the Swinne, a south moone.

It floweth at the Weast ende of the Norre, a south and by weast moone full sea.

It floweth at Graues ende, a south south weast moone.

It floweth at London brydge a South weast moone.

It floweth at the North forelande, a south south east moone, and so alongest the coast, tyl you come to Bechy, and in the Oftonne from the North forelande to the South forelande, it runneth halfe tyde, and from the South forelande to the Nasse, the tyde runneth halfetyde halfe quarter. And from the Nasse to the fayrly, it runneth half tyde. And Fayrly to Beche, it runneth quarter tyde vnder other.

It floweth to the Weastward of Bechy a kenyng, a south east and by south moone.

It floweth at Portes mouth, a south and by east moone.

It floweth at Saint Ellens, a south south east moone.

It floweth on the Sea side of the Iland, a south east and by south moone, and so on the lande, and at the Neadels, and runneth quarter tyde in the Oftunne.

It floweth at Pooll in the hauen, a south east moone.

It floweth at Wamouth, a east & weast moone.

It floweth at Portlande, a southeast moone.

It floweth from the Weast part of Portlande till you come to Plymmouth an east & west moone

It floweth on the shore from Plymmouth to the Lizarde, a weast and by south moone, and in the Oftonne, a southeast moone.

It floweth at Mouth baye, an East and Weast moone.

It floweth at Selly, a weast & by south moone.

It floweth at the landes ende of goolfe, a weast south weast moone, and all alongest the coste vp to Brystowe, and the coaste of Irelande, from Waterfoord to Kynsale, a weast and by south moone.

Nowe furthermore, it floweth for the most part from the Polle head of Burdeaux, all alongest the coaste of Byskey, Galyza, Portingale, tyll you doe come to the straightes of Malyga, a South weast and Northeast moone.

It floweth at Floushing, a Southweast and by South moone.

It floweth at Anwarpe, an East and Weast moone.

It floweth all alongest the Coast of Flaunders from the Wyldinges to Calys, a South and by East moone, and so runneth halfe a tyde vnder the other.

Nowe here is one speciall thinge to be noted, and that is this, it floweth one poynt of the Compas more in the spryng streames then that it doth in any of the quarters of the moone, so that it be a Ryuer where there is any indraft, hauinge dystaunce from the Sea, when there is neyther rage of wyndes nor no cause, neyther to hynder nor forder the sayd effect. As for example, thus it floweth at Grauesende at the chaunge of the moone or full, a South south weast moone, but in any of the quarters of the Moone, it scant floweth a south and by weast moone, and this is generally for euer.

⁋ The fifth Rule, teacheth of the Sunnes and
Moones course in the zodiake, and howe
you shall knowe at what houre the
Moone shall ryse, and at what
point of the compas, with
other necessary
thinges.

Furthermore, the Sunne by his naturall mouing through the .12. Signes in the zodiake, in the yeare doth cause the height and lowenes of his declination, which is necessary for the Sea faring men, to knowe in which declination they doe take from Equinoctiall to Equinoctiall. And this is to be noted, that as the Sunne hath declination, so in like maner the Moone hath declination, and by hir declination, and also of the Sunne, is knowen the tyme of her shining, or biding aboue our horison, the Sunne or moone in the first minute of Aries, they ryse east and set weast, & shine .12. houres In the first minute of Taurus, they ryse neare the east, north east, and sette neare the weast north weast, and shine .14. houres: In the signe of Gemini, they ryse neare the north east, and by east, and settes neare the northweast and by weast, & shyne 16. houres: In the signe of Cancer the first minute, they make their greatest declination to the north wardes, and then they ryse neare the northeast, & sette neare the north weast, and shyne neare .xvii. houres: In the first minute of Leo, descending towardes the Equinoctiall as they did in Gemini, & in the signe of Virgo, as they did in Taurus: and in the first minute of Libra, Equinoctiall, beginning south declination as in Aries: And in the first minute of Scorpio, they ryse neare the east, south east, and settes neare the weast south weast, and shineth .10. houres. In the first minute of Sagittarius, they ryse neare the southeast and by east, and setteth neare the south weast & by weast and shineth. 8. houres: In the first minute of Capricornus, then they haue their greater declination to the south, and beginneth to retourne to the Equinoctiall, rising neare the south east, and setteth neare the south weast, and shineth more than .vii. houres: In the first minute of Aquarius, as in Sagittari⁹: In the first minute of Pisces, as in Scorpio. And now by this rule you may knowe the rising and setting of the Moone for euer: as this, as I haue shewed you before in the shiftinge of the Sunne and Moone. That for euery daye of the age of the moone, the moone goeth to yᵉ eastwarde one point and .3. minutes, and two daies .2. pointe and .6. minutes. Nowe when you liste to knowe the very houre and tyme of hir rising, looke howe many daies the moone is olde, and then put so many pointes and so many .3. minutes, thē loke what that cometh vnto, and nowe for your better example, I will shewe you the moones beinge South for euery daie of the age of the moone. The moone being one daie olde, the moone is South at .12. of the clocke .48. minutes. The moone being twoo daies olde, wouth at one of the clock .36. minutes in the after noone. Three daies olde, south at twoo of the clocke .24. minutes. Four daies olde, at .3. of the clocke .12. minutes. Fiue daies olde, at .4. of the clocke iust. Sixe daies olde, at .4. of the clocke .48. minutes. Seuen daies olde, at .5. of the clocke, 36. minutes. Then when the moone is iust a quarter olde, south at .6. of the clocke at night. Then at 8. daies olde, the moone is south at .6. of the clocke 24. minutes. At .9. daies olde, at .7. of the clocke .12. minutes. At .10. daies olde, at .8. of the clocke iust. At xi. daies olde. at .viii. of the clock .48. minutes. At .xii. daies olde, at .ix. of the clocke .36. minutes. At .xiii. daies olde, at .x. of the clocke .24. minutes. At .xiiii. daies olde, at .xi. of the clocke .xii. minutes. At .xv. daies olde, the full moone, then the moone is South at midnight: then one daie after, the ful moone South at .xii. of the clocke .48. minutes in the morning. Twoo daies after the full, at one of the clocke .36. minutes. Three daies after, at twoo of the clocke .24. minutes. Foure daies after, at .3. a clock .12. mi. Fiue daies after, at .4. of the clocke iust in the morning. Sixe daies after, at .4. of the clock .48. minutes. Seuen daies after, at .5. of the clock .36. minutes. Then when the moone is three quarters olde, south at .6. a clock in the morninge. At .8. daies after, at .6. a clock .24. minutes .ix. daies after, at .7. a clock .12. minutes .x. daies after, at .8. a clock iust .xi. daies after, at .8. a clock .48. min .xii. daies alter south, at .9. a clock. 36. minut .xiii. daies after south, at .10. a clock in the fore noone .24. mi. xiiii. daies after, at .11. of the clock .12. min. then at 15. daies after the moone doth chaunge being then with the Sunne. For the chaunge of the moone is when the moone and the Sūne be both vnder one like degree and minute of any signe of the zodiack. And the full moone is, when that the Sunne and moone be appositiue, the one directly against the other iust .6. signes asonder, as you may perceiue at the full moone, for then when the moone riseth the sunne setteth, and when the Sunne riseth the moone setteth: and then in any of the quarters the sunne and moone be iust .3. signes asunder, that is iust .90. degrees. Nowe when you liste for to know the very time of the moones rising or setting, then loke in your kalender in what signe & degree the moone is in, then according to the rule of shining deuide that into two equall partes then from the South, so shall you see at what houre the moone riseth: as for example this. In Marche alwaies the Sunne is in Aries, then the moone beinge in her first quarter, thē she is .6. houres to the eastwardes of the Sunne, then the moone must needes be in Cancer, then shineth the moone in our horizon .17. houres, then the moone is south at .6. of the clocke then she shineth .viii. houres and a halfe after .vi. of the clock, so that she setteth at twoo of the clock and halfe an houre past: then she riseth in the daye viii. houres and a halfe before .vi. of the clock, that is at. ix. of the clock and halfe an houre past. Nowe at the last quarter in Marche, then the moone must nedes be in Capricornus, then shineth the moone but .vii. houres, then the moone is south at .vi. of the clock in the morning, then the moone riseth .3. houres and a half before, that is at two of the clock and half an houre past in the morning, then she setteth by day at .9. of the clock & halfe an houre past: and this rule wil serue for euer without any great error. But yet there is a further matter for yᵉ epact doing, which is the Latitude of the moone, frō the head or taile of the Dragon, but that is but a trifle in the respect of much error, & therfore I will not trouble you with yᵗ, yet there is one thing which I wold seafaring mē shold cōsider, although a great nōber be expert in yᵗ, yet it is mete to be spokē of as this, the Sunne beinge in Cancer, or moone in like maner, or in Gemini, or any time when the Sunne or moone hath north declination, they wil sette their compasse before them, and when they see the Sunne to giue an east shadowe, they wyll saie that it is .vi. of the clocke, whiche and if the Sunne be in Cancer, it is not muche past .v. of the clocke, and the more to the southwardes, the more they doe erre. And in lyke case of the Moone being in Cancer, when they doe see the moone geue an east shadowe by their compas, they will saye the moone is weast, but they doe not consider that the Sunne and Moone being in Cācer, be exsentricke and make their senter without the earth, which is the very height of their declination, comminge so neare to them, therefore they must iudge the east or weast from the pole or north starre. If that they will iudge truly, therefore I doe much commende the Equinoctiall dialles, for the exact truthe: For the common people cannot iudge the truuhe by their compas, so that the Sunne or moone, or any other starre, be excentricke, being in Cancer. And you must consider this in lyke maner, the Sunne hauing north declination, the further you doe go to the northwardes, the longer is your daye, and shorter is your nighte, and towards the southwardes the shorter daies and longer nightes. Nowe contrariwyse, the Sunne hauing south declination, the more to the northwardes, the shorter daies and longer nightes, the further to the southwardes, the longer daies and shorter nights, and vnder the Equinoctiall, the nightes and daies all one, what declination soeuer the Sunne hath. But this rule y^t I haue geuen you, is for Londō or any other place that hath that Latitude or eleuation of the pole articke, at .51. or .52. degrees.

⁋ The sixt Rule, is of a tabell of declination
for .iii. yeares, exactly calculated for
euery daye of the moneth.

Nowe shall folowe a table of Declination for iii. yeares, beinge exactly calculated for Englande, and will serue all Europe without muche errour, or any other contrey or place that hath our longitude, as the most part of Africa, as Ginny and these partes to the South, as farre as the anterticke pole being done for euery daie of the moneth, very necessary for Nauigation, and more exact then the regimentes for foure yeares, or any other tables of declynation, for this you must consider, that by the tabels of declination, you cannot knowe what declination the Sunne hath, except you doe knowe what degree and minute that the Suune is in at noone of the eclip-

ALMANACKE FOR THREE YEARES, 1571

ticke lyne, which I am suer that a great number of the Sea men doe not knowe, although certaine of them can calculate the Sunes declination out of the Ephimerides, the greatest nomber can not. Therefore I thought it conuenient to calculate these tables following, and the first rowe towardes your left hande, be the daies of the moneth, the next be the degrees of declination, and the thirde, the odde minute belonging to declination. Nowe, there is twoo tymes in the yeare, that the Sunne hath no declination. Nowe this yeare. 1567. the .xi. daye of Marche, at. vi. of the clocke at after uoone, the Sunne is equinoctiall, beginning North declination, then the .xiiii. of September at twoo of the clock in the morning, the Sunne is equinoctiall beginning south declination. Nowe the yeare. 1568 the .x. of Marche at xii. of the clocke at midnight, the Sunne is Equinoctiall, then the .xiii. of September in lyke maner equinoctiall at twoo of the clocke at after noone, then the yeare .1569. the .xi. daye of Marche at .vi. of the clocke in the morning, the Sunne is Equinoctiall, then the .xiiii. of September at .iiii. of the clocke in the morning, the Sunne is equinoctiall, beginneth south declination.

1567. Jan.			Februa.			Marche.			Aprill.		
D.	G.	M.	D.	G.	M.	D.	G.	M.	D.	G.	M.
1	21	57	1	14	20	1	4	2	1	8	0
2	21	48	2	14	1	2	3	39	2	8	23
3	21	39	3	13	38	3	3	15	3	8	44
4	21	28	4	13	18	4	2	51	4	9	6
5	21	18	5	13	0	5	2	27	5	9	28
6	21	7	6	12	37	6	2	3	6	9	50
7	20	56	7	12	17	7	1	40	7	10	11
8	20	45	8	11	56	8	1	16	8	10	32
9	20	32	9	11	35	9	0	52	9	10	53
10	20	20	10	11	14	10	0	28	10	11	14
11	20	6	11	10	51	11	0	6	11	11	35
12	19	53	12	10	30	12	0	18	12	11	55
13	19	40	13	10	8	13	0	40	13	12	14
14	19	25	14	9	46	14	1	5	14	12	36
15	19	10	15	9	24	15	1	29	15	12	55
16	18	56	16	9	2	16	1	53	16	13	15
17	18	41	17	8	39	17	2	16	17	13	34
18	18	26	18	8	17	18	2	39	18	13	53
19	18	11	19	7	54	19	3	3	19	14	13
20	17	54	20	7	32	20	3	27	20	14	31
21	17	37	21	7	9	21	3	51	21	14	51
22	17	21	22	6	46	22	4	12	22	15	9
23	17	4	23	6	23	23	4	37	23	15	26
24	16	47	24	6	0	24	4	59	24	15	44
25	16	29	25	5	36	25	5	23	25	16	2
26	16	12	26	5	13	26	5	46	26	16	19
27	15	54	27	4	49	27	6	8	27	16	36
28	15	35	28	4	26	28	6	32	28	16	54
29	15	1				29	6	54	29	17	10
30	14	58				30	7	17	30	17	26
31	14	39				31	7	39			

ALMANACKE FOR THREE YEARES, 1571

May.			June.			July.			August.		
D.	G.	M.	D.	G.	M.	D.	G.	M.	D.	G.	M.
1	17	43	1	23	4	1	22	17	1	15	34
2	17	58	2	23	8	2	22	9	2	15	16
3	18	12	3	23	11	3	22	0	3	14	58
4	18	28	4	23	14	4	21	52	4	14	39
5	18	42	5	23	17	5	21	43	5	14	22
6	18	56	6	23	20	6	21	36	6	14	3
7	19	11	7	23	22	7	21	26	7	13	43
8	19	25	8	23	24	8	21	16	8	13	24
9	19	37	9	23	26	9	21	5	9	13	4
10	19	51	10	23	27	10	20	54	10	12	45
11	20	3	11	23	28	11	20	43	11	12	26
12	20	15	12	23	28	12	20	32	12	12	6
13	20	27	13	23	28	13	20	20	13	11	45
14	20	39	14	23	27	14	20	7	14	11	25
15	20	51	15	23	26	15	19	54	15	11	4
16	21	1	16	23	24	16	19	42	16	10	43
17	21	11	17	23	22	17	19	28	17	10	22
18	21	22	18	23	20	18	19	14	18	10	2
19	21	32	19	23	18	19	19	0	19	9	40
20	21	41	20	23	16	20	18	46	20	9	19
21	21	50	21	23	12	21	18	31	21	8	58
22	21	59	22	23	8	22	18	17	22	8	35
23	22	7	23	23	3	23	18	2	23	8	13
24	22	16	24	22	59	24	17	47	24	7	51
25	22	23	25	22	55	25	17	31	25	7	30
26	22	31	26	22	50	26	17	14	26	7	7
27	22	37	27	22	46	27	16	57	27	6	45
28	22	44	28	22	39	28	16	39	28	6	23
29	22	51	29	22	32	29	16	25	29	6	0
30	22	55	30	22	25	30	16	8	30	5	37
31	23	0				31	15	52	31	5	14

Septemb.			October.			Nouemb.			Decemb.		
D.	G.	M.	D.	G.	M.	D.	G.	M.	D.	G.	M.
1	4	52	1	6	45	1	17	17	1	22	58
2	4	29	2	7	8	2	17	34	2	23	3
3	4	6	3	7	31	3	17	50	3	23	7
4	3	43	4	7	53	4	18	6	4	23	12
5	3	21	5	8	16	5	18	22	5	23	15
6	2	57	6	8	38	6	18	37	6	23	19
7	2	33	7	9	1	7	18	52	7	23	22
8	2	10	8	9	23	8	19	7	8	23	24
9	1	48	9	9	45	9	19	21	9	23	25
10	1	24	10	10	7	10	19	35	10	23	26
11	1	11	11	10	28	11	19	49	11	23	27
12	0	36	12	10	49	12	20	2	12	23	28
13	0	15	13	11	11	13	20	16	13	23	28
14	0	10	14	11	32	14	20	29	14	23	28
15	0	34	15	11	53	15	20	41	15	23	27
16	0	57	16	12	14	16	20	53	16	23	26
17	1	20	17	12	35	17	21	4	17	23	24
18	1	44	18	12	55	18	21	14	18	23	21
19	2	8	19	13	15	19	21	25	19	23	18
20	2	31	20	13	35	20	21	35	20	23	14
21	2	53	21	13	55	21	21	45	21	23	10
22	3	17	22	14	15	22	21	54	22	23	5
23	3	41	23	14	34	23	22	3	23	23	1
24	4	4	24	14	53	24	22	11	24	22	55
25	4	27	25	15	12	25	22	18	25	22	50
26	4	50	26	15	30	26	22	26	26	22	44
27	5	14	27	15	49	27	22	33	27	22	37
28	5	37	28	16	7	28	22	40	28	22	32
29	5	59	29	16	25	29	22	47	29	22	25
30	6	23	30	16	42	30	22	52	30	22	17
			31	17	0				31	22	9

ALMANACKE FOR THREE YEARES, 1571

1568. Jan.			Februa.			Marche.			Aprill.		
D.	G.	M.	D.	G.	M.	D.	G.	M.	D.	G.	M.
1	21	0	1	14	21	1	3	45	1	8	15
2	21	50	2	14	4	2	3	22	2	8	37
3	21	41	3	13	44	3	2	58	3	8	59
4	21	31	4	13	26	4	2	34	4	9	21
5	21	21	5	13	3	5	2	10	5	9	43
6	21	10	6	12	42	6	1	47	6	10	4
7	20	59	7	12	32	7	1	23	7	10	26
8	20	48	8	12	12	8	0	59	8	10	47
9	20	35	9	11	40	9	0	36	9	11	9
10	20	22	10	11	19	10	0	12	10	11	29
11	20	9	11	10	58	11	0	12	11	11	50
12	19	56	12	10	36	12	0	36	12	12	10
13	19	43	13	10	15	13	1	0	13	12	30
14	19	28	14	9	55	14	1	24	14	12	50
15	19	14	15	9	31	15	1	48	15	13	9
16	19	0	16	9	8	16	2	11	16	13	29
17	18	45	17	8	46	17	2	34	17	13	48
18	18	30	18	8	23	18	2	58	18	14	7
19	18	15	19	8	0	19	3	22	19	14	26
20	17	59	20	7	37	20	3	45	20	14	44
21	17	42	21	7	15	21	4	8	21	15	3
22	17	26	22	6	52	22	4	32	22	15	21
23	17	9	23	6	29	23	4	54	23	15	39
24	16	52	24	6	6	24	5	17	24	15	56
25	16	34	25	5	42	25	5	39	25	16	14
26	16	17	26	5	19	26	6	1	26	16	31
27	15	59	27	4	56	27	6	25	27	16	47
28	15	39	28	4	32	28	6	48	28	17	3
29	15	20	29	4	9	29	7	10	29	17	20
30	15	1				30	7	32	30	17	36
31	14	42				31	7	54			

May.			June.			July.			August.		
D.	G.	M.	D.	G.	M.	D.	G.	M.	D.	G.	M.
1	17	51	1	23	6	1	22	13	1	15	24
2	18	7	2	23	10	2	22	5	2	15	6
3	18	22	3	23	13	3	21	58	3	14	48
4	18	37	4	23	17	4	21	49	4	14	29
5	18	51	5	23	20	5	21	40	5	14	12
6	19	5	6	23	22	6	21	30	6	13	52
7	19	18	7	23	24	7	21	20	7	13	33
8	19	31	8	23	26	8	21	9	8	13	13
9	19	44	9	23	27	9	20	58	9	12	54
10	19	58	10	23	27	10	20	47	10	12	35
11	20	9	11	23	28	11	20	36	11	12	14
12	20	22	12	23	28	12	20	24	12	11	54
13	20	34	13	23	27	13	20	12	13	11	36
14	20	46	14	23	26	14	19	59	14	11	15
15	20	57	15	23	24	15	19	46	15	10	54
16	21	8	16	23	22	16	19	32	16	10	32
17	21	18	17	23	21	17	19	19	17	10	12
18	21	29	18	23	20	18	19	6	18	9	50
19	21	38	19	23	17	19	18	52	19	9	28
20	21	47	20	23	13	20	18	37	20	9	6
21	21	56	21	23	10	21	18	22	21	8	46
22	22	4	22	23	6	22	18	7	22	8	24
23	22	12	23	23	3	23	17	52	23	8	2
24	22	20	24	22	58	24	17	36	24	7	40
25	22	27	25	22	52	25	17	21	25	7	19
26	22	34	26	22	46	26	17	6	26	6	57
27	22	41	27	22	39	27	16	48	27	6	34
28	22	47	28	22	31	28	16	33	28	6	12
29	22	53	29	22	29	29	16	16	29	5	48
30	22	57	30	22	22	30	15	59	30	5	26
31	23	3				31	15	41	31	5	4

ALMANACKE FOR THREE YEARES, 1571

September			October.			Nouemb.			December.		
D.	G.	M.	D.	G.	M.	D.	G.	M.	D.	G.	M.
1	4	41	1	6	58	1	17	26	1	23	1
2	4	18	2	7	20	2	17	43	2	23	5
3	3	55	3	7	43	3	17	59	3	23	10
4	3	32	4	8	5	4	18	15	4	23	13
5	3	9	5	8	28	5	18	31	5	23	17
6	2	45	6	8	51	6	18	46	6	23	20
7	2	22	7	9	13	7	19	1	7	23	22
8	1	59	8	9	35	8	19	16	8	23	24
9	1	36	9	9	57	9	19	30	9	23	26
10	1	12	10	10	18	10	19	44	10	23	27
11	0	52	11	10	40	11	19	59	11	23	28
12	0	26	12	11	1	12	20	11	12	23	28
13	0	1	13	11	23	13	20	23	13	23	28
14	0	24	14	11	44	14	20	35	14	23	27
15	0	50	15	12	4	15	20	48	15	23	26
16	1	9	16	12	23	16	20	59	16	23	24
17	1	33	17	12	46	17	21	11	17	23	22
18	1	56	18	13	6	18	21	22	18	23	20
19	2	20	19	13	25	19	21	33	19	23	17
20	2	42	20	13	45	20	21	43	20	23	13
21	3	5	21	14	5	21	21	53	21	23	10
22	3	29	22	14	23	22	22	0	22	23	5
23	3	53	23	14	44	23	22	9	23	23	0
24	4	16	24	51	3	24	22	17	24	22	54
25	4	39	25	15	22	25	22	25	25	22	49
26	5	2	26	15	40	26	22	32	26	22	43
27	5	26	27	15	59	27	22	39	27	22	36
28	5	48	28	16	17	28	22	45	28	22	28
29	6	11	29	16	35	29	22	51	29	22	20
30	6	35	30	16	52	30	22	56	30	22	12
			31	17	9				31	22	4

1569. Jan.			Februa.			Marche.			Aprill.		
D.	G.	M.	D.	G.	M.	D.	G.	M.	D.	G.	M.
1	21	56	1	14	8	1	3	51	1	8	11
2	21	45	2	13	48	2	3	28	2	8	33
3	21	36	3	13	28	3	3	4	3	8	56
4	21	26	4	13	8	4	2	40	4	9	18
5	21	14	5	12	47	5	2	16	5	9	38
6	21	3	6	12	27	6	1	51	6	9	59
7	20	53	7	12	6	7	1	30	7	10	21
8	20	40	8	11	45	8	1	6	8	10	42
9	20	25	9	11	23	9	0	44	9	11	3
10	20	12	10	11	2	10	0	18	10	11	23
11	19	59	11	10	40	11	0	6	11	11	44
12	19	46	12	10	19	12	0	32	12	12	4
13	19	32	13	9	57	13	0	58	13	12	23
14	19	18	14	9	35	14	1	18	14	12	45
15	19	4	15	9	13	15	1	40	15	13	3
16	18	48	16	8	51	16	2	5	16	13	22
17	18	33	17	8	28	17	2	28	17	13	42
18	18	18	18	8	6	18	2	51	18	14	1
19	18	2	19	7	43	19	3	15	19	14	20
20	17	45	20	7	21	20	3	38	20	14	38
21	17	29	21	6	58	21	4	1	21	14	56
22	17	11	22	6	35	22	4	24	22	15	15
23	16	54	23	6	12	23	4	47	23	15	32
24	16	37	24	5	48	24	5	11	24	15	50
25	16	20	25	5	25	25	5	33	25	16	8
26	16	2	26	5	2	26	5	55	26	16	24
27	15	44	27	4	38	27	6	19	27	16	40
28	15	24	28	4	15	28	6	42	28	16	57
29	15	6				29	7	5	29	17	14
30	14	47				30	7	27	30	17	30
31	14	27				31	7	48			

ALMANACKE FOR THREE YEARES, 1571

May.			June.			July.			August.		
D.	G.	M.	D.	G.	M.	D.	G.	M.	D.	G.	M.
1	17	45	1	23	2	1	22	17	1	15	36
2	18	1	2	23	6	2	22	9	2	15	18
3	18	17	3	23	10	3	22	1	3	15	0
4	18	31	4	23	13	4	21	52	4	14	42
5	18	46	5	23	17	5	21	44	5	14	24
6	19	0	6	23	20	6	21	35	6	14	6
7	19	14	7	23	22	7	21	26	7	13	47
8	19	28	8	23	24	8	21	16	8	13	28
9	19	41	9	23	26	9	21	5	9	3	8
10	19	53	10	23	27	10	20	54	10	12	48
11	20	5	11	23	28	11	20	44	11	12	29
12	20	17	12	23	28	12	20	32	12	12	9
13	20	30	13	23	28	13	20	21	13	11	49
14	20	41	14	23	27	14	20	8	14	11	29
15	20	52	15	23	26	15	19	55	15	11	8
16	21	3	16	23	24	16	19	43	16	10	47
17	21	13	17	23	22	17	19	29	17	10	26
18	21	23	18	23	20	18	19	16	18	10	4
19	21	33	19	23	17	19	19	2	19	9	43
20	21	42	20	23	13	20	18	48	20	9	22
21	21	51	21	23	10	21	18	34	21	9	0
22	22	0	22	23	7	22	18	19	22	8	37
23	22	9	23	23	4	23	18	4	23	8	15
24	22	17	24	22	59	24	17	48	24	7	58
25	22	23	25	22	56	25	17	33	25	7	35
26	22	31	26	22	50	26	17	16	26	7	13
27	22	39	27	22	45	27	16	59	27	6	50
28	22	44	28	22	40	28	16	45	28	6	27
29	22	49	29	22	32	29	16	28	29	6	4
30	22	55	30	22	25	30	16	12	30	5	40
31	22	59				31	15	54	31	5	17

WILLIAM BOURNE

Septemb.			October.			Nouemb.			Decemb.		
D.	G.	M.	D.	G.	M.	D.	G.	M.	D.	G.	M.
1	4	55	1	6	45	1	17	19	1	23	1
2	4	32	2	7	8	2	17	36	2	23	5
3	4	19	3	7	31	3	17	52	3	23	10
4	3	46	4	7	53	4	18	8	4	23	13
5	3	23	5	8	16	5	18	24	5	23	17
6	3	0	6	8	38	6	18	39	6	23	20
7	2	36	7	9	0	7	18	54	7	23	22
8	2	13	8	9	23	8	19	9	8	23	24
9	1	50	9	9	45	9	19	23	9	23	26
10	1	27	10	10	7	10	19	37	10	23	27
11	1	3	11	10	29	11	19	52	11	23	28
12	0	43	12	10	50	12	20	5	12	23	28
13	0	17	13	11	12	13	20	13	13	23	28
14	0	8	14	11	33	14	20	31	14	23	27
15	0	34	15	11	54	15	20	43	15	23	26
16	0	59	16	12	15	16	20	55	16	23	24
17	1	20	17	12	34	17	21	6	17	23	22
18	1	43	18	12	56	18	21	17	18	23	20
19	2	6	19	13	16	19	21	29	19	23	17
20	2	29	20	13	36	20	21	39	20	23	13
21	2	53	21	13	56	21	21	49	21	23	10
22	3	16	22	14	16	22	21	58	22	23	5
23	3	40	23	14	36	23	22	7	23	23	0
24	4	3	24	14	55	24	22	16	24	22	55
25	4	27	25	15	14	25	22	22	25	22	50
26	4	50	26	15	32	26	22	29	26	22	43
27	5	13	27	15	51	27	22	36	27	22	34
28	5	36	28	16	10	28	22	43	28	22	27
29	5	59	29	16	28	29	22	49	29	22	19
30	6	23	30	16	45	30	22	55	30	22	11
			31	17	2				31	22	3

ALMANACKE FOR THREE YEARES, 1571

⁋ The .vii. Rule shewed how to take the altitude of the Sunne, and by the height of the Sunne to knowe the Equinoctiall, to knowe the eleuation of the pole articke, and howe you shall behaue your selfe with the Astralabe, with an example of Graues ende, and also howe to get the true Meridian, and also of the northeastinge or north weasting of the Compas, necessary for Nauigation, or otherwyse called the variation of the Compas.

Nowe in this table you must consider that the xi. daie of Marche, the Sunne is Equinoctiall, entring then the first point of Aries, called the Equinoctiall of Spring time, then hauing no declination, then the .x. daie of Aprill the Sunne entreth into the first minute of Taurus, thē hauing declination to the northwardes .xi. degrees .30. minutes, then the .xii. daie of May, the Sunne entreth the first point of Gemini, hauing then declination .20. degrees .12. minut. the .12. daie of June, the Sunne entreth into Cancer, then the Sunne maketh his greatest prograce to the northwards, hauing .23. degrees .28. minutes of declinatiō now in this our time. But some doe affirme to be .23. degrees and a halfe, but there lacketh twoo min. Then the .14. daie of July, the Sunne entreth into Leo, coming downwardes to the equinoctiall, hauing .20. degrees .12. minutes. The .14. daie of August, the Sunne entreth into virgo, the declinatiō 11. degrees .30. minutes. Then the .14. of September, the Sunne entreth into Libra, then being Equinoctiall, hauing no declination called the equinoctiall of Autumne or haruest, then beginninge her south declination: then the .14. of October the Sunne entreth into Scorpio, the declination .11. degrees .30. minutes. Then the .12. of Nouember, the Sunne entreth into Sagittarius, the declination 20. degrees .12. minutes. Then the .12. daie of December, the Sunne entreth the first minute of Capricorne, then maketh the Sunne her greatest prograce to the southwardes and his declination .23. degrees .28. minutes, and then retourneth to the Equinoctiall againe. Then the .11. of January the Sunne entreth into Aquarius, and the declinatiō 20. degrees .12. minutes. Then the .10. daie of February, the Sunne entreth into the first minute of Pisces, and the declination .11. degrees .30. minut. then the .11. daie of March, the Sunne returneth to the self same place that it did depart from before. Wherfore the Egiptians did paint the yeare like to an Ader lightning her taile, hauing not the vse of letters, they made a ringe and named it Anulus as it weare annus, that is a yeare, because a ring doth turne round in it self as doth the yeare. Now you hauing your Astralabe, if you doe require to know how many degrees the pole artick is aboue your horizon, take your Astralabe and bange it vpon one of your fingers, and lift vp or put down the athladaie or rule with ye sightes till ye beames of the Sunne doth pearse both the sightes of the rule or atheladaye, the Sunne beames geuing shadowe through both the sightes, then looke in the table what declination the sunne hath, whether that the declination be towardes the south of the equinoctiall or towardes the north of it, then loke vpon your astralabe what altitude the Sūne hath vpon the meridian vpon that daye of the moneth in your table, then if that it hath north declinatiō subtract, or pull away your declination, if south declination, adde or put to your delination to the altitude of height of the Sunne, then that doth shew you the true equinoctiall: then when you haue the true height of the equinoctiall, looke how many degrees that cometh vnto, subtract or pull that sum out of .90. degrees, which degrees & minutes, then that doth remaine shalbe the height of the pole aboue your horizon. For this you must cōsider, that from the zeneth or prick ouer the crowne of your head to be .90. degrees downe to the horizon, then looke what height the equinoctiall is from the horizon, so much is the zeneth from the pole, thē must it nedes be said that that is the altitude of the pole to be iust the distaunce of the zeneth downe to the equinoctiall. As for an exāple, this at Grauesende the yeare .1566. I take the Sunne vpon the meridian the .10. daie of Aprill, & founde the altitude of the Sunne lifted aboue the horizon .49. degrees 49. minutes, then I toke the Sunne the next daie and founde the Sunne vpon the meridian .50. degrees .9. min. so I found the declinatiō of the sunne more the .11. daie then it was the .10. daie by .21. mi. which signifieth to me that the Sunne entred into the first min. of Taurus, at one of the clocke after midnight. The .x. daie of Aprill, the sunne hauing north declination of the equinoctiall, and the declination .11. degrees .40. mi. Upon the .11. daie of the moneth, then I pulled y̆ᵉ declinatiō .11. degrees 40. mi. out of .50. degrees .9. mi. the remainer was 38. degrees .29. mi. The altitude or height of the equinoctiall aboue the horizon: nowe I doe take or subtract .38. degrees. 29 .mi. out of .90. degrees, the remainer is the height of y̆ᵉ pole, being .51. degrees 31. mi. So in like case it is from the zeneth to the pole .38. degrees .29. min. & from the pole downe to the horizon .51. degrees .31. mi. as by the example of this figure.

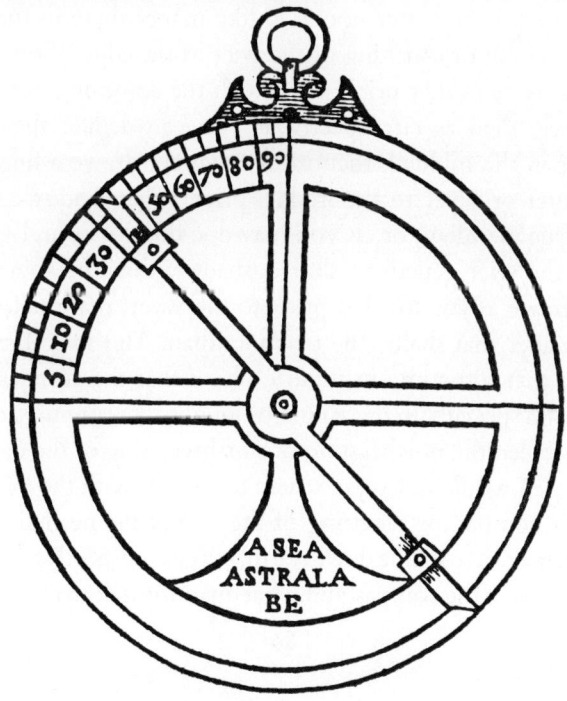

Now it is cōuenient to know the true meridiā or south, whiche you must doe either with a good compas or with a perfect diall or neadel, and if you be on the land, this you may doe vpō a pece of tymber that stādeth fast, or any other thing that standeth fast. First take a paire of compasses, then make a circle with the compasses, then in the middell where that the foote of the compas did stande, set a wyer vpright as circumspectly as you can, then you may doe this, looke in ye morning so that it be on plaine grounde, so that you may see the horizon circle without any let, then in the Sunne rising you must marke the shadow of the wyer, and there set a pricke, then at the setting of the sunne there set an other pricke euen at the circumference of the circle, then deuide that with your compasses euen in two peaces, then strike a straight lyne frō wyer or senter of the circle to the middell or deuided pricke, that shall be the true meridian, or els the wier standing vpright, first in the forenoone when the top of the wyer doth touche or be ready to come into the circunference or edge of the circle there make a prick, then in the after noone in like maner there in the very comming out or touching of the wier of the edge of the circle, there make an other prick, euen with the comming out of the shadowe, then as circūspectly as you can deuide these two prickes in the middell, then in like manner drawe a line from the senter or wyer to the middel pricke, that shadowe shalbe your true meridian, or els you may doe this, looke and watche when the wier geueth ye shortes shadow there make a prick, then drawe a lyne frō that prick to the wyer, that shadowe in lyke maner that shalbe the true meridian. This haue I said, to thende that sometime in sundrie places that the compas doth varie, and specially in the sailing of long viages runninge east or weast, called the northeasting or northweasting of the compas, therefore I would not wyshe them to meddle with the mending of their compas, or whetting of the side of the neadell, to the ende to make it to stande dewe north, but circumspectly to awayte the altering of the compas, and what quantitie it doth alter, as you may doe very well by daie by the altitude of the Sunne, and by night by the starres of the north or starres of the south, and then let your compas alone, although that it doth varie twoo or three pointes, you make accompt according to the variation as this I amu [sic] the northweast point, standeth dewe north, and my course is to goe dewe weast, then I will occupie the south weast point for the weast point, and this by obseruation and triyng of my compas, I care not what point standeth dewe north for it is all one, so that you consider what point standeth North.

The eight Rule is of the north starre, and howe he should be taken vpon any of the .viii. principall wyndes or pointes of the compas, with obseruation of the balastella or cros staffe.

Nowe further it is to be noted that sea men vse the north starre that standeth vpon the type of the tayle of Ursa minor, the little beare, but I am of the opinion that his distaunce is further from the pole then they make a counte of, for they saie that he is but three degrees and a halfe from the pole: but I suppose that he is .4. degrees from the pole, and goeth round about nere .24. degrees of the great circle or equinoctiall circle, but because I will not so muche contende with them for that they haue so long time obserued the custome of .iii. degrees and a halfe. I will shewe you my opinion of the starre. The northstarre is in the longitude of Aries, so that you doe reken him from the poles of the world and of declination aboue the equinoctiall .86. degrees, so that he is .4. degrees from the pole, therefore I would wishe those that haue experience, to take the starre at the hiest & at the lowest with a pretious instrument, and then put that nombre into two equall partes, and then you shal see what distaunce that the starre is from the pole, yet because that it hath bene of longe custome to a count by .iii. degrees and a halfe. I will declare the taking of ye starre vpō the .8. principal windes or pointes of the compas, and your markes that you shall haue shall be the twoo starres that stand vpon the foreshoulder of the great beare, called of the Mariners the pointers by caues that they doe alwayes pointe to the north starre, and of some men they be called two wheles of Charles wayne but I would haue pointed thee to Guarde starres, but I coulde not be suffered, and this you must cōsider because that it is towardes the north, they call the vppermoste part right ouer the pole starre north, and towardes the right hande, they call the east, and towardes the left hande the weast, and right vnder the starre south, and the other foure wyndes betwene them as foloweth. First, I saye that the pointers in the East, the north starre is halfe a degree aboue the pole the pointers in the north east, the north starre is one degree and a halfe vnder the pole, the pointers in the north, the starre is neare at the lowest .iii. degrees and a half vnder the pole, the pointers in the north weast, the north starre is .iii. degrees vnder the pole, the pointers in the weast, the north starre is halfe a degree vnder the pole, the pointers in the south weast, the north starre is one degree and a halfe aboue the pole, the pointers in the south right vnder the pole, the north starre is three degrees and a halfe aboue the pole, the pointers in the south east, the north starre is three degrees aboue the pole. Now there be .4. wyndes or pointes betwene the pointers and the Guardes, for if the pointers be east the gardes be south east: and if the pointers be northeast, the Guardes be east. Now some there be that will chuse their compas or mende their cōpas by the north starre, which sometime the starre is not due north. For when the pointers be east, then the north starre standeth the thirde parte of a point to the weastwardes of the pole, and whē the pointers be directly weast, the north starre standeth the third part of a point to the eastwardes of the pole, but when the pointers be either aboue the pole, or ryght vnder the pole, then the starre standeth dewe north. Nowe for the takynge of the altitude of the north starre, the sea men vse an instrument called a Balestela or a Bazoles Jacobe being a plaine crosestaffe set out with degrees. Nowe the north starre will serue them that trauell to the south wardes to any place on this side the equinoctiall, but to them that doe occupie to the north partes, the northstarre will not serue by caues that the altude of the pole standeth so hie, and that the crosestaffe commeth so neare to their face that with casting their eye vp to the star and downwardes to the horizon, and then the degrees be so short marked vpon the staffe that they may sone committe error and neuer be espied, therfore I doe meane to appoint certaine starres of the south for thē that doe occupie to the north partes, and as for the vse and the making of the balastela, you shall repare to the booke of Martyn Curtes, called the arte of Nauigation, for I must meddle with nothing contained in that booke.

℘ The nynth Rule is of sailinge vpon one quarter of the compas, in howe farre sailing you doe rayse or laie a degree, and what you doe departe from the meridian.

Furthermore, because some doe require to knowe the alteration of a point, that in the running of one point, you may rayse or laye a degree soner in one then in an other, as in the saylinge south or north you keepe one meridian, or rayse or laye the pole, as this, to the north you doe rayse the pole and laie the equinoctiall, and you go towardes the south you laye the pole, and raise the equinoctiall, but in the sayling or going east or weast, you doe not alter your pole nor parrel but onely your meridian, but in the sayling of any other point, you doe alter your pole and parrel and also your meridian. Therfore I wil open vnto you in the sayling vp on one of the quarters of the cōpas, what euery point doth raise or laie one degree, in howe farre saylinge, and howe many myles you be departed from the place that you did departe from, & what you be departed from your meridian. But here is one thing to be noted, as I suppose, in the moste parte of cardes, they doe alowe for euery degree but .17. leges and a halfe, because your cardes bee most comonly made in Lyshebourne in Portinggale, or els in Spaine or Fraunce. But as I suppose, that we in England should alowe .60. myles to one degree, that is after three miles to one leage of our English leages, therefore .20. of our English leages should aunswere to one degree for .3. of our myles will not make one of their leages, therefore they doe make their accoumpte by their leages in their cardes, but not for ours. Therefore I wyll showe you by our Englishe myles, an Englishe myle containeth .1000. paces, and euery pace .5. foote, & euery foote .12. inches. Nowe some thinke that a pace can not be .5. foote, but a pace Geometricall is twoo reasonable steppes, for it can not be a pace till the hinder foote be remoued forwardes, and those twoo stepes shall containe 5. foote, and so shall any man induce to go at pleasure. Nowe to our purpose, for the saylinge of one quarter of the compas that in sailing directly south or north, you doe raise or laie the pole in .60. miles going in the altering of one point from the southe or north .61. miles, and departed from the lyne of south and north, or the meridian .12. myles in the altering the second point, you do rayse a degree in sailing of .65. miles, and depart from your meridiā 25. miles in the altring of the third pointe, you doe rayse or laie one degree in the sailing of .72. myles and .9. part, and you doe depart from your meridiā 40. myles in yᵉ altering of the .4. point you do raise or laie a degree in the going of .85. miles, & departe from your meridian .60. myles, now in the altring of the .5. point or wynde, you doe raise a degree in sailing of .108. myles, and depart from your meridian .90. myles in the sailing by the .6. pointe, you raise or laie one degree in .157. myles, and departe from your meridian lyne .145. miles. Now in the sailing by the .7. point or wynd, you doe raise a degree in going of .308. myles, and depart from your meridian lyne .302. miles, and this you may consider of the other .3. quarters of the compas. And if you doe require to knowe the raising or laiyng of a degree by the legges of the cardes that is at .17. leages and a halfe, then reade the art of nauigatiō, and there shall you finde howe many degrees you be departed from your meridiā, and also from the place that you did depart from, but that serueth for no other place but only for vnder the Equinoctial, for he that maketh accompt of it in any other place, shall be deceiued. For as you goe to any of the twoo poles, so be your degrees shorter and shorter, till that your meridians meete vnder the twoo poles which I to treat of in the .11. Rule.

❡ The tenth Rule treateth of the Soundinges,
comming from any place out of the Occident
Sea for to seke vshant or the Lyzard, and
also all alongest till you doe come to
the coaste of Flaunders.

BEcause it is necessary to be had in memory, because that it is a daungerous place to hit or fal with, to enter into the sleue comming homewards out of Spaine or Portingall, or from Barbaria, or any place from the southwardes. A shippe that commeth from any suche place to seke the Iele of vshant, or the Lizarde in this Roote of soundinge of a .100 or .90. fadoms, and you shall finde bigge soundinges and shalbe nie about to the sainges, & in the root of .80. fadomes, ye shall finde cockle shelles and dentes in the talowe of the lead, and in this sounging hold on your course to the north. till you chaunge sounding, then if you be at .60. or .64 fadomes, you shall fynde small sande and mathey grounde, and you shalbe neare the Coaste of Uishaunt, and if you haue tyme and daye, goe seeke it in the northeast, and you shall be about tenne leages frō the Ile. If you come makīg your course about the base frede, you shall finde course sande, read and browne, and you shall haue soundinge at 40. fadomes, and if you be towardes the banke of Silley, you that haue soūdinges at .86. or .90. fadōs, and you shall finde in the tallowe stony grounde, and you shalbe well shotte towardes the banke of Silley. And when you be at .80. fadoms, you shall fynde small blacke sande, and you shalbe well towardes the Lizarde. And when you be at .60. or .64. fadomes, you shall finde whyte sande, & white softe wormes, and you shalbe very nie to the Lizarde. Betwene the cape of Cornewall and Uishant, amidde the chanell, you shall finde .70 fadomes. And neare yenowse betwene Dodna and the fourme in the channell, you shall haue .40. or 50. fadomes. If you be thwarte of Plymouth, or the starte, you shall fynde streamy grounde, and dentes in the tallowe, and soundinges of .41. or .42 fadomes, at the comming from porte lande, you shall haue .35. fadomes and small shingelles. And when you be nie to portelande .30. fadomes, and stones lyke beanes, and this soundinge will laste till saint Aldam: and in the saide soundinges you shall finde whyte stones lyke broken aules, and other that be bigger, and then you shalbe thwarte of Saint Aldame, or of the Ile of Wight, two or three leages from the Ile of Wight, and you shall finde .25. fadomes, with dentes and cleftes in the tallowe like small threedes. Twoo or three leages from the caskettes, you shall finde .40. fadomes, & bygge stones rugged and blacke. Betwene the Ile of wight and the Hagge, the deapest is but .35. or 40. fadomes. Betwene the Ile of wight & Lantri gate, ye depest is but .25. or .30. fadōs betwene Bechy and the Ile of wight, a leage frō the lande, you shall fynde .38. fadomes, and poppelles as bigge as beanes. Betwene Faierly & the water of Solent in the deapest but .25. fadoms. Betwene Folstayne and Bollayne, is a banke that is called Ryppe Rappe, and lyeth in the midde waye betwene Piccardie and Englande, and harde aborde by it, is 26. or .27. fadomes. In the straight of Callys, is .30. fadomes. In the rode of Callis, is .16. fadomes. And alongest the coaste of Flaunders is but .20. fadomes the deapest. This muche haue I sayde for the entraunce of the sleue to come to the ryuer of Thames, and as for daungers and suche lyke, I doe referre that to theim that haue more conning and experience then I haue. And in the entraunce in the midde waye betwene Ushante and the Lizarde, the pole articke is eleuated .50. degrees and a halfe, and the Equinoctiall is lifted aboue the Horizon .39. degrees and a halfe.

⁋ The eleuenth Rule, treateth of the Longitude, although that it be very tedious.

Nowe some there be that be very inquisatiue to haue a waye to gette the Longitude, but that is to tedious, for this they must consider, that the whole frame of the firmament is caried roūde from the east into the weast, in .24. houres, so there remayneth no light nor marke, but goeth rounde, sauing only the two poles of the world, and these twoo standeth faste. But as I saide before in the ix. Rule, he that goeth south or north, doth rayse or laye the pole, and in the like case of the Equinoctiall altering his parell, causing the lightes of the firmament to alter the time of their shining or byding aboue our horizon, and he that goeth directly east or weast, doth neither rayse nor delay the pole but still the lightes of the firmament, doth make one maner of arche, accordinge to their latitude or declination, but the going east or weast, doth alter the meridiane, causinge the Planes to haue their aspectes at an other hour or tyme, altering the tyme of the chaunges of the moone, and also the tyme of the Eclipses, whiche is necessary for all trauaylers by Sea or by Lande. Therefore I thought it neadefull to bee spoken of. For as countries haue Latitude from the poles, so in like manner they haue appointed longitude. But nowe you may get the Latitude with instrumentes, but the Longitude you must bringe from an other place, whiche you can not doe but with a Globe, or els a Mappe or Carde, & then you must measure from the meridian landes of the Canary Ilandes, or otherwyse called the fortunate Ilāds: and in our Latitude of London euery .555. myles, whiche containeth .15. degrees, will aunswere to one houre of tyme, and vnder the Equinoctial .900 myles to fiftene degrees, the degrees be as longe as the degrees of Latitude, but towardes the pole fewer and fewer, till they come to nothing, vnder the twoo poles. And nowe .37. myles with vs at London, will aunswere to one degree to our Latitude at .51. or .52. degrees of eleuation of the pole. But the cause why the Longitude was fechte frō the Canary Ilandes, I knowe not: Yet as I suppose, because that it was thē the westermost place then knowen. For Ptholomeus was the first that ordayned that rule. Nowe furthermore, because that you shall knowe the better, I wyll drawe out certayne of the chiefest places about this Realme of Englande, both their Longitude and Latitude, by whiche you shall knowe what maner of arche the Sunne with the other lightes doth make, and also by the Longitude to knowe at what tyme the Moone with any of the Planetes doth make any aspecte, & also the Eclipses of the Sūne or moone, with the chaunge, quarters, and full moone, by a true and epact Ephimerides through all Englād, to knowe the very true houre and minute of the tyme of the deametre, considering for what Longitude or place your Almanack was made for, & nowe to gette the Longitude, you may at the time of the Eclipse of the Moone, for the Eclipses of y[e] Moone be generall, so that she is aboue your Horizon in any place vpon the supersticial partes of the earth or sea, considering as I saide before, by your Almanack, at what tyme the Eclipse should happen the very houre & minute, knowinge the place that your Almanack was made for, and then according to this rule with a precise instrument the alteration of the time and houre and minute of the Eclipse. And furthermore, you may knowe your longitude by the Ephimerides by the coniunction of the moone with the other fixed starres, and by the distaunce betwene them with a precise instrument, considering the moones course with degrees and minutes, but I am of opinion that it is to tedious for to be done vpon the Sea, but it may be done vpon the land, for the Sea doth alwayes lift the shippe vp and down, and the least chop of a sea causeth a man to committe errour. Therfore lette no Sea men trouble them selfe with this rule, but according to their accustomed manner, lette them kepe a perfect accoumpt and

ALMANACKE FOR THREE YEARES, 1571

reckening of the way of his shippe, whether the ship goeth to lewardes or maketh her way good, cōsidering what thinges be against him or with him: as tydes, corrantes, wyndes, or suche like. As for the rule of Lōgitude it foloweth in the next Rule.

⁌ The twelfth Rule sheweth how many myles
will answere to one degree of Longitude in
euery seuerall Latitude betwene the
Equinoctiall and any of the
twoo Poles.

Now this Rule shall teache you to know how many myles will aunswere to one degree, for euery seuerall Latitude to any of the twoo poles, either the articke or anterticke. And first vnder the equinoctiall, two poles bein geuen with the horizon .60. myles to one degree as I saide in the .xi. Rule. And nowe shall folowe the reste where the poles be raised 21. degres .56. myles to one degree of Longitude. Nowe the poles being raysed .29. degrees .52. myles one degree, then at .36. degrees. 48 myles to one degree, thē at .42. degrees .44. myles to one degree longitude, then at .53. degrees .36. myles to one degree longitude. The pole raysed 57. degrees .32. myles to one degree. The pole raysed .62. degrees .28. myles to one degree. The pole raysed .66. degrees .24. myles to one degree. The pole raysed .70. degrees .20. myles to one degree. The pole raysed .74. degrees .16. myles to one degree. The pole raysed .78. degrees .12. miles to one degree. The poles raysed .82. degrees .8. myles to one degree. The poles raysed .86. degrees .4. miles to one degree. The poles being raysed to the hyghest at .90. degrees, being then your zeneth, there all the meridians mete. Nowe you must consider that euery houre of tyme in the chaunging of the moone or of the Eclipses, you must alowe .15. degrees, euery degree in myles as you do see in your Latitude of the coūtrey, as this, those places that be to the weastwardes of your towne or place, or countrey, by .15. degrees, the moone shall chaunge rather with them then with you by one houre, because that they shall touche your meridian before theirs by one houre. And if the towne or place be to the east wardes of you by .15. degrees, then shall the moone chaunge rather with you then with them by one houre, because the moone shall touche their meridian before yours by one houre: As for an example thus, with vs at London, the seconde daye of October .1567. the moone shall chaunge at xii. of the clocke at noone .5. minutes, nowe to the westwardes as farre as Lishborne in Portingall, the moone shall chaunge that same daie at .xi. of the clocke .8. minutes, the Longitude beinge there from the Canary Ilandes .5. degrees .36. minutes, nowe to the east wardes that same daye at Rome the moone shall chaunge at .1. of the clocke .12. mi. because that they haue longitude .36. degrees .40. minutes from the Canary Ilandes, and then by this accompt .7. degrees and a halfe, will aunswer to halfe an houre, and then .3. degrees and a quarter, will make a quarter of an houre, and then .9. myles and a quarter, will make one min. of tyme with vs at Londō in our latitude. So by this rule you may knowe at what tyme and minute the Eclipse or chaūges of the moone doth happen, knowing for what place your Almanack was made, for as commonly we here in Englande doe make them for the citie of London. Nowe the next Rule shall treat of the longitude and latitude.

⁋ The thirtenth Rule, treateth of the Longitude and the Latitude of certaine of the moste notable townes in Englande, and also how lōg the moone doth chaunge at the one towne before the o-
ther, and also the diuersitie of the lon-
gest daie in sommer, from Southhampton to the nethermost
place in Scotland.

Nowe in this rule shall folowe the Longitude and Latitude of the most parte, of the principall places in Englande, the

ALMANACKE FOR THREE YEARES, 1571

southermost place in Englande is the Lizarde in Cornewall, the Longitude .15. degrees .5. minutes, the Latitude .50. degrees 45. minutes. Saint Michaels mount .14. degrees .20. minutes. Latitude .51. degrees. 6. min. Falmouth Longitude .15. degrees. .12. minu. Latitude .51. degrees .0. minutes. Plymouth Longitude 19. degrees .7. minutes Latitude .51. degrees .1. mi. Southhampton Longitude .18. degrees .52. Latitude .51. degrees .2. minutes. Portesmouth Longitude .19. degrees .7. minutes Latitude .51. degrees 3. minutes. Rye Longitude .20. degrees .22. minu. Latitude .51. degrees .5. minutes. Douer Lōgitude 21. degrees .40. minutes Latitude .51. degrees .26. minutes. Caunterbury Longitude .21. degrees .25. minutes. Latitude .51. degrees .28. minutes. Sandwitche Longitude .21. degrees .38. minutes, Latitude .51. degrees .29. minutes. London longitude .19 degrees .54. minutes, Latitude .51. degrees .32. mi. Grauesende Longitude .20. degrees 14. minutes, Latitude .51. degrees .31. minutes. Bristowe Longitude .17. degrees .8. minuts, Latitude .51. degrees .42. minutes. Haruarde Longitude 17. degrees .0. minutes, Latitude .52. degrees 2. minutes. Saint Dauies head Longitude .15. degrees .5. minutes, Latitude .52. degrees .15. minutes. Oxforde Longitude .18 degrees .59. minutes, Latitude .51. degrees 50. minutes. Cambridge Longitude .20. degrees, 6. minutes, Latitude .52. degrees .0. minutes. Norwiche Longitude .21. degrees .20. minutes, Latitude .52. degrees .10. minutes. Lincolne Longitude 20. degrees .28. minutes, Latitude .53. degrees .6. minutes. Weshpole Longitude .16. degrees .40. minutes. Latitude .53. degrees .6. minutes. Westchester Longitude .17. degrees .29. minutes, Latitude .53. degrees .34. minutes. Hull Longitude .20 degres .54. minutes, Latitude .53. degrees .57. min. Yorke Longitude .20. degrees .0. minutes, Latitude .54. degrees .1. minute. Cockermouth Longitude .17. degrees .0. minutes, Latitude .55. degrees .8. minutes. Carleile Longitude .17. degrees .48. minutes, Latitude .55. degrees .2. minut. New castell Longitude .20. degrees .31 minutes, Latitude .55. degrees .0. minutes. Barwike Longitude

20. degrees .48. monutes, Latitude .56. degrees .23 minutes. Edenborowe in Scotlande Longitude .19. degrees .50. minutes, Latitude .57. degrees. 0 minutes. Nowe by the longitude and the latitude, you may knowe the lengthe of the daie both in sōmer and also in wynter, and also the perfect houre and minute of the chaūges of the moone, and how long the moone doth chaunge at one towne afore an other through the whole Realme of England. And nowe in order as I haue begonne before, I will shewe you the distaunce of tyme, and first at Saint michaels mount, the moone chaungeth rather then at London by .25. minutes.

Rather at Falmouth then at London by .20. minutes, at Plymouth rather then at London by 18. minutes, at Southhampton rather then at Lōdon by .v. minutes, at Portesmouth rather then at London, by .4. minutes, at Rye later then at London by one mintute and .$\frac{1}{4}$. at Douer later thē at London by .6. minutes and more, at Caunterbury later then at london by .5. minutes, at Sandwiche later then at london, by .6. minutes, Grauesende later then at london, by one minute & a half, Bristowe rather then at london, by .11. minutes, Haruard rather then at london by .12. minutes, S. Dauis head rather then at london by .19. minutes. Oxford rather then at london by .4. minut. Cambridge later then at london, by .$\frac{2}{3}$. partes of a mi. Norwiche later then at london, by fiue minut. and more, Lincolne later then at london, by .2. minut. Welshpole rather then at london, by .16. minutes Westchester rather then at london, by .10. minuts Hull later then at london, by .4. minutes, Yorke later then at london, by .$\frac{1}{4}$. of a minute, Cockmouth rather then at london, by .12. minutes, Carleile rather then at london, by. 9. minutes, Newecastell later then at london, by .2. minutes, Barwicke later then at london, by .3. minutes & more. Nowe in like maner I thinke that it is necessary to be spoken of, the difference of the longest day in sommer, in euery seuerall latitude in the whole Realme of Englande, from the southermost parte called the Lizarde, to the northermoste parte in Scotland,

and this is called the day frō the sunne rysing or appearing
aboue our horizon till the going downe of the Sunne in our
horizon, and first at Southhampton, the longest daye is .16.
houres long .26. minutes the shortest .7. houres .34. minu. at
london .16. houres .30. minutes lōgest 7. houres 30. minutes
shortest. At Lyncolne .16. houres .45. minutes longest .7.
houres .1. minutes shortest. Yorke the lōgest .17. houres, the
shortest .7. houres. Newecastell the longest .17. houres .12.
minutes, the shortest .6. houres .48. minutes. Barwyke the
longest .17. houres .30. min. the shortest .6. houres 30. min.
Edenborow in Scotland, the longest day in sommer .17. houres
.45. minutes, the shortest day 6. houres .15. minu. Now Catnesse
point being the northermost parte in all Scotland, the pole
being raised to .62. degrees, there the longest daye is .19. houres
.30. mi. the shortest day .4. houres .30. min. Now this you doe
consider, looke what the longest day doth contained, looke
what that lacketh of 24. houres, that is the shortest wynter daye.

⁋ The fourteenth Rule, is of the longitude and de
clination of .12. notable fixed starres for nauigatiō,
with tabels of their shining, and at what point of
your compas that they doe both ryse & set, and also
tabels for euery moneth of the yeare, declaring at
what houre and minute that they be south, running from the first daie of the moneth to the
15. and from the .15. to the last daye,
and wyll continue this .100.
yeares without much
error.

THis Rule containeth the Longitude and declination of .12.
notable fixed starres for Nauigation for them that trauell
to the northwardes or to the southwards, as farre as the Canary
Ilāds. The first rowe of this Table is the names of the Starres, the
seconde the signes that they be in, the third and fourth rowe,

the degrees and minutes in the signes: The fifth and sixt, the degrees & min. of declination: The seuenth sheweth towardes what partes they doe decline, & the letter, M. signifieth towardes the meridional or south. And the letter. S. signifieth the partes Septentrionall or north.

Names of the Starres.	Signes.	Degrees of signes.	Minutes of signes.	Degrees of declination.	Minutes of declination.	Towardes what partes they doe decline	⁋ The bignes of the starres.
The whales belly	Aries.	16	2	12	20	M.	A star of yᵉ .2. bignes.
The Bulles eye.	Gem.	3	42	15	24	S.	a great starre
Orions left foote.	Gem.	10	12	9	14	M.	a great starre
The first in Oriōs gyrdell.	Gem.	16	22	1	19	M.	The .2. big.
The great dogge.	Cācer	8	40	15	30	M.	a great starre
The little dogge.	Cācer	20	10	6	4	S.	a great starre
The brightest in Hidra.	Leo.	21	2	4	47	M.	The .2. big.
The Lions harte.	Leo.	23	32	14	1	S.	a great starre
The Lions tayle.	Virgo	15	32	16	46	S.	a great starre
Virgins spycke.	Libra	17	42	4	54	M.	a great starre
The scorpiōs hart	Sagi.	3	42	24	27	M.	The .2. big.
The Eagle.	Capri.	24	51	7	28	S.	The .2. big.

THis table is necessary for all men to knowe, doing as before is laid, as you do by the Sūnes declination, so doe by these starres, as if north declination pull the same awaye, if south declinatiō put to the degrees and minutes of declination, and that will shewe you the Equinoctial, and so by the altitude of the equinoctiall to knowe the eleuation of the pole euen as you doe by the Sunne in all pointes. And the .8. rowe sheweth you nothing but the bignes of the starres. And nowe shall folowe

ALMANACKE FOR THREE YEARES, 1571

certaine tables, for to know the time of their shining, and at what pointe and wynde that any of these Starres doth ryse and sette in our horizon, and also at what houre and minute that they doe touche our meridian or south, for this .x. yeares without muche error.

The whales belly ryse more then east and by south, and settes more than weast and by south and shineth .ix. houres .45. minutes. The Bulles eye ryse neare the east northeast, and settes neare the weast northweast, and shineth .14. houres .52. minutes. Orions lefte foote ryse east and to the northwardes, & settes weast & to ye northwardes, and shyneth .xii. houres .15. minutes. The firste in Orions girdell, ryse east and to the soutwardes, and settes weast and to the southwardes, and shyneth .xi. houres .52. minutes. The great dogge ryse east southeast, and settes weast southweast, and shineth .ix. houres .xviii. minutes. The lesser dogge ryseth east and to the northwardes, and settes weast and to the northwardes, and shineth .xii. houres .18. minutes. The brightest in Hidra, riseth east and to the southwardes, & settes weast & to the southwards, & shineth .11. houres .46. mi. The Liōs hart riseth neare east north east, & settes neare west northweast, & shineth .14 houres .30. mi. The lyons tayle, riseth east northeast, and settes weast north weast, & shineth .15. houres. The virgins spicke riseth east & to the southwardes, & settes west & to the southwardes, & shineth .11. houres .46. minu. The Scorpiones harte riseth south east, & settes south weast, and shineth .6. houres. The Eagle riseth east and to the northwardes, and settes weast & to the northwardes, & shineth .12. houres .26. min.

	Star							
	The whales belly	1	5	54	E	1	4	54	E
	The Bulles eie.	2	8	52	E	2	7	52	E
	Orions left foote.	3	9	23	E	3	8	23	E
	The first in Oriōs girdell.	4	9	50	E	4	8	50	E
	The gaeat dogge.	5	11	4	E	5	10	4	E
	The lesser dogge.	6	12	0	O	6	11	0	E
	The brightest in Hidra.	7	2	4	M	7	1	4	M
	The Lions harte.	8	2	13	M	8	1	13	M
	The Lions tayle.	9	3	42	M	9	2	42	M
	The virgins spike	10	5	51	M	10	4	51	M
	The scorpiōs hart	11	8	54	MD	11	7	54	DM
	The Eagle.	12	12	19	AD	12	11	19	DM

				☙ January frō the first day to ye. 15.				☙ January frō ye. 15. day to the last.			
	February frō the first day to the. 15.				February fro ye. 15. day to the last.				Marche frō the first day to the. 15			
1		3	54	DA	1	2	54	DA	1	1	54	DA
2		6	52	E	2	5	52	DA	2	4	52	DA
3		7	23	E	3	6	23	E	3	5	23	DA
4		7	50	E	4	6	50	E	4	5	50	DA
5		9	4	E	5	8	4	E	5	7	4	E
6		10	0	E	6	9	0	E	6	8	0	E
7		12	4	M	7	11	4	E	7	10	4	E
8		12	13	M	8	11	13	E	8	10	13	E
9		1	42	M	9	12	42	M	9	11	42	E
10		3	51	M	10	2	51	M	10	1	51	M
11		6	54	M	11	5	54	M	11	4	54	M
12		10	19	DM	12	9	19	DM	12	8	19	DM

ALMANACKE FOR THREE YEARES, 1571

	Marche frō the 15. to the last				April from the first day to yͤ. 15				April frō the 15. to the last.		
1	12	54	DA	1	11	54	DM	1	10	54	DM
2	3	52	DA	2	2	52	DA	2	1	52	DA
3	4	23	DA	3	3	23	DA	3	2	23	DA
4	4	0	DA	4	3	50	DA	4	2	50	DA
5	6	4	DA	5	5	4	DA	5	4	4	DA
6	7	0	E	6	6	0	DA	6	5	0	DA
7	9	4	E	7	8	4	E	7	7	4	E
8	9	13	E	8	8	13	E	8	7	13	E
9	10	42	E	9	9	42	E	9	8	42	E
10	12	51	M	10	11	51	M	10	10	51	E
11	3	54	M	11	2	54	M	11	1	54	M
12	7	19	DM	12	6	19	DM	12	5	19	M

	May frō the first to the. 15.				Aprill (sic) frō the 15. to the last.				June frō the first to the. 15.		
1	9	54	DM	1	8	54	DM	1	7	54	DM
2	12	52	DA	2	11	52	DM	2	10	52	DM
3	1	23	DA	3	12	23	DA	3	11	23	DM
4	1	50	DA	4	12	50	DA	4	11	50	DM
5	3	4	DA	5	2	4	DA	5	1	4	DA
6	4	0	DA	6	3	0	DA	6	2	0	DA
7	6	4	DA	7	5	4	DA	7	4	4	DA
8	6	13	DA	8	5	13	DA	8	4	13	DA
9	7	42	DA	9	6	42	DA	9	5	42	DA
10	9	51	E	10	8	51	DA	10	7	51	DA
11	12	54	M	11	11	54	E	11	50	54	E
12	4	19	M	12	3	19	M	12	2	19	M

June from the. 15. daye to the last.			July from the first day to the. 15.			July from the. 15. daye to the last.		
1	6 54	DM	1	5 54	DM	1	4 54	M
2	9 52	DM	2	8 52	DM	2	7 52	DM
3	10 23	DM	3	9 23	DM	3	8 23	DM
4	10 50	DM	4	9 50	DM	4	8 50	DM
5	12 4	DA	5	11 4	DM	5	10 4	DM
6	1 0	DA	6	12 0	O	6	11 0	DM
7	3 4	DA	7	2 4	DA	7	1 4	DA
8	3 13	DA	8	2 13	DA	8	1 13	DA
9	4 42	DA	9	3 42	DA	9	2 42	DA
10	6 51	DA	10	5 51	DA	10	4 51	DA
11	9 54	E	11	8 54	E	11	7 54	DA
12	1 19	M	12	12 19	M	12	11 19	E

August frō the first day to the. 15.			August frō the. 15. daye to the last.			September frō the first day to ye. 15.		
1	3 54	M	1	2 54	M	1	1 54	M
2	6 52	DM	2	5 52	DM	2	4 52	M
3	7 23	DM	3	6 23	DM	3	5 23	M
4	7 50	DM	4	6 50	DM	4	5 50	M
5	9 4	DM	5	8 4	DM	5	7 4	DM
6	10 0	DM	6	9 0	DM	6	8 0	DM
7	12 4	DA	7	11 4	DM	7	10 4	DM
8	12 13	DA	8	11 13	DM	8	10 13	DM
9	1 42	DA	9	12 42	DA	9	11 42	DM
10	3 51	DA	10	2 51	DA	10	1 51	DA
11	6 54	DA	11	5 54	DA	11	4 54	DA
12	10 19	E	12	9 19	E	12	8 19	E

ALMANACKE FOR THREE YEARES, 1571

	Septēb. frō the. 15. daye to the last.			October frō the first day to the. 15.			October frō the. 15. daye to the last.		
1	12	54	M	1	11	54	E	1	10	54	E
2	3	52	M	2	2	52	M	2	1	52	M
3	4	23	M	3	3	23	M	3	2	23	M
4	4	50	M	4	3	50	M	4	2	50	M
5	6	4	M	5	5	4	M	5	4	4	M
6	7	0	DM	6	6	0	M	6	5	0	M
7	9	4	DM	7	8	4	DM	7	7	4	M
8	9	13	DM	8	8	13	DM	8	7	13	M
9	10	42	DM	9	9	42	DM	9	8	42	DM
10	12	51	DA	10	11	51	DM	10	10	51	DM
11	3	54	DA	11	2	54	DA	11	1	54	DA
12	7	19	E	12	6	19	E	12	5	19	E

	Nouēber from the. 1 to the. 15.			Nouēber frō the. 15. to the last.			Decēber from the. 1 to the. 15.			Decēber frō the. 15. to the last.		
1	9	54	E	1	8	54	E	1	7	54	E	1	6	54	E
2	12	52	M	2	11	52	E	2	10	52	E	2	9	52	E
3	1	23	M	3	12	23	M	3	11	23	E	3	10	23	E
4	1	50	M	4	12	50	M	4	11	50	E	4	10	50	E
5	3	4	M	5	2	4	M	5	1	4	M	5	12	4	M
6	4	0	M	6	3	0	M	6	2	0	M	6	1	0	M
7	6	4	M	7	5	4	M	7	4	4	M	7	3	4	M
8	6	13	M	8	5	13	M	8	4	13	M	8	3	13	M
9	7	42	M	9	6	42	M	9	5	42	M	9	4	42	M
10	9	51	DM	10	8	51	DM	10	7	51	M	10	6	51	M
11	12	54	DA	11	11	54	DM	11	10	54	DM	11	9	54	DM
12	4	19	DA	12	3	19	DA	12	2	19	DA	12	1	19	DA

Now this Table serueth for euery moneth of the yeare being exactly calculated their tyme of their being south, or touchinge our meridian, or as some terme it the noonesteade, seruing very well the sea mē to be taken with their instrumētes vpon the Sea, referring it vnto the table of declination that goeth before the first is the houres, the second the minutes, the thirde beinge the letters, doth shewe you whether they be south by daye or by night, in the euening or morning, in ye forenone or in after noone. And the E. doth signifie euening. The letter M. signifieth the morning. And the letters DM. signifieth day in the morning. And the letters DA. signifieth daie in the after noone, ss I saide before: the very hour & minute of their being south. Now you doe see that I haue put to their being south in the daie as wel as in the night to the intent to knowe the houre of the nighte, as well by their setting, as also by your compas as I shewed you in the second Rule. To bring your .32. pointes into .24. houres. And in like maner in the fifth Rule or shining, to deuide the shining into .2. equall partes: And those partes beinge equaly deuided with the houres and mnutes, thē that time before their being south, put to that halfe that shineth, that sheweth the iust rysing of those starres: then the other time of their shining after their being south, sheweth the setting, as I declared in the rule of shining of the moone. Nowe you see that the table runneth from the first daye of euery moneth to the .15. & from the .15. to the last day. Nowe yow must consider, that if you will knowe the exact time betwixt the first day and the fiftene day, or betwixt the. xv. daie and the last: doe this, looke how many daies of the moneth is past, either frō the first daie or .xv. daie, pull .4. minutes from that nomber, for so many daies as is past for euery day that shall shewe you the true time of their beinge south, and then doing as aforesaid for their rising and setting. Now this I make an ende for breuitie, or els I would haue written the circles of the Spheare, with the orbes of the lightes of the firmament, and the courses of the seuen lightes, or

ALMANACKE FOR THREE YEARES, 1571

planetes in the zodiack, but that woulde make to great a volume. And furthermore, I am not worthy to make any rehersall of it. For there be a nōber of moste prudent and famous Autours, that haue written both in the Greeke tongue, and also in the Latine tongue, that be of great antiquitie. And also of late wryters most famous mē, in these our daies, as Johannes de Sacro Bosco, and Horōtius, Jewafritius, and also in the English tong Doctor Recorde, with a great nōber more, whiche I passe ouer, notably seene in the Mathematicall sciences.

⁋ The fifteenth Rule, sheweth howe to sayle by the Globe.

Nowe to sayle by the Globe, it is conuenient to be spoken of, for that generally the moste part of the sea men make their accompt as though that the earth ware a platte forme, for thei do not cōsider that the earth is a Globe, and that the Meridians doth growe narrowe & narrowe towardes the two poles, for it is vnpossible to drawe yᵉ face of the earth and the sea true vpon a platte forme or if that you will describe the land true, then shal not the Sea be tue. For as you doe go towardes the north partes, your meridians growe together, so shall not your lynes or pointes be accordinge to the arte of Hydrographie, for the sea shall be broader to the north partes thē that it is. Now & if you should describe the Sea true with lynes, courses, distaunces, hauēs & daungers, then should your land be broader to yᵉ north partes the it is, as for exāple. This England & Scotlād being both one Ilād in al your cardes of nauigation, yᵉ north part of Scotlande is drawen much bigger then it is, for els the lines of south & north, should not be according to the trentting of the lande: for if that you vewe it well, you shall finde the north ende of Scotlāde muche more in distaunce then it is, as you maye measure it by the trounke of your carde. Therfore for your better vnderstanding, I will shewe you the compas of the earth vnderneath sundry parrelleles or circles, how many myles that the earth doth contayne in compasse. First vnder the Equinoctiall where that the earth is at the greatest cōpasse in the going directly east or weast, that is by a right line ouer the sea and lande, the twoo poles being euen with your horizon, it is .21600. myles to come to the place that you did depart from. thē vnder the tropicke of Cancer, the north pole being raysed .23. degrees and .28. minutes, goynge directly east and weast .19800. myles in compasse. Then in our artike circle of London, where the pole articke is raysed .51. degrees .32. minutes, going directly east and weast .13320. myles in cōpas, then vnderneath the pollard circle where the pole is raysed .66. degrees .32. minutes .8460. myles in compas, so you see that the compas of the east and weast lyne coming from the equinoctiall, is muche lesser to the northwardes thē that it is to the southwardes, therefore when that you shall haue anye occasion to atempt any viage to the north partes, it is best to sayle by a globe, for so shal you better se the distaūces and bignes of the landes, and in like case your lines and courses as this first, according to the accustomed maner, kepe a perfect accompte, and rekening the way of the shippe, by what lyne or point your ship hath made her waye good, then must you resorte to your globe, and then consider in what place and parrell you be in, as you maye doe by the Sunne by daye, and by the Starres by nyght, then considering in what place and parrel you be in, set your globe to your eleuation of your pole, then turne to the place of your zeneth, & seeke the aposite of your zeneth in your parrell, for then you doe knowe that in that parrel is your east and weast lyne, then in the iust quarter of that circle to the pole, deuide into your .8. pointes of your compas, and so on the other side, and in like case if you come to the southwardes, then deuide your eight wyndes from your antertike pole to your parrell circle, and this must you doe euer, and anone for the oftener that you doe obserue this custome, the better and parfiter shall your course be. Now this briefly I do make an ende of sailing by the globe, but as for them that doe occupie the southpartes, nothing is better than their cardes, and because that I haue declared vnto you the lengthe of certaine of the parrelles, what myles the earth doth containe in compas vnder thē. Nowe will I shew you how many myles distaunce is betwene euery one of them, and first from the Equinoctiall to the Tropycke of Cancer, whiche is there where that the Sunne maketh his furdest prograce to the north partes, it is .1408. myles betwene them, thē betwene the Tropyke of Cancer and our articke circle of London, it is .1684. myles: Then betwene our articke circle and the pollare circle, is .900. myles. Then betweene the pollard circle and the pole, is .1408. myles, so that it is in all from the Equinoctiall to either of the twoo poles .5400. myles, whiche is the fourth parte of the compasse of the whole earth.

¶ The sixtenth Rule, declareth howe to knowe the houre of the daye by the Compas.

Nowe for to make your instrumentes for the Sea with their vses, you shall repayre to the booke of Nauigation, made by Martine Cortis a Spanyarte, Imprinted by maister Jugge printer to the Queenes maiestie, whiche booke hath bene very chargeable to him, therefore it is not for me to medle with nothing contained in that booke, or els I would haue shewed you the makinge of the Equinoctiall diall with his vse, whiche is very profitable to knowe the houre of the daie by, for your compas is not to knowe the houre of the day by in sommer, not in the morning and eueninge, neither can you know when that the moone is east or weast. When that she hath north declination, being in the signe of Taurus, Gemini, and Cancer, or Leo, because that your compas stādeth flat as doth your horizon, therefore I will shewe you what you shall doe, take an olde flie or carde of a compas, then pull out the brasse that the carde did hange on, then take a wyer and put it through the carde, that the one ende be as long as the other, & put a litle waxe about the wyer to make it stande fast and vpright, then whē you would know what that it is a clock, set your compas afore you, then take the olde flie of your compas and set it downe vpon the glasse of your compas, the north pointe right with the north, & the south point south, then according to the eleuation of your coūtrey or place that you be in, lift vp the south side of the olde flie, euen with your equinoctiall, & let the north point lene vpon the glasse, so shal the wyer point euen to the north pole, then looke what shadowe that the wier doth make that shalbe a true shadow, either by the moone or the Sūne, so shal you see the perfit houre of the day better then by any other dyal, then when that the Sunne or moone hath south declination, then must you obserue the shadow vnderneath the flie or carde, but it ware better to be made in metall, the. 32. wyndes or pointes, and thē you may in like maner put to the. 24. deuisions equall to know the houre of the day, and then you may make the northside square for to stande fast, for a round thing if you take not hede to it, it will not stande vpright.

⁋ Nowe foloweth the rising noonestead or being south, and setting of the seuen starres, as long as they giue light by the night, being calculated for the latitude of London, and wil continue this .100 yeare without muche error. And here with vs they ryse neare the north east, and settes neare the northweast, and shineth or abideth aboue our horizon 16. houres. 20. minutes.

⁋ January.

THe seuen starres south at .8. a clock .12. mi. and setteth at .4. a clocke .22. mi. the first daye.

The seuen starres south at 7. of the clocke .32. minutes. and settes at .3. a clock .42. mi. the .10. day

The seuen starres south at .6. a clock. 52. minu. and settes at .3. of the clock .2. min. the .20 daye.

⁌ February.

The seuen starres south at .6. a clocke .12. minu. and settes at .2. a clock 22. min. the first day.

The seuen starres south at .5. a clock .32. mi. and settes at .1. a clock .42. mi. the 10. day.

The seuen starres setteth at .1. a clocke .2. min. the .20. daye.

⁌ Marche.

The seuen starres setteth at .12. a clock .22. min. the first daie.

The seuen starres setteth at .11. a clock .42. min. the .10. daie.

The seuen starres setteth at .11. a clocke .2. min. the .20. daye.

⁌ Aprill.

The seuen starres setteth at .x. of the clock .22. minutes.

The seuen starres setteth at .ix. of the clocke .42 minutes.

The seuen starres will not be seene at the latter ende of Aprill.

⁌ May.

In the moneth of May, you can not see the seuē starres.

⁌ June.

The seuen starres ryse at twoo of the clocke .2. minutes, the first daie.

The seuen starres riseth the .x. day at one of the clocke .22. minutes.

The seuen starres riseth the .20. daye at .12. of the clocke .42. minutes.

⁌ August.

The seuen starres riseth the first daye at .x. of the clocke .2. minutes.

The seuen starres riseth the .x. daie at .ix. of the clocke .22. minutes.

The seuen starres ryse the .xx. daie at .viii. of the clocke .42. minutes, and in nonesteade or south at .iiii. of the clock .52. minutes in the morning.

⁌ September.

The seuen starres riseth the first daye at .viii. of the clocke .2. minutes, and south at .4. of the clocke 12. minutes in the morning.

The seuen starres ryseth the .x. daye at .vii. of the clocke .22. minutes, and south at .iii. of the clock 32. minutes.

The seuen starres ryseth the .20. day at .6. of the clocke .42. minutes, and south at two of the clocke 52. minutes.

⁋ October.

The seuen starres ryseth the first daye at .6. of the clocke, twoo minutes, and south at two of the clocke .xii. minutes.

The seuen starres riseth the .x. daie at .v. of the clock .22. mi. & south at one of the clock .32. minuts.

The seuen starres riseth the .20. daie at foure of the clocke .42. minutes, and south at .12. of the clock. 52. minutes, and settes at .ix. of the clocke .2. minutes in the morning.

⁋ Nouember.

The seuen starres ryseth the first day at foure of the clocke twoo minutes, and in the south at .12. of the clocke .12. minutes, and settes at .viii. of the clocke .22. minutes in the morning.

The seuen starres riseth the .x. daie at .iii. of the clock .22. min. and south at .11. of the clocke .32. mi. and settes at .vii. of the clock .42. minutes.

The seuen starres in the South, the .20. daie at x. of the clocke. 52. minutes, and setteth at .vii. of the the clocke, twoo minutes in the morning.

⁋ December.

The seuen starres the first day at .x. of the clock 12. minutes, and settes. at .vi. of the clocke .22. min.

The seuen starres south, at .ix. of the clock .32. minutes and settes at .v. of the clock .42. minutes.

The seuen starres be in the meridian or south, the .20. day at .8. of the clock .52. minutes, and settes at .5. of the clock .2. minutes in the morning.

⁋ Finis.

⟨ Faultes escaped in the printing.

The seconde Rule, the seconde page the thirde line, reade that is to saye. The thirde Rule the first page in the fifth line, reade houres for daies. The third Rule the second page the first line, take 30. for .39. in the same page the .6. line. reade prime and Epact. The fourth Rule the .7. page the third line, reade take foure of these partes. The fourth Rule the first page the second line, reade what for when. The fourth Rule the .12. page the .7. line, reade take. The fourth Rule the fourth page the 8. line, reade faster for farther. The fourth Rule the seuenth page, the .3. line, reade mountes bay for moūthbay. The .7. Rule, the seconde page the 20. line, reade bytinge her tayle for litening her tayle. The seuenth Rule the .3. page, the .25. lyne take .48. for .49. The .10. Rule, the seconde page the .10. line, reade neare enough for nere Inowse. The .11. Rule the .3. page, the .12. line reade exacte for Epact. The .11. Rule the .3. page the .19. line, reade superficiall for supersticiall. In the .12. Rule the first page, there lacketh these .6. wordes, yᵉ pole raysed .48. degrees .40. myles to one degree of longitude.

⟨ Imprinted at Londō in Paules
churcheyarde, at the signe of the Lucrece
by Thomas Purfoote.
1567.

Fig. 7. Tail-piece of *An Almanacke and Prognostication for three yeares*, by William Bourne, 1571

The tail-piece is the printer's device of Thomas Purfoote

Fig. 8. Edward Fiennes, Lord Clinton and Saye,
Lord High Admiral, 1562

Oil-painting in the Ashmolean Museum, Oxford. Lord Clinton, created
Earl of Lincoln in 1572, was again Lord High Admiral 1558–85

II

A Regiment for the Sea (1574)

EDITOR'S NOTE

William Bourne spoke of himself as a gunner, and it was as a gunner that Gabriel Harvey commended him; nevertheless it is by his services to navigation that he deserves recognition to-day. His simple manual, *A Regiment for the Sea*, was re-edited or re-printed at least ten times,[1] and was even translated into Dutch, although the Dutch were reckoned in the sixteenth century to be our masters in navigation techniques. His *Regiment* or Rule for the Sea contained the substance of the earlier Rules, some of them repeated verbatim, but in style and format, as well as in its enlarged content it is decidedly an improvement on its predecessor. Not only was the author now more confident and more mature, he had secured an unusually excellent printer-publisher in the person of Thomas Hacket. Hacket (or Haquet) was an immigrant Frenchman who had come over from Normandy in 1534 and established himself as a printer and stationer near the Royal Exchange. He produced an attractive and well-set title-page for the first edition of Bourne's book, and adorned it with an interesting woodcut of a sea astrolabe. On the verso of the page there was the woodcut portrait of a ship which is undoubtedly the Lord High Admiral's flagship, for it carries his standard.[2] It was to Admiral Lord Clinton, recently created Earl of Lincoln, that the work was dedicated by his 'poore

---

[1] The known editions and reprints are dated 1574, 1577, 1580, 1587, 1592, 1596, 1601, 1606, 1611, 1620 and 1631. The Dutch translation was printed three times, and the *Regiment* was included in the very short list of text books which Captain John Smith advised the young seaman to read in 1626. See the bibliography, Appendix C, below.

[2] See Fig. 9. The ship is a galleon, of which the prototype, the *Foresight*, was laid down for the Queen in 1570. The proportion of length to beam is greater than in the old 'high-charged' ship, while the height of forecastle and poop are much reduced. Guns are mounted on the lower as well as on the upper deck. The *Edward Bonaventure*, which sailed with Edward Fenton as vice-admiral in 1582, was built at Rochester on the

Fig. 9. The Lord High Admiral's flagship

Woodcut on verso of title-page of *A Regiment for the Sea* (1574); reprinted on the title-page of subsequent editions.

servant', as Bourne describes himself. And this can be no figure of speech for he writes, 'all my labours be due unto your honorable Lordship.' It may be inferred that he was in some way attached to the Earl's household, whether salaried or no. It is, however, often necessary to allow for verbal exaggerations in his mode of writing, as when he terms his book not only 'simple' (as it was intended to be) but 'barbarous'. This, however, was in accordance with the custom of his day.

In the Preface to the Reader the importance of navigation to an island kingdom is emphasized, a point still novel but one which became a commonplace in all subsequent works on ships

same lines in 1574, and the *Revenge* (with some modifications) in the following year. This woodcut, above, showing the Royal Standard, may well represent the *Foresight*. See E. G. R. Taylor (ed.), *Voyage of Edward Fenton* (1959), p. 154.

and seamanship. There follows Bourne's apologia for attempting what 'excellent learned men' had already done so well. The educated seafarer may turn to them, for his own care is only for the 'simplest sort'. He disclaims any intention (for reasons already explained) to write what had been set out in the English translation of Cortes, but in fact, so far as actual navigation is concerned, his book is fairly complete. It is probable that he really had no desire to go fully into the subject of instrument-making or compass-making, which were already established as specialized crafts in England, while there were also now a few professional chart-makers, so that to duplicate Cortes's detailed description of the chart was unnecessary. At the close of the Preface his readers are told that if this book pleases them, they may shortly look for others, but it is only in the concluding passage of the actual text that the titles of these are revealed. They are *A Treasure for Travellers* and *The Arte of Shooting in Great Ordnaunce*, writings which had been substantially complete in the manuscript their author had presented to Lord Burghley very recently. As already mentioned, they were both published in 1578.

As was customary at that period, a number of laudatory verses by the author's friends preceded the text. The third of these, by an unidentified A.R., takes up at length Bourne's diffidence in the face of that adverse criticism to which he himself had referred in the Preface. But again it must be remembered that at that date a writer was expected to show modesty and reluctance, whatever he might actually feel.

In the *Regiment* the Kalendar is now clearly and correctly printed. But the key numbers to the moon's cycle are there as before, and are still neither explained nor used. On a later page a table of the Prime or Golden Numbers with the Epacts is provided for the period 1574 to 1592, and the instructions for finding the age of the moon are repeated from the Rules of 1567. The names of the black-letter saints in the Kalendar differ considerably from those used in the earlier book, and there are other minor changes—the Dog Days for example begin and end three days later, and the faulty date of the Queen's accession is corrected. The moveable Feasts for the years 1574 to 1603 appear in a separate table, as do the dates of the Law Terms and those of the accessions of the monarchs reigning since the Conquest. Bourne also repeats a note on the length of day and night at London which he declares is commonly reckoned wrongly.

Before turning to the text it is necessary to say something about the change of printer. It proved unfortunate that the original copy had been given to Thomas Hacket despite his excellent workmanship, for he was an elderly man, and within two years had to give a power of attorney to his wife to wind up his business. She sold the copyright and the wood-blocks of the *Regiment* to John Wight,[1] who in 1577 issued a reprint without consulting the author. This he had a legal right to do, but Bourne declared that not only had Wight omitted to correct the misprints in the first edition, but had introduced fresh ones. The author therefore rejected the book, and reckoned as the second edition the issue of 1580, to which he made a number of textual additions (p. 296) besides the notable addendum of the essay on *Five Ways to Cathay*. This will be considered separately (p. 285). The book was still being printed for Wight in 1580, and it is remarkable that he apparently raised no objection to Bourne laying his complaint of discourtesy over the first reprint in an additional Address to the Reader. This Address, however, afforded the author an opportunity to explain the points in which the text had been augmented, no doubt in response to criticisms and requests from readers (p. 292).

For the modern reader the most misleading error which

---

[1] 'Jhon Wight. 8 Januarij. A⁰. 19 Reg. Elizabethe 1576/7. Tho. Hacket, At a court holden this day by assent of the m^r. wardens and assistantes. The said Thomas Hacket hathe sold and assigned unto ye said Jhon Wight theise ij copies viz. The Regiment for ye Sea and all the pictures belonging to ye same.' A marginal note says that Hacket acts through his wife who holds his power of attorney. W. W. Greg and E. Boswell (eds.), *Records of the Court of the Stationers' Company, 1576–1602* (London, 1930).

Fig. 10. The seaman's instruments
Title-page of *The Mariners Mirrour* (London, 1588), engraved by T. de Bry

Wight had introduced in 1577 was the misprint 'a minute *or* an hour glass' instead of 'a minute *of* an hour glass', when the author was describing the measure of time to be used with the new English log. A 'minute of an hour' is of course one sixtieth, and the use of a minute sand-glass is implied. Since, however, there is no copy of the first edition in any public library[1] in this country readers were puzzled as to how an hour-glass could be useful (see p. 237).

The text opens with a set of definitions necessary for the understanding of the celestial sphere, the starry heavens by which the sailor was to find his way across the pathless ocean. He must, for example, distinguish between the two Arctic Circles. The Arctic Circle proper is that which bounds the portion of the sky always to be seen from any particular latitude. It determines the declination of the circum-polar star which will just touch the horizon but never set. The Polar Arctic Circle is that which appears on our maps to-day, bounding the area within which the midnight sun appears. For an observer at the Pole the celestial equator is his Arctic Circle, and all the stars are circum-polar. They neither rise nor set, but only fade out in the sunlight. For an observer at the Equator there is no Arctic Circle, and there are therefore no circum-polar stars. All the stars rise and set, remaining twelve hours above and twelve hours below the horizon.

Since each star rises and sets daily at the same point on the horizon, according to the latitude of the observer, it serves him as an index to direction. And since it rises four minutes earlier every day it can serve also as an index to time.

Bourne explains the different usages of the terms latitude and longitude when terrestrial and celestial positions respectively are in question, and the word 'declination', the celestial equivalent to terrestrial latitude, is defined. In effect, the 'declination' of sun or star is its distance in degrees from the equinoctial or

---

[1] A copy is to be found in the Scott Library of the Royal Institution of Naval Architects. See Fig. 1.

Celestial Equator. Celestial longitude is measured along the ecliptic, the mid-line of the Zodiac marked out by the sun's path. The initial point is where the sun enters Aries, that is to say where he crosses the equinoctial from south to north. Each sign contains 30 degrees, and the sun's entry into each in succession is marked in the Kalendar.

It is evident that some of the definitions which follow those explaining the various circles left readers puzzled, for in the 1580 edition Bourne tried to make them clearer by explanations of the words 'excentric' and 'parallax' (p. 296). Yet these new definitions will possibly still further confuse anybody unfamiliar with the general Ptolemaic theory of the earth-centred universe. It had long been observed that there were irregularities in the motions of the planets (among which was then included the sun) along their supposed circular orbits. This anomaly could be partially accounted for by the theory that the centre of a planet's orbit did not coincide with the centre of the earth. It was excentric. One part of the orbit was consequently nearer the earth than the opposite part, and here the planet was in its slow motion. When it was farthest from the earth it was in its swift motion, and this was when it was said to be in 'auge'. If a line was drawn through the earth's centre and the centre of the planet's orbit, and thence extended to the circumference at its most distant point, this furthest point was called the point of auge. From Bourne's standpoint, the most important example of the effect of an excentric orbit was the case of the moon. Tide-tables were calculated on the basis of her mean motion through the month, but in fact the interval between high tides grew shorter when she was in her swift motion, longer when she was in her slow motion, and this had to be allowed for (p. 179).

Bourne's addition in 1580 of a definition of parallax (p. 296) may also be bewildering to the unmathematical. If two people look at a distant object from points some distance apart their lines of sight converge on the object and they will give different

A REGIMENT FOR THE SEA, 1574

readings for its height above the horizon. When, however, the object observed is as distant as are the sun or the stars the convergence of the lines of sight from the most widely separated points on the relatively small earth is imperceptible. The lines can therefore be treated as parallel, and observations from whatever point they are made will not sensibly differ. The earth is treated as a point. The moon, however, is sufficiently close to the earth for the convergence of the lines of sight towards it as from the centre and the surface of the earth respectively to be measurable. The angle at which they meet (varying of course according to the horizons of reference of different observers) is termed the moon's parallax. The fact that lunar observations must be corrected for parallax was an additional obstacle to their effective use in finding the longitude.[1]

The wording of Bourne's definition of navigation confirms what he specifically states elsewhere, that the author had read and used John Dee's famous *Preface* to the English Euclid. But the attractive description that he gives (p. 170) of the character that the master-navigator should bear is largely his own, although it strangely resembles that set out by Ibn-Majīd, the so-called 'Pilot of Vasco da Gama', who led the Portuguese to India in 1498.[2] The master or pilot must be a man of even temper, who has learned by self-control to control others, a man who could mete out justly both praise and blame, a man who could command the respect of those under his orders. His professional qualifications had been set out in Bourne's earlier book. First and foremost came his knowledge of the tides, and if he were a coaster, his knowledge of soundings, ground, leading marks, and landmarks. But if he is to be an ocean voyager, he must also be skilled in handling the table of declinations and able to work out his latitude from an observation of sun or star.

---

[1] The Sun's parallax is in fact a few seconds of arc, but it was not measurable until the latter part of the eighteenth century, when instruments had attained sufficient precision for the task.

[2] T. A. Chumolsky (ed.), *Tres roteiros desconhecidos de Ahmad Ibn-Madjid o piloto arabe* (Lisbon, 1960).

The first four chapters that follow are similar to the opening Rules in the earlier book, and deal with calculating the age of the moon and the tides. The fifth chapter now contains a four-year cycle of solar declinations such as Barlow had presented to Henry VIII in his *Brief Summe of Geographie* a generation earlier. Bourne also adds a drawing of the cross-staff, showing the two moveable sights on the 'transitory'. These could be covered with dark glass when observing the sun, although this involved the danger of distortion by refraction owing to the poor quality of glass at that date. Bourne does not, however, raise this point, but deals with what Thomas Hariot called 'parallax of the eye'. This is the error which arises from the fact that the pupil of the observer's eye does not coincide with the mid-line of the staff in respect of which the scale is marked. To correct this our author suggests paring away the corner of the staff, a suggestion which brought a sharp rebuke from Thomas Digges.[1] It was Hariot who introduced a method of numerical correction of the observed angle.[2]

Another new point is made in Chapter 6. It is with regard to observations made with the sea-ring or astrolabe. The instrument now shown has a double scale from horizon to vertical, and by taking the mean of the altitudes found on each scale any error is eliminated which may arise from the astrolabe not hanging true. It must have been difficult, however, to bring home the dangers of 'instrumental error' to men only newly introduced to instruments and often self-taught in their use. Nor was the possession of suitable instruments to be assumed. Scholars like Dr Nunes or Dr Dee might design, for example, azimuth compasses, and teach their use to master-pilots, but for the most part seamen merely pointed their compasses towards the North Star and judged the 'north-easting and north-

---

[1] Thomas Digges in describing the ten-foot *Radius Astronomicus*, a giant cross-staff with a diagonal scale, as used by Dr Dee, remarks: 'Mirium in modum haec baculi rectificatio Nautis prodierit, qui maxime ex oculi in Polis altitudinii deprehendenda falluntur....' His instrument had sighting pins (*Alae* (1573)).

[2] D. W. Waters, *Art of Navigation*, App. 30.

A REGIMENT FOR THE SEA, 1574

westing' of the needle accordingly.[1] Yet as Bourne points out, the Pole Star is 'a third of a point' (over $3\frac{1}{2}°$) away from the Celestial Pole as it passes to the east or west of it on its circumpolar orbit. If it is necessary to use the method it should be done only when the Star is directly above or below the true Pole, positions which are indicated by the Pointers of the Great Bear. He himself, he declares, is not convinced by any of the theories about the variation. It was said that it was proportional to the longitude east or west of the place where the particular mariner's compass was made, but having doubtless been already subjected to criticism as an armchair sailor, he leaves the matter to be tested by experience.

Three chapters (pp. 213–222) are now devoted to the use of the declination tables, assuming all possible relative positions for and between ship and sun. All the solutions depend on the same simple propositions. Latitude is directly given by the height of the Celestial Pole above the observer's horizon. The Pole is by definition always 90° from the equinoctial, therefore by finding the height of the equinoctial above the horizon and subtracting it from 90° the latitude is obtained. The number of degrees between the sun and the equinoctial at noon on any given date is to be found in the Declination Table. Its height above the observer's horizon can be instrumentally measured, and so a simple addition or subtraction sum gives the required height of the equinoctial. What the rules teach is when to add and when to subtract, for ship and sun may be in the same or opposite hemispheres, while the ship may be between the sun and the equinoctial or on the poleward side of the sun. It may even be on the equinoctial itself. Each case is explained with the help of a well-drawn diagram, and at the close Bourne suggests that it was because of their ignorance of how to deal with their observations in the Southern Hemisphere that English seamen

---

[1] This was all that the scholar William Cuningham suggested in his *Cosmographical Glasse* (1559), for he was more interested in general principles than in practice, so far as sea matters were concerned.

had so far feared to go beyond the Gulf of Guinea and cross the Equator.

But the sailors whom Bourne knew best, and whom he always had in mind, were those who travelled north, the servants of the Muscovy Company. The route to Russia round the North Cape took them well within the Polar Arctic Cirle, and a contrary wind might carry them further north still. He therefore added a special chapter on taking the sun not at noon but at midnight. This could be done with the cross-staff, as the altitude to be measured was only a few degrees. But unless the date was near midsummer day, a time of year when the declination barely altered for days, it was necessary to find what the correct figure was at midnight. This was done by taking the mean of the noon figures for the preceding and following days as shown in the table.

Having demonstrated the possibility of astronomical navigation in high latitudes, Bourne raises the point of the probability of finding open water there during the summer and early autumn, and so of discovering passages round Asia or North America.[1] His mention of C. Paramantia shows that he knows Ortelius's world map of 1564, on which alone this cape is marked. It was a map that was also used by Humfrey Gilbert and by Dr Dee. Bourne's argument was that there was no 'Frozen Sea' debarring mankind from the Arctic as the ancient geographers had declared, and as was still taught in the Schools. The continuous sunlight must render the region temperate for part of the year. He added the reminder that a high latitude passage would be short, for the whole circuit of the globe in latitude 80° was only 1250 leagues. He was to develop this theme more fully in the edition of 1580 after Frobisher's failure, and he carried his arguments still further in the *Five Ways to Cathay* (p. 301).

Despite his agreement with Richard Jugge[2] that he would not

---

[1] This section is expanded in the edition of 1580. See pp. 299, 300.
[2] Richard Jugge died in 1577, but his business was continued by a son.

include any matter 'sufficiently declared' in the English *Cortes*, Bourne could no longer omit the traditional pair of diagrams considered essential to a sea-manual. These were the Regiment of the North Star, and the Compass Circle which showed the course made good along each rhumb when raising or lowering the Pole (i.e. changing latitude) by one degree. On the first diagram the position of the Celestial Pole in relation to the Pole Star was now set out in the customary way, as indicated by the Guards of the Lesser Bear (*Ursa Minor*), but as the necessary explanatory text was worked into the diagram it could be considered in a certain sense original and not plagiarized. Similarly, the second diagram differed from that of Cortes in giving the distances to be sailed in English miles, as well as in Portuguese or Spanish leagues. But it must have puzzled many users, for in the lower half of the circle the figures do not represent the distances to be sailed along the rhumbs against which they are written in order to raise a degree. They are the distances in leagues to which the ship will have been carried east or west of the meridian from which she started when she has raised or laid the Pole one degree. In other words they give the change of longitude, and the diagram becomes a 'distance and departure' table. Cortes provided these 'departure' figures in a separate diagram in terms of the 'great degree' or degree of longitude measured at the Equator. Bourne is wrong, however, (as already explained) in supposing that the Spanish writer's diagram served only for a ship at the Equator, for he supplied a further table showing the number of lesser degrees at successive latitudes which correspond to the 'great degree'. At latitude 60°, for example, the distance between two meridians is half what it was at the Equator, or in other words two degrees of longitude at that latitude make one 'great degree'.[1]

The linear measure of a degree of a great circle (i.e. a com-

---

[1] Bourne added a chapter on the measure of degrees of longitude at latitudes up to 80° in the 1580 edition of the *Regiment*. For John Dee's contribution to the longitude problem see Appendix A, below.

plete circumference of the globe of the earth) is of course a fundamental figure for the navigator and the cartographer alike. When Bourne wrote, it was already accepted as a length of sixty miles, or one mile for one minute of arc. This figure was in fact much too small, but the convenience of the ratio of 'mile to minute' led to its establishment as the 'nautical mile', the length of which was progressively adjusted to the true measure of a minute of arc as and when this was more accurately determined. For Bourne it measured 5000 feet, but today it is known to measure 6080 feet.

It will be appreciated that the diagram for 'raising a degree' gives the solution for only seven special cases of the nautical triangle. Not until the sailor could read trigonometrical tables could he find his distance and 'departure' for any course whatsoever that he was following, and this was not until the seventeenth century.

It is difficult to find any clear pattern in the sequence either of Bourne's *Rules* or of the chapters of his *Regiment*. The two standard diagrams are now followed by an explanation (Chapter 14) of how the ship-master can 'set the coast' with his compass and his cross-staff—in effect how he can make a rough survey or sketch for his journal. Where observations are to be made from two points, measuring the distance between them depends upon measuring the ship's way, or rate of sailing. It is here that Bourne quite casually introduces to the world the English log—'Some do this (which I think is very good),' he writes. The age-old method had been to throw some floating object overboard at the prow, and either pace it to the stern or have a watcher there to call out when it arrived, i.e. when the ship had sailed past it. It can never be known who first thought of throwing out a log of wood which was tethered to the ship, and veering out the long fine line which held it for a fixed interval of time. It would seem that the smallest sand-glass at that period measured out one minute, and as this was rather too long an interval the use of a formula of words or syllables was considered preferable. The line used was already, when Bourne wrote, marked by twists of cord into sub-divisions, but that these were at the 'middle' and the 'end' makes no sense, since the line was allowed to run out from the cry 'Turn' until the cry 'Stop' indicated that the chosen time interval had elapsed. As the line was drawn in its length was measured in fathoms, no doubt by the stretch of the arms. Knowing the fraction of an hour which the time interval indicated, a simple multiplication and division sum gave the distance in leagues which the ship was covering in a whole hour, i.e. the 'way' of the ship. For the

Heures.	Nœuds.	Brasses.	Routes. Rumbs.
2	3	2	Cap au Nort $\frac{1}{4}$ du Nordeſt.
4	2	4	Cap au Nort-nordeſt.
6	4	2	Cap au Nordeſt.
8	5	3	Cap au Nordeſt.
10	2	3 $\frac{1}{2}$	Cap au Nort $\frac{1}{4}$ du Nordeſt.
12	3	5	Cap au Nort-nordeſt.
2	2	3.	Cap au Nordeſt $\frac{1}{4}$ de l'Eſt.
4	2	4	Cap au Nordeſt.
6	6	1	Cap au Nort.
8	6	3	Cap au Nordeſt $\frac{1}{4}$ du Nordeſt.
10	6	2	Cap au Nort $\frac{1}{4}$ du Nordeſt.
12	3.	4	Cap au Nort-nordeſt.

Fig. 11. Log and log-line, and sand-glass
From Samuel de Champlain, *Voyages* (Paris, 1632)

number of fathoms to a league was known. Such is the information that is supplied, but it is unlikely that any novice could follow so terse an explanation. In the 1580 edition, therefore, Bourne elaborates his description (p. 297) and works out an example. First of all he notes that 'stray' must be allowed for (measured by a mark on the line), so that the count does not begin until the log is clear of the eddy of the ship's wake.

Actually his allowance for 'stray' is considerably less than what became customary, but his most probable informant had sailed in a very small ship. From his worked example it is clear that the half-minute had now become the time interval actually used, so that the number of fathoms of line run out had to be multiplied by 120. These fathoms had next to be turned into leagues, and if the wind, and therefore the ship's course and way, continually changed, the amount of arithmetic to be done was decidedly daunting.

The identity of the mathematician who came to the rescue, like that of the sailor who had first tied a line to the log he threw overboard, can never be known.[1] What distance run in half a minute is equal to a mile an hour? It is, of course, $\frac{1}{120}$ of a mile. Ignoring Bourne's statement that a mile contains 5000 feet,[2] and taking the statute mile of 5280 feet, the answer obtained is 44 feet, but with the shorter mile it is approximately 42 feet. The instrument-maker in fact knotted the log-line at every 7 fathoms or 42 feet. The sailor had only to count the passing knots during the half-minute he veered out the line, and he at once had a figure of approximate 'miles an hour' that he could enter in his 'book' or journal, and use to prick his chart. He must multiply it, of course, by the number of hours during which the wind held steady. Within half a generation the log and line had come into general use in North-West Europe, although the Spaniards and Portuguese for long would have none of it. The 'way' of his ship, it seems, was something an old Iberian seaman 'knew', as a driver knows the speed of his car.

The next few chapters deal with the problem of longitude, which Bourne rightly concludes at that date could only be determined at sea by dead-reckoning. His graphical device (p. 241) for measuring the length of a degree of longitude at any particular latitude may, however, puzzle the reader. This

---

[1] Presumably a billet of wood such as was used to stoke the galley fire was always handy. A handful of ashes thrown on to the surface of the water indicated by its drift the direction of a current, so we are told elsewhere.

[2] This was the old 'geometric' mile of medieval writers.

device depends upon the mathematical relationship between latitude and longitude on a sphere. The longitude is the trigonometrical ratio termed the 'cosine' of the degree of latitude, and if the length of the degree of latitude (the 'great degree') is set out as the diameter of a semicircle, then a thread laid from one end of the diameter to the circumference measures the cosine of the particular angle which the thread makes with the diameter. Thus the length OA (Fig. *a*) set off as the line OB will be

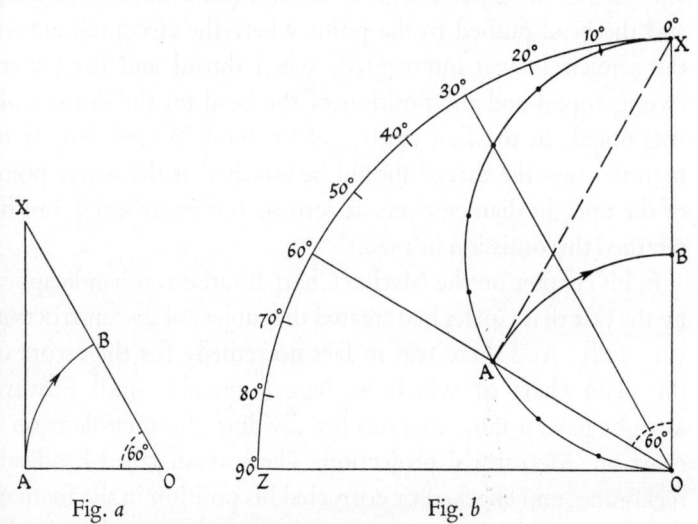

Fig. *a* Fig. *b*

found to be half OX, since, in the right-angled triangle OAX, OA makes an angle of 60° with OX, and the cosine of 60° is one half. In this case, if OX is one degree of the meridian, the answer is half 60 nautical miles. In the figure (Fig. *b*) a quadrant of a circle is drawn with radius OZ equal to the diameter OX of the semicircle OAX, and with its centre at point O. The scale of miles is marked along OX from zero to 60. The quadrant can be marked off in degrees from X round to Z at any selected interval, say 10°, from 0° to 90°. It will be found that the radii of this quadrant (e.g. at 10°, 30°, 60°, 70°) divide up the circumference of the semicircle equally. Bourne therefore omits this construction, and simply marks off equal divisions, 0 to 90, on the semicircle. If the thread is laid from the lower end of the diameter to division 30, for example, it is lying at an angle of 30° with the diameter, and its measure is the length of a degree of longitude (on the scale marked along the diameter) at latitude 30°. The original device, as described by Pedro Nunes in his *Tratado em defensam da carta de marear* (1537), carried a thread (attached at O) with a tiny sliding bead. The thread was stretched to the desired angle of latitude (on a one-degree scale) and the bead pushed to the point where the circumference of the semicircle was intercepted, when thread and bead were swung round and the position of the bead on the linear scale was noted. In the first edition of his book Bourne forgot to mention that the thread should be attached at the lower point of the upright diameter (i.e. at zero on the linear scale), but he rectified this omission in 1580.[1]

In his chapter on the Marine Chart Bourne was handicapped by the fact that Cortes had treated the subject of its construction very fully. And there was in fact no remedy for the errors of the plain chart of which he here complains until Edward Wright gave a table in 1599 for dividing the meridians on a chart on 'Mercator's' projection. The seaman sailed by dead-reckoning, and checked or corrected his position in the manner that Bourne describes on p. 253 whenever he was able to take an observation for latitude. But it has to be remembered that an overcast sky may persist for days together. No opportunity could therefore be missed of taking an altitude, and so in the *Regiment* the tables of the fixed stars are now enlarged to give a choice of thirty-two 'lights' as they used to be called. Unfortunately the figures are far from accurate, and in the case of

---

[1] 'And now shall follow a demonstration of half a circle, and that shall shew you how many miles will make a degree, according unto any latitude that you are in, by the replying of a payre of compasses, or a thread made fast at the lower corner at 90, and there in like maner at one of the pointes of the Compass and the other point unto the latitude that you are in, for all Circles is according unto theyr diameters.' At 90°, i.e. at the Pole, a degree of longitude is zero.

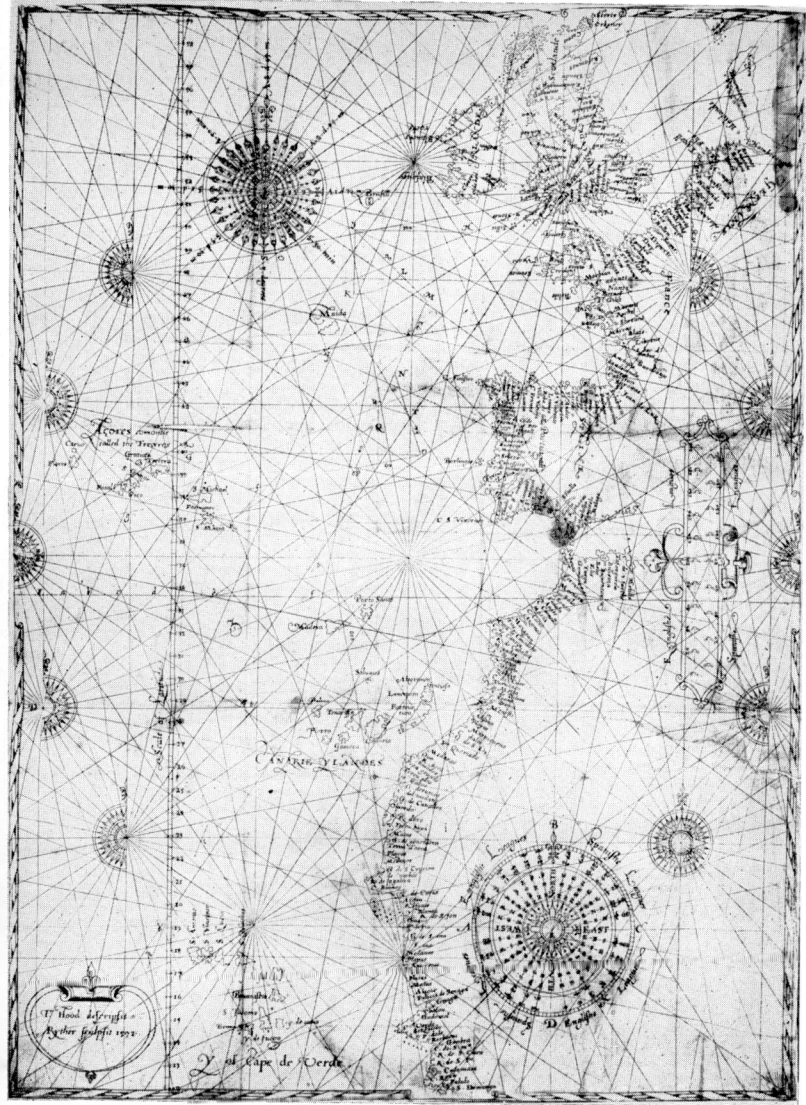

Fig. 12. Chart of the north-east Atlantic by Thomas Hood, engraved by Augustine Ryther, 1592

Accompanying *The Mariners guide*, added by Hood to his edition (1592) of Bourne's *A Regiment for the Sea*

the Virgin's Spike an arithmetical mistake in computing the declination from the celestial latitude of the star has introduced a total error of over 4°. When it is recalled that an error of even half a degree of latitude means an error of position of thirty sea-miles the success actually achieved in early ocean sailing seems almost miraculous.

Attention may here be drawn to some sensible suggestions that Bourne made (p. 249) for minor improvements to the plain chart. In the hands of professional chart-makers it had become elaborately illuminated and ornamented to no purpose. It would be useful, he commented, to have the ports lettered (with a key) according to their tidal 'establishments', while the pilot would be assisted by the addition of shore profiles and sketches of harbour entries. The first suggestion was adopted on one of his charts (1596) by Thomas Hood,[1] while the second soon became normal practice.

In Chapter 21 Bourne returns to the subject that has constantly troubled him—the method of finding time at sea by the sun or moon. And despite his repeated assurance that he is not going to encroach on Cortes's book, he now gives instructions for making a more finished Equinoctial Dial than the one he had described in the *Rules*. While valuable on land, such a dial would in fact be difficult to use on ship-board, even if there were only a slight swell. And it is doubtful whether the sailor would grasp the idea of taking the mean position of the constantly swaying shadow, although Thomas Hariot later pointed out that this could be done to get an instrumental reading. His teaching, however, was never public but remained limited to the seamen in Ralegh's service.[2]

Chapter 22 deals with the final and always dangerous end-phase of an English voyage—finding the entry into the Channel, which must be searched out by sounding. At $50°\frac{1}{2}$ latitude the ship was reckoned to be midway between the Lizard and Ushant, and had crossed the 100 fathom line. Depth and

[1] See Fig. 12. [2] D. W. Waters, *Art of Navigation*, App. 30.

'ground' must now be the guides. Nothing is more amazing than the faulty latitudes which appear to have been accepted for the English Channel entry. Reference to Chapter 17 will show that a principal landmark, the Lizard, was placed 47′ (equivalent to 47 miles) too far north, i.e. in 50° 45′ instead of 49° 58′. St Michael's Mount is given as 53′ north of its true position, Falmouth 51′ and Plymouth 39′. The errors in longitude are less than half as great in these particular cases, although elsewhere they may be gross, e.g. Edinburgh was placed more than 3° west of the meridian of London instead of a mere 4′.

Finally Bourne returns yet again to the debatable question of compass variation, and outlines the various theories then held. When they have been considered one by one, and that of Martin Cortes at great length, the final conclusion is a very sensible one: Masters and pilots should accumulate observations in their journals, and these on some future occasion would help them to judge their position. No theory had been established. In the edition of 1580 Bourne could report that Robert Norman, the nautical instrument-maker, sold a 'double-fly' compass, one which could be set according to any local variation, and so eliminated errors of calculation.[1] His remarks about his own failure, in spite of repeated inquiries, to find out anything about the behaviour of compasses and dials made in the West Indies are valuable as showing clearly his method of obtaining information. Bourne did not go to books, as (say) John Dee would do. He interrogated sailors, for which his situation at Gravesend gave him unique opportunities. Yet that the men who had been across the Atlantic with John Hawkins, or with Francis Drake—to name but two notable leaders—had apparently shown no inquisitiveness about the local variation of the compass, or compared colonial instruments with their own, will not surprise us. Men worked then, as the great majority work to-day, by rule of thumb, accepting current methods and

---

[1] 'Wherefore the Compasses that is devised by Norman, is very good to reforme those causes.'

tools without curiosity. Sailors of Bourne's day were quite accustomed to interrogation when they came home, but what their hearers wanted was a tale of adventure, or (where an Eden or a Hakluyt was the interlocutor), a straightforward narrative of events and experiences. To ask them technical questions must usually have been to court frustration. But William Bourne was a persistent as well as an exceptional man, and there are not many gaps in his book. Nor should his sound common sense be overlooked: '... it were twentie times better [he wrote] to be thoroughly persuaded that he knoweth it not, than to think he doth know, it not being that place.' And this had a wider application than simply to the man who would swear that he recognized a landmark but yet was mistaken, as William Bourne was aware.

'If these my labours [he concludes] may profite my Countrey, then have I my desire. And thus I bid thee moste hartily farewell.'

¶A REGIMENT for the Sea:

Conteyning moſt profitable Rules, *Mathematical experiences, and perfect* knovvledge of Nauigation, for all Coaſtes and Countreys: *moſt needefull and neceſſarie for all Seafaring men and Trauellers, as Pilotes, Mariners, Marchants. &c. Exactly deuiſed and made by* VVilliam Bourne.

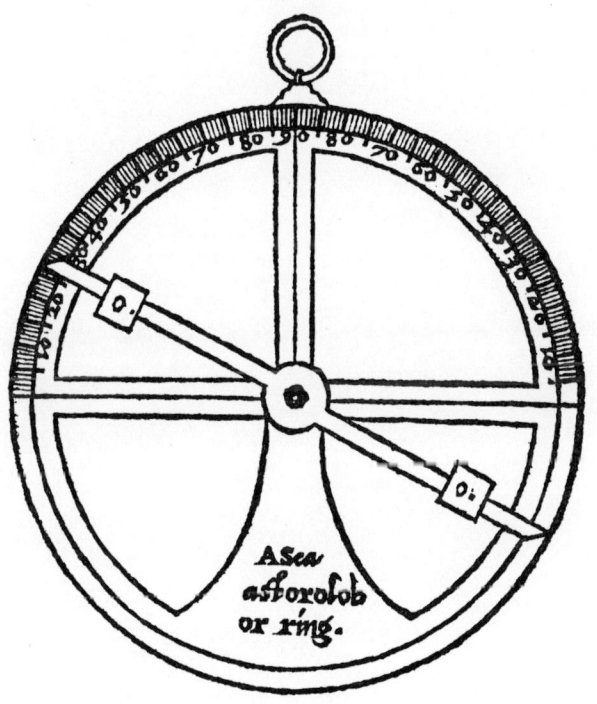

A Sea aſtorolob or ring.

¶ Imprinted at London by Thomas Hacket, and are to be ſolde at his ſhop in the Royall Exchaunge, at the Signe of the Greene Dragon.

TO THE RIGHT
Honorable, Edwarde Earle of Lincolne,*Baron of Clinton and Say,Knight*
of the Noble order of the Garter;Lorde highe Admirall of Englande,Irelande,and Wales, and of the Dominions and *Iles thereof, of the Towne of Calice, and*
Marches of the same, Normandie,
Gascoygne and Guyone,
and Captayne generall of the Queenes Maiesties Seas and Nauy Royall: *William
Bourne* wisheth increase of honor in perfect health.

Righte honorable and my singular good Lord and Master, when I had often repeated and called to my remembrance the opinion and sayings of the sage and auncient Writers, that one man should be an instructer to another, by seeking and paynestaking to doe them good: so at sundry times haue I studied and deuised with my selfe what thing to take in hande that might most profite my friends; and my natiue countrey: and at the length it came vnto my remembrance how necessarie a thing it was for Seafaring men to haue some good instructions, wherevpon I haue written this base and simple Regiment for the Sea, and Rules of Nauigation, for that I knowe it to be so needefull and necessarie for all sortes of Sea men. Therefore at sundrie times as I haue had leasure, I haue compyled and written this base and simple worke, calling to remembrance the saying of Plinie, who thought all that time lost which he did not bestowe at his booke: I beeing of all other most simple yet notwithstanding this enterprise haue I taken in hande, to publishe this simple booke vnto all men. And for that, all my labours be due vnto your Honorable Lordship, according to my bounden dutie I preferre it vnto your Honor, hoping that your Lordship will voutchsafe to take it in good parte, and to receyue this barbarous worke, more to take it as my goodwill (whiche is to offer things of much more excellencie) than the finenesse of the worke, for that it is but simple. And so shall I not onely be satisfied, but also further encouraged heereafter to trauell, according to the simple gifte and talent that God hath giuen vnto me: for that it is not altogither gathered out of other bokes, but that the greatest part is deuised and practised by me. Therefore I trust my labours (suche as they be) shall not hynder the cunning and learned sorte, but further the late beginners that are as yet not well instructed. And thus I cease to trouble your honorable Lordeship any longer, desiring you to take this simple thing in good part, as a true token and signe of my goodwill, beseeching God of his grace to prosper your Lordship in honor and vertue, with perfect health. Amen.

By your Honors poore seruant
William Bourne.

The Preface to
the Reader.

In my opinion (gentle Reader) which also is the saying and writing of all the Philosophers, those thinges are moste principally to be taught and maynteined, whiche in the commonwealth are moste profitable and necessarie. Then may I boldely say (without iust cause of reproofe) and affirme, that Nauigation is not the least but one of the principal matters to be knowne, as this time dothe require: Considering the state and scituation of our countrie, for that we be inuironed rounde aboute with the Sea, so that we neither can go out of our countrie, neyther they that are of other countries can come at vs, but onely by Sea. These things (I say) considered, what can there be more necessarie to be taught in our common wealth than Nauigation, considering also what Nauigation is: as Nauigation is how to direct ones course vpon or thorow the sea, where he findeth no path to any place assigned, and how to attayne the porte or place appointed in shortest time, how also to preserue the shippe and goodes in al common disturbances, as stormes, daungers by the way, and such otherlike &c. Moreouer and besides that, it is not vnknowne howe necessarie Nauigation is, both for the transportation of our commodities, to find vent for them in other countries (whereby no small numbre of people is set a worke in England) and also the bringing of other commodities (that we haue neede of) vnto vs, by which meanes the Queenes Maiestie receyueth no small benefite for hir customes, &c. And furthermore, for that Nauigation is the chiefe force and strength of our countrie, which whether it be true I referre to the iudgement of all men, and although I be but simple (gentle Reader) & a great number of excellent learned men in the Mathematicall Science haue written diuerse bookes of Cosmographie and Nauigation, yet notwithstanding I haue written this Regiment for the Sea with a fewe rules of Nauigation, as it were a nosegay whose floures are of mine owne gathering. And albeit the learned sorte of Seafaring men haue no neede of this booke, yet am I assured that it is a necessarie booke for the simplest sort of Seafaring men: for that they shal finde here the names of the circles in the sphere, with the names of diuerse things meete for Nauigation, togither with their vses, which the most part of Sea men do mistake or missecall: neyther do they know the vse of them being yet most necessarie for them that vse Nauigation, in whiche also there is a table of declination calculated for .4. yeres, (that is to say, for the yeare of our Lord .1573. the firste after Bissextilis, the yeare .1574. beyng the second yeare, & the yeare .1575. which is the third yeare, with the year .1576. whiche is the yeare of *Bissextilis* or leape yeare itselfe) whiche the Sea men do call a Regiment, and will serue for .24. yeare without any great errour: and is exactly calculated for the Longitude of London for the instāt time of noone, and will serue all Europe and Affrica, neare vnto the coast of America without much errour, sauing in Februarie, Marche or September, whilest the sunne hath swifte declination. But in June and December it will serue al the world ouer: bycause the sunne hath but slowe declination, &c. And also there be other necessarie rules of Nauigation to know how to handle the Sunnes declination, to knowe the altitude of eyther of the .2 Poles, (as the contentes of the booke do shewe) with other necessarie things meete to be knowne in Nauigation, and not mentioned in the booke of *Martin Curtise* called the Arte of Nauigation. Neyther doe I meane to write of anything mentioned in that booke: for that it is there sufficiently declared already. And thus (gentle Readers) I desire you to beare with my rudenesse, that I shoulde take vpon me to open any science, for that I am vtterly vnlearned, and without helpe of any learned persons, desiring you not to conceyue any euil opinion of me, but to take it as my good will, minding to profite my natiue Countrey as muche as lyeth in me. Notwithstanding it is possible that some people will be offended with me, that I shoulde write this simple Treatise, but then I consider agayne, and knowe, that vertue lacketh no enimies and defacers, and vyce lacketh no friendes and maynteyners, so that knowledge lacketh no contempt, neyther ignorance lacketh furtherance, and especially among all people there is none more ready to contemne, than the ignorāt sort: for ignoraunce is the father of all errours and the mother of contention. And thus I drawe to ende, desiring you to take this simple worke in good part, being willing to pleasure my natiue countrie according to the simple talent that God hath giuen me. And whereas you finde any errour I pray you let me gently vnderstand, for I thinke not that I can so circumspectly worke but I may be deceyued, for man cannot be so precise but he may erre, and I haue seldome heard of any the best Authours but he hath erred in some poynt: therefore in those things that he knoweth not of himselfe he muste needes follow his Authour, and if his Author doe erre he must needes fall into that errour that his Author dothe. And furthermore, a numbre of people there be that deuise nothing els but lies and slaunders, yea, and those which cannot attayne to anything themselues, doe hate all those that be not ignorant as they themselues be: for the corrupt nature of man is suche, that it is a corsey to their harts that any should be commended before themselues, for generally amongst all people of the earth (whiche is innumerable) euery seuerall person thinketh himselfe most worthie, imagining themselues to haue no fellowes: suche is the Diuill in the harte of man, pampering mans hart so with pryde to thinke he hath no fellow, whereas man of himselfe is not able to do any good thing, no not to thinke one good thought, but by the only might and prouidence of almighty God, therefore of ourselues we can do nothyng that is good. And thus gentle Reader I make an end. If this simple and barbarous thing be taken in good parte, then looke for other of my workes shortly, and heare him good will that studieth for the benefite of his natiue countrie, desirying

God of his grace, that I and you may do that thing that may be to the laude, prayse and glory of God, to our commoditie and soules health, to the profite of our brethren, and the common wealth of this our realme.

Thus I betake you to Almightie God the
creator of all things, praying him that
both I & you may after this life rest
in the kingdome of heauen, with
Abraham, Isaac and Jacob,
there to remayne world
without ende.
Amen.

I.H. *In commendation of the Booke.*

Wʜᴏ so thou art that mindst to passe the seas,
  By Compasse, Carde, the Sunne, or starrie skie,
Marke well this worke, and gayne thereby such ease,
As shall attayne thee profite great perdie,
Such rules hath *Bourne* directed to thine eye,
  That euen by them, if saylings art were gone,
  Thou mightst by these direct thy course alone.

T. H. *In prayse of the Author.*

Wʜᴏ trauels Countries gaine is worth of great prayse:
  as those yᵗ were before our time & yᵗ in sundry ways.
Whose actes do so excell, they pierce the loftie skies
  that in good artes for cōmon weale, both wit & will applies
For those that were tofore, haue bene aduanst by fame,
  by due desert, by doing well, haue merited the same.
As Authors old can tell, who list in them to reade
  who were inuēters of the same which dayly now proceede

A REGIMENT FOR THE SEA, 1574

In rule of publike weale, our loue it first began
   and plast it here in all estates, for the behoofe of man.
So now thou Seaman eke, that spredst abroad thy sayle
   be thankfull for thy Author here, whiche is for thy auayle.
Whose trauaile and whose toyle is thy behoofe and gayne,
   if thou dost reape what he did sow, it quiteth wel his paine,
And thankfulnesse is due, to euery liuing wight,
   and doth pertyne to euery man, but yet to God by right.
To whō be praise for euermore, which ruleth globe & sphere,
   who graūt vs grace to do his will, while we be liuing here.

FINIS.

A. R. *To the Author.*

Why does thou *Bourne* thy selfe hold backe
   not doing what you shouldst?
Me thinkes I heare thee Ansuere make
   that if thou durst thou wouldst.
Whereof art thou afrayde? tell forth
   to me thy doubtfull case:
To vtter truth no man there is
   that ones will hide his face.
Perhaps thou fearst the scoffing kind
   of *Momus* dearlings deare,
Perhaps againe thou standst in doubt,
   and art now dasht with feare.
To see these shaking quaking reedes
   that bend with euery blast,
Looke frowning on this booke, in which
   great paine bestowd thou hast.
Why did not then *Demosthenes*
   his workes hide out of sight?
Why did not *Tullie* stay his pen,
   when he began to write?

If taunting tongue of *Momus* then
  had bene so rife as now
Thou thinkst perchance they would haue feard
  the same as well as thou.
No sure thou art deceyud: there were
  as many lightbraynes then,
As there be now in these our dayes
  to carpe at painfull penne.
But Countries profite lo it was
  that caused them to write,
And prayse of good men did prouoke
  their workes to come to light.
And hast not thou spent all the time
  of writing this thy booke
For countries sake, to profite all
  that will vouchsafe to looke
Thereon? behold what prayse he reapt
  that ship did first inuent:
It cannot be but they which reade,
  perceiue shall thine intent,
Can any deeme amisse of thee
  that vse of ship hast told,
When ships inuentor gayned hath
  such prayses manifold?
Doest thou not know inuention
  what of it may be thought,
When vse and sauegarde of the same
  there is none knoweth ought?
The Prouerbe sayth, a thing that is
  to big to gripe in hand,
Can not be holden lenger than
  the siefe can holde the sand.
In booke it cannot be denied
  but thou hast taken payne

To set forth playne the vse of sayle
    for Countries common gayne.
Although I know how odious
    comparisons be still,
Be sure examples take thou mayst
    and vse them at thy will.
Sith therefore thou example hast
    of famous memorie,
Demosthenes and *Tullie* eke
    extold vnto the skie,
Wh' excelling farre all other men
    in Greeke and Latine phrase
Were subiect yet to *Sicophantes*
    and under *Momus* blase.
Thou hast besides all this, the truth
    by practise truly tride,
Whereby if any kicke at thee
    they may be soone espide,
Of good men I dare boldly say
    that good will thou shalt haue,
For euill of thee they none will speake,
    and prayse thou doest not craue,
Therefore I wishe thee naught to feare
    the force that tongues can bende
But still the worke thou has begonne
    to bryng to perfect ende.

FINIS.

The Kalender.

Ianuary hath .xxxj. dayes.

3	1	A	*Newyeres day.*
	2	b	Octa. Stepha.
11	3	c	Octa. John.
	4	d	Octa. Inno.
19	5	e	Thelosopho. vi.
8	6	f	*Twelfth day.*
	7	g	Julian mart.
16	8	A	Seuerine bish.
5	9	b	Martian Virg.
	10	c	Paule first her.
13	11	d	*Sun in Aquari.*
2	12	e	Satire Mar.
	13	f	Oct. Epiphani.
10	14	g	Isidore martyr.
	15	A	Maurice.
18	16	b	Anthonie Abbot.
7	17	c	Marcelle bish.
	18	d	Prisce Virg.
15	19	e	Mari. and his fel.
4	20	f	Fabian and Sa.
	21	g	Agnus virg.
12	22	A	Vincent mar.
1	23	b	Emerice.
	24	c	Timothie disci.
9	25	d	*Con. of Paule.*
	26	e	Policarp. mart.
17	27	f	Chrysost. Doct.
6	28	g	Theodore.
	29	A	Valerie bish.
14	30	b	Tran. S. Mark.
3	31	c	Ciri. and Ian.

February hath .xxviij. dayes, and in the yere of Bissextilis .xxix. dayes.

	1	d	Briget. Fast.
11	2	e	*Purific. of Mary.*
19	3	f	Blase mart.
8	4	g	Gilbert confes.
	5	A	Agathe virgin.
16	6	b	Dorothe virgin.
5	7	c	Amandus bish.
	8	d	Salomon.
13	9	e	*Sun in Pisces.*
2	10	f	Sother bishop.
	11	g	
10	12	A	Eufrase virgin.
	13	b	Valentine bishop.
18	14	c	Faustine bishop.
7	15	d	Julian virg.
	16	e	Constance virgin.
15	17	f	Simeon martyr.
4	18	g	Sabine Priest.
	19	A	
12	20	b	60. Martyres.
1	21	c	70. Martyres.
	22	d	Peters chayre.
9	23	e	Sirener. Fast.
	24	f	*Mathie Apostle.*
17	25	g	Policar. bishop.
6	26	A	Victor and his fel.
	27	b	Augustine bishop.
14	28	c	Oswald bishop.

The Kalender.

			Marche hath .xxxj. dayes.				Aprill hath .xxx. dayes.
3	1	d	Dauid bishop.		1	g	Theodore virg.
	2	e	Basilic mart.	11	2	A	Mary Egypti.
11	3	f	Maxime mart.	19	3	b	Richarde bish.
	4	g	Lucius mart.	8	4	c	Ambrose bish.
19	5	A	Focius mart.		5	d	Marci and Ma.
8	6	b	Vict. and Venin.	16	6	e	Sextus mart.
	7	c	Tho. de. Aquin.	5	7	f	Euphemi vir.
16	8	d	Apoline mart.		8	g	Denise mart.
5	9	e	40. Martyres.	13	9	A	Perpetuus bish.
	10	f	Gregorie bishop.	2	10	b	Marcus mart.
13	11	g	*Sun in Aries.*		11	c	*Sun in Taurus.*
2	12	A	Zacharie bish.	10	12	d	Appoline mart.
	13	b	Longine mart.		13	e	Sother martyr.
10	14	c	Patricius bish.	18	14	f	Tyburt mart.
	15	d	Gertrude vir.	7	15	g	Osmond bishop.
18	16	e	Anselme.		16	A	Isidore bishop.
7	17	f	Edward king.	15	17	b	Anicete bishop.
	18	g	Joseph. spon.	4	18	c	Cluther bishop.
15	19	A	Cutbert bishop.		19	d	Tiburtius con.
4	20	b	Benedict. Ab.	12	20	e	Hermegenes.
	21	c	Astrodose bishop.	1	21	f	Quintine.
12	22	d	Pigment bish.		22	g	Clete bishop.
1	23	e	Theodore.	9	23	A	Gorge mart.
	24	f	Fast.		24	b	Wilfride con.
9	25	g	*Annun of Mary.*	17	25	c	*Marke Euan.*
	26	A	Castore mart.	6	26	d	Anastace bish.
17	27	b	John Heremi.		27	e	Vitalis mart.
6	28	c	Dorothe mart.	14	28	f	Peter of Mi.
	29	d	Eustace.	3	29	g	Clete bishop.
14	30	e	Sabine vir.		30	A	Dep. of Erker.
3	31	f	Balbine vir.				

The Kalender.

			May hath .xxxj. dayes.				Iune hath .xxx. dayes.
11	1	b	*Philip and Iacob.*	19	1	e	Nicodeme.
	2	c	Athanasius bish.	8	2	f	Erasmus.
19	3	d	Inu. of the crosse.		3	g	Basill.
8	4	e	Christopher.	16	4	A	Marcel. martyr.
	5	f	S. Augustine.	5	5	b	Petrotius con.
16	6	g	John port lat.		6	c	Boniface bish.
5	7	A	John of Beuer.	13	7	d	Medard and Gil.
	8	b	Appe. of Mich.	2	8	e	Trans. Edmond.
13	9	c	Trans. of Ni.		9	f	Yuan conf.
2	10	d	Gordiane.	10	10	g	Tran. of Wol.
	11	e	*Sun in Gemini.*		11	A	Barnabe Apo.
10	12	f	Victorius mart.	18	12	b	*Sun in Taurus.*
	13	g	Seruacius conf.	7	13	c	Anthonie conf.
18	14	A	Boniface mart.		14	d	Basilides conf.
7	15	b	Sophia virgin.	15	15	e	Vate modestre.
	16	c	Brandon bishop.	4	16	f	Trans. Richar.
15	17	d	Trans. of Bar.		17	g	Botulphe conf.
4	18	e	Dioscor. mart.	12	18	A	Exuperie bish.
	19	f		1	19	b9	Geruasius mar.
12	20	g	Dunstan con.		20	c	Trans. Edwar.
1	21	A	Barnardine.	9	21	d	Walburge virg.
	22	b	Helene queene.		22	e	Albane mart.
9	23	c	Petronill.	17	23	f	Fast.
	24	d	Julian virg.	6	24	g	*Iohn baptist.*
17	25	e	Desiderie mart.		25	A	Trans. of Elig.
6	26	f	Adelme conf.	14	26	b	John and Pa.
	27	g		2	27	c	Crescens mart.
14	28	A	Germaine bish.		28	d	Fast.
3	29	b	Necomede.	11	29	e	*Peter and Paule.*
	30	c	Corone martyr.		30	f	
11	31	d	Felix bishop.				

The Kalender.

			July hath .xxxj. dayes.				August hath .xxxj. dayes.
19	1	g	Octa. John Bap.	8	1	c	Lammas.
8	2	A	Visit. of Mary.	16	2	d	Steuen bishop.
	3	b	Gregorie bishop.	5	3	e	Finding of Ste.
16	4	c	Demitius mart.		4	f	Justine Priest.
5	5	d	Parthene con.	13	5	g	Festum nivis.
	6	e	Procope mart.	2	6	A	Trans. demi.
13	7	f	Zenone mart.		7	b	Feast of Jesu.
2	8	g	Paternian Bish.	10	8	c	Cirack. & his fel.
	9	A	Pius bishop.		9	d	Roman mart.
10	10	b	*Dog bayes be*.	18	10	e	Laurence mart.
	11	c	Hermaco. for.	7	11	f	Tiburt and Su.
18	12	d	Anaclete. bishop.		12	g	Clare virgin.
7	13	e	Quirine and Ju.	15	13	A	Ypolite virgin.
	14		*Sun in Leo*.	4	14	b	*Sun in Virgo*.
15	15	g	Marine Vir.		15	c	Assump. of Mary.
4	16	A	Symph. cum. 7.	12	16	d	Roche confess.
	17	b	Arlene herem.	1	17	e	Octa. Laurence.
12	18	c	Praxede vir.		18	f	Agapite mart.
1	19	d	Margar. vir.	9	19	g	Lewes bishop.
	20	e	Praxede vir.		20	A	*Dog dayes ende*.
9	21	f	Appoline bishop.	17	21	b	Anastase mart.
	22	g	Mary Magda.	6	11	c	Timo. and Hip.
17	23	A	Christian.		23	d	Eleazor. Fast.
6	24		Fast.	14	24	c	*Barthol. Apostle*.
	25	c	*Iames Apostle*.	3	25	f	Lewes king.
14	26	d	Anne mo. of Ma.		26	g	Zepherine bish.
3	27	e	Panthalion.	11	27	A	Rufus mar.
	28	f	Sampson bish.	19	28	b	Augustine bish.
11	29	g	Marie virgin.		29	c	Johns behead.
	30	A	Abbon and Sen.	8	30	d	Felix and Audact.
19	31	b	German bishop.		31	e	Cuthbur virg.

The Kalender.

September hath .xxx. dayes.

16	1	f	Giles Abbot.
5	2	g	Anthony mart.
	3	A	Eupheme.
13	4	b	Moyses Pro.
2	5	c	Venturine.
	6	d	Zacharie pro.
10	7	e	Enurce bishop.
	8	f	Natiuitie of Ma.
18	9	g	Gorgone mart.
7	10	A	Nicholas de Tol.
	11	b	Protece and Hi.
15	12	c	Sire bishop.
4.	13	d	Philip bishop.
	14	e	*Sun in Libra.*
12	15	f	Nicomede priest.
1	16	g	Edith vir.
	17	A	Lambart bishop.
9	18	b	Victor and Coro.
	19	c	Eustace.
17	20	d	Fast.
6	21	e	*Mathew Apostle.*
	22	f	Maurice.
14	23	g	Line Mart.
3	24	A	German Abbot.
	25	b	Cleophin and Ap.
11	26	c	Ciprian and Ju.
19	27	d	Cosme and Da.
	28	e	Exupere bishop.
8	29	f	*Michaell arch.*
	30	g	Hierome doct.

October hath .xxxj. dayes.

16	1	A	Remigius bi.
5	2	b	Leodegare mar.
13	3	c	Candide mar.
	4	d	Francis mart.
	5	e	Faith virgin.
10	6	f	Gerionis.
	7	g	Marce and Mar.
18	8	A	Apolinaris mar.
7	9	b	Pelagi virgin.
	10	c	Linus conf.
15	11	d	Denice & his fe.
4	12	e	Nichasius bish.
	13	f	Wilfride bish.
12	14	g	*Sun in Scorpio.*
1	15	A	Calixt bishop.
	16	b	Wolfran. bish.
9	17	c	Micha. of the mo.
	18	d	*Luke Euange.*
17	19	e	Etheldred virg.
6	20	f	Frideswide vir.
	21	g	Austrebert virg.
14	22	A	xi. M. virgins.
3	23	b	Mary Salome.
	24	c	Romaine bishop.
11	25	d	Maglore bish.
	26	e	Crispi and Cris.
19	27	f	Fast.
8	28	g	*Simon ad Iude.*
	29	A	Narcissus bish.
16	30	b	Germaine conf.
5	31	c	Fast.

The Kalender.

			Nouember hath .xxx. dayes.				December hath .xxxj. dayes.
	1	f	All Saincts.		1	f	Elegi bishop.
13	2	g	All Soules.	13	2	g	Liban mart.
2	3	A	Wenefride virg.	2	3	A	Dep. of Osmo.
	4	b	Amantius.		4	b	Barbara virg.
10	5	c	Lete priest.	10	5	c	Sabba bishop.
	6	d	Leonard.		6	d	Nicholas bish.
18	7	e	Wilbrode.	18	7	e	Octa. Andrew.
7	8	f	Fower cround.	7	8	f	Con. of Mary.
	9	g	Theodore.		9	g	Cyprian bish.
15	10	A	Maxime.	15	10	A	Eulalie vir.
4	11	b	Martine bishop.	4	11	b	Antippe.
	12	c	Brise bishop.		12	c	Damase con.
12	13	d	*Sun in Sagit.*	12	13	d	*Sun in Capricor.*
1	14	e	Tran. Erkenw.	1	14	e	Nicasius vir.
	15	f	Macute bishop.		15	f	Otholie vir.
9	16	g	Dep. of Edmond.	9	16	g	O Sapientia.
	17	A	*Ini reg. Eliza.*		17	A	Lazarus con.
17	18	b	Octa. Martine.	17	18	b	Gracian bish.
6	19	c	Elizabeth mart.	6	19	c	Venetia vir.
	20	d	Edmond king.		20	d	Fast.
14	21	e	Pres. of Mary.	14	21	e	*Thomas Apost.*
3	22	f	Ciceli virgin.	3	22	f	xxx. Martyrs.
	23	g	Clement mart.		23	g	Victor virg.
11	24	A	Grisogen mart.	11	24	A	Fast.
19	25	b	Katharine virgin.	19	25	b	*Christmas day.*
	26	c	Line mart.		26	c	*Stephen mart.*
8	27	d	Vitales conf.	8	27	d	*Iohn Euang.*
	28	e	Rufus mart.		28	e	*Innocents day.*
16	29	f	Saturni. Fast.	16	29	f	
5	30	g	*Andrew Apostle.*	5	30	g	Tran. of Jame.
				13	31	A	Siluester mart.

A Table or Kalender for .30. yere, shewing the Prime, the Sundays letter, and Leape yere, and the mouable Feasts, as the first Sunday in Lent, and Easter day, Assention day, and Whitsonday.

The Yere of our Lorde.	The Prime.	Dominicall letter.	First sunday in Lent.	Easter day.	Assention day.	Whitson-day.
1574	17	c	28. Febr.	11. April.	20. May.	30. May.
1575	18	b	20. Febr.	3. Aprill.	12. May.	22. May
1576	19	Ag	11. March.	22. April	31. May.	10. June
1577	1	f	24. Febr.	7 Aprill	16. May	26. May
1578	2	e	16. Febr.	30. Mar.	8. May	18. May
1579	3	d	8. March.	19. April	28. May	7. June
1580	4	cb	20. Febr.	3. Aprill	12. May	22. May
1581	5	A	12. Febr.	26. Mar.	4. May	14. May
1582	6	g	4. March.	15. April	24. May	3. June
1583	7	f	17. Febr.	31. Mar.	9. May	19. May
1584	8	ed	8. March.	19. April	28. May	7. June
1585	9	c	28. Febr.	11. Aprill	20. May	30. May
1586	10	b	20. Febr.	3. Aprill.	12. May	22. May
1587	11	A	5. March.	16. April	25. May	4. June
1588	12	gf	24. Febr.	7. Aprill	16. May	26. May
1589	13	e	16. Febr.	30. Mar.	8. May	18. May
1590	14	d	8. March.	19. April	28. May	7. June
1591	15	c	21. Febr.	4. Aprill	13. May	23. May
1592	16	bA	12. Febr.	26. Mar.	4. May	14. May
1593	17	g	4. March.	15. April	24. May	3. June
1594	18	f	17. Febr.	31. Mar.	9. May	19. May
1595	19	e	9. Marche	20. April	29. May	8. June
1596	1	dc	28. Febr.	11. Aprill	20. May	30. May
1597	2	b	13. Febr.	27. Mar.	4. May	15. May
1598	3	A	5. Marche	16. April	25. May	4. June
1599	4	g	25. Febr.	8. Aprill	17. May	27. May
1600	5	fe	9. Febr.	23. Mar.	1. May	11. May
1601	6	d	1. Marche	12. April	21. May	31. May
1602	7	c	21. Febr.	4. Aprill	13. May	23. May
1603	8	b	13. March.	24. April	2. June.	12. June

FOR that the common people do fall into such a numbre of errours as touching the length of the day, holding an opiniō that in euery .15. dayes, the day is an hour longer or shorter, the truth is this: the day dothe keepe no such proportion in the lengthening and shorting, but dothe length and shorte according vnto the swiftnesse and the slownesse of the sunnes declination, for when the Sunne hath swifte declination, then doth the day lengthen and shorten apace; and when that the Declination is slowe, then dothe the day lengthen or shorten but slowly. And yet the most parte of the common people do holde an opinion, that at Christmasse or els at New yeares day at the furthest the day must needes be an houre longer, & yet the Sunne hath not declined or come towardes the Equinoctiall .2. degrees and a halfe, whiche will not make halfe an houre in the length of the day. Wherefore I do thinke it good to declare thorowe the whole yeare when the day is an houre longer or shorter here in this place for the Latitude or heigth of the pole Articke at London, the Pole beyng raysed .51. degrees and .32. minutes, or .34. minutes: and our longest Somer day is .16. houres and a halfe and our shortest winter day is .7. houres and a halfe from the rising of the Sunne vnto the setting of the Sunne: and first this, the shortest winter day is the .11. or .12. day of December, and then the Sunne hath his greatest declination vnto the Southwardes. And then the .29. day of December the day is a quarter of an houre longer, then riseth the Sunne at .8. of the clocke and settes at .4. And then the 17. or .18. of Januarie the day is an houre longer and not before, for the Sunne must be declined from hir Solstick of winter .5. degrees and .12 minuts before the day is lengthned an houre, so that I do affirme that from the .4. or .5. day of Nouember, vnto the .17. or .18. day of January, in all that time the day is but one houre shorter and longer, which is the time of 10. weekes. And then the .27. or .28. of Januarie the night is 15. houres long, then riseth the Sunne half and houre after .7. and setteth halfe an houre after foure of the clocke. And then the .11. or .12. day of

Februarie the day is .10. houres long, then riseth the Sunne at .7. and setteth at .5. of the clocke. And then the .26. day of Februarie the day is .11. houres long, then riseth the Sunne halfe an houre after .6. and setteth halfe an houre after .5. of the clocke. And then the .11. day of Marche the sunne is vpon the Equinoctiall and the day iuste .12. houres long all the world ouer. And then the .24. day of Marche the day is .13. houres long, and then riseth the Sunne halfe an houre before 6. and setteth halfe an houre after .6. of the clocke. And then the .7. day of April the day is .14. houres long, and then riseth the Sunne at .5. of the clocke iust, and setteth at 7. of the clocke iuste. And then the 23. day of April the day is .15. houres long and there riseth the Sunne halfe an houre before .5. and setteth halfe an houre after .7. of the clocke. And then the .15. day of Maye the day is .16. houres long, then riseth the Sunne at .4. of the clocke and setteth at .8. of the clocke iuste. And then the .11. of June the Sunne hath hir greatest declination to the Northwarde, and then is our longest Somer dayes, and then it is .16. houres and a halfe from the Sunne rising vnto the Sunne setting, so that the Sunne riseth a quarter of an houre before .4. and setteth a quarter of an houre after eight of the clocke. And then the .10. day of Julie the day is .16. houres long, then riseth the sunne at .4. and setteth at .8. of the clocke. And then the laste July the day is .15. houres long. And then the .16. day of August the day is .14. houres long. And the the last day of August the day is .13. houres long. And then the .13. or .14. of September the sunne is vpon the Equinoctiall, and the day iuste .12. houres long. And then the .27. day of September the day is .11. houres long. And then the 11. of October the day is .10. houres long. And then the .26. day of October the day is .9. houres long. And then the .15. day of Nouember the day is .8. houres long, and so vnto the .11. or .12. of December, and then the day is at the shortest (as before is declared). Thus much haue I sayde as touching the length of the day by euen houres, whiche some people will haue at the entrance of the Sunne into the .12. signes, of which in the lengthing and shorting of the day there is no such matter, but onely this looke, when that the Sunne hath declined .5. degrees and .12. minutes in this our Latitude, then is the day an houre longer or shorter, as you shall finde this matter more larglier spoken of in all places thorowe the worlde, in the .11. chapter of the booke.

Faultes escaped in the Printing.

Fol .2.b. lin .30. after oblique, leaue out equinoctiall, fol .8.b. lin .30. for crossing in, reade crossing the equinoctiall in, fol .3. a. lin .3. for .21. read .12. fol .eod. lin .10. for respectes, read aspects, fol .3.b. lin .18. for placing, read passing, fol .9.a. lin .11. for Northeast, read Northwest, fol 12.b. lin .20. for rarer, read rather fol .13.a. lin .22. for Nas. read Naase, fol .28.b. lin .2. for pointes, read pointers, fol .35.b. lin .11. for vacula, read Bacula, fol .41.a. lin .13. for North North, read North Northeast, fol .42.b. lin .14. for .250. read .2500. fol .43.a. lin .15. for whiche are, reade with vs, fol .45.a. lin .20. for noone, read Rome, fol .eod. lin .24. for a quarter, read .3. quarters, fol .46.a. lin .13. for .52. read 53 fol eod lin 15 for 15 read 17 fol 47 a lin penult, for treating, reade, trenting, fol .48.a. lin .24. for whole, read holde, fol .eod. b. lin .3. for middle of the, head [sic] middle-most, fol .52.a. lin .13. for port, read part.

A Table of the reigne of Kings since the Conquest.

Number of Kings and Queenes.	The names of the Kings of England.	Beginning of their Reigne.	Time of their death.	The place of their buriall.
1	William Conqueror.	14. Oct.	9. Sept. 1087	Cane in Norm.
2	William Rufus.	9. Sept.	1. August 1100	Westminster.
3	Henry the first.	1. Aug.	2. Deceb. 1136	Reding.
4	Stephan.	2. Dece.	25. Octob. 1154	Feuersham.
5	Henry the second.	25 Octo.	6. July. 1189	Fonteuerard.
6	Richard the first.	6. Julie.	6. Aprill. 1199	Fonteuerard.
7	John.	6. April	19. Octob. 1216	Worcester.
8	Henry the third.	19. Octo.	16. Nou. 1272	Westminster.
9	Edward the first.	16. Nou.	6. July. 1307	Westminster.
10	Edward the second.	6. July.	25. Janu. 1327	Glocester.
11	Edward the third.	25. Jan.	21. June. 1377	Westminster.
12	Richard the second.	21. June.	16. Sep. 1400	Westminster.
13	Henry the fourth.	16. Sep.	20. Mar. 1413.	Canterbury.
14	Henry the fifth.	20. Mar.	31. Augu. 1422	Westminster.
15	Henry the sixt.	31. Aug.	4. Mar. 1461	Windesor.
16	Edward the fourth.	4. Mar.	9. Aprill. 1483	Windesor.
17	Edward the fifth.	9. April	22. June. 1484	Westminster.
18	Richard the third.	22. June.	22. Aug. 1486	Lecester.
19	Henry the seuenth.	22. Aug.	22. April. 1509	Westminster.
20	Henry the eyght.	22 April	28. Janu. 1547	Windesor.
21	Edward the sixt.	28. Jan.	6. July. 1553.	Westminster.
22	Queene Mary.	6. July	17. Nou. 1559	Westminster.
23	Queene Elizabeth.	17. Nou.		

A REGIMENT FOR THE SEA, 1574

¶ *A profitable and necessarie rule to know the
beginning and ending of euery Terme,
with their returnes.*

Hillarie Tearme, beginneth the .xxiij. of Januarie, if it be not Sunday, which then is referred vntill the next day after, and endeth the .xij. of February, and hath foure returnes, that is to saye:

    Octauis Hillarij   Crastino Purific
    Quind. Hillarij   Octauis Purific.

Easter Tearme, beginneth .xvij. dayes after Easter, and endeth the Monday nexte after the Assention day, and hath fiue returnes, that is to say:

    Quind. Pasch.   Mense   Quinque Paschæ.
    Tres Paschæ   Paschæ.   Crast. Ascention.

Trinitie Tearme, beginneth the friday next after Trinity sunday, and endeth the wednesday fortnight after, and hath foure returnes, that is to say:

    Crast. Trinitati.   Quind. Trinitat.
    Octauis Trinita.   Tres Trinitat.

Michaelmas Tearme, beginneth the .9. day of October, if it be not Sunday, and endeth the xxviij. or .xxix. of Nouember, and hath eyght returnes, that is to say:

    Octauis Micha.   Crast. Anima.
    Quind. Michae.   Crast. Martini
    Tres. Michaelis.   Octa. Martini.
    Mense Michael.   Quind. Martini.

Note also that the *Eschequer* openeth eyght dayes before any Tearme begin, except *Trinitie Tearme which* openeth but foure dayes before.

Thirtie dayes hath September: Apryll, Iune, and Nouember, Februarie hath .xxviij. alone: and all the rest thirtie and one.

Except the leape year, wherin, Februarie hath .xxix.

¶ An Introduction vnto the Regiment for the Sea

The names of certaine things necessarie to be know of them that are Mariners or Seafaring men, meete to bee knowne of them that doe practise Nauigation, as this: the names of the circles of the Sphere, and what they are, and their vses: and also the names of other things belonging therevnto, and what they are, and their vses.

First what the Horizon circle is.

THe Horizon is the parting of the earthe or the Sea and the skye, that is to say, the halfe of the heauens being aboue ouer your heade, and the other halfe hidden with the earth or Sea vnder them: and this Horizon circle dothe moue as you doue moue: for as you doe by trauell chaunge your place, so doth the Horizon chaunge in all points.

The vse of the Horizon circle.

THe vse of the Horizon circle is this, to take the heigth of the Sunne or any starre, with the crosse staffe, setting the one ende with the Horizon, and the other ende with the Sunne or starre, so that you haue a true Horizon: and that must be doone vpon the Sea, or else it must be a very playne grounde vpon the toppe of a hill, else it is no true Horizon. And also if the Sunne or Moone, or any starre be to be seene, thē they be aboue the Horizon: if they be not to be seene, then they be under the Horizon.

2. What the Meridian circle is.

THe Meridian is a circle beginning due South, and so passing by youre Zenith that is right ouer the crowne of your head, and so by the two Poles of the worlde: and if you doe trauell due South and North, you doe not chaunge youre Meridian: but in the going or trauelling any other way you do chaunge it.

The vse of the Meridian circle.

THE vse of the Meridian circle is, to knowe the iust tyme of noone by the Sunne: for as soone as the middle of the Sunne is vpon the Meridian, then it is noone, and when the Sunne, Moone, or any Star is vpon the Meridian, then they be farthest from the Horizon, and it is a meete time to take their heigth for to know the altitude or heigth of the Pole of the worlde, whereby you may perfitly knowe howe farre you bee too the Southwardes or Northwardes of any place.

3. What the Equinoctiall circle is, being a Paralell line or circle fixed.

THE Equinoctiall is a fixed circle in the Heauens equally distant from both the Poles, and doth passe directly ouer the middle of the earth rounde about, and is called the Equinoctiall, for that if the Sunne be there, then thorowe all the whole world the Sunne is twelue houres aboue the Horizon, and twelue houres vnder the Horizon sauing vnder the two Poles, and there the Equinoctiall is with the Horizon. So they shal see halfe the Sunne and no more, till the Sunne be departed from the Equinoctiall. And also to them that do inhabite or dwell in any place vnder the Equinoctiall, the Sunne, Moone, and all the Starres be twelue hours aboue the Horizon, and twelue houres vnder the Horizon.

The vse of the Equinoctiall circle.

THE vse of the Equinoctiall, is to knowe what declination the Sunne or any other Starre hath from it, and of whiche side, and by that is known the heigth of the Equinoctial, and by the heigth of that is known the heigth of either of the two Poles of the world.

4 What the circle or Tropicke of Cancer is, being a Paralell circle fixed.

THE Tropicke of Cancer is the greatest declination that the Sunne doth come vnto the Norwards, and then is our longest Sommer dayes, and shortest nights.

5. What the circle or Tropick of Capricorne is, being a Paralell circle fixed.

THE Tropicke of Capricorne, is the greatest declination that the sunne doth go vnto the Southwards, and then is our shortest Winter dayes, and longest nights.

The vses of these two circles be but smal, but that the days beeing at the longest or shortes, the Sunne dothe returne backe againe . &c.

6. What the Articke circle is, beeing a Paralell circle.

THE Articke circle doth touch the Horizon due North, and is according to the place that you are in, of any place vpon the face of the earth, and doth wyden and narrow according vnto the altitude or heigth of the Pole: for as you doe goe vnto the South partes, then dothe your Articke circle grow narower and narower, vntill you come right vnder the Equinoctiall line, and then haue you no Articke circle: and if that you do goe vnto the North partes, then doth your Articke circle growe wider and wider: and where the North Pole is raysed .66. degrees and a half, there the Artick circle is iust with the Tropick of Cancer, and then vnder the North Pole, there your Artick circle is with the Equinoctial.

The vse of the Articke circle.

THE vse of the Articke circle, is to knowe what Starres doe neuer set vntoo you, for all those Starres or lyghtes that you do see under the Pole, doe not set: and if that you bee vnto the North wardes, of the height of the Pole, more than .66. degrees and a halfe: if the the Sunne or Moone be in the Tropicke of

Cancer, they shall not goe downe vntoo you vnder the Horizon, but shall bee still in sighte vnto you, so that they be not let by the cloudes and other accidentes.

7. *What the Antarticke circle is, beeing a Paralell circle.*

THE Antarticke circle doth touch the Horizon due South, and is opposite or right agaynste the Articke circle, and dothe wyde and narrowe in all poyntes, and dothe not differ from the Articke circle, sauing the Articke circle is aboue the Horizon, and the Antartike circle is vnderneath the Horizon.

The vse of the Antarticke circle.

THE vse of the Antarticke circle is as the Articke is in all poyntes, to knowe what starres will not appeare aboue your Horizon, and in like manner, to the Northwardes of 66. degrees and a halfe, (the Sunne or Moone being in the Tropicke of Capricorne) then they wyll not ryse aboue the Horizon.

8. *What the Zodiacke is, beeing a circle.*

THE Zodiacke is the greatest circle in all the Heauens, wherein all the wandering lightes or Planets doe keepe theyr courses, that is to say, the Sunne and Moone, and the other fiue Planets or Starres, that is to say, *Saturne, Iupiter, Mars, Venus,* and *Mercury* . &c. which circle is deuided into twelue equall partes, called the twelue signes, as *Aries, Taurus, Gemini, Cancer, Leo, Virgo, Libra, Scorpio, Sagitarius, Capricornus, Aquarius, Pisces,* the which circle standeth oblique equinoctiall or awrye, crossing the middle at two places: the Northermost parte is the middle of the Zodiacke, and that is the Tropicke of Cancer: and the Southermost parte is the tropicke of Capricorne, the very midle of the zodiack: and that line in the midle of the zodiack, is called the ecliptick lyne, and the zodiack is .12 degrees broade, that is to say, sixe degrees from the eclipticke line vnto the north parts, and sixe degrees vnto the South parts.

The vse of the Zodiack.

The vse of the Zodiack is, through the mouing of the Sunne and Moone & the other Planets, to know in what signe they be, and also to know the time of the chaunge of the Moone, with all the other Aspectes: and in like manner to know the aspects of all the other planets vnto the Moone, and also the planets amonst themselues: and by the aspectes in the .12. signes is gathered their effects, and in what countrey it may happen.

9. What the line Ecliptick is.

The line ecliptick, is a circle in the very middle of the Zodiack, the whiche the very midle or center of the Sunne doth go vpon.

The vse of the line Ecliptick.

The vse of the line Ecliptick is this, if that the Moone or any other starre be vnto the North part therof, then it is sayd that they haue North latitude, and if vnto the Southe part, then they haue south latitude: and also by this circle called the line ecliptick, is knowne the eclipse of the Sunne and the Moone.

10. What the artick polare circle is, being a paralell circle fixed.

The artick polare circle is made by the pole of the Zodiack, or pole of the circle ecliptick .23. degrees and a halfe in the heauuens from the poles of the world aboue the horizon.

11. What the antartick Polare circle is, being a Paralell circle fixed.

The antartick Polare circle is iust opposite vnto ye artick polare, made by the antartick pole vnderneath our horizon. The vse of them I will declare, when I speake of the poles of the Ecliptick or Zodiack.

12. What the two circles called Colures be . &c.

The .2. circles called Colures, be those that do deuide the

Zodiack, and all the other paralell cicles into .4. equall parts, the one of the circles doth crosse the Zodiack in the first point of Aries and Libra, and so passeth by the .2. poles of the world, and is called the equinoctiall colure: and the other colure circle doth crosse the Zodiacke in the first pointe of Cancer and Capricorne, and so passeth the .2. poles of the world, and there at the .2. poles the one circle doth crosse the other; and that is called the Solstitiall colure.

The vse of these two circles.

THe vse of the .2. colure circles is this, the Sunne passing by them doth deuide the yeare into .4. partes: as this, the Sunne in the first point of Aries, is Spring time. &c.

13. What the .2. Poles of the world is, imagined to be as an axiltree.

THe .2. poles of the world, imagined to be as an axiltree, (that is to say, the North pole called the pole artick, and the South pole called the pole antartick) the one is directly against the other: the North pole always aboue our horizon, and the South pole antartick always vnder our horizon, being fixed fast in the heauens, and the equinoctiall iust and equally betweene them: and the cause why that it is imagined too bee an axiltree is thys, for that the whole heauens and all the lyghtes of the Firmamente be caried rounde aboute from the East vnto the West in .24. houres: so that no light nor place remayneth vnremoued, but onely the .2. poles of the world.

The vse of the Poles of the world.

THe vse of the .2. Poles, is this, to knowe how farre we do transporte our selues, and to know what climate, and temperatnesse we be in as touching heate and colde.

14. What the .2. Poles of the Zodiack is, imagined to be an axiltree in the heauens.

THe .2. Poles of the Zodiack, or Ecliptick, imagined to bee as an axiltree, (the artick pole of the Zodiack, or rather the Ecliptick, and the Antartick pole of the Zodiack) the one being directly againste the other, and the Zodiack or rather the middle thereof, called the ecliptick, to be iust or equall betweene them, are called the Poles of the Zodiacke: for that the Sunne and the Moone, and the other planets and fixed starres do moue vnto the eastward, according to the standing of the Zodiac &c.

The vse of the Poles of the Zodiack.

The vse of the two Poles of the Zodiack is this, (as it is before declared) that the Zodiack is deuided into 12. equall partes, called the .12. signes, and those diuisions by imagination do passe vnto the poles of the Zodiack, in suche forme as the meridian lynes do all meete at the poles of the world, and so do all those diuisions meete at the two poles of the Zodiack, and then any starre, that is out of the Zodiack, eyther vnto the Southwards, or northwardes, (according vnto those diuisions) they be called in the signes.

15. *What the Zenith or verticall point is, imagined to be as an axiltree.*

The Zenith or vertical point, is imagined to be a pricke in the heauens right ouer the crowne of your head, and is moueable as we our selues be, and is as an axiltree vnto the horizon circle: and as you do transport your selfe from one place vnto another, so doth your Zenith or verticall poynte, and your horizon circle also.

The vse of the Zenith or verticall poynt . &c.

The vse of the Zenith or verticall point is this, to knowe howe neere or farre off any starre is from your zenith, by taking the true heigth of any starre with an instrumente, for that from your zenith is always .90. degrees down vnto the horizon on euery side round about you, as it shall more plainely appeare hereafter where I speake of degrees.

16. *What a Degree is.*

A Degree is the part or diuision of a whole circle, into .360. equall parts, how bigge or small soeuer the circle be.

The vse of the Degrees is manyfold.

THE vse of the degrees is to knowe by the Sunne and Moones course in the zodiack, or any other of the planets or mouable starres, how many degrees they be asunder: whereby is knowne at what time they haue any aspecte the one with the other. And also by the degrees it is knowe, what latitude and what declination any light or starre hath from the ecliptick or equinoctial: and also the degrees wil shewe vnto you, howe many myles that you do transporte your selfe vpon the earth to the South or North partes, for that euery degree doth aunswer vnto .60. english miles, in the going South and North: which is knowne by the altitude of the North pole or the numbre of degrees betwene the equinoctiall and your zenith or verticall point, for from your zenith vnto the horizon, is .90. degrees to the southwards, and 90. degrees vnto the Northwards, which is halfe the compasse of the heauens for twice .90. is .180. and then the earthe doth hide the other halfe of the heauens: and twice .180. maketh .360. the whole coutents of the compasse of euery greate circle in the heauens.

17. *What a Minute is.*

OF Minuts there by two sortes, minuts of time, and minuts of measure, and is no other thing but the lesser part of tyme or measure, whiche is the 60. parte of a degree, or the .60. parte of an houre: and all the diuisions in these matters, is by .60. For as .60. Minuts is a degree or an houre, so .60. seconds is a Minute, and .60. thirds is a seconde, and 60. fourths is a third, &c.

18. *Altitude is heigthe: the vse thereof.*

Altitude is the heigthe of any thing taken, as the heigthe of the Sunne, of any Starre, or the heigth of the Pole, aboue the horizon: or the heigth of a steeple, or a tower, or such other lyke.

19. Latitude is widenesse: the vse thereof.

Latitude is in the heauens: if the Moone, or any other Starre be vnto the South parts or the North partes of the ecliptick, that then it is sayde, to be so manye degrees in latitude or widenesse, from y^t line eclipstick to the South or North part: and also latitude is counted vpon the earthe in like manner, if that you be in any place betweene, from vnder the equinoctiall, either to the South or North part, betweene any of the 2. Poles, that you are so may degrees in latitude from the equinoctiall. &c.

20. Longitude is length: the vse thereof.

Longitude in the heauens is, if the Sunne or Moone or any other Starre, be in such a signe, & so many degrees; that then it is said: that they haue longitude, in such a signe and so many degrees. And also longitude vpon the earth, is counted from the Canarie Ilands vnto the Eastward, as this, if that any towne or cittie be vnto the Eastwards so may degrees from the Canarie Ilands, then it is sayde, that the cittie or towne is so many degrees in Longitude, whereby is knowne the time of the chaunges of the Moone, or any other aspecte, or anye Eclipse of the Sunne or Moone, at the cittie or towne.

21. Declination is leaning: the vse thereof.

Declination is counted in the heauens, if that the Sunne or any other Starre be vnto the North part, or South part of the equinoctiall, then it is saide, that the Sunne or Starre hath so many degrees of declination to the South or to the North parts, as it happeneth. &c.

22. Circumference is the compasse of a circle by the outer edge.

Diameter is the bredth of a circle, passing right ouer the center or midle thereof, from outside vnto outside.

23. *Center is the middle pricke in any circle, equally*
distant from the edge of the circle
in euery place.

A Parelell line or circle is, if two lines or more (how many soeuer there be) be equall distaunt in euery place alike, being right lines.

24. *Auge what it is.*

Auge is a point in the heauens, whē the Sunne or Moone is excentrick, going neerer vnto the heauens, and further from the earth than hir common order is: and the opposition thereof is, when that the Sunne and Moone do come nearer vnto the earth than they do at any other time.

The vse thereof.

The vse thereof is, to knowe when that thy be in theyr swift motion, of in their slow motiō: in the point of Auge, they be in their slow motiō, in the opposition thereof in their swift motion.

25. *What the head or tayle of the Dragon is.*

The head of the Dragon, is the place where that the Moone dothe come ouer the line Ecliptick, from the South part, vnto the North part: and the tayle of the Dragon is, where the Moone passeth ouer the line ecliptick from the Northe part, vnto the South part.

The vse of the head and tayle of the Dragon.

The vse of the head and tayle of the Dragon, is to know, when that there is any eclipse of the Sunne or Mone: and of what quantitie or greatnesse the eclipse is.

26. *What Nauigation is.*

Nauigation is this, how to direct his course in the Sea to any place assigned, and to consider in that direction what things may stande with him, & what things may stand against him, hauing consideration how to preserue the ship in all stormes and chaunges of weather that may happen by the way, to bring the ship safe vnto the port assigned, and in the shortest time.

The vse of Nauigation.

The vse thereof is this, fyrste to knowe how that the place dothe beare from him, by what winde or poynte of the compasse, and also how farre that the place is from hym, and also to consider the streame, or tide gates, Currents, which way that they do set or driue the ship, and also to consider what daungers is by the waye, as rockes and sandes, and suche other lyke impedimentes, and also if that the wynde chaunge or shifte by the waye, to consider which way to stand, and direct his course vnto the most aduantage to attayne vnto the port in shortest time: and also if anye stormes doe happen by the way, to consider how for to preserue the shippe and the goodes, and too bring hir safe vnto the porte assigned. And also it is moste principally to be considered and foreseene, that if they haue hadde by occasion of a contrarye tempest, for too goe very muche out of the course or way, too knowe then howe that the place dothe then beare, that is to say, by what poynte of the compasse the place dothe stande from you: and also how farre it may be from you. Whyche way to bee knowne is this: firste to consider by what poynte that the shippe hath made hir way by, and how fast and swiftly that the shippe hathe gone, and to consider how often that the shippe hath altered hir course, and how muche that she hathe gone at euery tyme, and then to consider all thys in youre platte or carde, and so you may gyue an neere gesse, by what poynte or wynde it beareth from you, and also howe farre it is thither. And also you may haue a greate helpe by the Sunne or Starres, to take the heigthe of the Pole aboue the horizon, and also in some place you may gesse by the sounding, bothe by the depth, and also by the grounde. And also it is very meete and necessarye to knowe any place, when that hee dothe see it.

27. Of instrumentes to vse at the Sea for to take the heigthe of the Sunne or any Starres.

All instrumentes too take the heighte of the Sunne or anye Starre, the originall of the making thereof, it is eyther a circle or the parte of a circle, whose division is the .360. parte of a circle what forme soeuer that it hathe, as your crosse staffe, it is marked according vntoo the proportion of a circle, and euery one of the degrees, is the equall parte of a circle, the three hundred and sixtie part. &c.

The vse of the Instruments.

The vse of the Instrumentes, as Astrolobes or common Rings, or the crosse staffe, is to take the heigth of the sūne or other stars, whose vses doe folow heere after in the boke.

28. What maner of persons be meetest to take charge of Shippes in Nauigation.

As touching those persons that are meete to take charge, that is to say, to be as maister of ships in Nauigation, he ought to be sober and wise, and not to be light or rash headed, nor to be to fumish or hasty, but such a one as can wel gouern himselfe, for else it is not possible for him to gouerne his cōpany well: he ought not to be to simple, but he must be suche a one as must keepe his companie in awe of him (by discretion) doing his companie no iuiurie or wrong, but to let thē haue that which men ought to haue, and then to see vnto them that they doe their laboure as men ought to doe in all points. And the principall point in gouernment is, to cause himself both to be feared & loued, & that groweth principally by this meanes, to cherishe men in well doing, and those men that be honestly addicted, to let them haue reasonable preheminence, so that it be not hurtfull vnto the Marchaunt nor to himselfe, and to punishe those that be malefactors and disturbers of their company, and for smal faults, to giue them gentle admonition to amende them: and principally these two pointes arte to be foreseene by the maisters. (that is) to serue God himselfe, and to see that all the whole companie do so in like maner, at suche conuenient time as it is meete to be done: the second point is, that the master vse no play at the dise or cards, neither (as near as he cā) to suffer any, for yᵉ sufferance thereof may do very much hurt in diuers respects: And furthermore, the maister ought to be suche a one, as dothe knowe the Moones course, whereby he doth knowe at what time it is a full Sea, or a lowe water, knowing in what quarter or part of the skye, that the Moone doth make a full Sea at that place, and also the master ought to bee acquainted, or knowe that place well, that he doth take charge to goe vnto (except that he haue a Pilot) and also he that taketh charge vpon him, ought to be expert, how the tydegates or currentes doe set from place vnto place: and also not to bee ignorant of such daungers as lyeth by the way, as rocks, sandes, or bankes, and also most principally he ought to bee such a one, as can very well directe his courses vnto any place assigned, and to haue capacitie howe for to handle or shift himselfe in foule weather or stormes. And also it behoueth him too be a good coaster. that is to say, to knowe euery place by the sight thereof. And also he that taketh charge for long voyages, ought to haue knowledge in plats or cardes, and also in such instrumentes as be meet to take the heigth of the Sunne or any Starre, and to haue capacitie to correcte those instrumentes, and also he ought to be such a one, that can calculate the Sunnes declination, or else to haue some true regiment, and also he ought to knowe howe to handle the Sunnes declination, when that he hath taken the heigth of the Sunne.

⁋ *Nowe beginneth the Regiment
for the Sea, the first Chapter or rule of Nauigation, and sheweth what the .32. pointes
of the Compasse is, and to what
vses they do serue.*

The first & most principall thing for any seafaring mā or traueller, is to know toward what part of the Earth he meaneth to go, & then being vpō the sea, there he seeth no path nor mark to trauell by, but only the vse of the Nedle or compasse. And to shewe the cause how they in olde time did finde them or called them, is sufficiently declared by other, but this is to be noted: There be eight capitall or head windes or poyntes, and foure of them haue their names properly of themselues, and the other foure of them, are deriued, or take their names of the other foure, as this, South commeth directly from the Meridian, and North is directly againste it, and East commeth from the Equinoctiall poynte, towardes the partes of the Sunne rysing, and Weast is right against it, Northeast is in the midway betweene the Easte and the North, and Southeast in the midway betweene the East and the South, and Southwest betweene the Weast and the South, and Northweast in the middle betweene the North and the Weast. And then there be eight inferior points, or winds, halfe way betweene euery one of those .8. Capitall or head poynts or winds, and that is Northe Northeast, East Northeast, East Southeast, and Southe Southeast, and South Southweast, and Weast Southweast, and Weast Northweaste, and Northe Northweast: and nowe detweene euerie one of these inferioure poyntes, and euerye one of the heade wyndes there is a by poynt or winde, and he is called a by point, for that he is not named but by the name of one of the heade points next adioyning. There be .16. of them in nūber, so that there be .8. capitall or head points, and .8. inferior points, and 16. by pointes or windes, so that in all there

8. Capitall or head pointes.

8. Inferior pointes or winds.

16. by pointes or windes.

be .32. of them. The vse of these points is, to direct the shippe to what quarter of the world you do assigne, to keepe that course to find the place so assygned, for that the propertie of the Needle or Flye, is alwayes to stand due South and North.

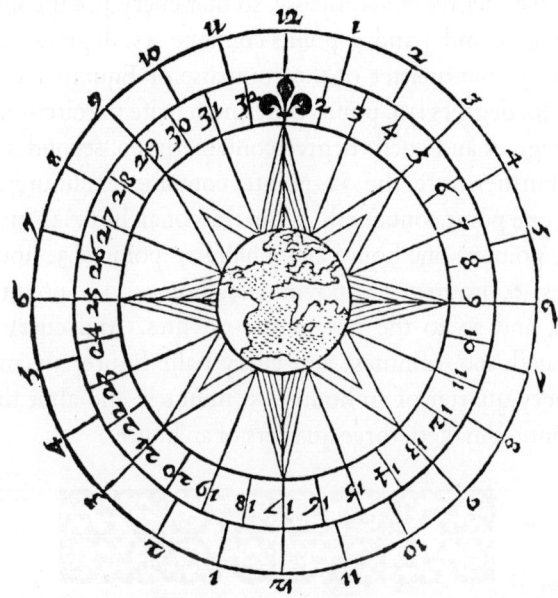

As touching Nauigation, for the instructions of the ineanest I haue set this figure or compasse, where first is to be noted the .32. winds and poynts of the compasse aboue made, The flouredeluce is the first pointe, and these be the names, beginning at the North, and so with the course of the Sunne to say North .1. North and by East .2. North noreast .3. North east and by North .4. Northeast .5. Northeast and by East .6. East Northeast .7. East and by North .8. East .9. East and by South .10, East Southest .11. Southeast and by East .12. Southeast .13. Southeast and by South .14. South southeast .15. South and by East .16. South .17. South and By Weast .18. South Southwest .19. Southweast and by South .20. South Weast .21. Southwest and by Weast .22. Weast Southwest .23. Weast and by South .24. West .25. Weast and by North .26. Weast Northeast .27.

The names of the .32. pointes of the cōpasse.

Northweast and by Weast .28. Northweast .29. Northeast and by North .30. North Northweast .31. North and by Weast .32. This is the whole contents of the .32. windes, and there is in the compasse the contents of the great circle, or Equinoctiall circle being .360. degrees in compasse, so that euery point containeth .11. degrees, and ¼ and 4. points containe .45. degrees .8. points containeth one quarter of the compasse or Equinoctiall circle, being .90. degrees .16. points containeth halfe the circumference .180. degrees and euery degree containeth .60. secondes and so forth. Furthermore, the .32. pointes containe .24. houres, that is to say, one point containeth .3. quarters of an hour .45. minutes: and .2. pointes. one houre and a halfe .4. pointes .3. houres: 8. poyntes .6. houres .12. poyntes .9. houres .16. poyntes .12. houres, and so to the rest of the poyntes. And euery houre contayneth .60. minutes: and euery halfe houre .30. minutes, and euery quarter of an houre .15. minutes: and after that rate .45. minutes maketh three quarters of an houre.

The contents of the Equinoctiall circle 360. de-grees one point of the cōpasse contayneth 11. degrees and a quarter.

The .32. pointes brought into .24. houres.

¶ *The second Chapter or rule treateth of the Golden number or Prime, shewing the Epacte, and by the Epacte to knowe the Age of the Moone.*

It is necessarie and conuenient for the Seafaring men, to knowe the Prime or Golden number: for by the Golden number is knowne the Epacte, and the Epacte sheweth the age of the Moone or chaunge day, within .12. houres vnder or ouer: and by the age of the Moone, you may know at what a clocke it doth showe in any place that you doe knowe that Moone doth make a full Sea: therefore it is meete to know the Epacte, and

A REGIMENT FOR THE SEA, 1574

that is knowne by the Pryme, or Golden number. The cause why it was called the Golden number, was bycause it was sent out of Egypte in letters of golde, too the Romaines or Citie of Rome. The cause why that it is called the Pryme, was for that it was the first order that the Moones course was known by, and it is thus knowne. Adde one to the yeare of our Lord that you would knowe the Golden number or Pryme of, then deuide the number by .19. the remainer is the Pryme: and multiply that by .11. and looke what the number commeth vnto, deuide that by .30. the remayner is the Epact. Then when you haue once the Epact, adde .11. to your Epact for euery yere more, and looke what that commeth to, that is your Epact: and if it do passe .30. put that away, and keepe the remainer for your Epact. And thus this rule will serue for euer, sauing when the Pryme beginneth at one, for then the Epacte is .11. and then doe (as aforesayde) as you may perceyue by this table heere following.

The cause why that it was called the Pryme or Golden number.

To knowe howe many the Epact is

¶ The Table of Pryme and E-
pacte for .19. yeares, and when those .19.
yeares be ended, then beginne againe,
and so it will serue for
euer . &c.

The yere of the Lorde.	Pryme	Epact	The yere of the Lorde.	Pryme	Epact
1574	17	7	1584	8	28
1575	18	18	1585	9	9
1576	19	29	1586	10	20
1577	1	11	1587	11	1
1578	2	22	1588	12	12
1579	3	3	1589	13	23
1580	4	14	1590	14	4
1581	5	25	1591	15	15
1582	6	6	1592	16	26
1583	7	17			

> The Pryme or Golden number, is the time of .19. yeares, in the which time the Moone maketh all hir chaunges or coniunctions with the Sunne, and when all these .19. yeares be expired, then she beinnneth againe: as for example. This yeare being the yeare of our Lord .1574. she chaunged the .22. day of March, and euery yere doth alter .11. days of hir change till the yere .1593. and then she chaungeth the sayd .22. daye of March againe, as I shewed you before. The Epacte is the putting to .11. for euery year. Nowe furthermore to knowe the age of the Moone, do thus: take the number of the Epact for your yere (beginning at March alwayes) and recken how many monthes it is from March, (counting March for one) then recken howe many dayes of the moneth it is in whiche you would knowe the age of the Moone: Then put all your numbers togither, (that is to say, your moneth from March, and euery day of the moneth), then looke howe many it acounteth vnto, that is the age of the Moone, but if it passe .30. throwe all the .30. away, and keepe that that will not be .30. for when the age of the Moone is iust .30. then is it the chaunge daye: and if it be the fifteenth daye of the age of the Moone, then the Moone is at the full. When the age is betweene seuen dayes and eight, then is the first quarter. And if it be, xxij dayes olde, then the Moone is at the laste quarter: as for example, this yeare .1574. I looke and finde the Epact .7. for the year, nowe I woulde knowe the age of the Moone, the .13. daye of June. Nowe I recken how many monthes it is from March, reckning March for one, and I finde it is foure monethes, then I take and adde all these togyther, that is to say, seuen for the Epacte, and foure for the monethes (that is to say, March, April, May, June) and then .13. for the dayes of the moneth, and all commeth to .24. So that you may conclud: that the Moone is .24. days olde, and was at the last quarter two dayes before.

The pryme is the time of 19 yeres.

To knowe the age of the Moone by the number of the Epacte.

A REGIMENT FOR THE SEA, 1574

¶ *The thirde Chapter or rule trea-*
teth, how to know by the age of the Moone
what houre it dothe flowe, or is full Sea at
any place, where you do knowe
what Moone maketh
a full Sea.

Nowe by the age of the Moone you may knowe at what houre it floweth in any place, where you do know what Moone maketh a full Sea, which rule commonly the Sea men cal the shifting their Sunne and Moone: and many wayes there be too doe it, for thus they may doe it: Let them deuide one houre into .5. parts, and the take .4. of those parts, and put the fifth part away, that serueth for the alteration of 24. hours. & the foure fift parts of an houre, are .48. minuts, and the .5. part of an houre is .12. minuts. A floud and an ebbe, dothe alter .24. minuts forwards: as this for example: it floweth at .12. of the clocke at the Landsend vpon the chaunge day, the Moone being in the South: at all times a full Sea. The Moone being one day old, it floweth at .12. of the clocke .48. minuts .2. dayes olde it floweth at one of the clock .36. minuts .3. days old it floweth at .2. of the clock .24. minuts: four dayes old it floweth at .3. of the clock .12. minuts: fiue dayes old, it floweth at .4. of the clocke iust: Sixe dayes old, it floweth at 4. of the clocket .48. minuts: Seuen dayes old at .5. of the clocke .36. minuts: Eight dayes old at .6. of the clocke .24. minuts: Nine dayes old, at .7. of the clocke .12. minuts: Ten dayes old, it floweth at .8. of the clocke iust: Eleuen dayes old at .8. of the clocke 48. minuts: 12 dayes .9. of the clocke .36. minuts: 13. dayes old .10. of the clocke .24. minuts: 14. days old, it floweth at .11. of the clocke .12. minuts: 15. dayes old, it floweth at .12. of the clock iust, then being the full Moone: and so begin againe as you did be-fore at one day old, and so foorth. For the course of the tides is nothing else but to adde for euery daye of the age of the Moone one houre, pulling backe the fifth part of an houre (being .12.

To knowe the alteration of the tides in .24 houres.

An ensample for the full Sea vppon the Landsend for euery day of the age of the Moone.

minuts) and by this accompt you maye at all times knowe at what a clocke it doth flowe, by putting to euery floude and ebbe .24. minuts, and to .2. flouds and .2. ebbes putting to .48. minuts. Now furthermore the Sea men vse to make their accompt by this meanes (but it is all one) they do allow for euery day of the age of the Moone, one point and 3. minuts: for a point of the compasse conteineth .45. minuts that is .3. quarters of an houre. Then they put .3. minuts to 45. minuts, which maketh .48. minuts, the sayd .3. minuts be the .15. part of a point, and from the chaunge to the full is .15. days, so that (the halfe compasse being .16. pointes) they breake the odde point into .15. partes, and that commeth to .3. minuts, so that the alteration of the tides, for euery .24. houres, be .48. minuts, or y̌e .4. fifth parts of an houre. Wherefore there shall follow a table of tides about certain places of this realme: for euery Moone conteineth .29. dayes .12. houres .44. minutes from chaunge to chaunge: the whole contents of the houres of the Moone, be .708. houres, and .44. minuts. And there is in euery yeare .12. changes of the Moone: and the yeare conteineth .365. days .5. houres .55. minuts .13. seconds. Yet some do affirme to be odde .6. houres, but there lacketh .4. minuts .47. seconds in the tropicall yeare. Likewise in the yeare be .12. monethes agreable to the .12. Moones: the 12. Moones conteine but .354. dayes, so that there be .11. dais more in the year, than there be in the .12. moones. The yeare also is deuided into .12. mooneths, which mooneths haue taken their names at the will and pleasure of menne: as first January, was so called, of *Ianus* bycause of .2. heades, for the month of January beholdeth the end of the year past and the beginning of the yeare to come. February tooke his name of certaine romaine sacrifices called *Februa*. March is so called of *Mars*. for *Romulus* so named it after his father. Aprill comes of *Aperio*, bycause that then the earth is opened. Maye of *Maia*, the mother of *Mercury*, June so called by preparing to the warre, July of *Iulius Cesar*, and Augustus of *Augustus Cesar* for in that month he entred the cosulship: then

To shift the Sunne and the Moone by the points of the compasse.

The contente of the numbre of dayes and houres in one moone: y̌e houres in euery mone be .708. 44 minuts. The contente of a yeare is .365 dayes .5. hours .55. Minuts. How the mooneths tooke their names.

the rest of the months toke their names of their number frō March. Now these .12. months which maketh the yeare, the Sunne dothe passe or go through the Zodiack called the .12. signes which is the occasion of the year, for this is to be noted, that the sunne as I saide before, doth go by his naturall mouing in .365. days .5. houres .55. minuts .13. seconds, through the Zodiack, conteining .360. degrees, his course being against the 24. houres. going from the Weast into the East, against the course of *primum mobile*, or first mouer, being moued by the mighty prouidence of God, which maketh the .24. houres: and so dothe all the seuen lights, or planets, (except) that it be in their retrogratiō: but the Sunne and the Moone, be neuer retrograt, as the other .5. planets or lights be. And this is to be noted, that the Moone goeth faster thā the Sunne, for she goeth through the whole Zodiack in .27. dayes and .8. houres. Now in that same time the sunne is remoued by his natural mouing from that place of the Zodiack neare .27. degrees: and then bycause that the Moone hath not found the Sunne ther, it is .2. dayes foure houres foure and forty minuts more before that the Moone ouertaketh the Sunne againe, so by that meanes it is .29. dayes twelue houres and .44. minuts betweene the chaunge of the Moone and the next chaunge, one Moone with and other thorowe the year, although that the Moone may chaunge sometime in lesse time and sometime in longer time, that is by the meanes of the .3. motions of the Moone, that is to say hir swift motion and hir midle motion and hir slow motion, which groweth by the meanes of the moones Auge or opposition thereof. The Moone being in Auge, goeth but little more than .12. degrees in 24. houres. And in the opposition of Auge neere .15. degrees in .24. houres, and in hir midle or equall motion .13 degrees, 12. minuts. So this is the occasion why sometime the Moone may chaunge sooner or be detracted longer than the time of .29. dayes .12. houres and 44. minuts. This point of Auge is mouable, and doth passe thorough the Zodiack in the time of .19. yeare: and it causeth sometime the

The Zodiack conteyneth .360. degrees.

The moouing of .24. houres

The tyme that the Moone goeth thorow the .12. signes.

The .3. motions of the Moone.

Of Auge.

The cause why the Moone chaungeth rather or later.

full of the Moone to happen sooner and later. In like manner also the quarters of the Moone, with al the other aspects that the Moone hath with the Sunne, or any other of the planets, according to the moones motion. In like manner (by the meanes of the .3. motions of the Moone) sometime the Moone goeth more thā one point and .3. minuts in .24. hours, and sometimes lesse than one point and .3. minuts, as this for example: the Moone being in hir slow motiō, goeth but little more than .12. degrees in .24. hours, and then the Sunne in that time doth go one degree: and then is there but .11. degrees between the Sunne and the Moone (that is but .44. minuts) So that the Moone is not one point in .24. houres from the sunne, But being in hir swift motion she goeth neere .15. degrees in .24. houres, and the Sunne goeth one degree in that time: so that there is .14. degrees in .24. hours, between the Moone and the Sunne, (that is .56. minuts) which is a pointe and .11. minuts .23. But notwithstādīng I would not wish the common Marriners to trouble themselues with these matters, but followe their accustomed order, to allow for euery day of the age of the Moone, one pointe, and .3. minutes, &c. And this muche haue I said of the Moones motion: for that some Sea men will take vpon them to correct ye Almanacks as touching the chaunge and quarters of the Moone: holding this opinion, that euery Moone ought to be equal in the number of the dayes and houres: and the full moones to be iust the halfe contents. And the quarters in like manner, the iust .4. parte in days and hours, so that some of them will take vpon them to tel (by the rule of the epact,) the true houre of the change, quarters and full of the Moone. Wherein they are notably deceiued. Againe, sometime in the yeare you shall see the Moone rather thā at some other time, as this for example: from January to June you shall see the Moone within .24. houres after the chaunge: bycause she hath North declination of the Sunne, and maketh a bigger arche thā the Sunne, from July to December you shall not see the Moone .3. dayes after the change: bicause hir declination is to

The mone goeth in .24. hours sometimes more degrees and sometime fewer degrees.

The mone is not one point asunder from the Sunne in .24. houres.

The mone is in .24. houres a point and .11. minuts asunder frō the Sunne.

Error of Marriners.

the South part of the Sunne: but you may see hir in .24. houres, before hir chaunge. Now, the Sea men do imagin a prime day, which is the halfe quarter of the Moone, that is: when the Moone is thre days and .18 houres old, (the Moone being then .4. points to the Eastward of the Sunne, which is 3 houres) the same rule may they in like case obserue when the Moone is paste the full .3. days and .18. houres, and also in the middes of the quarters.

Here followeth a table of Tides.

First, the Moone South or North: on Landes ende full Sea,
    The Moone South and by East: at the Gore ende full Sea.
    The Moone South southwest: betweene holy Iland and Tinemouth full Sea.
    It floweth between Tinemouth and Flambrough head, Southwest and Northeast Moone.
    It floweth betweene Flambrough head and Bridlington in the bay; a Southwest and by West Moone.
    The Moone in the West Southwest: betweene Bridlington and Laurenas full Sea.
    It floweth betweene Laurenas and Cromer all along the well: an East and West Moone.
    It floweth between: Cromer and Yarmouth rode, to Laystow North rode: a Southeast Moone.
    It floweth betweene Laistowe rode and Orfordenas; a Southeast and by South Moone.
    It floweth betweene Orford, and Orewel wands: a South Southeast Moone.
    It floweth betweene the Nase & the Ware head of Colne: a South and by East Moone.
    It floweth at the Spittes and at the Sheue and al alongst the Swinne: a South Moone.
    At the West end of the Norre: a Southe and by West Moone, full Sea.

It floweth at Grauesend: a South Southwest Moone.

It floweth at London Bridge: a Southwest Moone.

It floweth at the North forlande: a South Southeast Moone, & so alongst the coast till you come to Bechy. And in the ofton from the North forland to the South forland: it runneth halfe tide. And frō the South forland to the Nas: the tide runneth halfe tyde halfe quarter. And from the Nas to the Fairely: it runneth halfe tide, and from Fairely to Beche: it runneth quarter tide under other.

It floweth to the Weastward of Beche, a kenning: a Southeast and by South Moone.

It floweth at Portesmouth: a Southe and by East Moone.

It floweth at S. Elens: a South Southeast Moone.

It floweth on the Sea side of the Iland: A Southeast and by South Moone: and so on the Lande, and at the Needles, and runneth quarter tide in the oftonne.

It floweth at Poole in the hauen: a Southeast Moone.

It floweth at Waymouth: an East and West Moone.

It floweth at Portland a Southeast Moone.

It floweth from the Weaste parte of Portlande, till you come vntoo Plymmouth: an East and Weast Moone.

It floweth on the shoare from Plymmouth to the Lizard: a West and by Southe Moone. And in the oftonne a Southeast Moone.

It floweth at Mountes baye: an East and Weaste Moone.

It floweth at Selly: a West and by South Moone.

It floweth at the Landes ende of Goolfe: a West Southwest Moone.

It floweth all alongst the coast vp to Bristowe, and the coast of Ireland, from Waterford to Kinsale: a West and by South Moone.

Furthermore it floweth (for the most part) from the poll head of Burdeaux all alongst the coast of Biskey, Galiza, Portingale, till you come to the straightes of Maliga, a Southwest and Northeast Moone.

It floweth at Flushing: a Southweast and by Southe Moone.
It floweth at Antwerp: an East and west Moone.

It floweth all alongest the coast of Flaunders, from the Wyldings to Calys: a Southe and by East Moone: and so runneth halfe a tide vnder the other.

Nowe heere is one speciall thyng too bee noted, and that is thys: it floweth one poynte of the compasse more in the Spring streames, than it doothe in any of the quarters of the Moone (so that it be a riuer where there is any indrafte, hauing distaunce from the Sea) when there is neyther rage of wyndes nor anye cause eyther too hinder or further the sayde effect. As for example thus: it floweth at Grauesend at the chaunge of the Moone or full: a Southe Southwest Moone. But in any of the quarters of the Moone it skante floweth a Southe and by West Moone: and this is generally for euer.

It will flow a point of the compasse more in y^e spring tides than in the neap tides: in a Riuer that hath any distance vnto the Sea.

*The fourth Chapter treateth of
the Sunne & moones course in the Zodiack:
and how you shall know what houres
the Moone shall rise and set at: and at
what poynte of the compasse:
wyth other necessarye
thynges.*

Furthermore the Sunne (by hys naturall moouing thoroughe the twelue Signes in the Zodiack, in the yeare) dothe cause the heigth and lowenesse of his declination: whiche is necessarie for the Seafaring men to knowe, in whiche declination they do take from equinoctiall to equinoctiall: and this is to be noted, that as the Sunne hathe declination, so in like manner hathe the

Moone, for by hir declination, and the Sunne, is knowen the tyme of hir shyning or abiding aboue our horizon. The Sunne or Moone in the first minute of *Aries* do rise East, and set West, and shyne .12. houres. In the first minute of *Taurus* they rise neere the East Northeast, and set neere the West Northwest, and shyne .14. houres. In the signe of *Gemini*: they rise neere the Northeast and by East, and they set neere the Northwest and by West, and shyne .16. houres. In the signe of *Cancer* the firste minute: they make their greatest declination to the Northwards, and they rise neere the Northeast, and set neere the Northweast and shyne .17. houres. In the fyrste minute of *Leo* (discending towardes the equinoctiall,) as they dyd in *Gemini*. And in the signe of *Virgo*, as they dyd in *Taurus*. And in the firste minute of *Libra*, equinoctiall: beginning South declination, as in *Aries*. And in the fyrste minute of *Scorpio*: they rise neere the Easte Southeast, and sette neere the Weast Southweast, and shyne .10. houres. In the fyrste minute of *Sagittarius*: they rise neere the Southeast and by East, and set neere the Southwest, and by weast, and shyne .8. houres. In the fyrste minute of *Capricornus*, they haue their greatest declinatiō to the South, and begin to returne to the equinoctiall, rising neere the Southeast and setting neere the Southwest, and shyne more than .7. houres. In the firste minute of *Aquarius*: as in *Sagittarius*. In the firste minute of *Pisces*: as in *Scorpio*. Nowe by this rule you may knowe the rising and setting of the Moone foreuer: as thus: I haue shewed you before in the shifting of the Sunne and Moone, that for euery day of the age of the Moone, the Moone goeth Eastward one point & .3. minuts: in .2. days .2. points and .6. minuts . &c. Nowe when you list to knowe the very houre and time of hir rising: Looke howe many dayes the Moone is olde, then put so many points, and so many .3. minutes, and looke what it amounteth vnto. Which for your better vnderstanding, I will shew by example: and first of the Moones being South, by euery day of the age of the Moone. The Moone being one daye olde: is South at .12. of the clocke.

To know how long the Mone shineth.

To knowe what houre or point the Moone ryseth or setteth.

A REGIMENT FOR THE SEA, 1574

48. minutes. The Moone being .2. dayes olde, is South at one of the clocke .36. minuts in the afternoone. Three days old: South at .2. of the clock. 24. minuts .4. days olde, at .3. of the clock .12. minutes .5. days olde: at .4. of the clock iust .6. days olde at .4. of the clock .48. minuts .7 days olde at .5. of the clock .36. minutes. When the Moone is iust a quarter old, she is South at 6. of the clock at night. at .8. dayes olde: the Moone is South at .6. of the clocke .24. minutes. at .9. dayes olde at .7. of the clock .12. minutes. at .10. dayes olde: at .8. of the clocke iust. At .11. dayes olde at .8. of the clock .48. minutes. at .12. dayes olde at .9. of the clocke .56. minutes, at .13. dayes olde at .10. of the clock .24. minutes. at .14. dayes olde at .11. of the clocke .12. minutes. at .15. dayes olde (being the full Moone) she is then South at midnight. One daye after the full Moone: she is South at .12. of the clocke .48. minutes at midnight. Two dayes after the full: at one of the clocke .36. minutes. Three dayes after, at .2. of the clocke .24. minutes. Foure days after, at .3. of the clock .12. minutes. Fiue dayes after at .4. of the clocke, iust in the morning. Sixe dayes after, at .4. of the clock .48. minutes .7. dayes after, at .5. of the clocke .36. minutes. When the Moone is three quarters olde, she is South at .6. of the clocke in the morning. At .8. dayes after the full (being the firste daye after the quarter) at .6. of the clocke .24. minutes .9. days after: at 7. of the clocke .12. minutes .10. dayes after, at .8. of the clocke iust .11. dayes after, at .8. of the clocke. 48. minutes. 12. dayes after, South at .9. of the clocke, 36. minutes. 13 dayes after, South at .10. of the clocke in the forenoon .24. minutes .14. dayes after, at .11. of the clocke .12. minutes. at .15. dayes after the Moone dothe chaunge (being then with the Sunne) for the chaunge of the Moone is, when the Moone and the Sunne be bothe vnder one like degree and minute of any signe of the Zodiack. The full Moone is, when the Sunne and the Moone be opposite (the one being directly against the other, and iust .6. signes asunder) as you maye perceiue at the full Moone: for then when the Moone ryseth, the Sunne setteth: and when the

To knowe what houre the Moone is South for euery day of the age of the Moone.

Of the chaunge.

Of the full Moone.

Quarter of the Moone. Ensample of the moones rysing & setting.

sunne ryseth, the Moone setteth. The quarters be, when the Sunne and Moone be iust .3. signes asunder (that is, iust .90. degrees) Nowe when you list to knowe the very time of the Moones rysing or setting, looke in your Kalender what signe and degree the Moone is in: then according to the rule of the shining, deuide that into .2. equall partes, then from the South, so shall you see at what houre the Moone ryseth, as for example this. In March alwayes the Sunne is in *Aries*, then the Moone being in hir first quarter, then she is 6. houres to the Eastward of the Sunne, then the Moone must needs be in *Cancer*. Then shineth the Moone in our Horizon 17. houres, then the Moone is South at .6. of the clock, then she shineth .8. houres and a halfe after .6. of the clock. So that she setteth at .2. of the clock and halfe an houre past, then she ryseth in the day .8. houres and a half before .6. of the clock, that is at .9. of the clocke and halfe an houre past. Now at the last quarter in March, then the Moone must needes be in *Capricornus*, then shineth the Moone but .7. houres, then the moone is South at .6. of the clock in the morning, then the Moone riseth .3. houres and a halfe before, that is, at .2. of the clock and halfe an houre paste in the morning, then she setteth by day at .9. of the clocke and halfe an houre past, and this rule will serue for euer without any great error. But yet there is a further matter for the exacte

The Mone hath latitude.

doing, which is the Latitude of the Moone from the head or tayle of the Dragon, but that is but a trifle in respecte of muche error, and therefore I will not trouble you with that: yet there is one thing whiche I would Seafaring men should consider, although a great nū be expert in that, yet it is meete to be

You cannot know what a clock it is by the compasse, the Sun being in North signes.

spoken of, as this. The Sunne being in *Cancer* or Moone in like maner, or in *Gemini*, or any time when the Sunne or Moone hath North declination, they wil set their compasse before them, and when they see the Sunne giue an East shadowe, they will saye that it is .6. of the clock, which and if the Sunne be in *Cancer*, it is not muche paste fiue of the clocke, and the more to the South wardes the more they doe erre. And in like case, the

Moone being in *Cancer* when they doe see the Moone giue an East shadowe by their compasse, they will say the Moone is Weast, but they do not consider that the Sunne and the Moone being in *Cancer*, commeth so neare our Zenith or Verticall poynte right ouer our heads, which is the verie heigth of their declination comming so neare them, therefore they must iudge the East or Weast from the Pole or North starre if they will iudge truely. Wherefore I do much commende the Equinoctiall Dyals for the exacte truth, for they can not know the truth by their compasse, so that the Sunne or Moone or any other Starre haue any great declination being in *Cancer*: and you must consider this in like manner. The Sunne hauing North declination, the further you doe goe to the North wardes, the longer is youre daye, and the shorter is your nightes, and to-wardes the Southward, the shorter dayes and longer nightes. Nowe contrarywise, the Sunne hauing South declination, the more to the Northwardes, the shorter dayes and the longer nightes, the further to the Southwards, the longer days and shorter nights, and vnder the Equinoctiall, the nightes and dayes all one what declination soeuer the Sunne hath: but this rule that I haue giuen you is for London, or any other place that hath that Latitude or eleuation of the Pole Articke at .51. or .52. degrees.

Error of ye shadow of the Moone

The Equinoctiall dyals be very good.

As touching the length and shortnesse of the day and night.

> ¶ *The fifth Chapter or rule, is of a table of declination commonly called of Seafaring men, a Regiment of the Sunne, exactly calculated for .4. yeres, and wil serue for .24. yeres, for euery day of the moneth.*

Now shall folowe a table of declination or Regiment for 4. yeres, being calculated for England, and will serue all Europe without much error, or any other countrey or place that hath our Longitude, as the most part of Africa, as Ginnie and those partes to the South wards, as farre as the Antartick pole, seruing for euery day of the moneth, very necessarie for them that do vse to trauell either by sea or by land, and is one of the principall pointes in Nauigation for long voyages, and the cause why I haue written this Regiment for the Sea, or tables of declination is for that I do knowe that euery person that goeth vnto the Sea as maister of a shippe, hath not capacitie to calculate the Sunnes declination by the place of the sunne, although they haue the tables of declination, as the Ephemerides, or Martin Curtyse, otherwise called the art of Nauigatiō. Wherefore I haue written these notes, & Regiemnt or table of declination for .4. yeres, and the first row towards your left hand, is the dayes of the moneth: the next rowe is the degrees of declination that the Sunne hath at the instant time of noone: and the thirde rowe is the odde minutes of declination belonging to the degrees. Nowe there be two times in the yere that the Sunne hath no declinatiō, as this. For the first yere after *Bissextilis*, (which was in ye yeare of our Lorder .1573. the .11. day of March, at .4. of ye clock in the morning) the Sune was vpō the Equinoctiall beginning North declination. And in like maner the 13. day of September at noone, the Suune was vpon the Equinoctiall beginning South declination, and also the second yere after *Bissextillis*, which is the yere of our Lorde .1574. the sunne is vpon the Equinoctiall, the .11. day of Marche, betwene 10. and .11. of the clocke before Noone, beginning North declination: and in like maner the .13. day of September at .6. of the clocke in the after Noone, beginning South declination, Furthermore in the thirde yere after *Bissextillis*, whiche is the yere of the Lorde. 1575. the sunne is vpon the Equinoctiall the 11. day of Marche, betweene foure and fiue of the clocke in the after Noone, beginning North declination: & so in like maner the .13. day of September at .12. of the clocke at midnight, beginning South declination. Lastly, in the yere of our Lorde

Euery person cannot calculate ye Sunnes declination.

Two times in the yeare the Sunne hath no declination. 1573.

1576. that is the yere *Bissextilis* it selfe vpon the .10. day of Marche the sunne shall be vpon the Equinoctiall betweene 10. and .11. of the clocke at night, beginning North declination: and in like maner the .13. day of September at .6. of the clocke in the morning, beginning South declination: Nowe these foure yeres beeing expired, you must after the yere of *Bissextilis*, beginne agayne at the yere one, as heer dothe followe for example.

Yeare 1.	Yeare 2.	Yeare 3.	Yeare *Bissextilis*
1573	1574	1575	1576
1577	1578	1579	1580
1581	1582	1583	1584
1585	1586	1581	1588
1589	1590	1591	1592

1573. The first yeare.

Ianuarie.			Februarie.				Marche.		
D.	G.	M.	D.	G.	M.		D.	G.	M.
1	21	52	1	14	7	South declination.	1	3	49
2	21	43	2	13	47		2	3	26
3	21	33	3	13	26		3	3	2
4	21	23	4	13	6		4	2	38
5	21	12	5	12	46		5	2	14
6	21	1	6	12	26		6	1	51
7	20	49	7	12	5		7	1	27
8	20	37	8	11	44		8	1	3
9	20	25	9	11	22		9	0	39
10	20	12	10	11	1		10	0	16
11	19	59	11	10	39	Equino-	11	0	8
12	19	46	12	10	18		12	0	32
13	19	32	13	9	56		13	0	55
14	19	17	14	9	33		14	1	19
15	19	3	15	9	11		15	1	42
16	18	47	16	8	49	ctiall.	16	2	6
17	18	32	17	8	26		17	2	29
18	18	17	18	8	4	North declination.	18	2	53
19	18	1	19	7	41		19	3	17
20	17	45	20	7	9		20	3	40
21	17	28	21	6	56		21	4	3
22	17	11	22	6	33		22	4	36
23	16	54	23	6	10		23	4	49
24	16	37	24	5	46		24	5	12
25	16	19	25	5	23		25	5	35
26	16	1	26	5	0		26	5	58
27	15	42	27	4	36		27	6	21
28	15	23	28	4	13		28	6	44
29	15	5					29	7	6
30	14	46					30	7	28
31	14	26					31	7	50

(Column between Februarie and Marche: "South declination." / "Equino-" [sun figure] "ctiall." / "North declination.")

A REGIMENT FOR THE SEA, 1574

1573. The first yeare.									
Aprill.			May.				Iune.		
D.	G.	M.	D.	G.	M.		D.	G.	M.
1	8	13	1	17	49		1	23	8
2	8	35	2	18	5		2	23	12
3	8	57	3	18	20		3	23	15
4	9	19	4	18	35		4	23	18
5	9	41	5	18	49		5	23	22
6	10	2	6	19	4		6	23	24
7	10	23	7	19	17		7	23	26
8	10	44	8	19	31		8	23	27
9	11	6	9	19	44	Solstic.	9	23	27
10	11	25	10	19	57		10	23	28
11	11	45	11	20	8		11	23	28
12	12	9	12	20	21		12	23	28
13	12	26	13	20	33		13	23	28
14	12	47	14	20	45		14	23	27
15	13	6	15	20	56		15	23	26
16	13	26	16	21	6		16	23	25
17	13	45	17	21	17		17	23	24
18	14	4	18	21	27		18	23	22
19	14	23	19	21	37		19	23	19
20	14	41	20	21	46		20	23	15
21	15	0	21	21	55		21	23	12
22	15	18	22	22	3		22	23	8
23	15	25	23	22	12		23	23	3
24	15	53	24	22	19		24	22	59
25	16	11	25	22	27		25	22	54
26	16	29	26	22	33		26	22	48
27	16	45	27	22	40		27	22	42
28	17	2	28	22	47		28	22	35
29	17	18	29	22	52		29	22	29
30	17	34	30	22	57		30	22	22
			31	23	3				

(April and May columns: North declination. June column: North declination.)

1573. The first yeare.

July.			August.				September.		
D.	G.	M.	D.	G.	M.		D.	G.	M.
1	22	13	1	15	23	North declination.	1	4	39
2	22	5	2	15	5		2	4	16
3	21	56	3	14	48		3	3	53
4	21	47	4	14	30		4	3	31
5	21	36	5	14	11		5	3	7
6	21	27	6	13	51		6	2	44
7	21	19	7	13	33		7	2	20
8	21	8	8	13	13		8	1	58
9	20	57	9	12	54		9	1	34
10	20	47	10	12	34		10	1	10
11	20	35	11	12	14	Equino-	11	0	48
12	20	24	12	11	53		12	0	24
13	20	12	13	11	33		13	0	0
14	19	59	14	11	14		14	0	24
15	19	46	15	10	54		15	0	47
16	19	33	16	10	32	ctiall.	16	1	11
17	19	19	17	10	12		17	1	34
18	19	5	18	9	50	South declination.	18	1	58
19	18	56	19	9	28		19	2	21
20	18	37	20	9	7		20	2	44
21	18	22	21	8	46		21	3	8
22	18	9	22	8	24		22	3	32
23	17	53	23	8	2		23	3	55
24	17	37	24	7	39		24	4	18
25	17	22	25	7	18		25	4	41
26	17	5	26	6	55		26	5	3
27	16	49	27	6	33		27	5	27
28	16	22	28	6	11		28	5	50
29	16	7	29	5	47		29	6	13
30	15	59	30	5	25		30	6	36
31	15	41	31	5	2				

A REGIMENT FOR THE SEA, 1574

1573. The first yeare.

October.			November.				December.		
D.	G.	M.	D.	G.	M.		D.	G.	M.
1.	6.	59	1.	17	26		1	23	3
2	7	22	2	17	43		2	23	8
3	7	44	3	17	59		3	23	12
4	8	6	4	18	15		4	23	15
5	8	29	5	18	31		5	23	19
6	8	51	6	18	46		6	23	22
7	9	13	7	19	1		7	23	24
8	9	34	8	19	16		8	23	25
9	9	56	9	19	30		9	23	26
10	10	18	10	19	44		10	23	27
11	10	40	11	19	58	South declination.	11	23	28
12	11	1	12	20	10		12	23	28
13	11	23	13	20	22		13	23	28
14	11	44	14	20	36		14	23	27
15	12	5	15	20	48		15	23	26
16	12	26	16	20	59		16	23	25
17	12	44	17	21	10	———	17	23	23
18	13	7	18	21	21	Solstic.	18	23	21
19	13	27	19	21	33		19	23	18
20	13	47	20	21	41		20	23	14
21	14	7	21	21	51		21	23	11
22	14	26	22	21	59		22	23	6
23	14	45	23	22	8		23	23	1
24	15	4	24	22	17		24	22	55
25	15	23	25	22	25		25	22	50
26	15	41	26	22	32		26	22	43
27	16	0	27	22	39		27	22	36
28	16	17	28	22	46		28	22	28
29	16	35	29	22	52		29	22	2
30	16	52	30	22	57		30	22	13
31	17	9					31	22	4

1574. The seconde yeare.

January.			February.				March.		
D.	G.	M.	D.	G.	M.		D.	G.	M.
1.	21	56	1	14	12	*South declination.*	1	3	55
2	21	46	2	13	52		2	3	32
3	21	36	3	13	32		3	3	8
4	21	26	4	13	11		4	2	44
5	21	15	5	12	51		5	2	20
6	21	4	6	12	31		6	1	57
7	20	52	7	12	10		7	1	34
8	20	41	8	11	49		8	1	10
9	20	28	9	11	27		9	0	46
10	20	16	10	11	6		10	0	22
11	20	3	11	10	44		11	0	21
12	19	49	12	10	33	Equino-	12	0	25
13	19	36	13	10	1		13	0	49
14	19	21	14	9	39		14	1	13
15	19	7	15	9	17		15	1	36
16	18	52	16	8	55		16	2	0
17	18	37	17	8	32	ctiall.	17	2	23
18	17	17	18	8	10		18	2	47
19	18	1	19	7	47		19	3	11
20	17	49	20	7	25	*North declination.*	20	3	34
21	17	32	21	7	2		21	3	56
22	17	15	22	6	39		22	4	20
23	16	57	23	6	16		23	4	43
24	16	40	24	5	52		24	5	7
25	16	23	25	5	29		25	5	29
26	16	5	26	5	6		26	5	52
27	15	47	27	4	42		27	6	16
28	15	28	28	4	19		28	6	38
29	15	10					29	7	1
30	14	51					30	7	23
31	14	31					31	7	46

1574. The seconde yeare.

Apryll.			May.				June.		
D.	G.	M.	D.	G.	M.		D.	G.	M.
1	8	9	1	17	46	North declination.	1	23	6
2	8	30	2	18	1		2	23	11
3	8	51	3	18	17		3	23	14
4	9	14	4	18	32		4	23	17
5	9	35	5	18	36		5	23	20
6	9	56	6	19	1		6	23	23
7	10	18	7	19	14		7	23	25
8	10	39	8	19	28		8	23	26
9	10	59	9	19	41		9	23	27
10	11	20	10	19	54		10	23	27
11	11	41	11	20	6		11	23	28
12	12	1	12	20	18		12	23	28
13	12	21	13	20	30		13	23	28
14	12	41	14	20	41		14	23	27
15	13	1	15	20	53		15	23	26
16	13	21	16	21	3		16	23	25
17	13	40	17	21	14	Solstic.	17	23	24
18	14	0	18	21	25		18	23	22
19	14	18	19	21	34		19	23	20
20	14	37	20	21	43		20	23	16
21	14	55	21	21	52		21	23	12
22	15	13	22	22	1		22	23	9
23	15	30	23	22	9		23	23	5
24	15	48	24	22	17		24	23	0
25	16	6	25	22	25		25	22	54
26	16	23	26	22	31		26	22	49
27	16	40	27	22	38		27	22	43
28	16	57	28	22	45		28	22	36
29	17	13	29	22	52		29	22	29
30	17	30	30	22	58		30	22	22
			31	23	1				

1574. The seconde yeare.									
July.			August.				September.		
D.	G.	M.	D.	G.	M.		D.	G.	M.
1.	22	14	1	15	28	North declination.	1	4	45
2	22	6	2	15	10		2	4	22
3	21	58	3	14	51		3	3	58
4	21	49	4	14	33		4	3	36
5	21	40	5	14	16		5	3	13
6	21	31	6	13	58		6	2	49
7	21	21	7	13	38		7	2	26
8	21	11	8	13	18		8	2	4
9	21	0	9	12	58		9	1	42
10	20	49	10	12	39		10	1	18
11	20	38	11	12	19		11	0	56
12	20	26	12	11	59	Equino-	12	0	32
13	20	13	13	11	39		13	0	7
14	20	2	14	11	19		14	0	17
15	19	55	15	10	58		15	0	41
16	19	37	16	10	36	octiall.	16	1	3
17	19	23	17	10	16		17	1	27
18	19	9	18	9	54		18	1	51
19	18	55	19	9	34	South declination.	19	2	15
20	18	42	20	9	12		20	2	38
21	18	26	21	8	50		21	3	1
22	18	12	22	8	28		22	3	24
23	17	56	23	8	7		23	3	48
24	17	41	24	7	45		24	4	11
25	17	25	25	7	24		25	4	34
26	17	9	26	7	2		26	4	57
27	16	52	27	6	39		27	5	20
28	16	36	28	6	16		28	5	44
29	16	20	29	5	53		29	6	7
30	16	2	30	5	31		30	6	30
31	15	45	31	5	8				

1574. The seconde yeare.

October.			November.				December.		
D.	G.	M.	D.	G.	M.		D.	G.	M.
1.	6.	53.	1	17	22		1	22	2
2	7	16	2	17	39		2	23	7
3	7	39	3	17	55		3	23	12
4	8	0	4	18	11		4	23	15
5	8	23	5	18	27		5	23	18
6	8	45	6	18	42		6	23	22
7	9	8	7	18	57		7	23	25
8	9	30	8	19	11		8	23	26
9	9	52	9	19	25	Solstic.	9	23	26
10	10	13	10	19	39	———	10	23	27
11	10	35	11	19	53		11	23	28
12	10	56	12	20	6		12	23	28
13	11	18	13	20	19		13	23	28
14	11	39	14	20	32		14	23	27
15	12	0	15	20	44		15	23	26
16	12	21	16	20	56		16	23	25
17	12	42	17	21	6		17	23	24
18	13	2	18	21	17		18	23	22
19	13	22	19	21	28		19	23	19
20	13	42	20	21	38		20	23	15
21	14	2	21	21	48		21	23	12
22	14	22	22	21	57		22	23	8
23	14	41	23	22	6		23	23	2
24	15	0	24	22	15		24	22	56
25	15	19	25	22	23		25	22	51
26	15	37	26	22	31		26	22	45
27	15	56	27	22	37		27	22	37
28	16	14	28	22	44		28	22	30
29	16	31	29	22	51		29	22	23
30	16	48	30	22	57		30	22	15
31	17	5					31	22	7

South declination. (October)
South declination. (November/December)

1575. The thirde yeare.

Ianuarie.			Februarie.				Marche.		
D.	G.	M.	D.	G.	M.		D.	G.	M.
1	21	57	1	14	17	*South declination.*	1	4	2
2	21	48	2	13	57		2	3	38
3	21	38	3	13	37		3	3	15
4	21	28	4	13	15		4	2	51
5	21	18	5	12	56		5	2	27
6	21	6	6	12	35		6	2	3
7	20	55	7	12	15		7	1	40
8	20	44	8	11	54		8	1	16
9	20	31	9	11	33		9	0	52
10	20	19	10	11	12		10	0	28
11	20	5	11	10	51	Equino-	11	0	4
12	19	52	12	10	29		12	0	20
13	19	39	13	10	7		13	0	44
14	19	24	14	9	45		14	1	8
15	19	10	15	9	22		15	1	32
16	18	56	16	9	0	ctiall.	16	1	55
17	18	40	17	8	38		17	2	18
18	18	24	18	8	15	*North declination.*	18	2	41
19	18	9	19	7	53		19	3	5
20	17	53	20	7	30		20	3	29
21	17	36	21	7	8		21	3	52
22	17	20	22	6	45		22	4	14
23	17	2	23	6	22		23	4	38
24	16	45	24	5	59		24	5	1
25	16	27	25	5	35		25	5	24
26	16	10	26	5	12		26	5	47
27	15	51	27	4	49		27	6	10
28	15	33	28	4	25		28	6	33
29	15	13					29	6	56
30	14	55					30	7	19
31	14	35					31	7	40

A REGIMENT FOR THE SEA, 1574

1575. The thirde yeare.

April.			May.				June.		
D.	G.	M.	D.	G.	M.		D.	G.	M.
1	8	1	1	17	43		1	23	5
2	8	24	2	17	59		2	23	10
3	8	46	3	18	14		3	23	13
4	9	8	4	18	28		4	23	16
5	9	30	5	18	42		5	23	20
6	9	52	6	18	57		6	23	23
7	10	12	7	19	11		7	23	24
8	10	34	8	19	24		8	23	25
9	10	57	9	19	38	Solstic.	9	23	26
10	11	16	10	19	51		10	23	27
11	11	36	11	20	3	———	11	23	28
12	11	56	12	20	15		12	23	28
13	12	17	13	20	28		13	23	28
14	12	37	14	20	39	North declination.	14	23	27
15	12	57	15	20	51		15	23	26
16	13	16	16	21	1		16	23	25
17	13	35	17	21	12		17	23	24
18	13	54	18	21	22		18	23	22
19	14	14	19	21	32		19	23	20
20	14	32	20	21	42		20	23	17
21	14	51	21	21	51		21	23	13
22	15	10	22	22	0		22	23	10
23	15	27	23	22	8		23	23	6
24	15	46	24	22	16		24	23	1
25	16	4	25	22	24		25	22	55
26	16	22	26	22	30		26	22	50
27	16	38	27	22	37		27	22	44
28	16	54	28	22	43		28	22	37
29	17	10	29	22	50		29	22	31
30	17	27	30	22	55		30	22	24
			31	23	0				

(North declination. — April column)

1575. The thirde yeare.

	July.			August.				September.	
D.	G.	M.	D.	G.	M.		D.	G.	M.
1	22	16	1	15	30	North declination.	1	4	54
2	22	9	2	15	13		2	4	28
3	22	0	3	14	56		3	4	5
4	21	51	4	14	49		4	3	41
5	21	43	5	14	20		5	3	18
6	21	33	6	14	1		6	2	55
7	21	23	7	13	42		7	2	31
8	21	12	8	13	22		8	2	8
9	21	2	9	13	3		9	1	47
10	20	52	10	12	43		10	1	23
11	20	42	11	12	23	Equino-	11	0	59
12	20	30	12	12	2		12	0	36
13	20	18	13	11	42		13	0	12
14	20	6	14	11	23		14	0	12
15	19	57	15	11	2	ctiall.	15	0	36
16	19	40	16	10	41		16	0	59
17	19	26	17	10	20	———	17	1	23
18	19	13	18	9	58	South declination.	18	1	47
19	19	0	19	9	38		19	2	10
20	18	45	20	9	18		20	2	33
21	18	30	21	8	56		21	2	56
22	18	15	22	8	33		22	3	20
23	18	0	23	8	12		23	3	43
24	17	45	24	7	50		24	4	6
25	17	29	25	7	28		25	4	30
26	17	14	26	7	5		26	4	52
27	16	57	27	6	43		27	5	16
28	16	40	28	6	20		28	5	39
29	16	24	29	5	58		29	6	2
30	16	6	30	5	35		30	6	25
31	15	49	31	5	14				

(July column: North declination. August column: North declination.)

1576. The yeare of Bissextilis.

July.			August.				September.		
D.	G.	M.	D.	G.	M.		D.	G.	M.
1	22	10	1	15	17		1	4	33
2	22	2	2	15	0		2	4	10
3	21	53	3	14	42	North declination.	3	3	47
4	21	45	4	14	23		4	3	24
5	21	36	5	14	5		5	3	0
6	21	26	6	13	46		6	2	37
7	21	16	7	13	26		7	2	13
8	21	6	8	13	7		8	1	52
9	20	55	9	12	48		9	1	28
10	20	44	10	12	28		10	1	4
11	20	32	11	12	8		11	0	41
12	20	21	12	11	47	Equino-	12	0	18
13	20	9	13	11	28		13	0	6
14	19	56	14	11	7	North declination.	14	0	30
15	19	43	15	10	46		15	0	53
16	19	30	16	10	26	ctiall.	16	1	17
17	19	16	17	10	4		17	1	40
18	19	2	18	9	43	—	18	2	4
19	18	48	19	9	21		19	2	26
20	18	34	20	8	59	South declination.	20	2	50
21	18	19	21	8	37		21	3	13
22	18	4	22	8	16		22	3	37
23	17	48	23	7	56		23	4	0
24	17	33	24	7	33		24	4	23
25	17	19	25	7	11		25	4	46
26	17	2	26	6	49		26	5	9
27	16	45	27	6	26		27	5	32
28	16	28	28	6	3		28	5	55
29	16	11	29	5	40		29	6	19
30	15	53	30	5	19		30	6	42
31	15	36	31	4	57				

A REGIMENT FOR THE SEA, 1574

1576. The yeare of Bissextilis.

Apryll.			May.				Iune.		
D.	G.	M.	D.	G.	M.		D.	G.	M.
1	8	20	1	17	54	North declination.	1	23	8
2	8	41	2	18	9		2	23	12
3	9	3	3	18	24		3	23	15
4	9	25	4	18	38		4	23	19
5	9	46	5	18	53		5	23	22
6	10	8	6	19	7		6	23	24
7	10	29	7	19	21		7	23	25
8	10	50	8	19	34		8	23	26
9	11	11	9	19	48		9	23	27
10	11	31	10	20	0		10	23	28
11	11	51	11	20	12	North declination.	11	23	28
12	12	12	12	20	25		12	23	28
13	12	33	13	20	37	Solstic.	13	23	27
14	12	52	14	20	48		14	23	27
15	13	12	15	20	58		15	23	26
16	13	32	16	21	9		16	23	25
17	13	51	17	21	20		17	23	24
18	14	11	18	21	30		18	23	21
19	14	29	19	21	39		19	23	18
20	14	47	20	21	48		20	23	14
21	15	5	21	21	57		21	23	11
22	15	24	22	22	5		22	23	7
23	15	41	23	22	14		23	23	2
24	16	0	24	22	22		24	22	56
25	16	18	25	22	29		25	22	51
26	16	34	26	22	35		26	22	46
27	16	50	27	22	41		27	22	39
28	17	6	28	22	48		28	22	32
29	17	22	29	22	54		29	22	26
30	17	39	30	22	58		30	22	18
			31	23	3				

1576. The yeare of Bissextilis.

January.			February.				March.		
D.	G.	M.	D.	G.	M.		D.	G.	M.
1	21	59	1	14	21	*South declination.*	1	3	44
2	21	50	2	14	2		2	3	21
3	21	41	3	13	42		3	2	57
4	21	31	4	13	22		4	2	33
5	21	20	5	13	2		5	2	9
6	21	9	6	12	41		6	1	46
7	20	58	7	12	21		7	1	22
8	20	47	8	12	0		8	0	58
9	20	34	9	11	39		9	0	34
10	20	22	10	11	18		10	0	10
11	20	9	11	10	57		11	0	14
12	19	56	12	10	35	Equino-	12	0	38
13	19	43	13	10	13		13	1	0
14	19	28	14	9	51		14	1	24
15	19	13	15	9	28		15	1	48
16	18	59	16	9	6		16	2	12
17	18	44	17	8	44	ctiall.	17	2	35
18	18	29	18	8	21		18	2	59
19	18	14	19	7	59		19	3	22
20	17	57	20	7	36	*North declination.*	20	3	36
21	17	41	21	7	14		21	4	9
22	17	25	22	6	51		22	4	32
23	17	7	23	6	28		23	4	55
24	16	50	24	6	5		24	5	19
25	16	32	25	5	41		25	5	41
26	16	41	26	5	18		26	6	3
27	15	56	27	4	55		27	6	27
28	15	38	28	4	31		28	6	50
29	15	18	29	4	8		29	7	13
30	15	0					30	7	35
31	14	41					31	7	57

A REGIMENT FOR THE SEA, 1574

1575. The thirde yeare.									
October.			Nouember.				December.		
D.	G.	M.	D.	G.	M.		D.	G.	M.
1	6	48	1	17	16		1	23	0
2	7	10	2	17	33		2	23	6
3	7	34	3	17	49		3	23	11
4	7	55	4	18	5		4	23	15
5	8	18	5	18	22		5	23	18
6	8	40	6	18	37		6	23	21
7	9	3	7	18	52		7	23	24
8	9	25	8	19	7		8	23	26
9	9	46	9	19	21	Solstic.	9	23	27
10	10	8	10	19	35		10	23	27
11	10	30	11	19	49		11	23	28
12	10	53	12	20	2		12	23	28
13	11	13	13	20	15	South declination.	13	23	28
14	11	33	14	20	28		14	23	27
15	11	54	15	20	40		15	23	27
16	12	15	16	20	53		16	23	26
17	12	34	17	21	4		17	23	25
18	12	56	18	21	15		18	23	23
19	13	16	19	21	26		19	23	21
20	13	36	20	21	36		20	23	16
21	13	56	21	21	45		21	23	12
22	14	16	22	21	54		22	23	8
23	14	35	23	22	3		23	23	3
24	14	57	24	22	12		24	22	57
25	15	12	25	22	20		25	22	52
26	15	30	26	22	28		26	22	46
27	15	49	27	22	35		27	22	39
28	16	7	28	22	42		28	22	32
29	16	25	29	22	49		29	22	25
30	16	42	30	22	55		30	22	17
31	16	59					31	22	8

South declination. (October); *South declination.* (November)

1576. The yeare of Bissextilis.

October.			November.				December.		
D.	G.	M.	D.	G.	M.		D.	G.	M.
1	7	5	1	17	31		1	23	5
2	7	27	2	17	47		2	23	10
3	7	49	3	18	3		3	23	13
4	8	12	4	18	19		4	23	16
5	8	34	5	18	34		5	23	20
6	8	56	6	18	49		6	23	23
7	9	18	7	19	4		7	23	25
8	9	46	8	19	18		8	23	26
9	10	2	9	19	32		9	23	27
10	10	24	10	19	46		10	23	27
11	10	45	11	20	0		11	23	28
12	11	7	12	20	13	Solstic.	12	23	28
13	11	28	13	20	26	—	13	23	28
14	11	49	14	20	37	South declination.	14	23	27
15	12	10	15	20	50		15	23	26
16	12	31	16	21	1		16	23	25
17	12	51	17	21	12		17	23	24
18	13	11	18	21	23		18	23	21
19	13	31	19	21	33		19	23	18
20	13	51	20	21	43		20	23	13
21	14	11	21	21	52		21	23	9
22	14	30	22	22	1		22	23	6
23	14	50	23	22	11		23	23	0
24	15	9	24	22	19		24	22	54
25	15	27	25	22	27		25	22	49
26	15	46	26	22	34		26	22	43
27	16	4	27	22	41		27	22	35
28	16	22	28	22	48		28	22	28
29	16	39	29	22	51		29	22	21
30	16	56	30	22	59		30	22	13
31	17	14					31	22	4

South declination. (October column)

¶ The Balla Stella or Crosse staffe: to take the heigth of the Sunne or Starre.

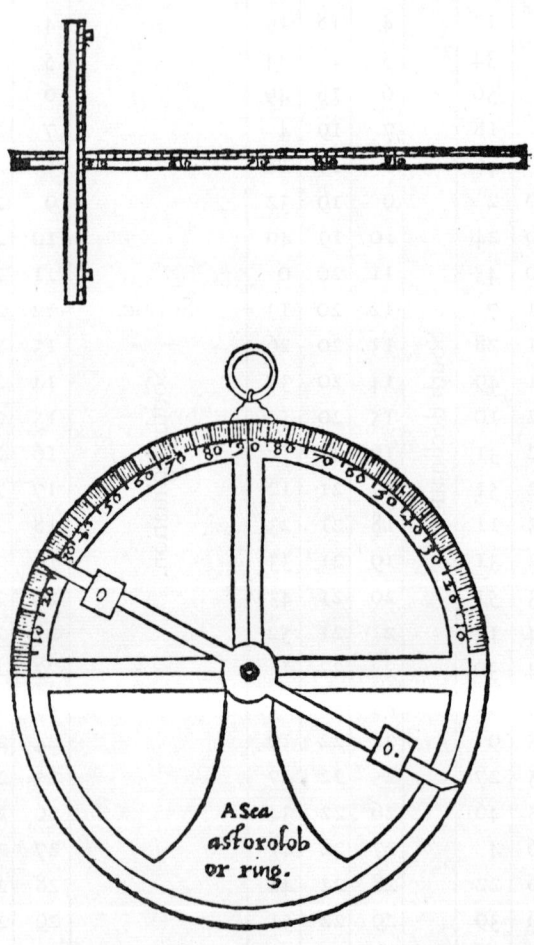

A Sea astrolob or ring.

¶ The sixt Chapter or rule sheweth, how to take the heigth of the Sun with the crosse staffe or with the Astrolobe, and also how to find the true Meridan, with other necessarie matters.

To take the true heigth of the Sunne at the Sea, the beste way is, to doe it with the crosse staffe: for that the Sea is moueable, and causeth the Shippe to heaue, and sette little or much: and also vpon the crosse staffe the degrees be larger marked than the Ring or Astrolobe: and in a large instrument an errour is seene sooner and better than it is in a small instrument.

Nowe to take the heigth of the Sunne, to knowe thy Altitude of the Pole aboue the Horizon, doe this: Firste set the Sunne with a compasse, to knowe when that the Sunne commeth near vnto the Meridian: as soone as you see that the Sunne is come vnto the South and by East, then beginne to take the heigth of the Sunne with the crosse staffe in this manner: Put the Transitorie vpon the long staffe, then set the end of the long staffe close at the corner of your eye, winking with your other eye, and remouing the Transitorie forwardes or backwardes, vntill you doe see the lower end of if (being iust with the Horizon) and the vpper ende of it, (being iust with the middle of the Sunne) both to agree with the Sunne and the Horizon at one time: and so haue you the true heigth of the Sunne: this done, Stil obserue ye same, vntil you see the Sunne at the highest and beginning to descende, and then haue you finished. Yet notwithstanding this is to be noted: that it is beste to take the heigth of the Sunne with the crosse staffe, when the Sunne is vnder 50. degrees in heigthe aboue the Horizon, for two causes. The one is this: till the Sunne be .50. degrees in heigthe the degrees be largely marked vppon the crosse staffe, but after (the Sunne being aboue .50. degrees high) they be lesser marked. The other is, for that the Sunne being vnder 50.

How to obserue ye sun.

To take ye heigth of the Sunne with the crosse staffe.

The cause why the crosse staffe is best to take the heigth of the Sun unto 50. degrees.

WILLIAM BOURNE

degrees in heigth, you may easily take the height, bycause you may easily see or viewe the vpper end and the nether end of the crosstaffe bothe at one time: but if it dothe exceede .50. degrees, then by the meanes of casting your eye vpwardes and downwardes so muche, you may soone commit error, and then in like manner the degrees be so small marked, that if the Sunne dothe passe .50. or .60. degrees in heigth, you must leaue the crosse staffe and vse the Mariners Ring, called by them the Astralaby, which they ought to call the Astrolobe. Nowe to take the heigth of the Sunne with the common Ring or Astrolobe, doe thus: The Sunne being (as before is declared) neare the Meridian or South, obserue it (vntill you haue the greatest heygth thereof) in this manner: Holde the Ring of the Astrolobe vpon one of youre fingers, and turne the Alhidada vppe and downe, vntil you see the shadowe of the Sunne pearse or passe thorough bothe the sightes thereof, being sure that the Astrolobe dothe hang vpright, whiche you may proue in this manner: Looke at howe many degrees and minutes the Alhidada dothe stande vppon the Astrolobe, then turne the Alhidada vnto the same number of the degrees and minutes on the other side of the Astrolobe, and then taking the heigth of the Sunne againe, if it doe agree as it did before, then the Astrolobe dothe hang vpright. but if it doe not, then it dothe not hang vpright. For knowledge of the true heigth of the Sun (the Astrolobe not hanging vpright) do thus: if the Astrolobe be truely marked, marke the diuersitie, that being knowne, rebate from the greatest beigth halfe the diuersitie, or else adde vnto the lesser heigth halfe the diuersitie, and that shall be the true heigth of the Sunne, although that the Astrolobe doth not hang vpright.

The Astrolobe is best to take the height of the Sun, if the Sunne be very high at .60.70. or 80. degrees, and the cause is this: the sunne coming so neere vnto your Zenith, hathe great power of light, for to pearce the .2. sights of the Alhidada of the Astrolobe, and then it is not good to vse the crosse staffe, for that the Sunne hurteth the eyes of a man, and besides that it is to

To take ye heigth of ye Sun with ye Astrolobe.

How to correct your Astrolobe if it dothe not hang vpright.

The astrlobe is best to take the heigth of the Sunne at .60. 70. or .80. degrees in heigth.

high to occupy the crosse staffe, (as before is declared) so that this way you may very much preserue your eyes. If you haue not glasses vpon your staffe (to saue your eyes in taking the heigth of the Sunne) but be vnprouided of them, do thus: take and couer the Sunne with the end of the transitorie of the crosse staffe, unto the very vpper edge or brinke of the Sunne (so shall you not neede to beholde the brightnesse of it) and with the other end of the transitorie to take the horizon truely, and that being done, for that the Sunne is .30. or 31. minuts in diameter or bredth, therefore you shall rebate .15. minutes from the altitude or beigthe of the Sunne, and then that whiche shall remaine shall be the true heigth of the Sunne from the center or middle of the Sunne. And furthermore there is some error in the taking the Sunne or Starre with the Ballastel or crosse staffe, and that groweth by this meanes: for that the true center (which is the sight of the eye) is within in the middle of the eye, and not in the outside of the eye: so that the end of the long staffe in the setting of it vnto the corner of your eye, dothe stande somewhat further out than the sight of your eye, that is too saye, that the sighte of the eye is somewhat further into the head, than the ende of the staffe dothe come: wherefore you must pare away a little of the ende of the staffe, for some mens vses more, and some mens vses lesse, for that it is according as you may set the staffe vnto your eye, for some mē neede pare away little or nothing, and some men must pare away .14. or .15. minutes as you may set the staffe: bycause some mens eyes be further into their head than other some mens are, and the bones of some mens face stand further out than other some do. It is moreouer conuenient to know the true meridian, or South, whiche you must do, either with a good compasse or with a perfyte diall or Needel: but if you be on the land this you may do: on a peece of timber, or any other thing that standeth fast, with a paire of compasses make a circle, then in the midle or center where the foote of the compasse did stand set a wire vpright (as circumspectly as you can) and then you may do this:

How to preserue youre eyes when you touch the Sunne with the crosse staffe and haue no glasses. The diameter of the Sunne is 30. or .31. minuts.

Some error in the crosse staffe and how to reforme it.

To get the true Medridian vpon the Land.

looke in the morning (so it be on plaine ground that you may see the horizon circle, without any let) at the Sunne rising, for the shadow of the wier, and there set a pricke: then at the setting of the Sunne you shall set another pricke; euen at the circumference of the circle, then deuide that with your compasses euen in .2. peeces, and strike a straight line from the wier or center of the circle, to the middle or deuided prick, & that shal be true meridian. Or else (the wier standing vprigth) first in the fore noone when the top of the wier doth touch, or is ready to come into the circumference or edge of the circle, there make a pricke: then in the after noone in like manner, at the very comming out or touching of the wyer, of the edge of the circle, there make an other pricke euen with the comming out of the shadow: this done (as circumspectly as you can) deuide these 2. prickes in the midle, then as before is said, drawe a line frō the center or wier, to the midle prick, and that shadow shal be your true meridian. After another manner you may doe this: looke and watch when the wyer giueth the shortest shadowe, and there make a pricke: then draw a line from that prick to the wyer, which shadow shall be the true meridian.

To knowe the true Meridian at the Sea, and also (if your compas be varied) and to know how much they be varied.

And yet furthermore, for y^t it is most cōuenient to know ye true Meridian at the Sea, bicause in long viages going far vnto the Westware or Eastward, the compasse doth varie: to find the true Meridian do this. Set the Sunne with your compasse at hir rising or appearing aboue ye horizon, & then (knowing what point & part the Sunne doth rise at) set the Sun with your compas at hir setting or departing vnder ye horizon & (that being known) you shal perfitly know, whether the compas be varied, & how much: for ensample this, I doe set the Sun at hir rising with the compas, & she doth rise vpō the East point: in like maner also I do set the Sun with hir compas at hir setting, & do find hir to set West Northwest: so I do see the compass to be varied one pointe, that is to say, the North point doth stand North and by East, &c. And furthermore (for that seldome times the Sun dothe rise and set cleere by the meanes of the cloudes, and other impediments neere the horizon) you may get the true Meridian thus: at any time in the fore noone, first set the Sunne with your compas, and then take the true heigth of the Sunne. Now you (knowing how many degrees yᵉ Sun was high at that point of the compas) may in like maner obserue the Sunne in the afternoon, vntill you do find the Sun iust at that heigth that it was in the forenoone, marking at what point of the compas the Sunne is, and so shall you see perfitely whether the compas be varied or no, and also howe much: for ensample thus: I take the Sun upon the Southest poynt .20. degrees aboue the horizon, & then in the after noone I do obserue the Sun vntil such time as I do find the Sunne iust .20. degrees aboue the horizon again, & then I set yᵉ Sun with the compas and do find yᵉ Sun to be at .20. degrees in heigth west Southwest, so that I see yᵉ compas to be varied one point, yᵗ is to say the North point doth stand North & by East. &c. Another way also to know yᵉ true meridian, is by the Sun: that is, to set yᵉ Sun with yᵉ cōpas at hir greatest heigth aboue the horizon, & so you shall know whither yᵉ cōpas be varied, & how much: & looke what is spokē of yᵉ Sun by day, you may do the like by night by any of the Starres yᵗ you perfectly do know, doing as you do by yᵉ Sun in all points: but you cannot do it so well and truly by the Moone, by the meanes of the swiftnes of yᵉ moones motiō in the Zodiack, you may also find the variatiō of yᵉ cōpas by the North Starre, as thus: set yᵉ North Star with the compas, if the North point do stande right with the Starre, then it is not varied, but if it dothe not stande ryghte wyth the Starre, then it is varied: and that must be done when the .2. Starres of Charles Waine called the pointes be right vnder, or right ouer the North Star, but if that the Starres be West from the North Starre, then the North Starre is the third part of a point vnto the Eastward of the North pole. If the .2. Starres of Charles Wayne called the poynters be due east from the North Starre, then the North Starre is the third part of a point vnto the westwarde of the North pole .&c. This

To find the variation of the compas in the night by yᵉ Starres but not by the Moone

haue I saide bycause that sometime in sundry places, the compasse doth varie, & especially in the sayling of long viages running East and West, (called the Northeasting or Northwesting of the compasse) therefore I would not wish them to meddle with the mending of their compasse or whetting of the side of the needell to the end to make it to stand due North, but circumspectly to awaite the altering of the compasse, and what quantitie it doth alter: as you may do very well, by the order before rehersed, and then let your compasse alone: for although that it dothe varie .2. or .3. poynts, you may make account according to the variation as thus: I admit the Northwest point standeth due North, and my course is to go due West, I will occupy the Southwest pointe in this case for the west poynte. And thus (by oberuation and trying of my compas) I care not what point standeth due North, for it is all one, so that you consider what poynt standeth North. And now furthermore, some are of that opinion, that (by the Northeasting or Northwesting of the compasse) you may knowe the Longitude: but I am not of the opinion, for I admit that it be so (as some do affirme) that the compasse doth varie, (as some haue said) that is, that you being .90. degrees vnto the Westwarde (from the place youre compasse was made at) youre North poynt should stand Northeast: and in like maner you being .90. degrees East, your North poynt should stand Northwest: then by that order the compasse should vary one poynt at .22. degrees and a halfe, and that commeth vnto .450. english leagues (if you be neere vnto the equinoctial:) wherefore no master or pilotte of a shippe, doth keepe so simple account of the shippes way, but that he may knowe what distance he hath vnto any place better than he shal know by the variing of the compas: & also whether it be so or not y^t the cōpas doth keepe any such proportion in the variatiō, I do refer that vnto them that haue tried the experience therof: for I for my part can say nothing in that matter. Wherfore I cease from writing muche thereof, althoughe the Sea men by very desirous to haue some way to get

Medell not with your compasse although it be varied.

To saile by the compas that is varied.

As touching Longitude to be found by the Northeasting or Northwesting of the compasse.

the Longitude. But if it be true that the compasse doth verie by that proportion, then it were very good for them to practise that matter that shoulde make any discouery vnto the Northwardes, for that the degrees be so short in those Paralels.

> *The seuenth Chapter sheweth how*
> *to handle the declination of the Sunne, to knowe*
> *the altitude of the North pole aboue the horizon, (the*
> *heigth of the Sunne being truely taken and kno-*
> *wen in any place betweene the North pole*
> *and the Equinoctiall) so that the Sunne*
> *be vnto the Southwards of you, at*
> *the taking of the Sunne vp-*
> *pon the Meridian.*

You must consider by the regiment or table of declination (going before) that the .11. day of Marche the Sunne is equinoctiall entring then the firste point of Aries (called the equinoctiall of spring time) where she hath no declination. The .10. day of Aprill the Sunne entreth into the firste minute of *Taurus*, then hauing declination to the Northwardes .11. degrees .30. minuts. The .12. day of May, the Sunne entreth the first poynte of *Gemini*, hauing then declination .20. degrees .12. minuts. The .12. day of June the Sunne entreth into *Cancer* where he (making his greatest progresse to the Northwards) hath .23. degrees .28. minuts of declination. But now in this our time, some do affirme it to be .23. degrees and a halfe, but it lacketh .2. minuts. The .14. day of Julie, the Sunne entreth into *Leo*. comming dounwards to the Equinoctiall, hauing .20. degrees .12. minutes of declination. The .14. day of August the Sunne entreth into *Virgo*, hauing declination, 11. degrees .30. minutes. The .14. of September, the Sunne entreth into Libra, (then being Equinoctiall, and hauing no declination) whiche is called the Equinoctiall of Autumne or haruest, where he beginneth his South declination. The .14. of October the Sun entreth into

The greatest declination of the Sunne.

Equinoctiall of Autumne.

Scorpio, where his declination is .11. degrees .30. minutes. The .12. of Nouember the Sun entreth into *Sagittarius*, his declination being .20. degrees .12. minutes. The .12. day of December, the Sunne entreth the firste minute of *Capricorne*, where the Sunne (making greatest progresse to the Southwards) hath of declination .23. degrees and .28. minutes. From whence he retourneth to the equinoctiall againe. The .11. of January the Sunne entreth into *Aquarius*, where his declination is 20. degrees .12. minutes. The 10. day of February the Sunne entreth into the first minute of *Pisces*, and hath of declination .11. degrees .30. minutes. The 11. day of March, the Sunne retourneth to the selfesame place that it departed from before, wherefore the Egyptians did paint the yeare like to an adder biting hir tayle, and (not hauing the vse of letters) they made a ring and named it *annulus*, as it were *annus*, that is to saye a yeare: bycause a ring dothe turne rounde in it selfe as dothe the yeare. The heigth of the Sunne beeing knowen, you (knowing the day of the mooneth, and what yeare it is after the *Bissextilis*) must turne to the day of the mooneth, in the regiment or table going before, where right againste the day of the mooneth you shall find the degrees of declination and the odde minuts belonging to the degrees of declination following: that being knowen (that is to say, the heigth of the Sun with the degrees and minutes of the declination) if the Sunne haue North declination, you shall subtract or take away the Sunes declination from the heigth of the Sunne, with the degree and minutes: and then that which remaineth shall be the true heigth of the Equinoctial: whiche being knowen, pulling that sūme out of .90. with the degrees and minuts, that whiche dothe remaine shall be the true heigth of the North pole aboue the horizon. But if that the Sunne hathe South declination, you shall adde or put that declination vnto the heigth of the Sunne, whiche shall shewe vnto you the true heigth of the Equinoctiall: of the which sūme (being taken from .90.) that which doth remain shall be the altitude of the North pole aboue the horizon. For this is to be

The greatest declination to the South.

The yeare is compared vnto a ring or an adder biting hir tayle.

The heigth of the Sun being taken and knowē then how to handle the declination to know the heigth of the pole.

noted: looke what heigth the Equinoctiall is aboue the horizon, it is equall or iust so much betweene the Zenith or verticall point and the North Pole. In like manner: looke how many degrees and minutes are betweene the Equinoctiall and your Zenith, iust that number of degrees and minuts is from the North pole, downe to the horizon, which is the cause that you must pull the heigth of the Equinoctial, from the horizon with the degrees and minutes. For that your Zenith is alwayes .90. degrees from the horizon as you see by this figure.

Things to be noted as touching the taking of the altitude of the pole.

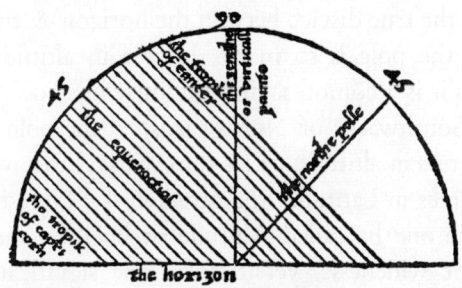

The .8. Chapter sheweth you how to handle the declination of the Sunne, when you are betweene the Equinoctiall and the Sunne: that is to say, the Sunne being to the Southwards or Northwards of you and the Equinoctial, or vnder the Equinoctiall: the heigth of the Sunne being truely knowen or taken.

Now furthermore if you be vnto the South parts neare vnto the equinoctiall, so that the Sunne haue any great declination either to the Southwards or yᵉ Northwards, you being between the equinoctial and the Sunne, when you haue taken the true heigth of the Sun with yᵉ Astrolobe, to know the heigth of any of the .2. poles do this: seeke the declination of the Sun for that day with the degrees & minuts, the declinatiō being known & the heigth of the Sunne in like maner, then adde yᵉ declinatiō of the Sun vnto the heigth thereof, & it will exceede or be more than .90. degrees, then againe looke how many degrees it is more thā .90. with degrees & minuts, that shall be the true heigth of the pole towards that side that the Sun is: bycause ye Equinoctial is ye number of degrees aboue .90. (which is your Zenith) to the contrary part frō the Sunwards. For (as I haue said in ye chapter going before & is general for euer) looke what heigth soeuer ye Equinoctial be frō ye horizo, that is the true distance betweene ye Zenith and the pole: in like maner looke what distance is betweene the Equinoctial & the Zenith, ye same is the true distāce betwen the horizon & the pole, that is to say, the pole is so many degrees in altitude aboue ye horizō. As it is a cōmon saying (in knowing how farre we be vnto the Southwards or Northwards) y^t the pole artick is so many degrees in altitude, or (as som wil say) that we are in so many degrees in Latitude: the question is all one in effect, although the one be called Altitude or heigthe, and the other Latitude or widenesse, yet it hathe one signification: for as when you say altitude or heigth of the Pole, you meane the Pole is raysed so many degrees aboue the Horizon. So likewise when you say Latitude, you mean you be so many degrees in widenesse frō the Equinoctiall: for that your Zenith or verticall pointe is so many degrees frō the Equinoct. Moreouer if you chaunce to be right vnder ye Equinoctial, as you cānot say that you haue any Latitude, so likewise cannot you say that you haue any Altitude, for that the two Poles be then iust with your Horizon, and in like maner the Equinoctiall is your Zenith or Verticall poynte. But when you will take the heigth of the Sunne with your Astrolobe, then looke what declination the Sunne hath, either to the Southwardes or Northwardes. Then put the declination of the Sunne vnto the heigthe of the same, and the number will be iust .90. degrees: if it lacketh any thing of .90. degrees, then it signifieth that the Equinoctiall lacketh so much of the Zenith, and so muche iust shal the pole be aboue ye Horizon towards that part that you be in from the Sunne

A thing to be noted.

Altitude or Latitude is all one question in effect.

Being under the Equinoctiall you haue neither Latitude nor altitude, for that the Equinoctial is your Zenith and the Poles your Horizon.

A REGIMENT FOR THE SEA, 1574

wardes. But contrarywise, if it dothe exceede or be any thing more than .90. degrees, then (as afore is declared) it signifieth that the Equinoctiall is as much as that number (both in degrees and minutes.) On the contrary side, from the Sunne wardes, that is to say, your Zenithe shal be betweene the Sunne and the Equinoctial, & the Pole shall be so many degrees or minutes aboue the Horizon, as is the distance betweene the Zenith and the Equinoctiall, towardes that part or side that the Sunne is on. Wherefore I do think it necessarie to giue certaine ensamples (and first take this for an ensample.) Admit I doe take the heigth of the Sunne vnto the Northwards .80. degrees aboue the Horizon, and the Sunne hathe declination vnto the Northwardes .20. degrees, to which I adde or put the heigth, that is to say .80. degrees (being the heigth of the Sunne) and .20. degrees. (being the declination of the Sunne) doe make .100. frō which I pull .90. away (which is my Zenith) and so ther remayneth .10. degrees. Wherefore you may conclude that the Equinoctiall is .10. degrees to the South parte of youre Zenith, and the Sunne to be .10. degrees to the North parte of your Zenith, so that the North Pole is .10. degrees aboue the Horizon, as by this example it is declared.

Of your zenith being y^e Equinoctiall and the Sunne.

An ensāple.

An ensāple where the pole is 10. degrees aboue the Horizon.

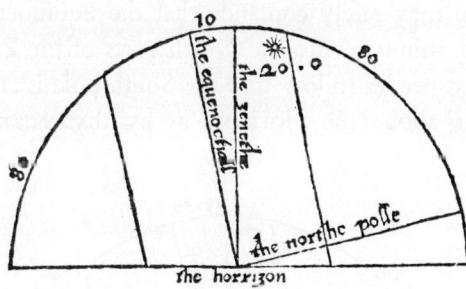

And for the second enzample, admit I take the Sunne vnto the Northwards .75. degrees and .20. minutes aboue the Horizon, the Sunne hauing North declination .14. degrees .40. minutes, I then do adde or put .14. degrees .40. minutes vnto

.75. degrees .20. minutes, and those .2. ioyned togither maketh .90. degrees, whereof you may conclude that the Equinoctiall is your Zenith, and then the .2. Poles be with your Horizon, as by this example it doth appeare.

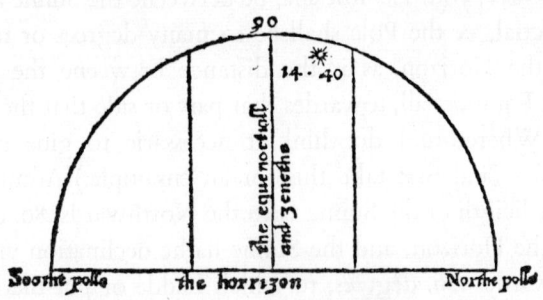

And now followeth the .3. ensample. I admit the Sunne be taken with the Astrolobe .81. degrees and .15. minutes aboue the horizon, and the same hathe South declination .22. degrees .35. minutes, wherefore I do adde or pute togither .81. degrees and .15. minutes (being the heigth of the Sunne) and 22. degrees .35. minutes (being the declination) and that maketh .103. degrees .50. minutes: from which I take away .90. degrees (which is my Zenith) so that there remayneth .13. degrees .50. minutes: so that you may safely conclude that the Equinoctiall is .13. degrees .50. minutes vnto the North parts of the Zenith, and then it must needes follow that the South pole is .13. degrees .50. minuts aboue the Horizon, as by thys ensample it is declared.

An ensáple.

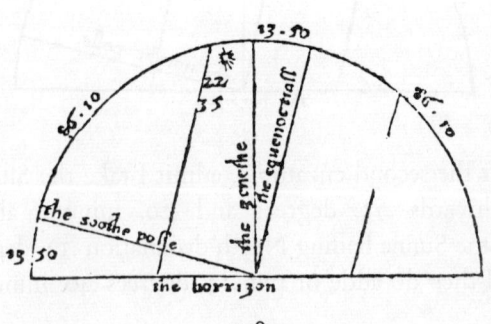

A REGIMENT FOR THE SEA, 1574

*The nynth Chapter sheweth how
to handle the declination of the Sunne, when
you are beyond the Equinoctiall, that is to say,
betweene the South pole and the Equinoctiall: with certaine ensamples
both for the South pole
and the North
pole.*

And furthermore if you be vnto yᵉ Southwards beyond yᵉ Equinoctial, as betweene yᵉ tropick of *Capricorne* & yᵉ South pole, then to vse the declination of yᵉ Sun to know yᵉ heigth of the South pole or antartick pole by the heigth of the Sun, there is no other matter in the doing thereof, but whereas we (being vnto the North partes) do adde the South declination vnto the heigth of the Sunne, and rebate the North declination from the heigth of the Sunne, so in like manner the contrary is to be vsed: that is to say, to rebate the South declination from the heigth of the Sunne, and to adde vnto the heigth of the Sun the North declination. As for ensample. I admit the heigth of the sun be taken .28. degrees aboue yᵉ Horizon due North, & the declination of the Sun be .21. degrees vnto the Nothwards, I do thē adde the declination of yᵉ sun which is .21. degrees vnto the heigth of the Sun (being 28. degrees) which maketh .49. degrees, & so many degrees yᵉ Equinoctial is aboue the Horizon vnto the Northwards, & then (as is before declared) pull that sum out from .90. degrees, and there remaineth .41. degrees, which is the distance betweene the Zenith and the Equinoctiall, whiche alwayes is equall with the distance betweene the Pole and the Horizon: so that you may conclude the South Pole to be raysed .41. degrees aboue the Horizon. As by this figure it is shewed.

To take yᵉ Sun to the Northwardes you being betweene the south Pole and the Equinoctiall.

An ensāple by taking yᵉ South pole 41. degrees aboue the Horizon.

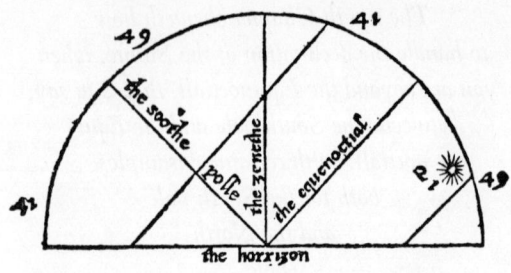

And furthermore, if the Sunne haue South declination, then (as before is declared) you must subtract or take away the Sunnes declination from the heigth of the Sunne: as for ensample. The heigth of the Sunne being taken at .50. degrees .30. minutes vnto the North partes, and the Sunne hauing .7. degrees and .15. minutes of declination vnto the southwards, from which heigth of the Sun (for that you are vnto the Southwards beyond the Equinoctial) you must rebate the declination which is .7. degrees and .15. minuts, and there resteth .43. degrees .15. minuts, for the true heigth of the Equinoctial, which summe you must take out of .90. degrees, that done, there remayneth .46. degrees .45. minutes, the true heigth of the South Pole aboue the Horizon, otherwise called the Antarticke Pole, as by ensample of this Figure is playnely shewed.

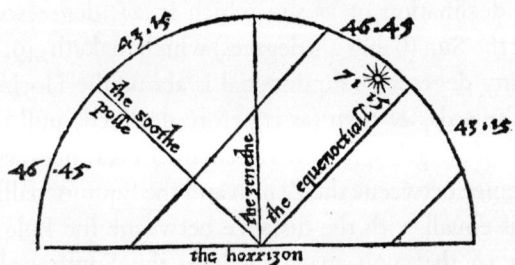

An ensāple by taking y^e north pole 60. degrees aboue the Horizon.

Yet furthermore I do thinke it conuenient to giue you an ensample vnto the North wardes, that you maye perfectly knowe the true order of the working, bothe for the North parte and also the South parte. Admit therefore I take the heigth of the Sunne due South, at .50. degrees aboue the Horizon the

Sunne hauing then north declination .20. degrees: Now (for as much as you haue the north Pole aboue the horizon) you must rebate the Suns declination frō the heigth: so that .20. degr. being taken away from .50. there resteth .30. whiche is the heigth of the Equinoctiall aboue the Horizon, and that .30. being taken from .90. there resteth .60. So that you maye boldly affirme the North Pole to be .60. degrees aboue the Horizon, as by this figure folowing it is shewed.

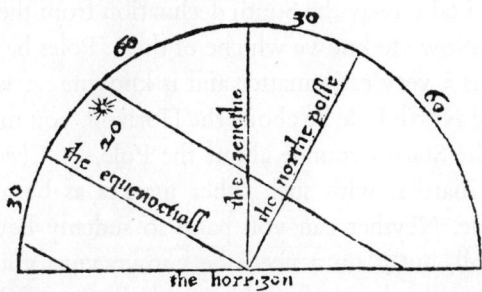

In like maner the Sunne being taken at the heigth and due South, hauing the like declination also to the Southwardes that it had before to the Nortwardes: that is to say, being .50. degrees in heigth, and hauing .20. degrees of declination vnto the South partes, you muste adde or put the declination of the Sunne vnto the heigth of the same, and if maketh .70. degrees which is the heigth of the Equinoctiall aboue the Horizon, this done, that .70. being taken out of .90. there remayneth but .20. so that the North Pole is but .20. degrees aboue the Horizon, as by the ensample of this figure it is shewed

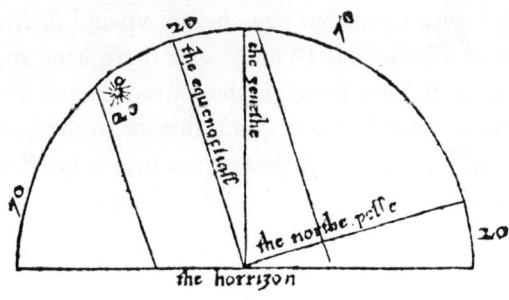

For in handling of the declination the true heigth of any of the Poles is knowne. Always hauyng this consideration, that if they haue the North Pole aboue the Horizon, they do alwayes adde or put too the heigth of the Sun, the South declination of the same. Or the Sunne hauing Morth declination, they pul away the Sunnes declination from the heigth thereof. Nowe contrarywise, if the South Pole be aboue the Horizon, you muste adde the North declination vnto the heigth of the Sunne, and take away the South declination from the heigth of the same. Nowe to knowe whiche of the 2. Poles be aboue the Horizon, is a very easie matter and is knowne .2. wayes. For firste if the North Pole be aboue the Horizon, you may knowe it by all the Starres rounde about the Pole, as *Charles Wayne* and the Guardes, with such other markes as be aboute the North Pole. Neyther can you passe so sudenly beyound the Equinoctiall, but it must needs be known vnto you, & then you must vse that kynd of working with the Sunnes declination that in the chapter or rule before is rehearsed: and also you may knowe it by the Arke or bearing of the Starres and lyghtes rounde aboute you. Thus much haue I sayd as touching the Suns declination, bycause I knowe that diuers English men would haue trauelled further beyonde the Equinoctiall than they haue done, but that they haue not had the capacitie to handle the Sunnes declination when they haue bene beyonde the Equinoctiall, that is to say, vnto the South partes, hauing lost the markes about the North Pole as the North Starre and other, and as for the Stars of the South, they haue not bene acquainted with them, but haue beaten vp and downe alongst the coast of Ginnie and Bynney, and there haue spoiled and consumed their men through the extraordinarie heat of the Sunne, not knowing that in going further to the South partes they should haue brought themselues into a good temperate clymate againe.

A thing to be noted in ye handling of the Sūnes declination.

Howe to know whiche of the .2. poles be vnder the horizon.

The cause why englishmē haue not traueled far beyonde the Equinoctiall.

An vntemperat place for extreme heate. Temperate clymate.

The 10. Chapter sheweth, howe to handle the Sunnes declination vnto the Northwards, where the Sunne doth not set vnder the Horizon, and also to take the Sunne at the lowest being due North.

For further vse of the Sunnes declination, if you haue any occasion to trauell vnto the Northwardes or Southwardes more than .67. degrees of Altitude of any of the .2. Poles, or if the sunne haue any great declination vnto those partes that you are in, thē shall not the Sun go down vnder the Horizon in a long time, after as you be in distance vnto the North parts, for if you were right vnder either of the .2. Poles of the world, then would not the Sunne go vnder the Horizon in halfe a yeare, so that there should be continually day: And now for the handling of the Sunnes declination, to knowe ye heigth of the Pole, & to take the Sun North at the lowest, do this: First with your crosse staffe obserue the Sun at the lowest, taking the true distance betweene the Horizon and the Sunne, that being truely done, looke what declination the Sunne hath, then haue you to consider, that except the Sunne be neare vnto hir greatest declination, that is to say, in the latter end of *Gemini*, or the beginning of *Cancer*) the Sunne dothe decline little in .24. houres: but if the declination be very swift, you must seeke the Sunnes declination vpon the day before, and the daye after, halfe the diuersitie of whych shall be the Sunnes declination: for that the sunne is at the angle of mydnight. The Sunnes true declination being knowne, rebate the heigth of the same from the declination of the Sunne, & so that you haue the true contente in degrees and minuts that the Equinoctiall is vnder the Horizon due North, and then pulling that sum from .90. that which remaineth shal be the heigth of the pole aboue the Horizon: for (as it is before declared) looke what heigth the Equinoctial is aboue the Horizon, that is equal the distance betweene the Pole and the Zenith, and looke what distance is betweene the Equinoctiall and the Zenith, the same distaunce is betweene the

Of being vnder either of ye poles.

Of taking the heigth of the sun due north at the lowest.

A thing worthy to be noted as touching ye sunnes declination.

A thing to be noted of the pole and the Equinoctiall the Zenith and the Horizon.

Pole and the Horizon; in like manner, looke howe deepe vnder the Horizon the Equinoctiall is vnto the Northwards, so far equall is the heigth of the Equinoctial vnto the southwards. As for ensample: admit I were vnto yᵉ Northwards of the North cape, the Sun being in hir greatest declination vnto the Northwards, whiche is about the .11. day of June .23. degrees and

The Sun taken due North at .6. degrees.

neere a halfe, this being knowen I take the Sunne due North at the lowest, iust .6. degrees aboue the Horizon, the declination being 23. degrees and .28. minutes. Wherefore I rebate from that .6. degrees and so there remayneth .17. degrees and .28 minutes. For the depth of the Equinoctiall vnder the Horizon, and then do I pull that sunne from .90. and there remayneth 72. degrees .32. minutes for the true heigth of the North pole aboue the Horizon, as by this ensample it is declared.

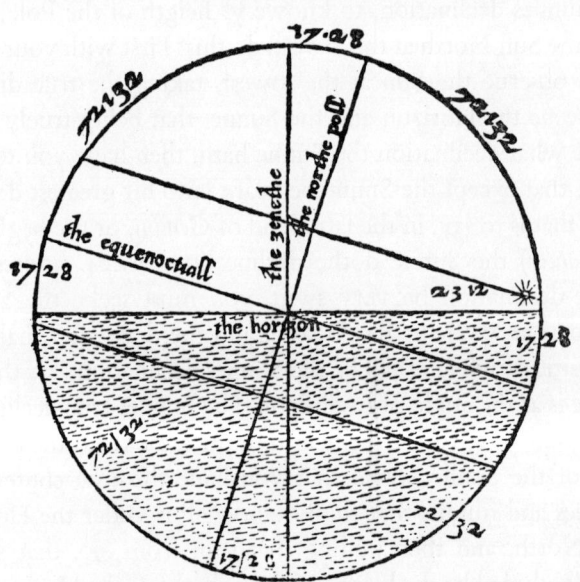

By this ensample you may also know the true heigth of any of the .2. poles, and how to obserue the Sunne at the lowest when the Sunne commeth neerest vnto the Horizon, as well as you may when the Sunne is vpon the Meridian at the greatest

A REGIMENT FOR THE SEA, 1574

heigth from the Horizon, which is very necessary for them that do occupy vnto the Northwardes of Sainct Nicholas in Rousey, it is also very necessary for them that would attempt any viages of discouery vnto the Northwards, as into the East by *Noua Zemla*, or to the West by cape de *Paramantia*, on the backe side of the North part of the tayle of *America*, otherwise called the backe side of *Bacula*, whiche if it were attempted, there is no doubt but they shoulde finde it nauigable eyther to the East parte or to the West part: and I am of this opinion, that the thing moste feared in making their discouery vnto the Northward, deserueth not so greatly to be feared as they do make it, the cause why they are so loth to go very farre vnto the Northwards is, for that is the frosen zone, but my opinion is, that in sommer tyme it is not to be feared, but the further vnto the Northwardes the more temperate warme, by meanes of the long continuaunce of the Sunne: for as we see by common experience that a thing once being made warme cannot sodenly be made cold, neither is there doubt of any great cold vntill the Sunne be vnto the Southwards of the Equinoctiall: for I admit that a ship should sayle vnto the Northwards, and not stay vntill the North pole were eleuated .80. degrees aboue the Horizon, I do thinke then they should find it very temperate and warme vnto the midle of September, for that by the space of .9. weekes togyther (that is to say from the .10. day of May, vnto the .12. day of July) the Sun should come no neerer vnto the Horizon due North that .10. degrees or .30. degrees vnto the South part aboue the Horizon: and yet is possible that it may be cold there vntill the ende of May, for that the Sunne must haue a time to make the aire warme. For like as a thing once beeing colde cannot bee sodaynely made warme, so in like manner a place being once made warme cannot bee sodainely made colde. And furthermore he that were in the Latitude of .80. degrees shoulde haue but a short paralele: for the whole compasse of the earth and Sea going East and West too come rounde about to that place agayne in the same paralele is but .1250.

Of viages for discouery to the Northwards eyther to the Eastward by Noua Zemla or to the West ward by cape de Paramantia.

Of temperatenesse the pole being raysed 80. degrees.

The length of the paralele at .80. degrees is but .1250. english leagues.

english leagues, euery league conteining .3. englishe miles: So that in sayling of lesse than 500. or .600. leagues, they myght see whether it were nauigable or not.

The eleuenth Chapter doth shew
how you shall know the length of the
day, and to knowe how much the day
is shortened or lengthened
by the Sunnes de-
clination.

Nowe I thinke it conuenient for Seafaring men to knowe the length of the day in anye place that they haue occasion too go vntoo: for that they haue occasion too trauell intoo all the climates and places, transporting them selues manye tymes quickly from one place vntoo another: and although the aunciente writers haue appoynted certayne climates, and other late writers in lyke manner haue made tables very exact for the longest or shortest day in anye of those climates, and other places, according to the eleuation of the pole: yet haue they not opened anye way vntoo them in gyuing anye order for them to knowe when the daye is an houre longer or shorter, whereby they might at all times knowe the length of the day, which notwithstanding is very necessary for them, for that they be abroad vnder sayle bothe night and day, and in like manner for that they must keepe account of houres and times exactly, in as muche as they ought to keepe an account of the shippes way: wherefore it must needes be most necessary for nauigation, to knowe the true time of the Sunne rising and setting, whiche you shall knowe by this meanes: first this is not vnknowne, that vnder the Equinoctiall the Sunne is .12. houres aboue the Horizon, and .12. houres vnder the Horizon, (what declination soeuer the Sunne hath) so that here the Sunne ryseth at .6. of the clocke and setteth at .6. of the clocke for euer. And where the pole is raysed .16. degrees and .44. minutes, there the

How necessary it is for a Seafaring man to know the lēgth of the day. Vnder the Equinoctial the day is always .12. houres lōg. The pole 16. degrees .44. minutes. the day .13. houres long when it is at the lōgest.

A REGIMENT FOR THE SEA, 1574

longest day is .13. houres, (the Sunne hauing hir greatest declination at .23. degrees .28. minutes) and the shortest day is 11. houres long: and then looke when the Sunne hath declined .23. degrres and a halfe eyther backwards or forwardes, for then the day is an houre longer or shorter and proportionable: when the Sunne hath declined .11. degrees .44. minutes then it is halfe an houre longer or shorter . &c. Moreouer wher the pole is eleuated .30. degrees .48. mintes, there the longest day is .14. houres and the shortest day is .10. houres long, the Sunne then rising at .5. of the clocke and setting at .7. of the clocke, and there when the Sunne hath declined .11. degrees and .44. minutes from the Equinoctiall . &c. vnto the greatest declination, then the day is an houre longer or shorter, and whē the Sunne hath declined .5. degrees .52. minutes then the day is halfe an houre longer or shorter . &c. Furthermore also, where the pole is raised .41. degrees .23. minutes, there the longest day is .15. houres, and the shortest .9. houres long, (the Sunne hauing hir greatest declination, and as thē rising at .4. of the clocke .30. minutes, and setting at .7. of the clock .30. minutes) so that there when the Sunne hath declined .7. degrees .49. minutes from the Equinoctiall, the day shall be an houre longer or shorter, and when it hath declined 3. degrees .54. minutes, the day shall be halfe an houre longer or shorter &c. And furthermore, where the Pole is raysed .49 degrees one minute there the longest day is .16. houres, and the shortest .8. houres long, the Sunne rysing at .4. of the clocke, and setting at .8. of the clocke, so that there when the Sunne hath declyned .5. degrees .52. minutes from the Equinoctiall, then shall the daye be an houre longer or shorter. And when the Sunne hath declyned .2. degrees .56. minutes, then the daye shall be halfe an houre longer or shorter . &c. Yet furthermore, where the Pole is raysed .54. degrees .30. minutes, there the longest day is .17. houres, and the shortest 7. houres long, the Sunne then rysing at .3. of the clocke .30. minutes and setting at 8. and .30. minutes: where when the Sun hath declyned .4. degrees & .41.

The pole 30. degrees 48. minuts the longest day .14. houres lōg.

The pole 41. degrees. 23. minutes the longest day .15. houres lōg.

The pole raised .49. deg. .1. mi. then the longest day is 16. houres long

The pole raised .54. deg. 30. mi. then the longest daye is 17. houres long.

minutes from the Equinoctial, to the greatest declynatiō, the day is an hour longer or shorter, and when she hath declined .2. degrees .21. minuts, the day is halfe an houre longer or shorter . &c. Where also the Pole is raysed .58. degrees .27. minutes, there the longest day is .18. houres long, and the shortest but .6. and there when the Sunne hath declined .3. degrees .55. minuts from the equinoctiall, then the day shall be an hour longer or shorter: and when the Sunne hath declyned .2. degrees lacking .2. minuts, then the day shall be halfe an houre longer or shorter. Furthermore also wher the pole is raised .61. degrees .18. minuts, there the longest day is .19. houres long, and the shortest but .5. houres: then shall the Sunne ryse at .2. of the clocke .30. minutes, and set .9. and .30. minutes, and there when the Sun hath declined .3. degrees and .21 minutes from the Equinoctiall, then shall the daye be an houre longes or shorter . &c. Furthermore, where the Pole is raysed .63. degrees .22. minutes, there the longest daye is .20. houres long, and the shortest but .4. houres, then shall the Sunne ryse at two of the clocke, and sette at tenne of the clocke, and when the Sunne hath declyned two degrees, and fiftie sixe minutes from the Equinoctiall vnto the greatest declination, ther shall the day be an houre longer or shorter &c. Now where the pole is raysed .64. degrees .49. minutes, there the longest day shall be .21. houres long, and the shortest but .3. houres: And there when the Sun hath declined but .2. degrees .36. minutes from the Equinoctiall vnto the greatest declination, the day shall be an houre longer or shorter. Where also the pole is raised .65. degrees, there the longest day shall be .22. houres and the shortest but .2. houres long, and when that the Sunne hath declyned but .2. degrees. and 20. minutes from the Equinoctiall &c. then the day shall be an houre longer or shorter . &c. And where the pole is raysed .66. degrees .20. minutes the longest day shall be .23. houres long and the shortest but one houre long. and then when that the Sunne hath declined but .2. degrees. and .8. minutes, then the day shall be an houre longer or shorter, and then where that the North pole is raysed .66. degrees and .32. minutes, there it is 24. houres long, for that when the Sunne hath hir greatest declination vnto the Northwardes, then at midnight you shall see halfe the Sunne, and then when that the Sun hathe the greatest declination vnto the South parts, then you shal see but halfe the Sunne at noone, and then in the going but 15. miles further vnto the Northwards, that is, but one quarter of a degree, then the Sunne shall be cleane aboue the Horizon at the due North, and not seene vnto the South at noone aboue the Horizon, the Sunne hauing hir greatest declination to the South, and then the day shal be an hour longer or shorter when that the Sunne hath declined one degree .57. minutes from the Equinoctiall and so foorth vnto the greatest declination. And thus much haue I sayd as touching the length of the daye, whereby you maye knowe at all times the true length of the day in any Latitude betweene the Equinoctiall and the eleuation of the pole at .66. degrees and 32. minutes, by knowing howe manye degrees the Sunne is declined, and that you may know on euery day by the regiment going before, hauing this consideration, that if the Sunne being vppon the Equinoctiall, and hauing no declination, that then in anye Latitude the daye is always iust .12. houres long. And you must note this, that it is called the day from the rising of the Sunne vnto the setting of the same vnder the Horizon and not from day light vnto day light. For before the Sun rise and after that the Sun is set it is counted for no parcell of the day but it is called the day light. And furthermore, the day light will appeare by that time that the Sunne doth touch the .17. degree of the Horizon before the Sunne rising, and also the day light will not be cleane gone vntill the Sunne be more than .17. degrees vnder the Horizon: for as you may perceiue here with vs at London that when the Sunne hath hir greatest declination vnto the Northwards in June that the day light remaineth all night, for that the Sunne goeth not vnder the Horizon, but .15. degrees and .2. minutes.

The pole 66. degrees 32. minutes then the Sun shall not set vnto them.

The Sun clean aboue the Horizon due North and not to appeare aboue the Horizon South at noone.

To knowe the length of the day at any time in any place. What the day is.

WILLIAM BOURNE

*The twelfth Chapter is of
the North Starre.*

As touching the North Starre I say but little thereof for that it is sufficiently declared in the art of nauigation, the Starre hathe Longitude vnto the signe of *Gemini*, and from the poles of the world in the signe of *Aries*, which Star standeth vppon the tippe of the tayle of *ursa minor* or little Beare, and hath Latitude frō the line Eclipticke .66. degrees 30. minutes, and declination from the Equinoctiall, 96 degrees or there aboutes. Heere followeth the note, by the guardes to knowe whether the North Starre be aboue the pole, or vnder the pole, and howe manye degrees and minutes . &c.

*The North
Starres
declination.*

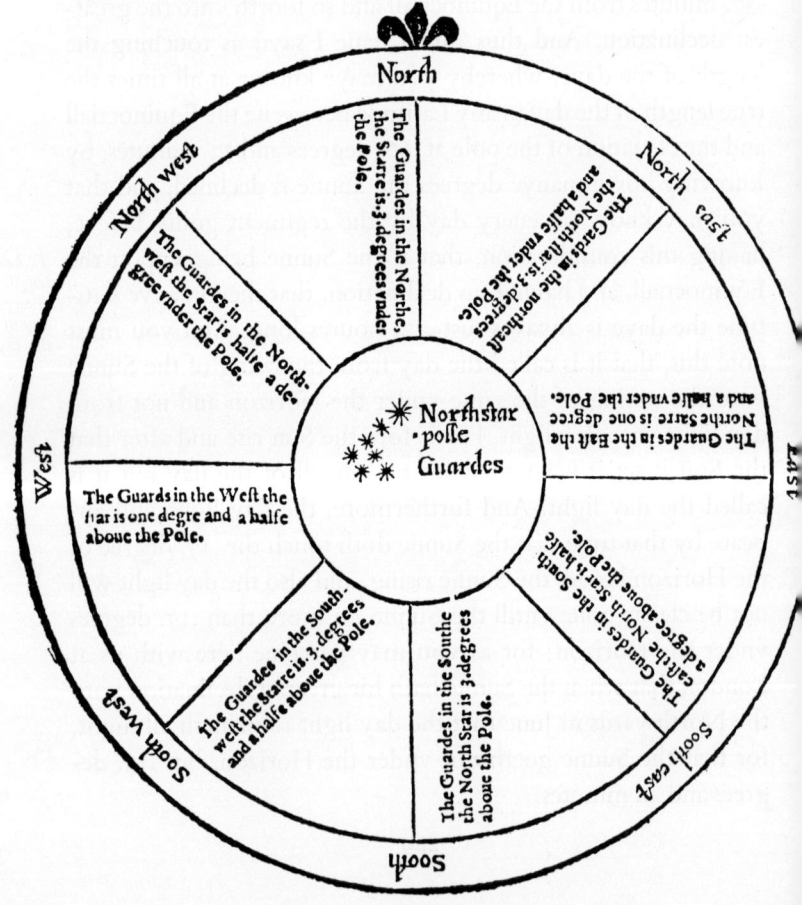

A REGIMENT FOR THE SEA, 1574

¶ *The thirteenth chapter dothe shewe you by the sayling vpon the quarter of your compasse, in how far sayling you do rayse a degree, and what you do departe from the Meridian, and in the ende there is a Demonstration therof.*

Furthermore, bycause there be some that desire to knowe the alteration of a point: to this ende, that in running of one poynte, they may rayse or lay a degree soner in one than in an other: as in ye sayling south or North, keeping one Meridian they rayse or lay the Pole. As this for your example. In going to the North, you doe rayse the Pole and lay the Equinoctial: Contrarywise, going towardes the South, you laye the Pole and rayse the Equinoctiall. But in sayling or going East or Weast, you do neyther alter your Pole nor Paralele but onely your Meridian. Whereas in sayling of any other poynte, you doe alter both your Pole and Paralele, and also your Meridian. Wherefore I will open vnto you (in sayling vppon one of the quarters of the compasse) what euery pointe dothe rayse or lay one degree, in how farre sayling, and howe many myles you be departed from the place you departed from, and what space you be departed from your Meridian. But heere is one thing to be noted (as I suppose) in the most part of cardes they allowe for euery degree, but 17. leagues and a half: your cards be most commonly made in *Lishborne*, in *Portugal*, in *Spayne*, or else in *Fraunce*. But as I take it, we in England should allowe 60 myles to one degree: that is after .3. miles to one of our Englishe leagues, wherefore .20. of oure English leagues shoulde answere to one degree, for that .3. of our myles will not make one of their leagues. And bycause they make their acountes by their leagues in the cardes and not by oures, therefore I will shew you by our Englishe myles. An English myle conteyneth .1000. pases, and euery pase .5. foote, and euery foote .12 ynches. Now some thinke

In going southwards you rayse ye equinoctiall & lay ye pole: in going to ye northwards you rayse ye pole and lay the Equinoctiall.

Of englishe leagues and spanish leagues.

A mile conteineth 1000. pases and euery pase .5. fote

that a pase can not be .5. foote, but a pase Geometrical is .2. reasonable steppes, for it can not be a pase vntill the hinder foote be remoued forwards, and those 2. steppes will containe .5. foote, and so maye any man endure to goe at pleasure. But nowe to our purpose. For the sayling of one quarter of the compasse, this is to be noted. First y^t in sayling directly south or North, you do raise or lay the Pole a degree in .60. myles going. In the altering of one point from the South or North in .61. myles: and you be departed from the lyne of East and Weast, or the Meridian .12. myles. In altering of the seconde poynt you rayse a degree in sayling of .65. myles: and departe from your Meridian .25. myles. In altering of the .3. poynte, you doe rayse or lay one degree in sayling .72. myles and a .9. part: and are departed from your Meridian .40. myles. Moreouer in altering of the 4. point, you do raise or lay a degree in the going of .85. myles: & depart from your Meridian .60. miles. In altering of the .5. point or winde, you raise a degree in the sayling of .108. miles: and depart from your Meridian .90. miles. In sayling by the 6. point, you raise or lay one degree in .157. miles: and depart from your Meridian line, 145. miles. Last of all, in sayling by the .7. pointe or winde, you doe raise a degree in going of .308. miles, and depart from your Meridian line 302. miles, and after this manner you amy consider of the other three quarters of the compasse. But if you require to knowe the raysing or laying of a degree by the leagues of the cardes: that is, at .17. leagues and a halfe: than reade the arte of Nauigation, and there shall you finde howe many degrees you be departed frō your Meridian, and also from the place that you departed from: and yet that serueth for no other place but onely for vnder the Equinoctiall, for he that maketh account of it in any other place, shall be deceiued. For euer as you goe to any of the .2. Poles, your degrees be stil shorter and shorter till such time as your Meridian meete vnder the two Poles, whereof I intreat in the .16. Chapter. For the better vnderstanding of y^e things aforesayd, looke on this figure folowing.

A degree is 60. miles or 20. englishe leagues.

A note to knowe in how far sayling you do rayse or lay a degree in the sayling by any one point of the compasse.

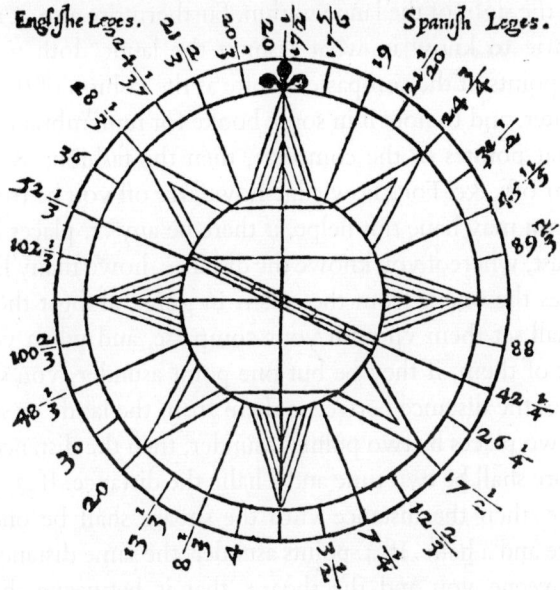

⁋ The .14. Chapter teacheth to know
how far any lande is off from you, knowing but
the distance betweene any two places: whither you
runne along by the lande, or directly to the
shoare or otherwise: with other necessarie things.

For that I know it very necessarie and profitable for Sea men, to knowe how neare or farre they be into the Sea, and how neare to the Lande, I will intreat thereof for diuers considerations: And first, bicause in rūning alongst the land there may be daunger, which may be such a certaine quantitie into the sea, that they may go both within them and without them. And also in like manner, for that being at one distance from the land, the land may rise in such a shape or fashion, whereas being nearer, the lande may rise in another forme or fashion: for being far off, you shall see the hils within the lande, and being neare, the hilles or cliffes neare vnto the Sea coast maye take awaye the sight of the lande within. Furthermore also, it is very necessarie to know in what fashion the lande doth rise vpō diuers points of the compasse, as ofte as the fashion of the lande doth alter, and to note it in some booke for remembrance. First by what pointes of the compasse, then the fashion, & last at how far off. &c. For knowledge how farre off you be from the land, you may haue this helpe, if there be any .2. places by the Sea coast, whereof you knowe the distance, howe many leagues or miles the one is from the other. In going alongst the coast you shall set them vp with your compasse, and when you are thwart of them, if they be but one point asunder, you shal be .5. times the distance betweene them from the lande or shoare. If the two places be two pointes asunder, then the distance vnto the shore shall be two time and a halfe the distance. If .3. points asunder, then the distance vnto the shoare shall be once the distance and a halfe. If .4. points asunder, the same distance shall be betweene you and the shoare, that is betweene the two markes. If .5. pointes asunder, then is it vnto the shore but .2. third partes of the distance between the .2. places. If .6. points asunder, (you being thwart of one of them) then shall the distance vnto the shore be, not halfe the distance betweene the .2. places. And in al these cases before rehearsed, the one place must be thwarte of you, the other must be ahead or sterne of you: and so it is exacte and true. As for ensample this: I (going alongst by any coaste) do know before hand how the one place doth beare from the other, besides this also I know the distance, that is to say, howe many leagues they be asunder. As for ensample, the .2. places assigned bear Easte and West the one from the other, I then (knowing that they be .3. leagues asunder) when I haue brought one of the places South or north of me, do set them with my compasse, the one being North of me, and the other bearing North and by east that is one point asunder: Now the distance vnto the shore, being .5. times the distance between the .2. places which be .3. leagues asunder, I knowe the shoare to be .15. leagues from me, which (if the places were but one

A note for the land rysing in diuers shapes or fashions.

To knowe how far the lande is frō you.
Where two lands be but one point asunder.

Of .2. places to be one point asunder.

league asuneder) should be but .5. leagues from the shoare. Furthermore if the places be .2. pointes asunder, that is to say, the one North, and the other North Northeast, then shall the distance vnto the shoare be 7. leagues and a halfe from me. Whereas if the 2 places were but a league asunder, it shuld be but .2. leagues & a halfe vnto yᵉ shore. And furthermore, if the places be .3. points asunder, that is to say, the one North, and the other Northeast & by north, the distance vnto the shore shal be .4. leagues & a half: whereas if the 2. places were but one league asūder, vnto yᵉ shore it should be but a league & a half. If .4. points asunder, that is to say, if the one place be due North, and the other place Northeast, then it is vnto the shore .3. leagues iust. If but one league asunder then but one league vnto the shore. Moreouer if the .2. places be .5. points asunder, that is to say, the one north and the other Northeast & by East, then yᵉ distance vnto the shore shall be but .2. leagues: whereas if the .2. places were but one league asūder vnto the shore should be but .2. miles. Last of al, if the .2. places be 6. points asunder, that is to say, the one north, and the other east northeast, then it shall not be a league and a halfe vnto the shore &c. But if you come directly to yᵉ land wards, hauing no cause to be thwart of none of those known places, then to know how far you be from the lande you must do as is by the places before spoke of. For if you go in due north the one place being north & by west, & the other north and by east: then (the .2. places being .3. leagues asunder) you shall be 7. leagues and a halfe from the shore: so that if you runne into the shore due north vntill they be .4. points asunder, that is to say, the one north northwest, and the other north northeast, then it shall be vnto the shore .3. leagues and 3. quarters. And furthermore, you still running in due north, till the 2. places be 6. pointes asunder, that is to say, the one place to be northweaste and by north, and the other place to be northest & by north, the distance vnto the shore shall be .2. leagues and a quarter. And again, if you runne in due north, vntil they be .8. points asunder, that is to say, the

To be two points asunder.

3. points asunder.

4. points asunder

5. points asunder.

6. pointes asunder.

Of going on sayling right into yᵉ shore.

one place northwest, and the other northeast: then the distance vnto the land or shore shall be but half the distance between the 2. places, that is, but one league and a half. Lastly, if you run to the land due north, vntill tho .2. places be .10. points asunder, that is to say, the one place northwest and by weast, and the other northeast and by east, then the distance vnto the shore shall be but one third part of the distance between the .2. places, that is, but one league from the land . &c. Thus much haue I saide as touching the bearing of the lande from you, by the points of the compasse, to know the distance or howe farre the land is of: which is very necessary for Seamen to know for diuers considerations, as I sayd before. If now therefore you knowe not howe one headland doth beare from another, doe thus: In running alongst the coast, when you see the appearing of any lande one before another, set them with your cōpasses, and looke how they beare from you, by what point of the compasse, and so shall you know iustly how the one lande doth beare or lye from the other. And by this order you may correct your plats, by doing this, as often as you see .2. notable places togither: as Ilands, rocks, headlands, mouthes of hauens, sandes, or what soeuer else be worthy of noting, this done, as often as you do see them togither, set them with your compasse, & that wil shew you most certainly, that so they do beare the one from the other. You may know the distance in like maner betweene them, if you knowe your ships way, as thus, whē you first see any .2. places togither, as .2. headlands, or .2. Ilands, hauing set them with your compasse, and knowing how the one beareth from the other then, for that you wil not come neare vnto them, you do hale off from the land, vntill that you haue brought your selfe farre inough off at youre discretion, and when you be thwart of the first headland, set the other land, and consider howe it beareth from you: then recken your ships way, how many leagues the shippe might goe vntill you come thwarte of the other headlande, keeping your course along as the .2. headlandes beare and so shall you both knowe the dis-

A way to knowe how one hedland beareth of another.

To knowe the distance at the Sea between any .2. headlandes.

tance between the .2. places, and also how farre you be off from them. In like maner, hauing consideration of the distance betweene the other places that you haue obserued both by your compasse and also by the shippes way, you may know how farre it is to the shore, going right to the lande wardes, by your crosse staffe, although you knowe not the distance between any two places. As thus: take the widenesse between any two places with your crosse staffe, bearing right to the land wardes, and then remoue the crosse staffe or transitorie halfe the length of the transitorie, that is to saye, the end next vnto you, and then by running in till the .2. ends of the transitorie doe agree with the two markes, you shall be halfe way to the shore: then looke howe farre the shippe hath gone in that time, for the same distance is vnto the land frō the ship. But if you remoue the transitory but a quarter ye length of the transitorie to youwards, then at the place wher the end of the transitorie doth agree with the .2. markes, shall be one quarter of the distance betweene the shore & you at the first obseruation: & it shall be .3. times that quantitie vnto the shore . &c. And to know the ships way, some do vse this which (as I take it) is very good: they haue a pece of wood & a line to vere out ouer borde, with a small line of a great lengthe whiche they make fast at one ende, and at the other ende and middle, they haue a piece of a line which they make fast with a small thred to stande like vnto a crowfoote: for this purpose, that it should driue a sterne as fast as the shippe doth go away from it, alwayes hauing the line so ready that it goeth out as fast as the shippe goeth. In like manner they haue either a minute of an houre glasse, or else a knowne part of an houre by some number of wordes, or suche other like, so that the line being vered out and stopt iuste with that time that the glasse is out, or the number of wordes spoken, which done, they hale in the logge or piece of woode againe, and loke howe many fadome the shippe hath gone in the time: that being knowne, what part of a league soeuer it be, they multiplie the number of fadomes, by the portion of tyme or part of an houre.

To knowe how far it is vnto the land another way.

To knowe the shippes way.

An englishe league .2500 fadome. A Spanish league .2857 fadome.

Whereby you may knowe iustly howe many leagues and partes of a league the ship goeth in an houre . &c. For an Englishe league doth containe .2500. fadome. And a spanish or portingale league doth contain .2857. fadomes . &c.

¶ *The fiftenth Chapter or rule treateth of the Longitude &c.*

Nowe some there be that be very inquisitiue to haue a way to get the longitude, but that is to tedious. For this they must consider, that the whole frame of the firmament is caried round from the east to the west in .24. hours, so as ther remaineth neither light nor marke, but goeth rounde, sauing only the .2. poles of the world, and theses .2. stand alwayes fast. But (as I sayd before in the .9. rule) of him that going South or North doth raise or lay the pole, and in like case of the Equinoctiall altering his paralele, and causing the light of the firmamēt to alter the time of their shining or abiding aboue our Horizon: so he that goeth directly east or weast, doth neither raise nor lay the pole, so that still the lights of the firmamēt doth make one maner of arch according to their latitude or declination: but the going East or Weast doth alter the Meridian, causing ye planets to haue their aspects at another hour or time, altering ye time of the change of ye moone & also the time of the Eclipses: which is necessary for all trauellers by Sea or by lande. Therefor I thought it needefull to be spoken of: for as countries haue Latitude from the pole so in like manner they haue appointed Longitude. Now therefore you may get the Latitude with instrumentes, but the Longitude you must bring from another place, which you can do but with a globe or else a mappe or card, and then you must measure from the Meridian of the Canarie Ilands, eitherwise called the fortunate Ilandes. And in oure Latitude of London euery .555. miles whiche conteineth .15. degrees wil aunswer to one houre of time: and vnder the Equinoctiall .900. miles to .15. degrees: the degrees be as long as

Altering ye time of rising and setting of the lights.

Altering the aspects.

Of latitude and Longitude.

15. degrees is an houre of time and at London it is .555. miles.

the degrees of Latitude, but towards the pole fewer and fewer till they come to nothing vnder the .2. poles. And now .37. miles which are at London, will aunswer to one degree of our Latitude at .51. or .52. degrees of eleuation of the pole, but the cause why the Longitude was fetched from the Canarie Ilands I know not, but it was as I suppose, bycause it was then the westermost place then knowen: for *Ptholemeus* was the first that ordeyned that rule. *Longitude beginneth at the Canarie Ilāds.*

Nowe furthermore bycause you shall knowe the better, I would draw out certain of the cheefest places about thys Realme of England, both their Longitude and Latitude, by which you shall know what manner of Arch the Sun with the other lights dothe make, and also by the Longitude you may know at what time the Moone with any of the Planets doth make any aspect. Besides this, the Eclipses of the Sun or Moone, with the chaunge, quarters, and full Moone, by a true and exact Ephemerides through all England to knowe the verie true houre and minute of the time of the diameter: considering for what Longitude or place your Almanacke was made. And now to get the Longitude, you may do it at the time of the Eclipse of the Moone, for that the Eclipses of the Moone be generall, so that she being aboue your Horizon in any place vpon the superficial parts of the earth or Sea, considering (as I said before) by your Almanacke, at that time when the Eclipse should happen, the very houre and minute, knowing also the place that your Almanacke was made for: that done, according to this rule, with a precise instrument you shall take the alteration of the time with the houre and minute of the Eclipse. And furthermore you might know your Longitude with the Ephemerides, by the coniunction of the Moone with other fixed Starres, if it were not for one great infirmitie, and that is the paralex of the Moone, whiche the semidiametre of the earth doth cause, by the neerenesse of the Moone vnto the earth: wherefore I woulde not any Sea men shoulde be of that opinion that they mighte get anye Longitude with instrumentes. Therefore let no Sea *To know the true time of the aspects of the Mone.*

The Longitude is not to be gotten with instrumēts on ye Sea.

men trouble themselues with anye such rule, but (according to their accustomed manner) let them keepe a perfite accompt and reckening of the way of their shippe, whether the shippe goeth to lewards or makith hir way good, considering alwayes what thinges be against them or with them: as tides, currents, winds, or such like. As for the rule of Longitude, it followeth in the next Chapter.

The .16. Chapter sheweth how many miles will aunswer to one degree of Longitude, in euery seuerall Latitude, betweene the Equinoctiall and any of the 2. poles: with the demonstration for that purpose: and the diuersities of aspectes of the Moone.

Now by this rule shal I teach you how many miles wil anwer to one degree, for euery seuerall Latitude to any of the .2. poles either articke or antarticke. And first, vnder the Equinoctial (the .2. poles being euen with the Horizon) 60. miles do answer to one degree, as I said in the .15. rule. And now shall follow the rest. Where the poles be raised .21. degrees .56. miles belongeth to one degree of Lōgitude. Now yᵉ poles being raysed .29. degrees .52. miles do answer to one degree. The poles being raised .36. degrees .48. miles do answer to one degree. The pooles .42. degrees raysed .44. miles goeth to one degree of Longitude. The Pole raised .52. degrees .37. miles to one degree. The Pole raised .57. degrees .32. miles to one degree. The Pole raised .62. degrees .28. miles to one degree. The Pole raised .66. degrees .24. miles to one degree. The Pole raysed .70. degrees .20. miles to one degree. The Pole raysed .74. degrees .16. miles to one degree. The Pole raysed .78. degrees .12. miles to one degree. The Pole raysed .82. degrees .8. miles to one degree. The Pole raysed .86. degrees .4. miles to one degree. The Pole being raysed to the hyest at .90. degrees (being then your Zenith) there all the Meridians meete.

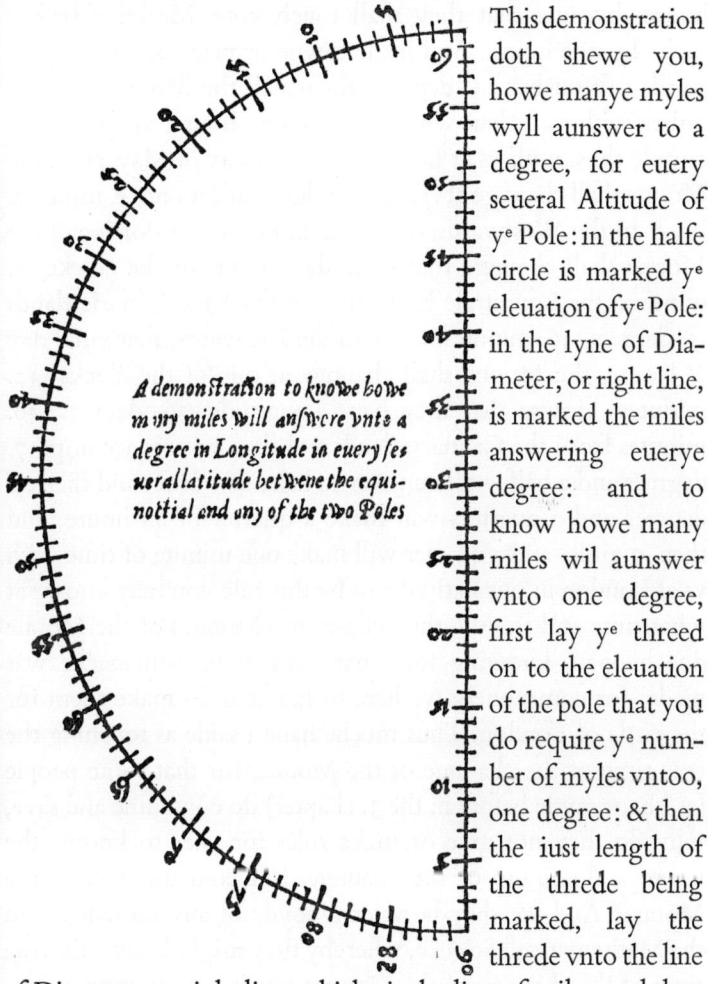

A demonstration to knowe howe many miles will answere vnto a degree in Longitude in every severall latitude betwene the equinoctial and any of the two Poles

This demonstration doth shewe you, howe manye myles wyll aunswer to a degree, for euery seueral Altitude of ye Pole: in the halfe circle is marked ye eleuation of ye Pole: in the lyne of Diameter, or right line, is marked the miles answering euerye degree: and to know howe many miles wil aunswer vnto one degree, first lay ye threed on to the eleuation of the pole that you do require ye number of myles vntoo, one degree: & then the iust length of the threde being marked, lay the threde vnto the line of Diameter, or right line, whiche is the line of miles, and then you shall see at that place is the number of miles vnto one degree &c. Now you must consider that euery hour of time in the chaunging of the Moone or of the Eclipses you must allow .15. degrees, euery degree in miles as you do see in your Latitude of the countrie, as thus: those places y^t be to the

15. degrees answereth vnto an houre of time.

Westwards of your towne, place or countrie by .15. degrees the Moone shall chaunge rather with them thā with you by one houre, bycause that they shall touch your Meridian before theirs by one houre. And if the towne or place be to the East-wards of you by .15. degrees, then shall the Moone chaunge rather with you than with them by one houre, as for an en-sample thus, with vs at London, the .xx. day of May 1574. the Moone shall chaunge at .12. of the clocke at Noone .5. minutes. Now to the Westwards as farre as Lishburne in Portingall the Moone shall chaunge that same day at .11. of the clocke .8. minutes, the Longitude being thereof from the Canarie Ilands .5. degrees .36. minutes. Now to the Eastwards, that same day at Rome, the Moone shall chaunge at one of the clocke .12. minutes, bicause that they haue Longitude .36. degrees .40. minutes from the Cannary Ilands and then by this accompt .7. degrees and a halfe will aunswer to halfe an houre, and then .3. degrees and a quarters will make a quarter of an houre, and then .9. miles and a quarter will make one minute of time with vs at London in our Latitude, so by this rule you may knowe at what time and minute the Eclipses or chaunges of the Moone doe happen, knowing for what place your Almanacke was made, for commonely we here in England do make them for the cittie of London. Thus muche haue I saide as touching the true time of the chaunge of the Moone, for that some people (as I haue sayde before in the 3. chapter) do contemne and saye, why do they not giue or make rules for euer to knowe the houre and minute of the chaunge, full, and quarters of the Moone? And yet they be vtterly voyde of any knowledge in the Mathematicall Science, whereby they might knowe the true time of the chaunge of the Moone: For it is a question Astro-nomicall, to know the Moones motion: a question Geometri-call, to know the true time of the aspectes, or measure betweene the Sunne and the Moone: and thirdly, it is a question Cosmo-graphicall, to knowe the true Longitude of the place he is in, at the time when the Moone chaungeth . &c. Nowe foloweth

To knowe ye true time of ye change & quarters of the moon is a question astro-nomicall, geo-metricall and cosmographicall.

A REGIMENT FOR THE SEA, 1574

the next rule whiche shall treate of Longitude and Latitude.

The .17. Chapter or rule treateth of
the Longitude and Latitude of certaine of the most
notable places in Englande: and also howe long the
Moone doth change at the one towne before the
other, with the diuersitie of the Longest day
in Sommer, from South Hampton
to the Northermost parte
in Scotland.

Nowe in this rule foloweth the Longitude and Latitude of the most part of the principall places in England. The Southermost place in England, is the Lizarde in Cornwal: the Longitude thereof is .15. degrees .5. minutes: the Latitude .50. degrees .45. minutes. S. Michaels Mount hath in Longitude .14. degrees .20. minutes: in Latitude .51. degrees .6. minutes. Falmouth hath Longitude .15. degrees .12. minutes: Latitude .51. degrees .0. minutes. Plimmouth hath Longitude 19. degrees .7. minutes: Latitude .51. degrees .1. minute. South Hāpton. Longit .18. degr .52. minuts: Latitude .51. degr .2. mi. Portsmouth Longitude .19. degrees .7. minuts: Latitude .51. degrees .3. minutes. Rye Longitude .20. degrees .22. minutes: Latitude .51. degrees .5. minutes. Douer Longitude .21. degr .40. minutes: Latitude .51. degrees .26. minutes. Canterburie Longitude .21. degrees .25. minutes. Latitude .51. degr .28. mi. Sandwich Longitude .21. degr .38. minuts: Latitude .51. degr .29. minutes. London. Longitude .15. degr .54. minutes: Latitude .51. degr .32. minuts. Grauesend Longitude .20. degr .14. minuts: Latitude .51. degr .31. minuts. Bristowe Longitude 17. degr .8. minutes: Latitude .51. degr .42. minuts. Haruarde Longitude .17. degr .0. minutes: Latitude .52. degr .2. minuts. S. Dauids head Longitude .15. degr .5. minuts: Latitude .52. degr .15. minuts. Oxford Longitude .18. degr .59. minut: Latitude .51. degr .50. minuts. Cambridge Longitude .20. degr .6. minuts: Latitude .52. degr .0.

WILLIAM BOURNE

minuts. Norwich Longitude 21. degr .20. minuts: Latitude .52. degr .10. minuts. Lincolne Longitude .20. degr .28. minuts: Latitude .52. degr .6. minuts. Welshpoole Longitude .16. degr .40. minutes: Latitude .53. degr .6. minuts. Westchester Longitude .17. degr .29. minuts: Latitude .53. degr .34. minuts. Hull Longitude .20. degr .54. minuts: Latitude .53. degr .57. minuts. Yorke Longitude .20 degr .0. minuts: Latitude .54. degr .1. minute. Cockermouth Longitude .17. degr. .0. minuts: Latitude .55. degr .8. minuts. Carlyle Longitude .17. degr .48. minuts. Latitude .55. degr 2. minuts. Newcastle Longitude .20. degr .31. minuts: Latitude .55. degr .0. minuts. Barwicke Longitude .20. degr .48. minuts: Latitude .56. degr .23. minuts. Edenborow in Scotlande, Longitude .19. degr .50. minuts: Latitude .57. degr .0. minuts. Now by the Longitude & Latitude you may know the length of the day both in Sommer and in Winter, with the perfit houre and minute of the changes of the Moone, and how long the Moone doth change at one town before another, through the whole realme of England. And now in order as I haue begon before, I will shewe you the distance of time. And first at S. Michaels Mount, the Moone changeth rather than at London by 25. minuts. Rather at Falmouth than at London by .20. mi. At Plimmouth rather than at London by .18. min. At South Hampton rather than at London by 15. minuts. At Portsmouth rather than at Lon. by .4 minuts. At Rye later than at London by one minute and $\frac{1}{2}$. At Douer later than at London by .6. minutes and more. At Canterburie later than at London by .5. minutes. At Sandwich later than at London by .6. minuts. Grauesend later than at London by one minute and a halfe. Bristow rather than at London by .11. minutes. Haruard rather than at London by 12. minutes. Saint Dauids head rather than at London by 19. minutes. Oxforde rather than at London by .4. minuts. Cambridge later than at London by .$\frac{2}{3}$. partes of a minute. Norwich later than at London by .5. minuts and more. Lincolne later than at London by .2. minutes. Welshpoole rather than at London by .16. minutes.

*To know y*ᵉ *diuersitie of the time of the chaunge of the moon through all England.*

Westchester rather than at London by .10. minutes. Hull later than at London by .4. minutes. Yorke later than at London by .¼. of a minute. Cockermouth rather than at London by .12. minutes. Carelyle rather than at London by .9. minutes. Newecastle later than at London by .2. minutes. Barwicke later than at London by three minutes and more.

The cause why that it is called the chaunge of the Moone, is for that the Moone chaungeth the sydes of the Sunne, for before the change the Moone is on the West side of the Sun: and after the chaunge, the Moone is on the Easte side of the Sunne . &c. Nowe in like manner, I thinke it necessarie to be spoken of the difference of the longest day in Sommer, in euery seuerall Latitude, through the whole Realme of England frō the Southermost part, called the Lizard, to the Northermost part in Scotlande: and this is called the day, from the Sunne rysing or appearing aboue the Horizon.

First at South Hampton the longest day is .16. houres long .26. minutes, the shortest .7. houres .54. minuts. At London .16. houres .30. minutes longest .7. houres .30. minuts shortest. At Lincolne .16. houres .45. minuts. longest .7. hours 15. minutes shortest. *To know yᵉ lēgth of the longest day through all England & Scotlande.*

At Yorke, the longest .17. houres, the shortest .7. houres. Newcastle the longest .17. houres .12. minutes, the shortest .6. houres .48. minutes. Barwicke, the longest .17. houres .30. minutes, the shortest .6. houres .30. minutes. Edenborow in Scotlande, the longest day in Sommer .17. houres .45. minuts, the shortest day .6. houres .15. minutes. Now Catnes point being the northermost part in all Scotlande, the Pole being raised to .62. degrees, there the longest day is .19. houres .30 minutes, the shortest daye .4. houres .30. minutes. Nowe this you doe consider, loke what the longest day doth containe, looke what that lacketh of .24. hours, that is the shortest Winter day, &c.

WILLIAM BOURNE

The eightenth Chapter or rule
sheweth howe to sayle by
the Globe.

Now to sayle by the Globe, it is conuenient to be spoken of. For that generally the most part of the seamen make their account as though the earth wer a platforme. For they do not consider that the earth is a Globe, and that the Meridians do growe narrower and narrower towardes the .2. poles, for it is vnpossible to drawe the face of the earth and the Sea true vpon a platforme, for it you wil describe the lande true, then shall not the Sea be true, for as you go towards the North partes, your Meridians growe togither, so as your lines or pointes be according to the arte of Hydrography, for the Sea shall be broader to the North partes than it is. Nowe and if you woulde describe the Sea true, with lines, courses, distances, hauens and daungers, then shoulde your lande be broader to the North partes than it is. As for ensāple, thus: Englande and Scotlande being both one Ilande, in all your Cardes of Nauigation, the North parte of Scotland is drawn much bigger than it is, for otherwise the lines of South & North shoulde not be according to the trenting of the lande, for if you viewe it well, you shall finde the North ende of Scotlande much more in distance than it is. As you may see in measuring it by the trunke of youre carde there. For youre better vnderstanding, I will shewe you the compasse of the earth vnder sundrye Paralels or Circles, howe many myles the earthe doth contayne in compasse. Fyrst, vnder the Equinoctiall (where the earthe is at the greatest compasse) in going directly Easte or Weaste, that is, by a ryghte line ouer Sea and Lande, the two Poles being euen wyth your Horizon: you haue .21600. myles to come to the place you departed from. Vnder the Tropicke of *Cancer*, the North Pole being raysed .23. degrees .28. minutes, going directly East & West: it is .19800. miles in compasse in our artick circle of London wher the pole artick is raised .15. deg .32. minuts. going East & West: it is

You cannot drawe the Lande & sea true vpon a flat thing.

To make a Sea plat or carde.

The compasse of the earth.

The compasse of the earth vnder ye tropick of Cancer. The artick circle of Lōdon vnder the Polare circle.

.13320. myles in compasse, then vnderneath the Polare circle where the Pole is raysed sixtie five degrees, thirtie two minutes: it is .8460. miles in compasse. by this you see that the compasse of the East and Weast lyne (comming from the Equinoctiall) is muche lesser to the North wardes than it is to the South wardes. Wherefore when you shall haue any occasion to attempte any voyage to the North parts, it is best to sayle by a Globe: for so shall you better see the distances and bigness of the landes, and in like manner your lines and courses. In this order, fyrste (according to the accustomed manner) keepe a perfitte accounte and reckoning of the waye of the shippe, by what lyne or poynte your Shippe hathe made hir waye good, then muste you resorte to youre Globe. After that consider what place and Paralell you be in, whiche you maye doe by the Sunne by daye, and by the Starres by nyght. Nowe (knowing what place and Paralel you be in) sette youre Globe to the eleuation of youre Pole: that doone, turne to the place of youre Zenith, and seeke the opposite of it in your Paralell: for then you knowe that in the same Paralell is youre Easte and Weaste lyne: that had, the iust quarter of that circle to the Pole, muste be deuided into the eight pointes of your compasse, doing so likewise on the other side. In like case if you come to the Southwards, deuide your .8. wyndes from your Antarticke Pole, to youre Paralell circle: and thus must you doe euer and anon, for the oftner you do obserue this custome, the better & perfiter shal your course be. Now thus briefly I make an end of ye sayling by the Globe. But for them that do occupie the Southpart, nothing is better than their cardes. Bycause I haue declared vnto you the length of certayne of the Paralels, what myles the Earth doth contayne in compasse vnder them, now wil I shew you how many myles distance is between euery one of them. And first, from the Equinoctial to the Tropick of *Cancer*, (which is there where the Sun maketh his furthest progresse to the North partes) it is .1408. myles. Secondly, between the tropick of *Cancer* & our Artick circle of Londō it is .1684. miles. Thirdly between our

How to vse the globe to direct your course, and to knowe how that any place doth beare.

The distāce between the equinoctiall and the tropick of Cancer. Between ye artick circle of London & the tropick of Cancer.

Artick circle & the Polare circle is .900. myles. Lastly, betweene the Polare circle and the Pole is .1408. myles. So that it is in all from the Equinoctiall to eyther of the two Poles .5400. miles: whiche is the fourth part of the compasse of the whole Earth. Furthermore, for that you may the better vnderstande that the Earth is a Globe or Circular. (which any person that dothe occupie the Sea, seeth most apparantly) you shall perceiue it thus, if you see a Shippe any thing farre off, you may perfitly see ye sayles of it, but not the whole, the cause whereof is the circularnesse of the earth and the water of the Sea: for that the water doth rise and swell between you and the other ship, according to the distance between both the ships: bicause the distance to the center of the earth or water, is in euery place alike. And he that hath desire to know further heerof, M. Dee hath made mention therof in *Euclides Elamentes* in his mathematical preface, & also in the .12. booke, whither you may haue recourse, yet notwithstanding I wil say a litle therof, wherby you may discerne how far it is possible to see a ship vpon the sea: as thus: if you be on ye sea in a ship, so y^t ther be but halfe a league betweene you and the other ship, the water wyll be fyue ynches and a halfe hygher in the middle of the waye betweene bothe the ships, for that the water is equall in euery place vnto the center of the earthe, and then the water going by a croked line, then to strike it by a right line, the middle of the line that shoulde come from the center of the earth, shall be shorter than the other .2. lines comming from the center of the earth betweene the .2. shippes by .5. ynches and a halfe, and then it must needes by sayde, that the water is hygher by the said .5. ynches and a halfe. And furthermore, if the two shippes were a league asunder, then the water by his circulernesse shuld be .22. ynches hygher than the leuell in the middle betweene both the shippes. Furthermore, if the .2. ships be 2. leagues asunder, then the water shall be higher than the leuell in the middle betweene bothe the shippes by .88. ynches, which is .7. foote and .4. ynches. If the .2. shippes be .3. leagues the one

The cause why that you may see the sailes of a ship & not the whole.

To knowe howe many foote and ynches that the water is higher than the leuell or the sea between two ships.

from the other, then the water shall be higher than the leuell in the midway betweene both the shippes, by .198. inches. which is .16. foote and a halfe. Furthermore if the .2. shippes be .4. leagues asunder, the water shall be higher than the leuell in the midway betweene both the shippes by .252. ynches, which is .29. foote and .4. ynches. And furthermore, if the .2. shippes were .5. leagues asunder, the water shoulde be higher than the leuell of the midway betweene both the ships by .550. ynches, which is .46. foote lacking .2. ynches. Yet furthermore, if the .2. ships were .6. leagues asunder, the water should be higher than the leuell in the middle way betweene them by .792. ynches, which is .66. foote. Furthermore also, if the .2. shippes were .7. leagues asunder, the water should be higher than the leuell in the midway between both the ships by .1878. ynches, and that is .90. foote, which is as farre & rather farther than it is possible to see any ship vpon the Sea: Neyther is it possible to see any lande further, but such lande as is very high lande, which for the greatnesse of the heigth you may see it, wherfore .7. leagues or .6. leag. is called a ken. Now the circularnesse of the earth is the cause that you may see a shippe or land further out of the top than, vpon the hatches: Wherefore it is a plaine case, that the Earth and Sea is not flat, but circular, as is aforedeclared. &c.

What a ken is, and the cause why you may see a ship further out of the top than vpon the hatches.

⸿ *The .19. Chapter, is as touching the making of Plats or Cardes for the Sea, and not to paint their cards as they do, but rather to supply the vacant places with other necessarie matters: & also of three necessarie things contained in the plats or cardes, and their vses, which is the most necessarie thing in Nauigation.*

For the making of Plats or Cards, as touching *Hydrographia* cōmonly called sea Cards, I meane to say litle therof: for that it is sufficiently declared in the booke called the art of Nauigation: Sauing this, I would wish thē that be the makers of plats and cardes for the Sea, not to paint their compasses with so many colours: neither vpon the Lande with so many flagges, for that it dothe rather hurte than good: althoughe it may be saide they be so painted in vacant places, those vacant places I would wish them to furnish with these 2. matters in this order. Firste in some vacant place with a compasse there, to place against euery point of the half of the compasse, letters, or some other figures or carecters, then in like maner, (according to that place where suche a Moone maketh a full Sea) to make that letter or carecter at the hauen, port, or place. As for ensample thus. I place A at the East point, B at the East and by South, C at the East southeast, D at Southeast and by East, and so consequently to all the pointes vnto the Weast, then that being doone, where it showeth an Easte Moone, I place A in the platte or carde, and where an Easte and by South Moone, I doe place B in the carde, and so forthe, according to the place of the Moone that maketh a full Sea. And where it runneth halfe tyde vnder other, to make some note vpon the poynt of the compasse . &c. This also is very necessarie to be done to furnishe vp all the vacant places of the plat or carde, to drawe the shape or fashion of euery headland or high lande alongst euery coast that is needefull to be knowne, and at what poynte of the compasse the lande is of that fashion: at howe farre off the lande ryseth in that fashion: and so to make the fashion of the lande as often as the lande altereth the forme and fashion: and last of all, at what poynte of the compasse the lande hathe that shape or fashion: for being vpon one side, the lande ryseth of one fashion, and on the other side of an other forme or fashion: Also being neare the lande it will be in one fashion, and being far off in an other fashion (as is before declared in the 14. Chapter) for there is nothing more needefull and necessarie for a Seaman, than this: to knowe the lande when he seeth it, and there is no way better to make him remember it, than to haue notes howe the lande dothe rise

Not to paint their Sea cards but to vse ye vacant places with other necessary matters.

To draw ye shape of the lād in their cardes.

A REGIMENT FOR THE SEA, 1574

vpon euery side: and what greater inconuenience may there growe by any meanes, than there may by mistaking of a place: for it were twentie times better to be throughly persuaded that he knoweth it not, than to thinke he doth knowe it not being that place. For whereas he doth thinke to preuent the dangers, be may willingly runne vpon the dangers not known of him. Therefore in my opinion they can do no better than to furnish their vacant places in their plats and cards with this matter: for there can be nothing better. The vse of the Sea cardes is most necessary for Nauigation for long voyages: fyrste for that it sheweth you howe one place beareth from another: secondly, the distance of any places howe farre the one is from the other. Of whiche the one is represented by the lines of the compasse: the other by the scale or trunke of measure, if the platte be truely made. Thirdly, it sheweth you in what Latitude from the Equinoctiall or Altitude of the pole any place is in, by the line of degrees. Now to directe youre course through the Sea by the carde to any place assigned, you must first looke by what poynte of the cōpasse it beareth from you, from the place you meane to sette off from the lande, vnto the place you would fyrst fall with. Which you shall know thus: seeke alyne from the next compasse vnto the place you meane to depart frō, then open your compasses vnto one of those lynes by your iudgement that falleth neare vnto your place assigned: and let the other foote of your compasses stande iust at that place where your ship is, when you direct your course: that doone, beare your hands forwardes euen, and let the one ende be still vpon the lyne to the whiche you did open your compasse, vntill you come to your place assigned. But if it falleth short of the place assigned, then take the nexte line nearer vnto the place you departed from: when you haue so done, if your compasses doe ouer reache the place assigned, then take a lyne further off from the place you doe meane to set off from: and so shall you see by what poynte of the compasse the place assigned dothe beare from you . &c. If you would knowe howe farre the place

Great infirmities by mistaking any place.

How necessary a thing the sea cardes be .3. necessarie thinges in y^e *sea cardes.*

To knowe howe any place dothe beare from you by the carde.

WILLIAM BOURNE

To knowe howe far it is vnto any place by the carde.

assigned is from you, set the one foote of the compasses vpon the place you departe from, and stretche out the other foote vnto the place assigned iuste, that doone (standing still vnremoued) sette them to the scale or trunke of measure, and that wil shew you iustly how many leagues it is iust frō the place of your departing vnto the place assigned. If the distance between the .2. places be more than the compasses will reach at once, then first set your compasses vnto the scale, opening the compasses vnto .100. leagues more or lesse, as your scale and compasses will giue you leaue at your discretion, after that set yᵉ one foot at the place of your departing, & the other foot of the cōpasses right towards the place assigned, as oftē times as yᵉ distance between the .2. places doth require, & thereof (the cōpasses being opened vnto .100. leagues) you may cōclude it to be so many .100. leag. vnto the place assigned as the cōpasses did shew vnto you: but if ther be any od mesure, thē opē your cōpasses to yᵗ quātity, & set to thē yᵉ scale, & it wil shew you yᵉ iust contente of that measure, more than so many .100. leagues &c. Furthermore touching the third commoditie,

To knowe what Latitude or heigth of yᵉ pole any place hath by the carde.

which is to knowe what Latitude any place assigned hath: set one foote of the compasses vpon the place assigned, and open the compasses vnto the nexte Easte and Weast line, then carie that vnto the line of degrees (keeping the foote of the compasses vpon the Easte and Weast lyne) it will shewe iustly the number of degrees that the Pole is aboue the Horizon. So of these three wayes, by the first is knowne by what poynt of the compasse any place beareth from you. By the seconde is knowne howe farre distance it is vnto any place assigned. And by the thirde is knowne in what heigth the Pole is in any place assigned. &c. Nowe (this being knowne) you may with the most ease know howe to attaine to come vnto the port or place assigned. Yet furthermore, there is to be considered (in directing the course of a ship

Things to be cōsidered by the M. or pilote of a ship.

to any place assigned) what impediments may be by the way: as tydes, currents, or the scantnesse of the wynde whiche may put the ship vnto the leewardes of his course, as also the surging

252

A Table of the fixed Starres.

The names of the Starres.	Signes	Longit. degr.mi.		Declin. degr.mi.		To what part they decline	Bignesse of yᵉ stars.
Whales backe.	Aries.	6.	6	12.	11	M	second bignesse
Whales belly.	Aries.	16.	2	12.	20	M	second bignesse
Rammes horne.	Aries.	27.	42	17.	19	S	thirde bignesse
Rammes head.	Taurus.	1.	46	21.	16	S	thirde bignesse
Bulles eye.	Gemini.	3.	42	15.	42	S	a great Starre
Orions left fote.	Gemini.	10.	2	9.	14	M	a great Starre
Orions left shoulder.	Gemini.	11.	26	4.	37	S	a Starre of the
First *Orions* girdle.	Gemini.	16.	22	1.	19	M	second light bo
Orions right shoulder	Gemini.	23.	6	6.	18	S	a great Starre
Great Dogge.	Cancer.	8.	40	15.	30	M	a very great sta
Lesser Dogge.	Cancer.	20.	10	6.	4	S	a great Starre
Brightest in *Hydra*.	Leo.	21.	2	4.	47	M	second bignesse
Lyons necke.	Leo.	23.	16	21.	59	S	second bignesse
Lyons heart.	Leo.	23.	32	14.	3	S	a great Starre
Lyons backe.	Virgo.	5.	16	22.	30	S	second bignesse
Lyons tayle.	Virgo.	15.	32	16.	46	S	a great Starre.
Rauens head.	Libra.	5.	6	19.	53	M	of the thirde bi
Rauens wing.	Libra.	9.	36	17.	8	M	nesse both thos
Virgins spike.	Libra.	17.	42	4.	54	M	a great Starre
twixt *Bootes* thighs.	Libra.	18.	6	22.	9	S	a great Starre
South balance.	Scorpio.	9.	2	13.	44	M	second bignesse
North balance.	Scorpio.	13.	12	7.	33	M	second bignesse
Scorpions heart.	Sagitari.	3.	42	24.	47	M	second bignesse
Hercules head.	Sagitari.	8.	42	15.	20	S	thirde bignesse
Serpents head.	Sagitari.	15.	42	14.	7	S	thirde bignesse
The Eagle.	Capricor.	24.	51	7.	28	S	second bignesse
Dolphins tayle.	Aquari.	8.	27	10.	1	S	thirde bignesse
Goates tayle.	Aquari.	17.	22	14.	13	M	thirde bignesse
Water pourers leg.	Pisces.	2.	20	15.	52	M	thirde bignesse
Pegasus shoulder.	Pisces.	17.	41	13.	1	S	second bignesse
Pegasus legge.	Pisces.	23.	10	26.	30	S	second bignesse
Whales tayle.	Pisces.	26.	21	21.	47	M	thirde bignesse

the North parts where the North pole is raysed more than .50. or .60. degrees, then the North Starre is too hye to be obserued or taken with the crosse staffe (as I haue declared in the .6. Chapter) and it may chaunce so that in the day the Sunne is not to be seene at noone, and then these Starres may serue your turne. And furthermore they be very good for them that haue occasion to trauell beyonde the Equinoctiall where the North pole is vnder the Horizon, in vsing their declination as they do the Sunnes declination in all points, whiche doth appeare in the .7.8. and .9. Chapters of this book. And furthermore they be very necessary for Seafaring men to knowe the houre of the night: both by their being vpon the Meridian, and also by their rising and setting: you may know the true time of their rising and setting in euery Latitude by their declination from the Equinoctiall, whether they decline to the South partes or North parts, as is declared by the declination of the Sun in the .11. chapter. And furthermore by any of these Starres you may trie the variatiō of your compas by night . &c. Now shal folow the table of all these Stars. The first row of this table conteineth the names of the Stars. The seconde, the signes, that they be in Longitude. The thirde, the degrees in the signes. The .4. the miutes belonging therevnto. The .5. the degrees of declination. The .6. the odde minuts belonging therevnto. The .7. sheweth towardes what part they decline by letters, of whiche S. signifieth Septentrionell or North declination. M. signifieth Meridionall or south declination: as in the table doth appeare. The .8. doth shew nothing but the bignesse of the Starres. Now followeth the Table.

If the pole be raysed more than .50 or .60. degrees, it is to hye to be obserued by ye crosse Staffe. These Starres will serue beyond the Equinoctiall.

To knowe the rising and setting of these Starres in all places by the order of the xi Chapter. The order of the table following.

the heigth of the pole doth shew vnto you, by the order before rehersed &c. Furthermore (as I haue declared vnto you in the .14. Chapter going before) to knowe howe farre the land is off from you, knowing (as before) the distaunce betweene any 2. places by setting the land with your compas, you may do the like by your card, as thus: you setting the .2. places with your compasse, do know that the .2. places be so many leagues asunder, then shall you repaire to the card, and according to the bearing of the .2. places by the points of the compas, you (being thwart of one of these .2. places) shall replie it with your compasses vnto your scale: But for that in the scale the leagues be so small, you may assigne .20. leagues to be but one league, and open the compasses vnto that proportion that the .2. place be asunder, and the one of them doth beare from the other: that done, open the compasses agayne from the center of the compas vnto the place that you do imagin to be the land, and then reply it vnto the trunk of measure, you shall see howe many leagues you bee from the shore and so foorth. So that you may see that the plat or card is one of the necessariest things that is to be vsed in Nauigation . &c.

To knowe howe far ye the lande is off from you by the sight of the lande with youre compasse & to do it upon the land.

⁋ *The .20. Chapiter is of the Longi-*
tude and declinatiō of .32. notable fixed Starres for Na-
uigation, with tables of their shining, and at what pointe of your
compas they do both rise and set: and also tables for euery mo-
neth of the yeere, declaring at what houre and minute they
be South, running from the first day of the moneth to
the .15. and from the .15. to the last day, and will
continue these 100 yeares with-
out muche error.

And furthermore I do thinke it conuenient for diuerse considerations to shew the Longitude and declination of certaine of the most notablest fixed Starres that are neere vnto the Equinoctiall, to the number of .32. of them, whiche are very necessary for Nauigation in diuers respectes, as this: if you be vnto

A REGIMENT FOR THE SEA, 1574

of the Sea: And all this muste be considered by the maister and Pilot of the ship. Likewise also in long voyages, the winde may oftē shifte vpon him, and sometime the winde may be such as he can not lye his course: wherefore he must keepe a perfite account of the ships way, and consider to know what point the ship hath made hir way good by. And at euery time that the wynde doth shifte, and the ship can not lye hir course, to note in the carde or plat in what place the ship may be: in hauing a speciall regarde vnto the way of the ship, as touching the swiftnesse or slownesse that the shippe goeth: and if so be the weather be cleare either by night or by day, to take the true Altitude of the Pole: for by that they may correcte the ships way, and giue a very neare gesse howe the place (assigned to go vnto) doth bear from them, as also how farre it is thither, sauing onely in the Easte and Weast course: and then they haue no other helpe but only the very account of the shippes way. And to correct their deade reckning by the altitude of the Pole they must do this: (especially if the shippe haue had often trauerse by the means of contrary winds, so that she could not lie hir course) consider vpon the cardes or plat how long the ship hath made hir way good for so many points as the ship hath sayld by: then (if by the altitude of the Pole the shippe hathe gone more than the dead reckning did shewe you) repaire vnto the line of degrees, and set the one foote of the compasses vpon the degree and place of the heigth of the Pole, and the other vpon the next east and west lyne: that done, bear it vnto the place you suppose the shippe to be in: & thē bring forwards with the other compasses, what point of the Compas the shippe hath sayled by, and at the meeting of the .2. paire of compasses make a note for the place that the shippe is in: from which place you may with your compasses see, how the place assigned dothe beare, and also how farre off you be from the same. Furthermore (if you find by the heigth of the Pole that you are not so farre shot as your reckning did shewe vnto you) you must pull backe so much from the point that the shippe hath sayled by, as

They may correct the shipes waye by the taking ye heigth of the Pole.

A REGIMENT FOR THE SEA, 1574

The vse of this Table is this: when you haue taken the heigth of any of these Starres vpon the Meridian, then loke what declination the Starre hath from the Equinoctiall: if the star haue North declination, then subtract or take away the stars declination from the heigth: if it haue South declination, then adde or put vnto the heigth of the starres declination, and that will shewe vnto you the heigth of the Equinoctiall, and then by the heigthe of the Equinoctiall the heigth of the Pole is knowne, as the .7. Chapter doth declare. And now I thinke it conuenient to make certaine Tables, to shew vnto you at what houre and time any of these Starres be vpon the Meridian, whereby they maye the better knowe these Starres. I will also shewe vnto you howe long any of these Starres doe shyne or tarry aboue the Horizon in this Latitude from the Equinoctiall of London, that is at .51. or 52. degrees. And also at what poynte of the compasse any of these Starres do ryse or set, which will serue this .100. years without much error.

How to vse the starres declination to know the Heigth of ye Pole.

⁋ *A Table to knowe the rysing and setting of these Starres, by what poynt of the cō-passe, and howe many houres they be aboue our Horizon, the Pole being raysed .51. or .52. degrees.*

The Whales backe ryseth East and by South, and vnto the South wards: and shyneth .10. houres and better.

The Whales belly (in a maner) as the whales backe.

The Rammes Horne riseth Easte Northeast, and setteth Weast Northwest: and shineth .15. houres .16. minuts.

The Rammes Heade ryseth East Northeast, and setteth Weast Northwest: and shineth .16. hours .4. minuts.

The Bulles Eye rysieth neare the Easte Northeast, and setteth neare the West Northwest: and shyneth .15. houres 2. minutes.

The Orions left foote riseth neare the East and by South, and setteth neare the West and by Southe: and shineth .10. houres and .6. minuts.

The Orions lefte shoulder ryseth East and to the Northwardes, and setteth West and to the Northwardes: and shineth .12. houres .45. minuts.

The first in Orions girlde doth rise a little to the Southwardes of the East, and setteth a little to the Southwardes of the West: and shineth .11. houres .46. minuts.

Orions right shoulder riseth East, & vnto the Norwardes, and setteth West and vnto the Norwardes: and shineth .13. houres .12. minuts.

The great Dogge riseth East Southeast, & setteth West Southwest: and shineth .9. houres.

The lesser Dogge riseth Easte and vnto the Norwards, & setteth West & vnto the Norwardes: & shineth .13. h .10. min.

The brightest in Hydra ryseth Easte and vnto the Southwardes, and setteth West and vnto the Southwardes: and shineth .11. houres .7. minutes.

The Lions necke riseth East Northeast and to the Norwards, and setteth West Norwest and vnto the Southwardes: and shineth .16. houres .16. minutes.

The Lyons hart riseth neare the East Northeast, and setteth neare the West Norwest: & shineth .14. houres .50. min.

The Lions backe riseth neare the Northeast and by East, and setteth neare the Norwest and by West: and shineth .16. houres .26. minutes.

The Lions tayle riseth neare the East Northeast, & setteth neare the West Norwest: and shineth .15. houres .12. minutes.

The Rauens head ryseth neare the East Southeast, and setteth neare the West Southwest: & shineth .8. hours .12. min.

The Rauens wing riseth neare the East Southeast, and setteth neare the West Southwest: & shineth .8. houres .50. mi.

The Virgins spike riseth East & to the Southwards, & setteth West & to the Southwards: & shineth .11. houres .4. min.

Betweene *Bootes* thyes riseth neare the Northeast and by East, and setteth neare the Northwest and by West, and shineth .16. houres .20. minutes.

The South Ballance ryseth neare the East Southeast, and setteth neare the West Southwest: and shineth .9. houres .36. minutes.

The North ballance riseth neare the East & by South, and setteth neare the west & by South: and shineth .10. hou .38. min.

The Scorpions heart riseth neare the Southeast and by East, & setteth neare the Southwest & by West: and shineth .7. houres .5. minutes.

Hercules head riseth neare the East Northeast, and setteth neare the West Northwest: & shineth .14. houres .56. min.

The Serpēts head riseth neare the east northest, & setteth neare the west northwest: & shineth .14. houres .40. minutes.

The Eagle riseth neare the East and by North, and setteth neare the West & by North: and shineth .13. houres .24. min.

The Dolphines tayle riseth East and by north, and setteth west & by North: and shineth .15. houres .57. minutes.

The Goates tayle riseth neare the East southeast, & setteth West southwest: and shineth .9. houres .20. minutes.

The water pourers leg riseth neare the East Southeast, & setteth West southwest: and shineth .8. houres .54. minutes.

Pegasus shoulders riseth neare the East Northeast, & setteth neare the West northwest: & shineth .14. houres .32. minutes.

Pegasus legge riseth neare Northeast, and setteth neare Northwest: and shineth .17. houres .6. minutes.

The Whales tayle riseth East Southeast, & setteth West Southwest: and shineth .7. houres .48. minutes.

Furthermore if you desire to know the time of any of these starres, beeing aboue the Horizon in all Latitudes, then repayre to the .11. chapter: so you shall know it there by their declination: euen by the same order that you know the sunnes beeing aboue the Horizon, by the sunnes declination.

The .11. chapter will shewe howe long any of these stars will shine in all places.

A Table of the fixed Starres.

	These stars being south from the first day of January vnto the .15. day			January frō the 15. day to ye last			February from ye 5. vnto the .15.			February fro 15. to the la	
1	Whalesbacke.	5.20	E	1	4.20	DA	1	3.20	DA	1	2.20	D
2	Whales belly.	5.54	E	2	4.54	DA	2	3.54	DA	2	2.54	D
3	Rammes horne.	6.28.	E	3	5.28	E	3	4.28.	DA	3	3.28	D
4	Rammes head.	6.45.	E	4	5.45.	E	4	4.45.	DA	4	3.45	D
5	Bulles eye.	8.52.	E	5	7.52.	E	5	6.52.	E	5	5.52	D
6	*Orions* left fote.	9.23.	E	6	8.23.	E	6	7.23.	E	6	6.23	E
7	*Orions* left shoulder.	9.28.	E	7	8.28.	E	7.	7.28.	E	7	6.28	E
8	First *Orions* girdle.	9.50.	E	8	8.50.	E	8.	7.50.	E	8.	6.50.	E
9	*Orions* right shoulder.	10.12	E	9	9.12.	E	9.	8.12.	E	9.	7.12	E
10	Great Dogge.	11.4	E	10	10.4.	E	10	9.4.	E	10	8.4	E
11	Lesser Dogge.	12.0		11	11.0	E	11	10.0	E	11	9.0	E
12	Brightest in *Hydra*.	12.4	M	12	11.4	E	12	10.4	E	12	9.4	E
13	Lyons necke.	2.12	M	13	1.12	M	13	12.12	M	13	11.12	E
14	Lyons heart.	2.13	M	14	1.13	M	14	12.13	M	14	11.13	E
15	Lyons backe.	3.0	M	15	2.0	M	15	1.0	M	15	12.0	
16	Lyons tayle.	3.42	M	16	2.42	M	16	1.42	M	16.	12.42	M
17	Rauens head.	5.2	M	17	4.2	M	17	3.2	M	17.	2.2	M
18	Rauens wing	5.19	M	18	4.19	M	18	3.19	M	18	2.19	M
19	Virgins spike	5.51	M	19	4.51	M	19	3.51	M	19	2.51	M
20	twixt *Bootes* thighs.	5.56	M	20	4.56	M	20	3.56	M	20	2.56	M
21	South balance.	7.16	M	21	6.16	M	21	5.16	M	21	4.16	M
22	North balance.	7.33	MD	22	6.33	M	22	5.33	M	22	4.33	M
23	Scorpions heart.	8.54	MD	23	7.54	MD	23	6.54	M	23	5.54	M
24	*Hercules* head.	9.14	MD	24	8.14	MD	24	7.14	MD	24	6.14	M
25	Serpents head.	9.41	MD	25	8.41	MD	25	7.41	MD	25	6.41	M
26	The Eagle.	12.19	DA	26	11.19	MD	26	10.19	MD	26	9.19	M
27	Dolphins tayle.	1.12	DA	27	12.12.	DA	27	11.12	MD	27	10.12	M
28	Goates tayle.	1.48	DA	28	12.48	DA	28	11.48	MD	28	10.48	M
29	Water pourers leg.	2.48	DA	29	1.48	DA	29	12.48	DA	29	11.48	M
30	*Pegasus* shoulder.	3.47	DA	30	2.47	DA	30	1.47	DA	30	12.47	D
31	*Pegasus* legge.	4.12	DA	31	3.12	DA	31	2.12	DA	31	1.12	D
32	Whales tayle.	4.24	DA	32	3.24	DA	32	2.24	DA	32	1.24	D

A REGIMENT FOR THE SEA, 1574

A Table of the fixed Starres.

March from the first to the .15.			March from the 15. to the last.			Aprill from the first day to the.15.			Aprill from the 15.day to the last.			May from the first to the .15.		
1.20	DA	1	12.20	DA	1	11.20	MD	1	10.20	MD	1	9.20	MD
1.54	DA	2	12.54	DA	2	11.54	MD	2	10.54	MD	2	9.54	MD
2.28	DA	3	1.58	DA	3	12.28	DA	3	11.28	MD	3	10.28	MD
2.45	DA	4.	1.45	DA	4	12.45	DA	4	11.45	MD	4	10.45	MD
4.52	DA	5.	3.52	DA	5	2.52	DA	5	1.52	DA	5	12.52	DA
5.23	DA	6.	4.23	DA	6	3.23	DA	6	2.23	DA	6.	1.23	DA
5.28	DA	7.	4.28	DA	7	3.28	DA	7	2.28	DA	7.	1.28	DA
5.50	DA	8.	4.50	DA	8	3.50	DA	8	2.50	DA	8.	1.50	DA
6.12	E	9.	5.12	DA	9	4.12	DA	9	3.12	DA	9.	2.12	DA
7.4	E	10.	6.4	DA	10	5.4	DA	10	4.4	DA	10.	3.4	DA
8.0	E	11.	7.0	E	11	6.0	DA	11	5.0	DA	11.	4.0	DA
8.4	E	12.	7.4	E	12	6.4	DA	12	5.4	DA	12.	4.4	DA
10.12	E	13.	9.12	E	13	8.12	E	13	7.12	DA	13	6.12	DA
10.13	E	14.	9.13	E	14	8.13	E	14	7.13	DA	14	6.13	DA
11.0	E	15.	10.0	E	15	9.0	E	15	8.0	E	15	7.0	DA
11.42	E	16.	10.42	E	16	9.42	E	16	8.42	E	16	7.42	DA
1.2	M	17.	12.2	M	17	11.2	E	17	10.2	E	17	9.2	E
1.19	M	18.	12.19	M	18	11.19	E	18	10.19	E	18	9.19	E
1.51	M	19.	12.51	M	19	11.51	E	19	10.51	E	19.	9.51	E
1.56	M	20.	12.56	M	20	11.56	E	20	10.56	E	20	9.56	E
3.16	M	21.	2.16	M	21	1.16	M	21	12.16	M	21	11.16	E
3.33	M	22	2.33	M	22	1.33	M	22	12.33	M	22	11.33	E
4.54	M	23	3.54	M	23	2.54	M	23	1.54	M	23	12.54	M
5.14	M	24	4.14	M	24	3.14	M	24	2.14	M	24	1.14	M
5.41	M	25	4.41	M	25	3.41	M	25	2.41	M	25	1.41	M
8.19	MD	26	7.19	MD	26	6.19	MD	26	5.19	MD	26	4.19	M
9.12	MD	27	8.12	MD	27	7.12	MD	27	6.12	MD	27	5.12	MD
9.38	MD	28	8.48	MD	28	7.48	MD	28	6.48	MD	28	5.48	MD
10.48	MD	29	9.48	MD	29	8.48	MD	29	7.48	MD	29	6.48	MD
11.47	MD	30	10.47	MD	30	9.47	MD	30	8.47	MD	30	7.47	MD
12.12	DA	31	11.12	MD	31	10.12	MD	31	9.12	MD	31	8.12	MD
12.24	DA	32	11.24	DM	32	10.24	MD	32	9.24	MD	32	8.24	MD

A Table of the fixed Starres.

	May from the 15. day to the last.			June from the first to the .15.			June from ye 15. day to the last.			July from the first to the .15.			July from ye 15 day to the last	
1	8.20	MD	1	7.20	MD	1	6.20	MD	1	5.20	MD	1	4.20	
2	8.54	MD	2	7.54	MD	2	6.54	MD	2	5.54	MD	2	4.54	M
3	9.28	MD	3	8.28	MD	3	7.28	MD	3	6.28	MD	3	5.28	M
4	9.45	MD	4	8.45	MD	4	7.45	MD	4	6.45	MD	4	5.45	M
5	11.52	MD	5	10.52	MD	5	9.52	MD	5	8.52	MD	5	7.52	M
6	12.23	DA	6.	11.23	MD	6	10.23	MD	6	9.23	MD	6	8.23	M
7	12.28	DA	7	11.28	MD	7	10.28	MD	7	9.28	MD	7	8.28	M
8	12.50	DA	8	11.50	MD	8	10.50	MD	8	9.50	MD	8	8.50	M
9	1.12	DA	9	12.12	DA	9	11.12	MD	9	10.12	MD	9	9.12	M
10	2.4	DA	10	1.4	DA	10	12.4	DA	10	11.4	MD	10	10.4	M
11	3.0	DA	11	2.0	DA	11	1.0	DA	11	12.0		11	11.0	M
12	3.4	DA	12	2.4	DA	12	1.4	DA	12	12.4	DA	12	11.4	M
13	5.12	DA	13	4.12	DA	13	3.12	DA	13	2.12	DA	13	1.12	D
14	5.13	DA	14	4.13	DA	14	3.13	DA	14	2.13	DA	14	1.13	D
15	6.0	DA	15	5.0	DA	15	4.0	DA	15	3.0	DA	15	2.0	D
16	6.42	DA	16	5.42	DA	16	4.42	DA	16	3.42	DA	16	2.42	D
17	8.2	DA	17	7.2.	DA	17.	6.2	DA	17.	5.2	DA	17	4.2	D
18	8.19	DA	18	7.19	DA	18	6.19	DA	18	5.19	DA	18	4.19	D
19	8.51	DA	19	7.51	DA	19	6.51	DA	19	5.51	DA	19	4.51	D
20	8.56	DA	20	7.56	DA	20	6.56	DA	20	5.56	DA	20	4.56	D
21	10.16	E	21	9.16	DA	21	8.16	DA	21	7.16	DA	21	6.16	D
22	10.33	E	22	9.33	DA	22	8.33	DA	22	7.33	DA	22	6.33	D
23	11.54	E	23	10.54	E	23	9.54	DA	23	8.54	DA	23	7.54	D
24	12.14	M	24	11.14	E	24	10.14	E	24	9.14	E	24	8.14	
25	12.41	M	25	11.41	E	25	10.41	E	25	9.41	E	25	8.41	
26	3.19	M	26	2.19	M	26	1.19	M	26	12.19	M	26	11.19	
27	4.12	MD	27	3.12	M	27	2.12	M	27	1.12	M	27	12.12	
28	4.48	MD	28	3.48	M	28	2.48	M	28	1.48	M	28	12.48	
29	5.48	MD	29	4.48	MD	29	3.48	M	29	2.48	M	29	1.48	
30	6.47	MD	30	5.47	MD	30	4.47	MD	30	3.47	M	30	2.47	
31	7.12	MD	31	6.12	MD	31	5.12	MD	31	4.12	MD	31	3.12	
32	7.24	MD	32	6.24	MD	32	5.24	MD	32	4.24	MD	32	3.24	

A REGIMENT FOR THE SEA, 1574

A Table of the fixed Starres.

August from ye first to the .15.		August from the 15. day to ye last.		September from ye 1. vnto ye .15. day.		September from ye 15. to ye last day.		October frō the .1. to the .15. day.	
3.20	M	1	2.20	M	1	1.20	M	1	12.20	M	1	11.20	E
3.54	M	2	2.54	M	2	1.54	M	2	12.54	M	2	11.54	E
4.28	M	3	3.28	M	3	2.28	M	3	1.28	M	3	12.28	M
4.45	MD	4	3.45	M	4	2.45	M	4	1.45	M	4	12.45	M
6.52	MD	5	5.52	MD	5	4.52	M	5	3.52	M	5	2.52	M
7.23	MD	6	6.23	MD	6	5.23	M	6	4.23	M	6	3.23	M
7.28	MD	7	6.28	MD	7	5.28	M	7	4.28	M	7	3.28	M
7.50	MD	8	6.50	MD	8	5.50	MD	8	4.50	M	8	3.50	M
8.12	MD	9	7.12	MD	9	6.12	MD	9	5.12	M	9	4.12	M
9.4	MD	10	8.4	MD	10	7.4	MD	10	6.4	MD	10	5.4.	M
10.0	MD	11	9.0	MD	11	8.0	MD	11	7.0	MD	11	6.0	M
10.4	MD	12	9.4	MD	12	8.4	MD	12	7.4	MD	12	6.4	M
12.12	DA	13	11.12	MD	13	10.12	MD	13	9.12	MD	13	8.12	MD
12.13	DA	14	11.13	MD	14	10.13	MD	14	9.13	MD	14	8.13	MD
1.0	DA	15	12.0		15	11.0	MD	15	10.0	MD	15	9.0	MD
1.42	DA	16	12.42	DA	16	11.42	MD	16	10.42	MD	16	9.42	MD
3.2	DA	17	2.2	DA	17	1.2	DA	17	12.2	DA	17	11.2	MD
3.19	DA	18	2.19	DA	18	1.19	DA	18	12.19	DA	18	11.19	MD
3.51	DA	19	2.51	DA	19	1.51	DA	19	12.51	DA	19	11.51	MD
3.56	DA	20	2.56	DA	20	1.56	DA	20	12.56	DA	20	11.56	MD
5.16	DA	21	4.16	DA	21	3.16	DA	21	2.16	DA	21	1.16	DA
5.33	DA	22	4.33	DA	22	3.33	DA	22	2.33	DA	22	1.33	DA
6.54	DA	23	5.54	DA	23	4.54	DA	23	3.54	DA	23	2.54	DA
7.14	DA	24	6.14	DA	24	5.14	DA	24	4.14	DA	24	3.14	DA
7.41	DA	25	6.41	DA	25	5.41	DA	25	4.41	DA	25	3.41	DA
10.19	E	26	9.19	E	26	8.19	E	26	7.19	E	26	6.19	E
11.12	E	27	10.12	E	27	9.12	E	27	8.12	E	27	7.12	E
11.48	E	28	10.48	E	28	9.48	E	28	8.48	E	28	7.48	E
12.48		29	11.48	E	29	10.48	E	29	9.48	E	29	8.48	E
1.47	M	30	12.47	M	30	11.47	E	30	10.47	E	30	9.47	E
2.12	M	31	1.12	M	31	12.12	M	31	11.12	E	31	10.12	E
2.24	M	32	1.24	M	32	12.24	M	32	11.24	E	32	10.24	E

A Table of the fixed Starres

October from ye 15. day to the last			Nouember from ye first to the .15.			Nouember the 15. day to the last			December from ye first to the .15.			December from ye 15. to the la		
1	10.20	E	1	9.20	E	1	8.20	E	1	7.20	E	1	6.20	
2	10.54	E	2	9.54	E	2	8.54	E	2	7.54	E	2	6.54	
3	11.28	E	3	10.28	E	3	9.28	E	3	8.28	E	3	7.28	
4	11.45	E	4	10.45	E	4	9.45	E	4	8.45	E	4	7.45	
5	1.52	M	5	12.52	M	5	11.52	E	5	10.52	E	5	9.52	
6	2.23	M	6	1.23	M	6	12.23	M	6	11.23	E	6	10.23	
7	2.28	M	7	1.28	M	7	12.28	M	7	11.28	E	7	10.28	
8	2.50	M	8	1.50	M	8	12.50	M	8	11.50	E	8	10.50	
9	3.12	M	9	2.12	M	9	1.12	M	9	12.12	M	9	11.12	
10	4.4	M	10	3.4	M	10	2.4	M	10	1.4	M	10	12.4	M
11	5.0	M	11	4.0	M	11	3.0	M	11	2.0	M	11	1.0	M
12	5.4	M	12	4.4	M	12	3.4	M	12	2.4	M	12	1.4	M
13	7.12	MD	13	6.12	M	13	5.12	M	13	4.12	M	13	2.12	M
14	7.13	MD	14	6.13	M	14	5.13	M	14	4.13	M	14	2.13	M
15	8.0	MD	15	7.0	M	15	6.0	M	15	5.0	M	15	4.0	M
16	8.42	MD	16	7.42	MD	16	6.42	M	16	5.42	M	16	4.42	M
17	10.2	MD	17	9.2	MD	17	8.2	MD	17	7.2	M	17	6.2	M
18	10.19	MD	18	9.19	MD	18	8.19	MD	18	7.19	M	18	6.19	M
19	10.51	MD	19	9.51	MD	19	8.51	MD	19	7.51	MD	19	6.51	M
20	10.56	MD	20	9.56	MD	20	8.56	MD	20	7.56	MD	20	6.56	M
21	12.16	DA	21	11.16	MD	21	10.16	MD	21	9.16	MD	21	8.16	MD
22	12.33	DA	22	11.33	MD	22	10.33	MD	22	9.33	MD	22	8.33	MD
23	1.54	DA	23	12.54	DA	23	11.54	MD	23	10.54	MD	23	9.54	MD
24	2.14	DA	24	1.14	DA	24	12.14	DA	24	11.14	MD	24	10.14	MD
25	2.41	DA	25	1.41	DA	25	12.41	DA	25	11.41	MD	25	10.41	MD
26	5.19	DA	26	4.19	DA	26	3.19	DA	26	2.19	DA	26	1.19	D
27	6.12	E	27	5.12	E	27	4.12	E	27	3.12	DA	27	2.12	DA
28	6.48	E	28	5.48	E	28	4.48	E	28	3.48	DA	28	2.48	DA
29	7.48	E	29	6.58	E	29	5.48	E	29	4.48	E	29	3.48	DA
30	8.47	E	30	7.47	E	30	6.47	E	30	5.47	E	30	4.47	
31	9.12	E	31	8.12	E	31	7.12	E	31	6.12	E	31	5.12	
32	9.24	E	32	8.24	E	32	7.24	E	32	6.24	E	32	5.24	

A REGIMENT FOR THE SEA, 1574

Now this table serueth for euery monthe in the yere (beeing exactly calculated) the time of their beeing South, or touching your Meridiā or (as some terme it) Noonestead, seruing very well the Seamen to take the heigth of them with their instruements vpon the Sea, referring it vnto the table of declination that goeth before: the first is the houres, the secōd the minutes, the thirde be the letters that shewe you whether they be South by day or by night, in the euening or morning, in the forenoone or after noone, of which the letter E doth signifie Euening, the letter M. signifieth Morning, the letters DM. signifieth day in the Morning, and the letters DA signifieth day in the after noone (as I sayde before) the very houre and minute of their beeing South. Nowe you see that I haue put to their beeing South in the day as well as in the nighte, to the intent to knowe the houre of the night as well by their setting, and also by your compasse, which I shewed you in the first chapter or rule, namely to bring your .32. poyntes into 24. houres: and in like maner in the fourth chapter by shining of the Moone to diuide the shining into two equall partes, then those parts (beeing equally deuided with the houre & minutes) and the time before their beeing South, put togither the halfe that shineth, and that sheweth the iust rising of those starres: and the other time of their shining after their beeing South, sheweth their setting (as I declared in the rule of the shining of the Moone.) Nowe you, seeing the table runneth from the first day of euery monthe to the .15. and from the .15. to the last day, you must consider (if you will knowe the exacte time betwixte the first day & the .15. day, or betwixt the .15. day, and the last) to do this, looke how many dayes of the monthe is paste eyther from the first day, or .15. day, and pull foure minutes from the number: for so many days as is past, for euery day that shall shew you the true time of their beeing South. That knowne, you shall doe (as is aforesayde) for their rising and setting.

The significa-tion of the letters in the table.

¶ *The .21. Chapter sheweth you the making of a generall instrument, to know the houre of the day by, throughout all the worlde.*

Nowe for the making of your instruments for the Sea, with their vses, you shall repayre to the booke of Nauigation made by Martin Curtise a Spaniarde, Imprinted by M. Jugge Printer to the Queenes Maiestie: else I woulde haue shewed you the making of diuers instruments, as also the making of the equinoctiall diall with his vse, whiche is very profitable to knowe the houre of the day by, in all latitudes through the whole worlde, for your compasse is not to knowe the houre of the day be in Sommer, neyther in the Morning nor Euening, neyther can you knowe when the Moone is east or West, she hauing North declination, as beeing in the signe of *Taurus, Gemini, Cancer,* or *Leo*: bicause your compasse standeth flatte as dothe your Horizon. Wherefore it is very good for Sea menne to vse the Equinoctiall dials, for that it sheweth them the true houre of the day in all Latitudes, and also the Moone dothe giue a true shadowe in that Diall in all Latitudes, for I doe knowe that Sea men are very many times deceyued where it dothe flowe an East and West Moone, or any poynt betweene the Southeast and North east. Bicause in setting the Moone with their compasse (beeing in the North signes) she seemeth to be East by the Compasse, when she is neare the East Southeast in hir course: and in like manner when the Moone seemeth West by the compasse she shall be a little more than West Southwest in hir course: which is a very perillous matter vnto them that should put into a tide, harborowe, or hauen, where he knoweth there is water inough for him if that he dothe come at a full Sea, and then by the error of the Moones shadowe of the compasse he is deceyued: and when he findeth the error he thinketh that the cause thereof commeth by the occasion of some storme of wynde that is lyke to followe, imputing vnto it that the tyde dothe not keepe hys course, whereas the uery cause groweth by

The sunne and moone doth giue a full shadow by the compasse. The Equinoctiall diall giueth a true shadow all the world ouer.

A perilous matter.

A REGIMENT FOR THE SEA, 1574

no other meanes but of receyuing a false shadowe by the Horizontall compasse: and especially if the Moone be neare hir greatest declination vnto the North partes, that is, in the signe of *Gemini* and *Cancer*. And also that effect is most preferred if the Dragons head be in the beginning of the signe of *Aries*: for that then if the Moone be in the beginning of *Cancer*, she shall haue .5. degrees more in declination from the Equinoctiall, than the sunne shall haue at their greatest declination vnto the North partes: so that reseruing the Moones Paralex, which is according vnto the Latitude of any place that the Moone shal be declined .28. degrees and a halfe vnto the North part of the Equinoctiall: so that for auoyding of these infirmities, I woulde wishe them to vse the Equinoctiall dials. And furthermore I do thinke that the Equinoctiall dials be not vsed amongst our Mariners heere in Englande for that the charges is so muche in the making of them, & yet it serueth no other turne but to know the houre of the day, & to shew the true shadowe of the Moone. I haue not knowne thē vsed by any English Master or Pylot, but only by one man, which person had not it for the proper vse therof, but rather had it, to say that he had suche an instrument as no English man had the like, & to bragge that he had such an instrument that he could do great feates therewith in the going of long viages &c. I would haue no man offended with me. I know the nature and qualitie of some that take charge: they will haue instruments & other things therunto apperteyning, & yet they thēselues do not know yᵉ vse of thē, yet they will seeme to be cunning, & that they neede no instructiōs of any man, for that they know all things, & yet in respect know nothing. (But not withstanding) I would wish them that be Sea faring men to vse themselues to the Equinoctiall dials: for that they doe serue two notable turnes, as well at home in these our chanels, as also in long viages: they may make them with a very easie charge: for whereas in the Arte of Nauigation it is shewed howe to make them in brasse, they may make them with wood in this manner: take a peece of bordes

The moon may decline 28. degrees and a halfe from the Equinoctiall.

Of mē that wil haue instruments and knowe not the vse of them.

An easie waye to make an equinoctiall diall with little charge

267

ende of sixe inches broad, more or lesse at your discretion, and halfe an inche in thicknesse, then hauing cutte it rounde, and playned it smoothe, you maye eyther graue in it the .32. poyntes of the compasse, or else paynt them vpon it with some colours, with the .24. houres vpon bothe the sides: as this figure sheweth.

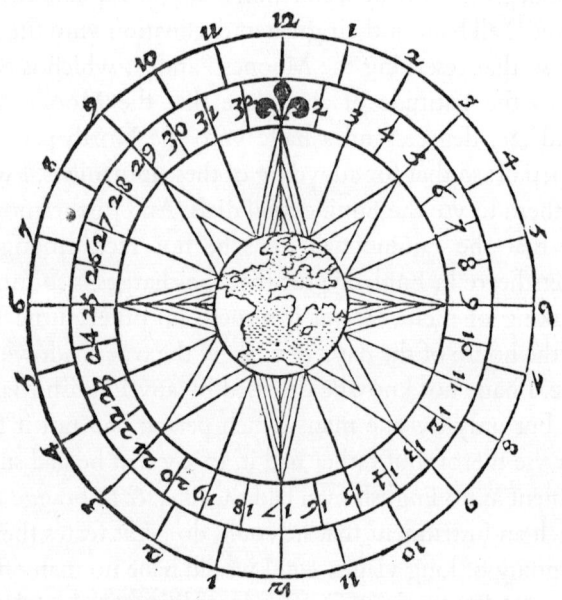

That done take a wyre of iust the Diameter of the Instrument and put it through the middle or centre of the Instrument, then make it faste that the one ende be halfe way thoroughe on the one side, and the other halfe on the other side, this done make a frame with three peeces of bordes endes to hang the diall or instrument vpō, with one pinne on the East poynt and an other on the West poynt: then take an other peece of boardes endes being square, and with a payre of compasses strike a quarter of a circle of iuste the bignesse of the quarter of the diall, and cutte all that away, and then the rest of the square that is left, (at the ende of the quarter of the circle) deuided into

.90. equall partes, marking it thus .10.20.30.40.50.60.70.80.90. as in this forme: last of all let this be placed in the middle of the frame, so that .90. may stand right vnder the verie middle of the diall and there made fast, in suche forme that the very ende of the wyer when the diall is put vp and downe may touche the hollow parte that you see cut away, which 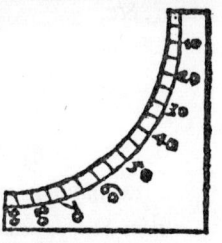 is called the Directer, and so it is finished, and will stand altogether in this forme.

The Equinoctiall Diall.

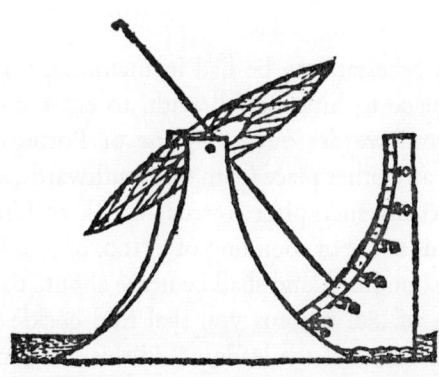

The vse of this Diall is most necessarie in a shippe, for that you haue occasions to transporte your selues into all the clymates. And to know the true houre of the day doe this: set this Diall by your compasse (the Directer vnto the Southewardes) and then (you knowing how hie the pole is abouc the Horizon) set the ende of the wyer right against that degree in the directer, and the other ende of the wier will poynt iuste vnto the pole, then looke what shadowe the wyer doth giue by the Sunne, that is the true houre of the daye. In lyke manner you may know the true houre of the night by the Moones shadowe, and also the Moone will giue a true shadowe of hir place . &c.

> ¶ The .22. Chapter treateth of the
> soundings, commying from any place out of the Occi-
> dent Sea, to seeke Vshant or the Lyzarde, and so all alongst
> till you come to the coaste of Flaunders: with other
> necessarie matters to be knowne, to them that
> be Channellers, that doth occupie, or
> deale amongst sandes, bankes,
> or such other like.

The sounding neare vnto Ushāt and the Lizarde.

Bicause it is necessarie to be had in memorie, for that it is a daūgerous place to hitte or fall with, to enter into yᵉ Sleue, comming homewardes out of Spaine or Portugall, or from Barbarie, or any other place from the Southwardes, a shippe that commeth frō any such place to seeke the Ile of Ushant, or the Lizarde in this roote of sounding of a .100. or .90. fadoms shall finde bigge soundings, and shall be neare aboute to the seames. In the roote of .80. fadoms you shal find cockle shelles, and dentes in the talow of the leade: & in this sounding holde on your course to the North till you chaunge sounding, then if you be at .60. or .64. fadom, you shall finde small sand and Mathey grounde, and shall be neare the coaste of Ushant. If you haue time and day goe seeke it in the Northeast, and you shall be aboute .10. leagues from the Ile. If you come making your course aboute Basefreede, you shall finde course sande, red and browne, and you shall haue sounding at .40. fadom: if you be towardes the banke of Silley, you shall haue soundings at .86. or .90. fadom, & you shall finde in the tallow stonie ground and shall be well shotte towards the banke of Silley. When you be at .80. fadome you shall finde small blacke sande, and shall

A REGIMENT FOR THE SEA, 1574

be well towardes the Lizarde. When you be at .60. or .64. fadome, you shall finde white sande & white softe wormes, and shall be verie nie to the Lizarde. Between the cape of Cornewall and Ushant amidde the channell, you shall finde .70. fadome, & neare inough. Betweene Dodman & the Forne in the channell you shall haue .40. or .50. fadome. If you be thwarte of Plimmouth or the Starte, you shal finde streamic ground & dentes in the tallowe, & soundings .41. or .42. fadoms. At the cōming from Portland you shall haue .35. fadoms, and small shingels. And when you be nie to Portland .30. fadoms, & stones like beanes: & this sounding will last till S. Aldam, & in the sayd soundings you shall find white stones like brokē Aules, & other that be bigger, & then you shalbe thwarte of S. Aldam or of the Ile of Wight. Two or 3. leagues frō the Ile of Wight, you shall finde .25. fadome, with dentes & cleftes in the tallow like smal threedes .2. or .3. leagues frō the Caskettes you shall finde .40. fadome & bigge stones ragged and blacke. Betweene the Ile of Wight & the hagge, the deepest is but .35. or .40. fadome. Betweene the Ile of Wight & Lantergate the deepest is but .25. or .30. fadomes. Betweene Beachy & the Ile of Wight, a league from the land, you shall finde .38. fadome and poppell as bigge as beanes. Betweene Fairely and the water of Summe in the deepest but .25. fadom, Betweene Folkestone and Bollayne is a banke that is called Rippe rappe: and lieth in the midde way betweene Pickardie and Englande: and harde aborde by it, is .26. or .27. fadome. In the straighte of Calice is .30. fadom, in the roade of Calice is .16. fadom. And alongst the coast of Flaunders is but .20. fadome the deepest. Thus muche haue I sayde for the entrance of the Sleeue, to come to the riuer of Thames, and in the entrance in the midway betweene Ushant and the Lizarde the pole Articke is eleuated .50. degrees and a halfe, and the Equinoctiall is lifted aboue the Horyzon .39. degrees and a halfe. And furthermore for them that are channellers and occupiers amongst sandes and banckes, and such other like, they must haue consideration of these things follow-

The sounding in the channell.

The higth of the pole at the entrāce of the Sleeue.

Necessary things to be noted for thē that are Chānellers & dealers amongst sandes.

ying. As this: first (if you knowe how the channell doth lie right betweene any .2. sandes) you must view the land to take some markes for it, in this manner to be a leadyng marke. And that you shall do thus: looke something that standeth farre into the lande, that you may knowe it well being right open with the channell of the sandes, then take an other marke neare vnto the water side, and the one to be right agaynst the other, when that you be in the middle of the channell, and then you knowing these twoo markes well, they will be leading markes vnto you for euer to keepe that channell. And then furthermore if it dothe so happen that the channell doth turne to keepe an other course, or els (some other daunger lying in the way) you muste haue a thwarte marke to know bothe when that you are cleare of any daunger, and also when that you are open of an other channell, and that you shall do as before is declared, to take some marke within the lande, and also an other neare vnto the sea, water or riuer side, to be your thwarte marke when you bring them both together. And this is most specially to be noted: that those markes be very yare and good when the one is farre distant from the other: and those markes very slowe and asketh some distance in sayling to open and shette them, whiche are neare together vpon the lande. And furthermore, for them that are Channellers or occupiers amongest sandes, for that the weather is not alwaies cleare, when they haue occasion to passe thorowe suche places, it is good for them to sounde the channelles perfitely, and to know the by depthe, what side of the channell they are vpon, and also howe farre they are shotte into that channell. And also in like manner to know by the sounding of any of the sides of the channell, whether they be neare any of the sandes or daungers, or any breadth of: for y^t some sandes or daūgers there be: hauing fayre or good soundings or shaldings, that they may borrowe of and on at their pleasure. There be againe some sandes and daungers that there is no borrowing nor sounding of them, and those be neall or deepe, harde vnto the sandes or daungers: for that the water is deepe harde vnto the sande: and these are verie daungerous sandes for any shippe to come neare, for that they shall haue the water verie deepe, and by and by be a grounde. Yet furthermore it is very good for them that be channellers and occupiers amongst sandes, to know whiche way the tide doth set at euery time of the tide: for that many times it happeneth so, that when the sandes be vnder the water, the tide doth set crosse the channell, which is a daungerous matter if it be not very well considered by the Master or Pilote. &c.

¶ *The .23. Chapter, is as touching the variatiō of the Compasse, called the Northeasting and the Norwesting of the Compasse: and how to giue a gesse to know the Longitude.*

As touching the variation of the cōpasse called the Northeasting or Norwesting, it is supposed that the Compasse doth varie by proportiō, in the sayling to the Eastwards or Westwardes: and (as I haue declared in the end of the .6. chapter) if it varieth by proportion that the Northpoint is varied one poynt from the North at .22. degrees and a halfe, and so vntill the North point doth stande Northeast or Norwest. And that is, when you are .90. degrees from the Meridian that the compas was made at to the Eastwardes or Westwards. Some also are of an other opiniō, that the compas doth varie by no proportion, but dothe varie according vnto the nature of some kinde of mineralles, that is, in some countrie or some kynde of Ilandes, that drawe the Compasse by the mines of the Loade stone or Magnes stone that they touche their compasse with when they make them. And furthermore the booke of Martine Curtise, (called the arte of Nauigation) sayeth that the compasse doth varie by proportion, in this māner: which is, by the proportion of a circle: for that the North poynt dothe alwayes poynt vnto a

Of the cōpasse to varie by euen proportion.

Of the cōpasse to vary by no proportion.

Of yͤ compasse to varie according vnto the proportion of a circle, that is swiftly & slowly.

place in the heauens that is vnmoueable, and therefore as you do transporte your selfe to the Eastwarde or Westwarde, the North poynt doth still poynt vnto that place in the heauen: wherefore (as he sayeth) when you be .90. degrees in Longitude from the place of the making of your compasse or that is, when you be one quarter of the circumference of the earth, in that paralell the compasse will be varied .4. poyntes from the North: and as you do transporte your selfe further, then the Northe poynt of the compasse will come nearer and nearer vnto the North: and when you are iust halfe the circumference of the earth, that then the North poynt will stande due Northe vpon the pole agayne: for that you are come to the same Meridian againe vpon the opposite part of the earth, (as it doth appeare in the third part and .5. chapter, of the saide booke of Martine Curtise) but if that be true then the compasse doth varie swiftely at the first and slowly afterwardes in order like vnto the Sunnes declination: by whiche (if it be true) they may very well knowe what order the compasse doth varie by, and so by the variation you may giue an neare estimation of the Longitude, and knowe in howe many degrees the compasse is varied one poynte, two poynts, three poynts, and so the greatest variation whiche is foure poynts. Nowe to know the proportion doe this: Firste, make a circle with a payre of compasses, and stryke a Line by the Center to the circumference, which shall be your Meridian lyne, then stryke an other lyne by the Center a crosse, that you may deuide the circle into foure equall

To knowe in how many degrees goyng vnto the Eastward: or Westwarde that the cōpasse doth varie one poynt or .2. points or .3. points &c.

partes, and then (for that fourtie fiue degrees is the greatest variation) sette fourtie fiue vnto the Easte parte and West parte, deuidying euery one of the quarters of the circle into fourtie fiue equall partes, according to the greatest variation then make an other circle of that Diameter, that the circumference touche the Center of the Circle: and deuide it as you deuide the Compasse after the rate of two and thirtie poyntes although you neede not deuide but that true to the Norwardes, and then the Northeast and Norwest point will fall vpon fourtie fiue degrees: that done drawe lynes according to the poyntes of the Compasse vnto the Eastwardes or Westwardes, and looke howe they fall vpon the lyne that commeth from the Center of the other Circle of which euery quarter is diuided into fourtie fiue equall partes: and then (at the very place that the lyne doothe touche) drawe paralell lynes in that Circle by proportion, at the very place to the Eastwardes or Westwardes that the lyne of the Compasse falleth vpon: and that will shewe you iustly howe many degrees you shall transporte youre selfe vnto the Eastwardes or Westwardes, for the varying of the first poynte, seconde poynte, and thirde poynte, and in lyke manner the greatest variation whiche is the fourthe poynte. So that (according to that order) it will fall out in this manner, that the Compasse will be varied one point at neare eleuen and $\frac{1}{3}$. It will be varied two poyntes neare aboute foure and twentie degrees and a halfe. It will be varied three poyntes at fourtie two degrees, and aboute a halfe. But it will not be varied the fourth point vntill you be full foure score and tenne degrees from the Meridian that the Compasse was made at: whiche is a very slow varying beyng .47. degrees and $\frac{1}{2}$ before the Compasse dothe varie one poynt, and betweene the thirde poynt and the seconde poynt beyng .18. degrees for the varying of the poynt, and then from the seconde poynte vnto the fyrste poynte, it is .13. degrees and better, and last of all from the varying of one poynt to the Meridian it is .11. degrees and $\frac{1}{3}$ parte, euery degree beyng according to the parralel you are in, which dothe alter according vnto your Latitude from the Equinoctiall: for vnder the Equinoctiall it is .60. Englishe miles, or .20. English leagues vnto one degree. In the Latitude of .60. degrees from the Equinoctiall there in that parralell it is but .30. myles, or .10. Englishe leagues vnto one degree . &c. as it is plainely shewed in the .16. chapter of this booke, wherein is an instrument shewing you howe many miles of Longitude will answere vnto a degree in euery seuerall Latitude by the replying of a threed at your discretion: so that I conclude if the compas doth varie by that

To knowe how many degrees is in the varying of one poynt.

If you wil knowe howe many leagues a degree is, repayre to the 16. chapter.

ordre of proportion that Martine Curtise dothe attribute vnto it, you may giue a neare ghesse to finde the Longitude by the varying of the compas beyng neare vnto the Meridian that the compas was made for. But if you be very farre from the Meridian that the compas was made for, then the variation is so slowe that you can haue no iudgement at all (by the variation of the compas) to finde any Longitude. And furthermore if the compas dothe varie by that proportion that Martine Curtise doth affirme, I am of that opinion that there may growe some errour in proportion in those compasses that are made for any Meridian: for those compasses that are made here with vs in Englande whereof the needle dothe stande .4. or .5. degrees vnto the Eastwards of ye North (as doth appeare by all the needles made for dials & also in the compasses) if they would haue the North point to stande due North, then the ende of the wyers vnder the carde of the compasse should stande foure or fiue degrees vnto the Eastwards of the Flouredeluce: wherefore it may be doubted that the compasse maye varie more the one way than it will the other way, by that proportion that the ende of the wyre dothe stande beside from the North poynt. For (if in the greatest variation) the ende of the wyre (vnder the carde of the compasse) dothe stande Northwest, the flouredeluce of the compasse sthould stande neare halfe a poynt to the Westwards of the Northwest. And in like maner at the greatest variation, if the ende of the wyre doth stande Northeast, then the Flouredeluce should stande neare halfe a poynt vnto the Northwards of the Northeast .&c. And furthermore heere is one thing that I could neuer vnderstande the truthe of, and yet I haue often-times demaunded the question of dyuers that haue beene in the West part, in the bay of *America*, and that is this: Whether in the compasse there made, or in the dials that are there made, the endes of the Nedles doe stande due North, or not? and yet it hath not beene my chaūce to meete with any that can tell. For if it be so that those Nedles that are there touched doe stande due North, then it were very good for them

There may growe some errour in ye proportion of the varying of the Compasse.

Thinges that I can not know.

A REGIMENT FOR THE SEA, 1574

that should occupie long trauerse vnto the Westwarde or Eastwarde, to haue diuers compasses ready made with the Needle of them vntouched, and to carie a good Lodestone with them to touche those compasses when the compasse hath the greatest variation. It is good for these two causes: the once cause: it is the better to direct your course by. But this cause is very speciall, to giue a neare gesse of the Longitude, that is to say, the compasse will varie more quickly (according to the order before written) by which you see they may transporte them selues further vnto the Eastwards or Westwardes before that the compasse dothe varie one poynt, that it dothe for the other three poynts, so that they are not able to giue any estimation at all, by the varying of the compasse, to knowe any Longitude: for that they may trauel more than the quarter of the circumference of the earth, before the compasse will be varied one poynt backewardes and forwardes. And I do very much maruell at this, (considering how many times English men haue bene in the west Indies) that I can meete with no man that can tell whether the needels of the Dials or compasses made there do stande due Northe or not: whiche is a thing that may be easily knowe. For the needels of the Dials it is soone seene, and in like manner of the Compasses: for if the Needle of the Compasses there made will not stande due North, then it is reformed vpon the Carde of the flye of the Compasse, as if the North ende of the wyers doe stande Northeast, then they will set Northeast ouer it, euen as we do set the ende of the wyres of the Compasses with vs made neare halfe a poynt to the Eastwardes of the North . &c. And furthermore it is very good for them that are Masters or Pylotes of shippes to note, when they doe fall with any lande where the Compasse is varied, to make a remembrance in a booke howe many poyntes and degrees the Cōpasse is varied in euery place where they come vnto, which will be a great helpe for them to finde that place againe. And to finde the variation it is declared in the 6. Chapter. And heere I leaue to trouble thee any further for this time:

Of slowe varying of the cōpasse.

How easy it is to knowe whether ye the cōpasses made in the West Indies do stād due North.

Of making notes of the variation.

but shortly after this, looke for the two other workes of myne,
the one called, *The shoting in great Ordinance*:
an other named. *A Treasure for Trauellers*: which
two Bookes will be profitable I trust for
all men. If these my labours my profite my Countrey, then haue I my
desire. And thus I bid thee
moste hartily fare-
well.

A REGIMENT FOR THE SEA, 1574

The Table of the contents of this booke.

The first chapter of Nauigatiō sheweth what the .32. poyntes of the compasse be, and to what vses they do serue. Fol.8.a

The .2. chapter treateth of the golden number or prime, shewing the Epact, and by the Epact to knowe the age of the Moone. Fol.9.b

The .3. chapter teacheth howe to know by the age of the Moone what a clocke it dothe showe, or is full Sea at any place where you do knowe what Moone maketh a full Sea. Fol.10.b

The .4. chap. treateth of the Sunne and Moones course in the Zodiacke, and howe you shall knowe at what houres the Moone shal rise and set at: and at what poynt of the Compasse, with other necessarie things. Fol.14.a

The .5. chapter is of a table of declination, commonly called of Seafaring men a Regiment of the sunne, exactly calculated for .4. yeres, and will serue for .24. yeres. for euery day of the monthe. Fol.16.b

The .6. chapter sheweth howe to take the height of the Sunne with the Crosse staffe . &c. Fol.26.a

The .7. chapter sheweth howe to handle the declination of the Sunne, to know the altitude of the north pole aboue the Horizon (the height of the Sunne beeing truly taken & knowne in any place betweene the North pole and the Equinoctial) so that the sunne be vnto the Southwards of you at the taking of the same vpon the Meridian. Fol.19.a

The .8. chapter sheweth you how to handle the declination of the Sunne when you are betweene the Equinoctiall and the sunne, that is to say, the sunne to the Southwardes or Northwards of you, and the Equinoctiall to the Northwards or Southwards, or vnder the Equinoctiall, the heigth of the sun being truly knowē or takē. f.30.b.

The .9. chap. sheweth howe to handle the declination of the sunne when you are beyonde the Equinoctial, that is to say, betweene the South pole, and the Equinoctiall: with certen ensamples bothe for the South pole, and the North pole. F.32.a

The .10. chapter sheweth howe to handle the sunnes declinatiō unto the Northward, where the sunne doth not set under the Horizō: and also to take the sun at the lowest due north. f.34.b.

The .11. chap. doth shew howe you shall know the length of the day, and to know how much the day is shortned or lengthened by the sunnes declination. Fol.36.a

The .12. ch. is of the North star. f.38.a

The .13. chap. doth shew you by the sayling vpō the quarter of your compasse, in how far sayling you do rayse a degree, and what you do depart from the Meridian . &c. Fol.39.a.

The .14. chapter sheweth howe to knowe howe farre any lande is off from you, if you knowe the distance betwene any two places, whether that you do runne alongst by the lande, or directly to the shore, or otherwise, with other necessarie things. Fol.40.a

The .15. chapter treateth of the longitude . &c. Fol.42.b

The .16. chapter sheweth how many miles will answere to one degree of longitude in euery seuerall latitude betweene the Equinoctiall and eyther of the two poles: with the demōstratiō for that purpose, & also the diuersitie of aspects of the Moone. fo.44.a

The .17. chapter treateth of the longitude and latitude of certayne of the most notable townes in Englande, and also how long the moone doth chaūge at one towne before an other: with the diuersitie of the longest day in sommer, from Southhampton to the northermost part in Scotland. Fo.45.b

The .18. chapter sheweth howe to sayle by the globe. And to know how much the water is hyer than the leuell betweene any two shippes on the Sea, which groweth by the roundnesse of the earth. Fol.47.a

The .19. chapter is as touching the making of plattes or Cardes for the Sea, and not to paynt their Cardes as they doe, important to sailors, as the changes of the moon, and therefore the tides, were accelerated or retarded according to her motion. The considerable elaboration (in this edition) of what Bourne had to say about the log and line has also already been discussed (p. 126), but the style of the first hundred or so words of this additional explanation (p. 297) deserves comment. It gives an irresistable impression of first-hand experience, and as Bourne had none, we must suppose a sailor at his elbow, very possibly James Beare, whose words he wrote down.

A further lengthy addendum (p. 299) is that on 'matters as tending discoveries unto the North parts', largely based on the experience gained during Frobisher's voyages. It is remarkable for the correct explanation offered for the accumulation of icebergs encountered off Labrador and Newfoundland. They are driven by a current coming from the north, and then 'stayed' by the Gulf Stream where it turns across their path towards Europe. The whole of this section should be read in connection with what was the most definitive feature that distinguishes the new edition, namely the *Hydrographicall Discourse* on the searoutes to Cathay discussed below (p. 301).

The purpose of this *Discourse* was evidently to attract the reading public, for it has no immediate relevance to the rules and methods of navigation. Richard Eden and his printer, Richard Jugge, had planned a similar addendum to help the sales of a second edition of the English *Cortes*. It was to be a translation of Taisnier's little book on the magnet which Eden had brought home from France. But in this case death intervened and the plan did not mature.[1] Bourne's choice of Cathay

---

[1] 'I chaunced in the meane tyme, to meete with my olde acquayntance and freend, Richard Jugge, Printer to the Queenes Majestie, who had many yeeres before, printed the Book of *Marten Cortes*, of the Art of Navigation, by me translated out of the Spaynish tongue. Whereof, having with him some conferences, he declared that he would prynt that booke agayne, yf I woulde take the paynes to devise some addition touchyng the same matter, that myght be joyned thereto.' Richard Eden's 'Epistle Dedicatorie to Syr William Wynter, Knight, Master of the Ordnaunce of the Queen's Majesties Shippes', 1572/3, prefixed to his translation of J. Taisnier's *De natura magnetis*, published separately in 1575(?) as *A Booke concerning Nauigation*.

III

A Regiment for the Sea (1580)

EDITOR'S NOTE

The second Address 'To the Reader' and the textual additions

The two printings of the *Regiment* (1574 and 1577) were exhausted by 1580, but as the book had proved successful the author was now given the opportunity of supervising a new edition. He used it (as already explained) to disclaim the second imprint, on the grounds that he was not told about it or asked to see it through the press. His complaint is made in the opening of a second Address *To The Reader* (p. 292). The earlier Address, together with the Dedication to the Lord High Admiral, appears unchanged, as does the Calendrical material and other Tables, save that the years 1574–8 are omitted from the list which gives the Prime, Epact, Dominical Letter and Moveable Feasts down to 1603. The time-table of Law Terms and 'Returns' was, of course, unchanged, and it may be noted that in some details it supplements the information to be found in Cheney's *Handbook of Dates* (R. Hist. Soc., 1945), the author of which did not have the opportunity to consult any Elizabethan almanac.

The changes made in the general text, which the author points out in his second Address, although comparatively few, are important. There are, in the first place, two additional definitions (p. 296) of astronomical terms, 'excentric' and 'parallax', no doubt asked for by pupils. These are, it must be admitted, rather fumblingly worded, and they have already been discussed (p. 120). The moon's alternate swift and slow motions are now more fully explained, both in relation to her excentricity and to the movement of her nodes through the Zodiac during the nineteen-year cycle. This was, of course,

but rather to fill the vacant places with other necessarie matters: and also of three necessary things conteyned in the Plattes or Cardes, with their vses. Fol.49.a

The .20. chapter is of the longitude and declination of .32. notable fixed starres for Nauigation, with tables of their shining, and at what poynt of the compasse they do both rise and set: it hath also tables for euery monthe in the yere, declaring at what time they wil be South . &c. which wil continue these .100. yeres without muche error.
Fol.51.b

The .21. chapter sheweth you the making of a generall Instrument, to know the houre of the day by through out all the worlde. Fol.57.b.

The .22. chap. treateth of the soundings cōming from any place out of the Occidental Sea, to seeke Ushant, or the Lizarde and so all alongst tyll you come to the coast of Flaunders: with other necessarie matters to be knowne for them that be Chanellers, that occupie or deale amongst sandes, bankes . &c. Fol.59.b.

The .23. chapter is as touching the variation of the Compasse, called the Northeasting and Northweasting of the Compasse: and howe to giue a gesse to know the longitude. Fol.61.a

FINIS.

as his subject could hardly have been bettered, for both in the City and at Court it was the topic of the day. The diversion of Frobisher's second and third voyages from the search for a Passage to the collection of ship-loads of supposititious gold ore was known to have led to heavy losses by the investors. The treasurer of the adventure, Michael Lok, found himself in gaol, and Dr John Dee (who had been on the Committee) was pressing for the resumption of exploration to the north-east. Nothing could have been more welcome to inquisitive and interested persons than a simple geographical survey of all the possible routes to the fabled El Dorado of Cathay as described by Marco Polo.

Bourne expected to be criticized for his new book as he had been for his earlier ones. But as he only wrote for the simplest sort of readers and not for the learned, he was not to be put off by the malice of the envious. It seems obvious, however, that sailors as well as educated men had been among his critics, for he castigates them for their self-esteem, recalling those 'ancient mariners' who mocked at the use of cross-staff and chart. The best-trained man might be the victim of ill-fortune (he said), but the untrained man, although he might boast his good fortune, could not for ever command it.

'Hydrographicall Discourse' of the Passage to Cathay

While by 1580 there was a growing volume of travel literature available in English, there was still no text-book of geography from which the student could obtain a clear picture of the world as a whole. Johann Honter's little *Cosmographia* (1541) was read, but it was old-fashioned and formal—hardly more than a catalogue of names. And it was in Latin. William Cuningham's *Cosmographical Glasse* (1559) dealt, and in highly academic style, only with topics which fall into the category of mathematical geography. Thus, neither book could present the reader with the 'freedom of the globe' in quite the way that he could acquire it from Bourne's rapid sketch of the world's great seaways—'known and supposed' as he classified them. And of course, his subject was highly topical.

His proposal to show the way to Cathay by five different routes instead of the expected four was a clever stroke to awaken the reader's curiosity. The courses that the Portuguese and the Spanish ships followed to the east and the west respectively had long been accepted as being their monopolies, to be challenged only at risk. The merits of the north-east and north-west passages had also in turn long been publicly discussed, and two books on the subject, those of Humfrey Gilbert and Richard Willes had quite recently been published. But what was the fifth way? It was one that few had dreamt of—it lay across the Pole, athwart the Frozen Zone. Yet it was only necessary to look for a moment at the globe to realize that this was the shortest and the most direct way of them all. For Cathay was what is now called Northern China. It was reckoned to lie midway between equator and pole, and to be almost on the opposite meridian to that of Britain, 180° away in longitude, but in latitude less than 90°.

It is not impossible that Bourne was aware that the idea of sailing due north to reach the east had been put forward two generations earlier, as the nearest way by which the English could reach the Spiceries. The proposal had been made by the merchant Robert Thorne to King Henry VIII, and was later revived by his friend Roger Barlow. Thorne had based his argument not only on the avoidance of any clash with Portugal or Spain, but on the advantage of sailing by the long drawn out summer daylight. It lasted six months at the Pole. And he believed that darkness was the sailor's worst enemy. Copies of Thorne's Address, and of the letter dated 1527 which he wrote to the English ambassador in Spain, were preserved by Cyprian Lucar, whose father Emanuel had been Thorne's apprentice. Cyprian brought the papers to the notice of Dr Dee in 1577, and also allowed Richard Hakluyt to copy them. He may have shown them to Bourne, for as both were 'mathematical prac-

Fig. 13. 'Sir Humfray Gylbert knight his chart', drawn c. 1582, perhaps by Dr John Dee

Original in the Free Library of Philadelphia. The polar projection illustrates Bourne's contention that the shortest way to Cathay lay across the Pole.

titioners', teaching and writing on similar subjects, an acquaintance between them may be surmised.

Bourne's discussion of the trans-Polar route is, nevertheless, much fuller and better informed than Thorne's. He had the advantage of his stepson's experience in high latitudes. James Beare gained an excellent reputation during the second and third Frobisher voyages in which he took part. This is evident from George Best's narrative published during December 1578. As master of the *Anne Francis* Beare served under George Best, her captain, and in such a small ship the master and captain were brought into very close association. It is safe to assume therefore that Beare was familiar with, and even supplemented, his superior officer's arguments when the latter urged the possibilities of high latitude navigation.[1] They were the arguments also used, though in more summary form, by Bourne. Both agreed that the great salt sea never froze. The icebergs round Meta Incognita which put the ships in such imminent danger were of land origin, or were formed in inshore waters. No ice was encountered for upwards of a hundred leagues to the north of North Cape in Norway, that is to say as far as 76° or 77° north. And this was taken to prove that there was no great land-mass still further north. Mercator's Arctic map of 1569 was at fault, and the Frozen Sea which earlier cartographers showed lying to the north of the Old World, likewise did not exist.

Such arguments were, of course, only partially correct, but it was a sound inference that it was the fog and the northerly winds that brought such severe weather in the much lower latitudes (62°–63°) which were being explored in the north-west. When the sun shone it was found warm and pleasant enough on land there. It had become obvious, in fact, that latitude was not the sole factor that determined climate, as the ancients taught. In particular the long days compensated for the low angle of the sun's rays as the latitude increased. But Bourne

[1] George Best, *A True Discourse of the late Voyage of Discovery* (London, 1578).

had met with practical arguments of another sort against his suggested polar passage. The magnetic compass, it was said, would fail the steersman so near the magnetic pole, while the sun, moving almost horizontally round the sky could not be used to mark the meridian line. And under the Pole itself every direction would be south. How could a ship set course? Bourne would not admit these difficulties save within five degrees, a mere hundred leagues, of the Pole. And within this area he suggests the use of a spring-watch with a twenty-four hour dial. Having oriented the watch in good time so that the hour hand pointed south at noon, the hand would point in succession to the quarters of the sky as the day passed. The usefulness of the spring-watch at sea had already been realized for a generation or more, and at this very time William Borough was giving advice on how to employ one as a chronometer to obtain the longitude at sea. But an Elizabethan watch was a very poor timekeeper, and was soon put out of action by damp or temperature change. Nor would Bourne's device serve if the ship was driven off course. Nevertheless English seamen were prepared to sail ever further north as John Davis was shortly to prove.

In describing the north-east passage Bourne did not consider that even Nova Zemla would prove an obstacle although it stretched to latitude 80° N. It must be rounded if there proved to be no strait through the Waigatz Is. Actually these straits were discovered, and the Kara Sea was entered, in the very year that his book was published. Classical geography, as taught at the universities, was breaking down quickly under the influence of the new navigations and of the 'unlearned' men who now had to review the subject. Little wonder that the younger Hakluyt's modern lectures on cosmography at Oxford were drawing eager audiences. Ocean currents, for example, had been explained by scholars as drawn by the Primum Mobile, or First Mover. Like the sky they always moved from east to west. Bourne, however, knows them only from sailors' experience. He remarks that the Spaniards going to the West Indies take

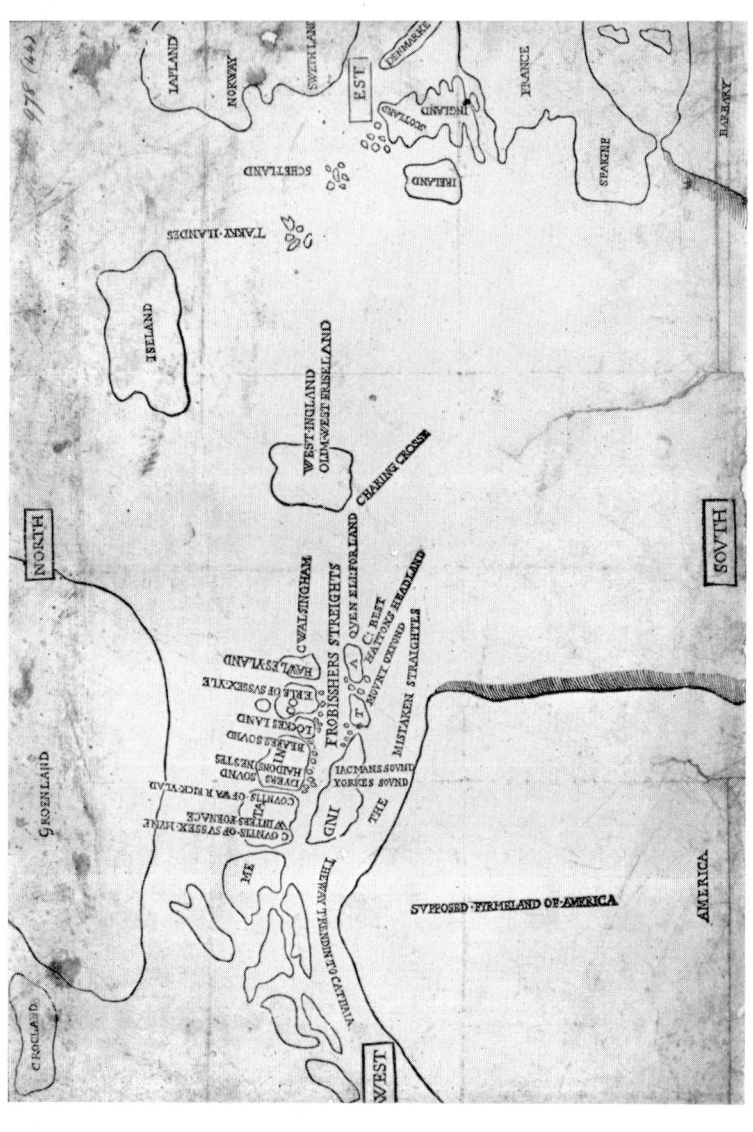

Fig. 14. George Best's chart of the North-west, with Frobisher's Straits

advantage of the current that sweeps into the Gulf of Mexico along the South American coast on their outward voyage, and of the current leaving the Gulf by the Strait of Florida on their return. The Portuguese, too, on their way to India, stood well out to sea as they rounded South Africa so as to avoid the Agulhas Current which runs strongly southward along the East African coast. But on their return voyage they followed an inshore course to take advantage of it, although (a point he does not mention) this not infrequently led to disastrous shipwrecks owing to their overladen ships. Those who had been to Magellan's Strait (and John Winter's ship had just passed through it in both directions) reported that there the water always ran from east to west.

It is worth remark that Bourne departs from his general scheme of describing the ways to Cathay in order also to outline that to Panama and that to Calicut. The former was the route which Drake actually took (although when Bourne wrote he was not yet home). The latter was the objective of a plan formed by the Queen's advisers early in 1580. This was to set up a trading station in the East by agreement with the Portuguese colonials who were expected to favour Don Antonio, the pretender to the Portuguese throne whom the English supported.[1]

The actual 'courses', i.e. directions and distances, which Bourne supplies are given in very broad terms, and the figures are, as he admits, only approximate. He probably measured the distances on a globe, taking a degree of a great circle as twenty leagues. But he certainly knew Ortelius's map of 1564, which Humfrey Gilbert had used in his discussion of the exploration of the north-west passage,[2] and shows himself very much at home with maps. It was no doubt, however, on his stepson's report that he concurs with the opinions of George Best and

---

[1] E. G. R. Taylor (ed.), *Voyage of Edward Fenton* (London, 1959), xxviii–xxx.
[2] Humfrey Gilbert, *A Discourse for a Discovery for a new Passage to Cataia* (London, 1576).

Frobisher's ship-master Christopher Hall that the so-called Frobisher's Straits were actually a gulf and not a passage to the eastern ocean. James Beare was a careful observer, and there was an occasion on the third voyage when the General actually sought his advice, as the fleet lay hemmed in by ice 'without sight of sun'. As George Best explains it, the master of the *Anne Francis* 'was knowen to be a sufficient and skilful Mariner, and having bene there the yere before, had wel observed the place, and drawen out Cardes of the coast'. Bourne did not, of course, deny that a passage might be found, but he makes the significant statement that the explorer must keep on his way westward for a thousand leagues before turning south. Otherwise he might be embayed in North America. This suggests that he was aware of Sebastian Cabot's voyage of 1508 which is mentioned by George Best. The evidence is that Sebastian on this occasion went through Hudson's Strait and entered Hudson's Bay (the nomenclature, of course, is of a later date), while Frobisher too went sixty leagues into the Strait, which Best in his sketch-map diplomatically marked as 'Mistaken Straits'.

The situation is obscured by the need which the discoverers felt to keep secret such facts as might lead interlopers to anticipate them. Bourne was no doubt correct in his statement that no Englishman had ever seen a Portuguese chart of the East Indies, for although detailed charts survive they were not allowed to get into alien hands. So far as it goes the course he describes to Ternate is correct, but throughout Bourne avoids speculation and waits on experience. As to the north-east passage, for example, he does not accept Dee's assurance that beyond Nova Zemla the Asian coast ran south-east to Quinsay. The scholar had assured himself that this was so because of a sentence he had read in an old book by an Arab writer, who spoke of the direction as seen from Cathay itself. The two men had discussed the whole problem in Dr Dee's library at Mortlake, when Bourne had been shown a volume of Marco Polo's *Travels*. And it is upon that Venetian's account of the wonders of the Grand Khan's shipping that the Gravesend man's *Discourse* ends. It was presently to be read not only by Englishmen, but in their own languages by the Dutch and also by the Spaniards, whose monopoly of half a world was so soon to be broken.[1]

---

[1] Dutch editions of the 1580 *Regiment* were published in 1594, 1599, and 1609. The Spanish translation of the *Discourse* appeared in 1585. See Appendix C.

1. *The second Address 'To the Reader'*

Gentle Reader, I haue thought it good now in this third Impression to mend or correct certeine faultes that were in the first, but most specially in the second Impression: for that it was printed the second time, I not knowing thereoff, so that it had not onely those faults that wer printed out of the first written Coppy, but a great number of new faultes more then that it had in the first.

Wherefore I haue not only mended and corrected those faults but in lyke manner I haue added other necessary matters, not before this time printed, as this.

What Excentrix is, and also what Paralex is, and his vse, as it doth appeare in the .6. folio of the booke. And also I haue in lyke manner shewed how that Sea-men shall know when that the Moone is in hir slow & swift motion, which is known by ye Prime, as it is declared in the thirde Chapter. And also how for to knowe the Moones latitude as it is shewed in the .4. Chapter. And also I doe shew in the .5. chapter, the cause that there is more dayes from the Equinoctiall of March vnto the Equinoctiall of September then there is from ye Equinoctiall of September vnto the Equinoctiall of March. And also I haue added vnto y^e .x. Chapter certeine matters as touching discoueries vnto the North parts. And furthermore, I haue shewed in the .14. chapter how for to know how fast or softly that any ship doth goe, and how for to keepe a perfect account of the ships way. And also I haue altered cleane the .17. Chapter, and shewed how that the Sea-men shal know what part or quantitie that they haue passed or gone of the whole earth, whereby that they shall know the diuersitie of aspects as the Eclipses of the Moone, and the alteracion of time and also I haue added diuers things in sundry partes of the booke, that I doe omit for breuitie. And in lyke manner I haue added vnto the ende of the booke, a Hidrographicall discourse for to goe vnto Cattay .5. seueral or sundry wayes that is to say, the first way is about by *Cape bone sperance*, which is that wayes that the *Portugalls* doth go vnto *Calicut* and vnto the *Moluccas* and other places in the East Indies, the second way is thorow the straights of *Magalenos*, into the South sea the third way is towardes the Northwest, where-as Captaine *Forbisher* and *Christopher Hall*, hath begon the discouerie now called *Meta Incognita*, and the .4. way is by the Northeast by the coast of *Noua Zembla*, that Master *Stephen* of *Borrose*, hath begon that discouerie. And the .5. way is by the North Pole if that it be nauigable, &c.

Now it is possible that I maye be enuied of diuers & sundry people for that I haue written this discourse of the passages vnto Cattay, for that the nature of a number of men is to dislyke of all things not done by themselues: But notwithstanding al is one vnto me whether they doe lyke or dislyke. For that I doe know some persons hath already made euill report of that I haue written before this time, yet notwithstandinge I will not stay my pen for their malice for although their skilles is much more then mine, my meaning is not to teach any of them but to instruct the simplest sort of Sea-men, for to shew vnto them such thinges as is necessary for them to know. And also some sort of people are of that nature, if that they write or talke of any things past their capacitie, then they will saye that he can talke well, but they themselues cannot talke but they can doe, but this is the truth, whatsoeuer hee be that will say that he can doe anything, and if that he cannot shew the Reason of the doing thereoff I doe say vnto you he cannot doe it and this is most certeine for if that he doth it, he doth it but by fortune: Euen as he that drewe his Bow by chaunce in the *Assirians* hoaste, and slewe *Achab* the king of *Israell*, as wee doe reade in the third booke of the Kings and the last Chapter, when that *Iosaphat* the King of *Iuda*, and *Achab* King of *Israel*, went to Battaile agaynst *Ramoth* in *Gilead*.

For this is generall amongest Sea-men and also Gunners how

simple or without skill soeuer that they be, if that they haue once taken charge to be the Master of a shippe he thinketh great scorne to learne at any mans hande, but will bragge of himselfe how long he hath bene a Master, and GOD knoweth vtterlye without skill, but that he is a Coaster, and doth knowe the markes for to carrie a shippe ouer the lands ende, and ouer the Naase.

But good simple men, if that they coulde not doe that, then there were nothinge in them: For euerye man must needes bee skilfull and know that place that a number of times he hath occupied & hath bene taught vnto him.

And who doubteth but a simple Fisher-man of Barking knoweth Barking Creeke, better then the best Nauigator or Master in this lande: so who doubteth but these simple men doth know their owne places at home. But if they should come out of the *Occean* sea to seeke our chānel to come vnto ye riuer of *Thames*, I am of that opinion, that a number of them, doth but grope as a blinde man doth, & if that they doe hit wel, that it is but by chaunce, and not by any cunning that is in him.

But I doe hope that in these dayes, that the knowledge of the Masters of shippes is very well mended, for I haue knowen within this .20. yeeres that them that were auncient masters of ships hath derided and mocked thē that haue occupied their Cards and Plats, and also the obseruatiō of the altitude of the Pole, saying that they care not for their Sheepes skins, for hee could keepe a better account vpon a boord.

And when that they did take the latitude, they would cal them starre shooters and Sunne shooters, and would aske if they had striken it. Wherefore now iudge of their skilles, considering that these two poyntes is the principal matters in Nauigation. And yet these simple people will make no small brags of themselues, saying: that he hath ben Master this .20. yeeres, and neuer had no misfortune, and also if that they could heare of any that did vse Plats and Instruments that had any misfortune, then they woulde not a little bragge of themselues what notable fellowes they themselues were.

O what a notable folly was in these men not considering what they thēselues were. For this is most certeine, that it is not wisedome nor cunning that canne preuent nor alter Gods prouidence, if that it pleaseth him to lay his scourge vpō vs. For if that men through cunning could prouide that no misfortune should happen vnto them, then were they Gods not men, and yet notwithstanding we must not condemn cunning & knowledge but put all things vpon Fortune, then you may take one from the Plough and make him Master of a ship, and say he hath good Fortune. And thus (gentle Reader) I cease, requesting thee to accept this as a simple present proceeding of good will.

Thine W.B.

2. The textual additions

(i) Excentric, what it is (p. 283)

Excentric is, when either the Sunne or Moone are towards the point of Auge, or the opposition thereof, and then the Center of the Sunne or Moones sphere is not in the Center of the Earth: the vse thereof is shewed in the Auge.

(ii) Paralax what it is (p. 283)

Paralax is, when that the Moone or the two Planets Venus or Mercurie, are in conjunction or neere any star, by the meanes of the Diameter or thicknesse, that the superficies is from the Center of the earth, and the nearnes of them vnto the earth, that so accordingly, that in some parts of the Skyes it shall seeme nearer or farther vnto those starres then in some parts, which reason groweth by the Simidiameter of the earth, for that you are not in the Center, when you do behold it.

(iii) [The Moon's Motion] (p. 283)

Where I do thinke it verie necessary for to show some what of the moones motion, that they may knowe when that the moone is either in hir swift motion or her slow motion, for that I do know that there is not in respect, no seaman that doth know it. For that I do know no one seaman that hath anye sight of knowledge in the Moones Theorat, therefore let them note these few words folowing.

When that the Prime is one, then the point of Auge is in the first part of Aries, then the moon being there, she is in her slow motion. So in like manner the moone being in Libra, is in her swift motion for that it is the opposition of the moones auge, and so in the time of 19 yeares, the point of Auge doth go through 12 signes. So that in 9 yeares and a halfe, the poynt of Auge is in Libra, and then the moone being in Aries, she is in her slow motion, going about 12 feared, but the further vnto the Northwards, the more temperate warme, by meanes of the long continuing of the sunne: for as we see by common experience, that a thing once being made warme, cannot sodenly bee made colde, neither is there doubt of any great colde until the sunne be into the southward of the Equinoctiall: for I admit that a shippe should saile into the Northward, and not stay vntill the North Pole were eleuated 80 degrees aboue the horizon, I doe thinke then they should finde it verye temperate and warme, vnto the middle of September, for that by the space of nine weekes together, that is to say, from the tenth day of May, vnto the twelfth day of July, the sunne shoud come no neerer vnto the Horizon due North than two degrees, and 30 degrees vnto the South part above the Horizon, and yet it is possible that it may be colde there vntil the end of Maye, for that the Sunne must haue a time to make the aire warme. For lyke as a thing once beeing colde cannot be sodainly made warme, so in lyke manner a place beeing once made warme, cannot be sodainely made colde. And furthermore has [those] that were in the Latitude of 80 degrees, should haue a short paralell: for the whole compasse of the Earth and sea going East and West, to come rounde about to that place againe in the same Paralel, is but 1250 English leagues, every league containing three English miles: So that in sailing of lesse than 500 or 600 leagues, they might see whether it were nauigable or not: For this is one principle, That if that they doe not meete with lande, then they shall finde sea, to accomplish the long desired passage to find out Cattaye.

which is a league, and then there will stande 13 in the quantitie lyne, and 1340 remaineth over. So that you may conclude, that the Shippe hath gone 13 leagues and a halfe, and 90 fadames: and by this order you may keepe a verie good order in your reckoning, and so note it in your Boke, and make a marke in your Cart, etc. And this is to be noted that a Spanish or Portugal league doth contain 2837 fadames, and an English league but 2500 fadames.

(v) [The North Parts] (p. 284)

... my opinion is, that it is not frozen there so much to have such huge quantity of Ise, but that it may be frozen more farther vnto the Northe partes, and so by some current or stream brought thether, and so is stayed upon the coast of Labrador and Baculayas by the meanes of the great current that commeth out of the Bay of Mexico all alongst the North side from Floriday vnto Baculayas or Newfoundland.

And yet notwithstanding it may be possible y^t if that they did discouer more vnto the Northwardes, that they should not meete with so much Ise. For at the North cape in Norway, which is much more vnto the Northwards, ther is seldome seene any great quantity of Ise, & yet some ships hath been beaten of vnto the north of ye Cape neere 200 leagues, so that they had often neere 80 Degrees of height of the North Pole aboue the Horizon, and yet they haue not met with Ise, and yet it is farther vnto the Northe partes by 17 degrees then that place that Frobisher was at.

Wherefore if it were attempted there is no doubte but they should finde it Nauigable eyther to the East part, or to the West parte: and I am of this opinion, that the thing most feared in making theyr discoverye vnto the Northwarde, deserueth not so greatlye to bee feared as they doe make it, the cause why they are so loth to go very farre vnto the Northwardes is, for that it is the Frozen Zone, but my opinion is, that in Summer time it is not to be suppose that your portion of tyme is a 120 part of an houre, more or lesse it maketh no matter, so that you know the portion of tyme.

And suppose that you haue veered five and twentye fadomes in the hundreth and twentie parte of an houre, therefore multiply a hundreth and twentie by fiue and twentie, and of that multiplication there commeth 3000 fadam, and nowe an English league is 2500 fadame so that the shippe hath gone one league and 500 fadames in an houre, and the said 500 fadames is the fifth part of a league so that the Shippe hath gone one league and one fifth part of a league in an houre. And thus by multiplying the portion of time by the number of fadames, you may kepe a verie good reckoning of your ships way having this consideration, that you doe make as oftentimes proofe as the winde doth increase or decrease.

And for good order in the keeping your account, doe this: Looke how longe time that the winde hath blown steddely without any increasing or decreasing, or altering of your course, then when you do see what or how many fadames that the Shippe hath gone in an houre, then multiplie it vnto so many houres as the Shippe hath gone so much by, and then diuide that summe by 2500 or else it is better to adde all your number of fadames as long as the ship hath gone on one course without altering: as for example this. The Shippe hath gone four times 25 fadames in the time of 120 parts of an hour, that is in four hours 12000 fadams, and the wind increasing, she went three times 34 fadames in 120 parte of an houre, that is in three hours 12240 fadames, and the Winde decreasing, the Shippe went five houres but 16 fadames in the 120 part of an houre, that is 9600 fadame in five houres, now adde all these numbers of fadames together, that is, 12,000 and 12240 and 9600, and all these makes 33840. So that the ship hath gone in 12 hours 33840 fadams, and now diuide this summe by 2500 degrees in XXIIII houres. So that then the moone being in Libra, she goeth XV degrees in XXIIII houres, for that there is the opposition of auge.

And also when the Prime is five, then the point of auge is in Cancer, and then there being in her slow motion. So that when the moone is in Capricorne, then in her swift motion. And when the Prime is XIIII or XV then the moones auge is in Capricorne, and then there the moone is in her slow motion, and also in Cancer her swift motion. And this by considering what the Prime is, you may know where that the Moones Auge is, which is very necessarie for sea-men to knowe in divers respects. For if that the moone doth come from her swift motion, then it causeth the change, quarter, and full of the moone to be the rather [earlier]. But contrairiwise, when that the moone cometh from her slow motion, then that doth detract the time the longer before the Moone doth change, or is at the full or any other aspect.

(iv) [The Log and Line] (p. 126)

As for example thus: I hauing a minute glasse, but it is better to have a porcion of time by some number of wordes, and the lesser part of time that you haue, it is the better, for if that the shippe doth goe verie fast, you shall not haue so much lyne out, and if that the ship doeth go but slowly, then you may double the lengthe of tyme by speaking the words twice or thrice over, and for to work it truely do this. First let down your logge handsomely into the water, and then let the line be marked according vnto the shippe, a two or three fadome from the logge accordingly, that it be so farre a stearne that it commeth into quicke water, that the edie of the stearne doth not staye it, and that done, then begin to speake your wordes, and so stayed at just the ende of the wordes and then hale in your logge againe, and measure how many foote or fadomes that you have veered or put out in that time, &

3. 'Hydrographicall Discourse' of the Passage to Cathay

A Hydrographicall discourse to shew the passage vnto Cattay fiue manner of waies, two of them knowen and the other three supposed, wherein you shall know the distance vnto Cattay, and also by what points or windes for the attaining thether, and also the rest of the East Indies.

Whereas it hath beene oftentimes in question of late yeeres nowe in this our age, for the discouerie for to finde out a way to come vnto *Cattay*, *China*, and the Islands of *Moluccas*: with other places in the East *Indies*, I haue thought it good to write this Hydrographicall discourse, to goe vnto *Cattay* fiue manner of waies, for that ther is some people that are doubtfull that there is no passage thether.

So some holding one opinion and some another, I haue taken vpon me for to shew vnto them the passage to go vnto *Cattay* fiue manner wayes, whereof two of them are knowen, and the other three supposed.

Wherein I haue set downe particularly the courses, that is to say, by what point of the Compasse that you must saile, and also the distance what number of leagues that it is from place to place. I haue perused the best Cosmographers, and for that we haue no Charts or Plats Hydrographicall that doth shew the true courses and distaunce, it is possible that is not exactlye true, but only to glaunce somewhat neere the matter. Therefore you must not looke to haue it so certaine that there is no errour in it, neither I am assured that it is not altogether vntrue, neither in the distance nor courses, but that you may haue some aide by this &c.

And first this, for to goe to *Cattay* that waye that the Portugalls doth goe vnto *Calicut* and the Ilands of *Moluccas*, which is about by *Cape bone sperance*, and nowe for to procede to go that waie, and first this, for to depart from the *Lizard* or Cape of *Cornewall*, being the Westerne part of *England* and for to make your direction from thence vnto the *Canarie Ilandes*, hauing latitude twentie eight and a halfe, the course is neere the South Southwest about five hundred leagues. And on the Starboard side is the West Ocean sea, and on the Larboord side, first the coast of *Fraunce*, and then the coast of *Spain* and *Portugall*, and then the coast of *Barbarie* in *Africa* etc. And from the *Canarie Ilands* into *Cape de varde*, in *Guiney*. The Latitude thereof is neare *15*. Degrees, and the course is South about *270*. leagues. and on the starboord side is the West Occeant Sea, and on the larboorde side the Coast of *Barbarie* and *Ginnie*, and from *Cape de Varde* vnto Cape *Palmas*, the Latitude is neere *4*. degrees, and the course is South and by East, about *230*. leagues, and on the Starboorde side is the Occeant Sea, and the larboorde side, the coast of *Ginnie*. And from thence for to make your direction with *Cape bone Speranca*, being the Southermost parte of all Aethiopia, forsaking the Coast, and to make your course thorowe the Sea, the course is neer the Southeast and by South. *1000*. leagues, and the Altitude is the Antarticke Pole about *35*. Degrees above the Horizon. and on the Starboorde side is *Brasile* in *America*, and the great River of *Platte*, and on the larboorde side is the coast of *Castill de Mine* in *Ginnie* and *Binney*, and the coast of *Aethiopia* &c. But if that you will keepe the coast of *Ginnie*, then for to depart from Cape *Palmas*, for to goe vnto the Iland of *Saint Thomas*, then your course is East and by South. neere *360*. leagues, and the Iland of Saint *Thomas* hath no Latitude, for that it is directly vnder the Equinoctiall, and on the starboord side is the Occeant Sea, and on the Larboore side the Coast of *Castell de Mine*, and the coast of *Binnie* &c. And from the Iland of Saint *Thomas*, vnto *Cape bone Sperance*, the course is South and by East, about *750*. leagues, and on the Starboord side is the Occeant Sea. and on the larboord side the coast of *Aethiopia*: and now from *Cape bone Sperance*, vnto yᵉ great Iland Saint *Laurence*, the Wester most parte of the Iland, and that hath latitude towarde the Antarticke Pole, about 28. degrees. and the course is from *Cape bone Sperance* Noreast and by East, about *550*, leagues and on the starboord side, is the vnknowen land that lyeth towards the Antarticke Pole, and the larboord side the coast of *Aethiopia*, and the length of the Iland is about *360*. or *400*. leagues and the longest waye of the Ilande doth lye East, Northest and West, Southwest, and is from mayne lande of *Aethiopia* about 80 or 100 leagues, &c. And furthermore by the waye, I doe think it good for to shew the course and distance vnto *Calicut*. And first this, for to set out your course for to go from the Eastermost end of the great Ilande of Saint *Laurence*, and that hath the Antarticke Pole raised *13*. Degrees. And for to go with the straights of the redde Sea the course is North and by East about *470*. leagues, and the latitude of the straights is about *10*. degrees, towards the North Pole & this straights is greatly occupyed, for that all the Spices that seruethe the Turkes dominions, and also some parte of Christendome, is brought from the Iland of *Moluccas* and other parts in the *East Indies*, as *Calicut*, and such lyke places and so by shipping transported into the redde sea, and so put on land in *Aegypt*, and then carried over a little part of the land, and then is newly embarked, and brought downe to the great River of *Nilus*, and put a land at *Alexandria* in *Aegypt*, that is a port in the middle earth Sea, and from thence it is transported by shipping into a number of places both in the Turkes dominions, and other places Christened &c.

And from the Straights vnto the hither end of the red sea in *Aegypt*, the course is for the most parte Norwest and Nore Norweste, about neere *500*. leagues, And going into the read sea, the starboord side is the coast of *Arabia* & yᵉ larboord side is first yᵉ coast of *Aethiopie*, as *Aegypt* &c.

And also if that you will goe from the East side of the great Iland of Saint *Laurence* into the famous merchaunt Towne called *Calicut* in *Indie* then your course is Northeast and to the Eastwarde about 860 leagues, and the latitude is fiue degrees to the Northparts, and on the starboord side is the Occean sea, and the larboord side is first the coast of *Aethiopia*, and the straights of the read sea, and the coast of *Arabia*, and the Straights of the Persian Sea, and the Ilands of *Ormuz* &c.

But if that you will holde on your course to goe vnto *Cattay*, then from the East end of the great Iland of Saint *Laurence*, for to go with the great Iland called *Trapobane*, your course is East Northeast or East, and by North about 1100 leagues, but it is possible that in these courses you maye meete with a number of Ilands, for that all this East Occean Sea is very full of great and small Ilands, and the middle of this great Iland [*Taprobane*] lyeth directly vnder the Equinoctiall, and the length of this Iland is neere *300.* leagues, and on the Starboord side is the vnknown lands, towards the Antarticke Pole, and on the larboord side the straights of the redde sea, Arabia, the Ilands of *Ormes*, the Persian sea, *Calicut* and the great river of *Ganges*. And now for to depart from the great Iland of *Taprobane*, to goe vnto yᵉ great Iland of *Gelilow*, being the greatest Iland amongst all the *Moluccas*, the course is East about *1000.* leagues, and there lyeth a number of Ilands in the way, and on the starboorde side is the Iland of *Jaue* and *Berno*, and on the larboord side the greatest heap of the *Moluccas* Ilands. The Iland of *Gelilow* hath no latitude, for that it lyeth directly vnder the Equinoctiall, and for to goe from the Iland of *Gelilow*, to go vnto the coast of *China*, the course is North and by West, about *500.* leagues.

The latitude of *China* is about *25.* degrees and on the starboord side is the South Sea, and *America*, and the larboorde side is the Ilandes of *Moluccas* but for to goe from the great Ilande of *Taprobane*, the next way to *China*, the course is Northeast and by East, *1000.* leagues, and then on the starboorde side, you shall have all the *Moluccas* Ilandes, and the larboorde side the maine land of *Asia* or *East India*, and then from the coast of

China, into the great Baye of *Quinsay* in *Cathay*. the course is North and by East about 100 leagues, and the entrance of the Bay of *Quinsay*, the latitude is 35. degrees and on the starboord side is the firme land of *America*, and the great iland of *Jupan*, and the larboorde side the coast of *China* and *Cattay* &c.

Now thus much have I sayd as touching the waye to come out of *Englande* to goe vnto *Cattay*, and East *India*, hopeing that the reasonable Reader will not enuie mee, for this vsing my discourse, neither you must not looke so exquisitely into it, for that it cannot be exact truth. for as I do suppose that no English man hath seene any true Charte or Plat of all the East *India*, wherefore I doe suppose that you will beare with this my discourse &c.

And now furthermore as touching the discourse for to come out of *England* to goe vnto *Cathay*, the seconde way, and that is known that the sea will let them passage, that is to say, through the straightes of *Magalenos*, and so vnto the south sea, as this, first to make their direction from the west part of *England* vnto ye straights of *Magalenos*, although that in deed ther can be no longe passage by sea, but that the ships are to seeke some places for to water at. and other easements, yet notwithstanding I do meane to make but one direction or course from *England* into the straightes of *Magalenos*, for that the Masters or the Pilots may seeke thier watring places most best for their purposes etc. And first, from y^e *Lizard* vnto the straights of *Magalenos*, the course is for the most part south southwest and to the Westwards, about 2400. leagues, and the latitude of the straights is 52. degrees and a halfe towards the Antarticke Pole, and on the starboord side is the firme land of *America*, & the Larboorde side *Europe* and *Africa* &c.

And through the Straights, the course may be West or West south west 100. or 140. leagues before that they be clearly in the South sea, and now being into that sea, they may goe either into *Cattay* or the *Moluccas*, or the Port of *Pannama*, that is the place that the king of *Spaine* hath all the treasure that commeth from *Pero*.

And from thence it is carried up a certain reuer, and then transported ouer the necke of a land, and then imbarcked. and brought down an other riuer, and so landed at *Nomber the Deas*, and from thence transported by shippes into Spaine &c.

And now they being through the straights of *Magalenos*, if that you will goe vnto the port of *Pannama*, then their course is for to goe Nornorwest, or Norwest and by Nore, or Nore and by West, as the land will give them passage for that ther hath not bene made any true Plats for that Coast in that Sea, and doth containe in leagues from the straights vnto the Porte of Pannama *1100*. or *1200*. leagues. But if that you wil goe from the Straights vnto *Cattay* as it is a Sea that is not vnto the South parts neere the straights not [sic] well knowen, so there may be many Ilandes in that sea that you maye meete with, and also there may be Rockes and daungers there in like maner that are not knowen, but the generall course is Norwest vnto *Cattay* or *China*, about 2800 leagues, hauing on the starboord side the maine land of America and on the Larboorde side the vnknowen land that lyeth towardes the Antarticke Pole, and also the Ilands of *Moluccas* and *Calicut*, and thus much haue I sayde as touching the passage vnto *Cattay* by these two wayes that are known. But heare is one thing to be noted, for as it hath bene reported, that when the Portugalls Carrickes doth goe vnto *Calicut*, that when that they be at *Cape bone sperance*, then they doe not directly set theyre course the next way, but standeth South ouer toward the land that lyeth to the Antarticke Polewards, and the cause thereof, is by the meanes of the great Current, that is at *Cape bon sperance* continually running from the East vnto the West, and then when that they haue gone a hundreth or a hundreth and fiftie Leagues vnto the Southwardes of the Cape, then they set theyr Course for to goe with *Calicut*, so that outwards that they doe not come neere the great

Iland of Saint *Laurence*, but goe a great deale to the Southward of it for that they will not be lette by the great currant: But when they doe come homewards, then they doe come hard by the Ile of Saint *Laurence*, and so directly with *Cape bone sperance*, for that they will haue all the helpe that they may with the Current, then they goe West Norwest into the Sea with the maine lande of *America*, till that they be halfe that Sea ouer, and then they doe set their course to goe homewards, as it is not vnknowen, that when the Spanish Fleete doth goe onto the West *Indies*, that when they goe outwardes, that they doe goe into the *Canaries*, and so West into the sea, and so holding in the south lande of the Baye of *Mexico*, for that they haue some helpe by the Current: but when that they doe come home, then they do come by the North land of the Baye of *Mexico*, betweene the Iland of *Cuba* and *Terra Florida*, for that they will haue the Current homewardes to helpe them. Also it is reported that in the straights of *Magalenos*, that the Current rūneth continually from the East into the west. Now this much haue I said, as touching the two waies vnto *Cathay*, for that it is knowen that there is passage by Sea, if that it were attempted, although the passage is very long, &c.

And now furthermore, for to discourse the third waye, that is not knowen, but supposed that it may be passageable, that is by the Northwest, as now of late Captaine *Forbisher* hath begun, and hath discouered as farre as a place nowe called *Meta Incognita*, which he himselfe did call *Forbishers Straights*, but yet notwithstanding it is doubtfull, whether that be a Straightes to giue passage to come into the East Occean Sea, or south sea, for any thing that is knowen yet, it maye bee as well a Baye as otherwise, but notwithstanding whether that bee a Straight or not, it is possible that there maye be passage there about, between the Norther parte of America, as betweene *Labradorre* and *Groynland*, and such landes as lyeth vnto the North Polewardes.

Wherefore now for to depart from *England* to go vnto

Cattay by the Norwest, first this for to make their direction from the West part of *England*, vnto the place called *Meta Incognita*, the course is West Norwest about *650.* leagues, and the latitude thereof *63*. Degrees, and on the Starboord is first *Ireland* and *Iseland*, and *Freeseland*, and on the Larboord side, is the Occean Sea. And now beeing at *Meta Incognita*, they must discouer there abouts, where that they may finde Sea for to giue them passage, & yet if they do finde sea, they must hold on their course West vntill y^t they haue passed *1000* or *1100* leagues. For if that they should hold on any Southerly course, then they should imbaye themselues in the maine land of *America*, for the extention of the backe Side, or North side of *America*, is not much lesse than 1000. leagues, before that they shal open ye way into the East Occean Sea, and in this West course on the Starboord side is the North Pole, and such lands as lyeth that way if there be any, and on the Larboord side, is the maine of *America*.

And after that they haue sailed West *1000.* leagues on the North part of *America*, they may then direct a more southerly course, for that then they may be open of the East Occean sea, for that the most parte of the best Cosmographers laye the opening of that sea opposite vnto vs in our Meridian, & then holding on a southerly course, then they may haue vnto the great bay of *Quinsay* about 400. or *500*. leagues. And the latitude of ye North part of ye Bay of *Quinsay* in *Cattay* is about 46. degrees, and on the Starboord side is the coast of *Asia*, as *Mangie* and *Cattay*, and on the Larboord side *America*. And thus much haue I saide as touching the third way to goe to *Cattay*, &c.

And now in like manner as touching the fourth way to go vnto *Cattay*, not knowne but supposed, and that is by the Northeast part or North part of *Russey*, about by that way that Master *Barrowes* began the discouery, about by a land that is called *Noua Zembla*, which is a coūtry or point of a land that extendeth to the Northwards, it is not knowen how farre, &

A REGIMENT FOR THE SEA, 1580

yet it may be possible that it is nauigable that wayes if it were attempted.

And now for to passe that waye vnto *Cattay*, I will a lyttle vse my discourse. The way and distaunce vnto the North Cape in Norway is not unknowen vnto a number of Sea menne, the Latitude thereof is *71.* degrees *.20.* minutes, therefore I doe thinke it best to beginne the direction and setting out the course East, vntill that they doe come with the lande of *Noua Zembla*, and then falling with that place to make theyr discouerie as the lande will giue them leaue, and so in this direction it maye be possible that they maye finde a Sea to giue them passage as it may be possible, that when they may meete with lande, that they shall be constrained to goe Northeast or North Noreast, vntyll that the North Pole bee raised eightie or eightie fiue Degrees, yet they may holde on their course vntill such time that they shall bee incombred with Ise, for it may bee so, that in the Latitude of *80.* Degrees, there shall bee no Ise, although that on the Coast of *Baculayas*, you maye haue Ise in the Latitude of *50.* Degrees, for no man can tell vnto such time as it hath beene put in experience, and now in this passage vnto the Eastwardes from the North Cape vntill that they shall haue the sea open to come into the Southwards in the sea of *Cattay*, it may be about *1000.* or *1200* leagues, and then in this passage on the Starboord side is first *Norway* and *Lapia*, and the Baye of Saint *Nicholas*, and the greate riuer of *Obe* and *Noua Zembla*, and the East parte of *Asia*, and on the Larboord side the North Pole, and those landes that lie that waies if there be any, and now in the following of the coast of the lande which may be Southeast or South Southeast or South, it may be *500* or *600* leagues vnto the Bay of *Quinsay* in *Cattay*, and on the Starboord side is *Asia* and the coast of *Mangie* & *Cattay*, & on the larboord side the maine land of America, &c.

And furthermore, it may be possible for to finde passage for to go to *Cattay*, betweene *Noua Zembla*, and the countrie of *Samwetes*, through the sea of *Vagates*, & this passage may be somewhat shorter, then for to go vnto the Norwards of Noua Zembla, & then you shall haue in this passage upon the starboord side, first the countrie of *Samwetes*, as *Pichora*, and the river of *Obe* and *Tartaria*, &c. And on the Larboord side, *Noua Zembla*, &c.

And this I doe ende as touching the Northeast passage to goe or attaine unto *Cattay* the fourth waie, &c.

And furthermore as touching the fifth waie to goe vnto Cattay, it is possible that in my discourse it is meere foolyshnesse and a thinge vnpossible for it to bee done, and yet notwithstanding no man can tell, before that it is put in experience, and yet it is the neerest way if that it bee nauigable, and my meaning is this, for to goe directly vnto the Pole, if so be that there is no land to let the passage. Now it is possible that some will say that it is the frozen Zone, but notwithstanding if that there is not land that waye, then it is not frosen, for the great salt Sea neuer freeseth, and for that you doe see the greate quantitie of Ise on the Coast of *Labradorre* and *Baculayas*, it is a token that there aboutes is much lande towareds the North Pole-wardes, and so is frosen in Soundes and Riuers, and so in the breaking vp of the yeare, that then it doth come driuing out to Sea: for in respect they doe seldome see any Ise at the North Cape, nor *100*. leagues North off from thence, which is a great token that there is no land towards the Pole-wards, and before that it hath bene put in proofe it cannot be knowen. But all the doubts for going vnto the Polewards, is for feare of to much colde, & yet notwithstanding it may be reasonable warme right vnder the Pole for any thing that is knowen vnto the contrary, by the long continuance of the Sunne in summer, for that in the tyme of *9*. weekes, that the sunne is neuer lesse than *20*. Degrees aboue the Horizon going round about them, so that the continuance of the sunne must inforce the aire to be reasonable warme, & especially if that ther is no Ise driuing in ye sea, for it is not so cold at *Meta Incognita*, if that they be not amongst the Ise, for if that they be at sea and not amongst Ise, then it is very warme, and also if that they be a shore, then it is warme in like maner, so that the cold is by no other meanes but the cold breath of aire that commeth from the Ise. And now for to proceede to go vnto *Cattay*, and to go directly North till that they be right vnder the Pole, and then to go south to the opposite part beyond the Pole, which is to be done if y^t they be not let by any land that lyeth in the way, then it may be possible for it to be done, and then the whole distance in this course from ye riuer of Thames vnto the Baye of *Quinsay*, is but *1680.* leagues, which is a very short way in respect of the other. But now it is possible that some will make argument and say, that it is not possible for any man to make any direction or set any course being directly under the Pole, for y^t it is not knowen which way that the compasse will stand, and also in like maner being vnder ye Pole, all places is south which way so euer you go, & also the sunne is equally one height, so that you can make no proofe which way is forwardes, & which way is backwards, therefore it is to be supposed, that some will say, that it is not possible to make any instruments to assigne any course to any place appointed, for truth it is, being vnder the Pole that any place assigned is South from them that is vnder the Pole, what quarter of the worlde soeuer that it is in, and if that the sea will giue them passage, their course is South to go vnto it, &c. Yet notwithstanding I will shew vnto you what you shall doe to make a perfect direction vnto any place appointed you beeing right vnder the Pole, that you shall knowe whether that you doe goe backwards or forwards or any other way that you shall appoint, so that you may see the Sunne, and that must be done, as this. First prepare a perfect good clocke that goeth with a Spring and to be made in that order that the director or pointer both goe round in *24.* houres, and so to be marked for to ende 24. houres at noone, and then to begin one, and this clocke or Diall being well made and both keepe the time truelye, then when that you doe approch neere the Pole within *100.* leagues, that is the latitude of *85.* degrees, and so farre the Compasse may serue, and also you may correct the Compasse well inough, for that the Sunne is *10.* degrees higher on the South part, than it is on the North part, and now going within *5.* degrees of the Pole, set your clocke to worke, and *24.* houres to be noone, and then when that you are directly vnder the Pole, looke if that the Pointer doth stand vpon *24.* houres, then that part or quarter that the sunne is in, is right back again, and if y*t* it point *12.* houres, then towards the sun-wards is right forwards, and if that it point *6.* houres, then towards the sunwards doth shewe, that if any place bee west from the place that you did come from, and is one quarter of the earth, that direction will set you right vpon it, & if *18.* houres, then towards the Sunne doth appoint you that place that is East one quarter of the earth, &c.

And nowe for to set any course to stirre the ship upon any place appoynted, then note this as for an ensample. I would goe directly homewardes, and then I will set the Flie of a Compasse before him that shall stir and then for that I come out North and I must go home South and lay the Card or Flye stedie before me, & the south point right with the ships head or stem, and so I do set the clocke by it, now if that the clocke doth point *22* houres for that afore was my noone, then I do stirre the ship right vpon the Sunne, and if the clocke doth appoynt *3.* hours, then he that doth stirre must keepe the Sunne vpon the southwest, and so shall the ship go that south that she came from, and if that the clocke doth poynt *6.* houres, then he that doth stirre, must keepe the Sunne vpon the west point, and if the clocke shewe *9.* then keepe the Sunne vpon the Norwest. If the clocke doth shew *12.* then the sun must be on the North poynt, that is right with the starne of the ship. And if the clocke doth shew *15.* houres, then he that stirreth must keep the sunne vpon the Northeast point, if *18.* then the Sunne on the East point, and if *21.* houres, then on the southeast point, &c. But now if y*t* you would goe directly forwards, then lay the North point right with the ships head, and when the clocke doth point *12.*

then stirre right vpon the sunne, and so in like manner to stirre by the sunne as I haue afore shewed you by ensamples, so that you may see by this clocke or diall, you may assigne your selfe to keepe any course into any place in the whole world, you being vnder the Pole, and then when that you are departed from the pole *100.* leagues, that is *5.* degrees, then you may vse your compasse, and correct it by the sunne at your plesure. And thus much I haue saide as touching the passages to goe vnto *Cattay*, wherefore gentle Reader beare with my rudenesse, for that I am so bold to use my discourse vpon the passage vnto *Cattay*. And furthermore, some men hath ben of that opinion, that when that they are in the East Occean sea that they shall meete with no shipping, as about *Cattay* and *China*, &c. But notwithstanding it is a sea that there is a huge number of ships both great and small, for this must be most certaine that wheras ther is such great trade of Marchandize, and also such a number of Ilands both great and small, and also such a number of commodities in these Ilands, so that any man may iudge that there is great store of ships, and also ordinance in their shipping, &c. And it is not vnknowen but that the great *Cane* of *Cattay*, is a Prince of great power as well by sea as by Lande, then iudge you whether that such a prince of such a force and welth but that they will prouide for all things meete for warres. Therefore as soone as they come into those coasts they must orderly vse the trade of Marchandize, & not to use force, &c. As vpon a time I being with Master *Dee* at his house at *Murclacke*, we falling in talke about the discouerie to *Cattay* & so talked as touching the shipping whereupon he opened a Booke and shewed me a note what number of ships that the great *Cane* had readie at one time to goe vnto sea about his affaires, surely you would thinke it vncredible, the number was *15000* surely a huge armie by Sea: and then I replyed againe that it might be that they were but small things, and yet they might call them shippes, and then he turned vnto another place where the great *Cane* did send one of his daughters by Sea, and did appoint *14.*

of his ships, and the least of the *14.* shippes had *250.* Mariners, beside all the rest of his daughters traine, and such Nobles as did accompanie hir, which must bee no small number. Therefore it is most manifest that the *Cane* is a great Prince of power as well by Sea, as by Land.

FINIS

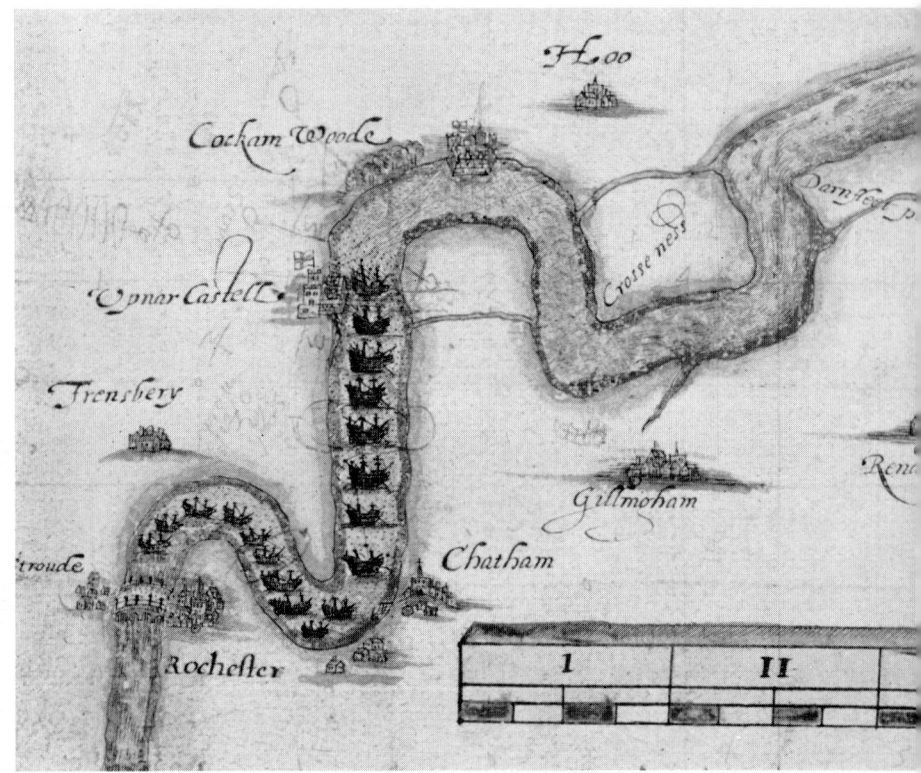

Fig. 15. Upnor Castle and the Medway: detail from an anonymous MS chart, c. 1580
Hatfield House maps, I. 47

IV

An almanacke & prognostication for x. yeeres (1581)

EDITOR'S NOTE

William Bourne completed his new Almanac for the years 1581–90 in December 1580, when he was in residence at the Queen's House, Upnor Castle. The House contained the apartments of the military Captain of the Castle, and doubtless Bourne was serving him as master-gunner. But of this there is no direct evidence. Drake's recent return with his looted treasure had set the whole nation agog for the sea, and there were various plans under consideration for taking up the treaty he had made with the local ruler in Ternate. Apart from this his circumnavigation had made clear that in future voyages lasting two years or more might be anticipated. Something more than an annual almanac had become necessary, although it might occur to the purchaser that only an intention of actual settlement in some distant trading-post could necessitate carrying with him a ten years' prediction of the moon's phases.

Bourne had to find a new publisher,[1] which explains why there are changes in the list of black-letter saints named in the Kalendar. The un-needed column of numerals relating to the nineteen-year cycle of the moon was now omitted. The prime, epact, dominical letter and dates of the moveable feasts were all given directly for each year. There were also predictions of eclipses to be seen at London (the meridian for which the Almanac was compiled), and in addition (p. 408) Bourne inserted notes on three very remarkable astronomical events that had occurred since the publication of his last Almanac. The first was the appearance, in 1572, of a new star in the constellation of

[1] Almanacs could only be printed by a stationer who held a special licence or privilege to do so. The privilege was held at this date by Watkins and Roberts.

Cassiopeia, a 'fixed' star of the first magnitude. It shone brilliantly for over a year and then wasted away. Bourne says nothing about the cosmic significance of this *Nova*, indeed he was probably unaware of it, but it was keenly discussed by contemporary astronomers. It was as though (he himself naïvely suggests) the star was let down from the heavens and drawn up again.

The second notable appearance was also strange and even alarming, but although rare it had occurred throughout the ages. It was a comet with a fiery tail which was first observed in 1577, and was to be seen for the next three months. And almost unbelievably a second comet began to move across the sky on 8 October 1580. It had not yet disappeared when Bourne was recording it. But its life was short, for Dr Dee in his diary says that he could no longer see it on November 22. The two statements are not inconsistent. Bourne's Preface to the Reader, dated December 1, would be the last part of the text of his Almanac to be written, and would complete the copy (including his mention of the comet) which he had already handed to the printer.

True to his resolution against prediction, Bourne draws no astrological conclusions from the appearance of these Blazing Stars. Yet despite his puritanical attitude and his perhaps genuine religious feeling, he cannot forbear to note that in 1583 (p. 359) there would occur a very sinister conjunction of the baleful Saturn with Jupiter, a situation apparently worsened by the fact that Jupiter would then be in a sextile position with regard to the sun. The consequence (save for God's Providence) would be disastrous floods. He did not live to see whether these actually occurred, but according to a tract by William Averall[1] it 'raigned wheat' in Suffolk and Essex that year—evidence of wild weather.

The great novelty that the author claims for his Almanac is

---

[1] William Averall, *A wonderful and strange news which happened in . . . Suffolk and Essex* (London, 1583).

way of reckoning the year is from the date of accession of the reigning monarch. In Bourne's day therefore the Regnal Year ran from 17 November 1558, when the first Elizabeth ascended the throne.

The *Almanacke*, like the *Regiment*, is dedicated to Bourne's 'master', Lord Clinton. And the author is proud to record that during the short period of seven years since the first publication of his navigating manual it had 'proved very necessary and profitable to seamen'. In consequence there had been a great advance in knowledge and skill. As he was now addressing the Lord High Admiral, it is unlikely that Bourne was making any idle boast, and he is confirmed by the contemporary statement of George Best.[1] Twelve years after his untimely death his *Regiment* was re-edited with new tables by his admirer Thomas Hood, a Cambridge man[2] who became a 'mathematical practitioner' under the patronage of Lord Lumley. The Hollanders, too, from whom English seamen, prompted by Lord Charles Howard, had so eagerly borrowed the 'Waggoner',[3] were as ready on their part to learn from the Gravesend innkeeper, and a Dutch translation appeared in 1594. The English revisions spread over half a century. This had been a book worth writing.

---

[1] 'Navigation whiche in the time of King Henrie the 7. was very rawe, and toke (as it were) but biginning ... is now in hir Majesties reign growen to his highest perfection.' George Best, *A True Discourse* (London, 1578).

[2] He was a Fellow of Trinity College, and was first engaged to lecture to the trainband officers in London when invasion threatened. He later devoted himself to chart and instrument making, and to teaching the art of navigation. (See E. G. R. Taylor, *The Mathematical Practitioners* (London, 1954).)

[3] A sea manual and chart book written by Lucas Waghenaer, whose name was thus corrupted into English.

passage of cold and warm 'fronts', of anti-cyclones and depressions. Many of them match the 'Shepherd of Banbury's Rules'. Of even greater interest, perhaps, are his remarks about the effects of strong winds on the floods and tides in the Thames estuary, with which he had been familiar all his life. A persistent south-west wind followed by a north-wester drives water into the North Sea, with the result that as the tide rises (and especially at spring tides) there are serious floods over the marshes. An easterly wind, on the contrary, blowing up-river checks the flow of the ebb-tide, which consequently does not run for its normal period.

The section on how to determine the Sign of the Zodiac through which the moon is passing on any given day was rendered necessary (for the Elizabethan 'common reader') because the age-old rules for purging, bathing, letting blood, and so on depended (it was believed) upon this relationship. So, too, the fortunes of cities and countries when an eclipse occurred, or a comet was seen, hinged upon the particular combination of sign and planet under the influence of which they lay. England in general was under Aries and Mars, London under Gemini and Mercury. This table Bourne ascribes to Cyprianus Leovitius of Augsburg;[1] and there is one, more useful to the modern reader, which should not be overlooked (p. 398). It is a list of the six different ways of reckoning the beginning of the new year. The first way, from New Year's Day, Bourne calls the 'general' reckoning. Lady Day is the first day of the year for the Church of England. St Matthew's Day, on February 24, starts the Bi-sextile or Leap Year, when the Sunday Letter changes. The fourth year is that which is used for calculating the age of the moon from the Prime and Epact: it begins on March 1, St David's Day. Fifthly, there is the astronomers' and astrologers' year, which is dated from the spring equinox, the day that the sun's path crosses the equinoctial, at the point termed the first point of Aries. This happens about March 10. Finally, the sixth

[1] Cyprianus Leovitius, *Ephemerides* (Augsburg, 1557).

the inclusion in the Kalendar itself of the daily solar declination, and also of the hours of sunrise and sunset at the beginning of each week. This was undoubtedly a great convenience to the seaman, but it involved making some small adjustments which arose from the neglect of the four-year cycle of declinations arising from Leap Year. Normal observational errors, however, were still of such an order as to make this of no great moment. A novelty that is perhaps of greater interest to the modern reader is the inclusion of an advertisement of other works written by the author. There were four of these, namely the *Regiment for the Sea* and the three books published in 1578. The earlier *Almanackes* containing the *Serten Rules* were clearly no longer 'extant in print', and would also, of course, be out of date. Advertising was then in its infancy, but the 'mathematical practitioners' were one of the earliest professional groups to make use of it, although the patent medicine vendors ran them close. Bourne merely advertises his own works, and he also refers the reader to his *Regiment* several times in the text of this Almanac. It was, however, natural for a writer from the leisure class, like William Barlow, to recommend a humble teacher of mathematics in his *Navigator's Supply* (1597), and for a surveyor like Aaron Rathborne to mention the particular instrument-makers whom he employed himself.[1]

There was another section of this Almanac, which according to Bourne had never appeared in such a publication before. This was the very interesting chapter on weather forecasting, not based astrologically on the stars, but on the signs afforded by the shift of the wind, the forms of the clouds, the appearance of lunar haloes and so on. It was derived, he said, from his own observations, and he obviously considered it more useful than the vague prognostics for the seasons which he had inserted in the yearly Almanac, although it was the latter which the 'common people' looked for. His own weather signs were such as any observant countryman can build up during the

[1] Aaron Rathborne, *The Surveyor* (London, 1616).

An Almanacke and Prognostication for x. yeeres, beginning

at the yeere of our Lorde 1581. and ending the yeere 1590. being calculated for the Meridian of London.

Wherein is set downe the change, quarters, and fulles of the Moone, with the Eclipses that doe happen in the said x. yeeres:

And also, according vnto the accustomable manner, the iudgement of the weather, and the moueable feastes, with diuers other necessary matters, before this time in no Almanacke and Prognostication.

Written by *William Bourne*, Student and Practicioner in the Mathematicall sciences.

Imprinted at London by Richard Watkins and Iames Robertes. 1581

Cum Priuilegio.

To the right honourable Edwarde,
Earle of Lincolne, Baron of Clinton & Say,
Knight of the noble order of the Garter, Lorde high
Admirall of England, Ireland, and Wales, and
of the Dominions and Iles thereof, the towne
of Calice, and Marches of the same, Norman-
dy, Gascoyne, and Goyne, and Captaine generall of
the Queenes Maiesties Seas, and Nauy Royal,
William Bourne wisheth increase of
honour and perfect health

Although a thing most simple, & not worthie to be presented vnto any person of noble personage, yet notwithstanding, my singular good Lorde & Maister, I doe present vnto your honour a rude and plaine Almanacke and Prognostication for x. yeres: And though that it be a thing not worthie to be preferred vnto any person of such worthie action, yet I do hope that your honour will not take it otherwise, but as a thing from me proceeding of good will. The cause that hath moued me to write this Almanacke & Prognostication for x. yeeres, is, for the vse of Seamen, for that they are oftentimes foorth, a yeere or two, so that it is necessary that they shoulde haue Almanackes for longer time then one yeere. Therefore such as it is, I hope that your Lordship will take it in no worse part then your honour did the booke that I presented to you before, called the *Regiment for the Sea*, the which book, hath proued very necessary and profitable vnto Seamen: for since the printing of the booke which lesse is then vii. yeeres past, it hath helped very much the knowledge and skil of the Mariners, to the great furtherāce of our English Nauigation. And thus I ceasse to trouble your honorable Lordship with any more circumstance, beseching the liuing God the Creator of al things to prosper you in all your affayres, in perfect health, with my good Lady, and all your family.

By your honours poore seruant,
duetifully at commandement,
William Bourne.

¶ *To the friendly and curte-
ous Reader*

Gentle Reader, I haue thought good for sundry causes to write this Almanacke or Prognostication for ten yeres, & especially for the vse of Seamen, for that oftentimes they haue occasion to be foorth out of Englande, a yeere or ii. more or lesse, so that then in their long absence, it is very meets and necessary, that they should haue Almanackes for longer time then for one yeere, for that euery Seaman hath not an *Ephemerides*, neither doeth euery Seamen knowe the vse thereof. And although that they may geue a very neere gesse of the change, and the quarter, and the full of the moone, by the rule of the epact, that may reasonably wel serue their turnes, yet it is very necessary, to haue an Almanacke for diuers necessary purposes, as the moueable feasts, and such other like causes. And also according vnto the ordinary custome, there is set downe the iudgement of the weather, according vnto the Authours that haue written in Astronomy and Astrologie, which I woulde not that any man should be of that opinion, for to looke that the weather should come so to passe, for it is God that determineth those causes: for that those that write the iudgements Astrological, haue made long obseruation from age vnto age, and accordingly vnto the aspectes of the Planets, the one with the other of them, and the planets with the fixed starres, and how that they haue byn angled in the houses of the heauens, and also the nature of the signes, & their cōbusting with the sunne occidentall or orientall, so that as they haue founde howe the weather hath followed oftentimes, so they haue written the iudgements &c. And although that it bee a methode that the weather should be so, yet God doth alter that vnto his will and pleasure. Therefore I did write the iudgement of the weather, to no other purposes but for the common people, who the most part of them are not satisfied, except they haue the iudgements of weather: & furthermore I haue written herehow for to iudge what weather shall followe by diuers significations of mine owne obseruatiō, not before this time printed, with diuers other necessary matters, as in the booke doth appeare. Therfore (gentle Reader) I desire you to take this rude thing in good part, although that it be not altogether to the satisfying of your minde, for that some people doth looke into Prognostications, for to heare what strange thinges should happen, which I doe thinke most vayne & foolish, for God doth determine al causes, therefore let us serue God, and geue him thanks for al the benefits wherwith God hath blessed this our countrie of England: as I cal vnto minde that *Plutarch* writeth of *Plato* the great Philosopher, that when *Plato* felt in himselfe that he was likely to die, hee beeing a heathen not knowing of God, as the accustomable manner of the heathen was, that they did attribute gods for sundry purposes, so they did attribute vnto *Genius* to be the God of reason, and nature, so as *Plutarch* writeth, That *Plato* gaue the God *Genius* thankes for three causes: the first was for that the God *Genius* had made him a man, and not a beast: The second was, he gaue *Genius* thankes for that he was a Grecian: the third was, hee gaue *Genius* thankes, for that he was in *Socrates* time, who was another Philosopher that *Plato* had oftentimes conference with all. Now seeing that *Plato* beying a heathen Philosopher and neuer hearing of GOD nor his lawes, and he so geuing the God *Genius* thankes, which was no God, but according vnto the inuenting or deuising of man, how much the more are wee bound to lawde, prayse, and thanke the liuing GOD that hath made heauen and earth, and all thinges therein contayned, for the vse and benefite of man, and hath redeemed vs from the originall sinne of *Adam*. Therfore how muche the more are wee bound to giue the Lorde God thankes that he hath made vs men or women, who might haue made vs any vile beasts, or wormes, as todes & such like? The second cause, how much are we bound to thank the liuing God, that we are Christians, and not heathen, as *Plato* did thanke *Genius* for that hee was a Grecian. The iii. cause that we haue to prayse the almighty God, is that we heere in England, are in such a most vertuous Princes time, that the Gospel of Jesus Christ is preached through the whole realme of England, and hauing liued in peace and tranquility with abundance of all necessaries for the vse of man. Therefore how much are we bounde to praise the euer liuing God the Creator of all things, that it is our fortune through Gods prouidence to liue in such a happy time. Therefore let us all earnestly pray for the Queenes Maiesties long life, & to continue in this happy gouernment many yeres longer, yea, if it were possible that she might liue the yeres of Methuselah, and to continue in this her most godly peace. Then how happie are we that are borne in such a floorishing, peaceable, and prosperous time, wherfore we are much bound to thanke the liuing God, as well for that which is past, as for that which is to come: and there is no doubt, but that the Lord God will continue that same godly peace if we turne vnto him with al our heartes and mindes, and be sory for our sinnes and wickednes, but otherwise if we doe not repent vs of these our filthie liues and liuing, the Lorde will powre downe the abundance of his wrath upon vs, for there is not doubt, but that God hath spared vs for the vertuousnes of the Queenes Maiesties sake. And thus gentle reader I desire you to take this simple Almanacke and Prognostication in good part.

> From the Queenes house called Vpnor Castle
> in Kent, the first of December. 1580.
> Thy friende W.B.

*A note of such bookes as haue
beene written by the Authour William
Bourne, that are extant in Print.*

First, the Regiment of the Sea, *newely corrected and amended, wherevnto is added a Hidrographicall discourse, as touching the passages vnto Cataya, China and Molockus, with other places in the East Indies.*

The Treasure for Trauellers, *diuided into fiue bookes. The first booke sheweth the conclusions of the staffe and the crosse staffe, shewing how for to finde distances. The second is of* Cosmographie. *The third is of* Geometrie. *The iiii. is of the* Staticke. *The v. is of* Naturall Philosophie.

A booke called the Art of Shooting in great Ordenaunce.

A book called Inuentions or Deuises, *and the first is al deuises of Shippes, and then deuises of ordenance, and then deuises of walles, of fortes, and deuises of engins for sundry purposes . &c.*

The xi. sheweth the rising, Noonesteed, and setting of the Pliades commonly called the seuen starrs.

The Table of the contents of this Almanacke and Prognostication as foloweth.

First a Kalender of the Festiuall dayes, wherevnto is added the Sunnes declination for euery day of the yeere; where by taking the true height of the Sunne vpon the Meridian, you may knowe the altitude of the Pole aboue the Horizon.

The second, the Almanacke and Prognostication for x. yeeres, euery yeere particularly by it selfe, conteining first the Prime, and Epact, the Sundaies letter, the moueable feasts, the change, quarter, and full of the Moone, the iudgement of the weather, the Eclipses of the Sunne and the Moone, & the disposition of the weather for the iiii. seasons or quarters of the yeere.

The iii. is a meane and way how for to know in what signe & degree that the Moone is in for euer, not before this time printed.

The iiii. sheweth the beginning of the yeere for diuers purposes, as the yeere hath vi. seuerall beginninges according vnto the times appointed.

The v. is how for to iudge what weather shalbe by diuers significatiōs, with other necessary thinges meete to be noted.

The vi. is of letting of blood, purging, bathing, setting, sowing, and planting.

The vii. sheweth the nature and qualitie of the xii. signes.

The viii. sheweth the nature, course and qualitie of the vii. wandering lights or Planets.

The ix. sheweth according vnto sundry Authours that haue written of Astronomie and Astrologie, what countries, cities or townes are subiect vnder the xii. signes, and the vii. Planets.

The x. sheweth what Comets or Blazing starres haue happened since the yeere of our Lord 1572. with the place of their appearing and walke, and continuance and going out.

Ianuarie hath xxxj. dayes.

First day, Sun riseth at viii.of the clocke, and setteth at iiii. The viii.day, Sun riseth 50.min.after 7.set.10.mi.after 4.

The xvi.day Sun riseth xl.min.after 7.setteth xx.min.after 4. The 24.day, Sunriseth xxv.mi.after vii.set.xxxv.mi.after.4

			The Sunnes declination.	
i	A	*Newyeeresday.*	21	52
ii	b	Octa.Steph.	21	43
iii	c	Octa.John.	21	33
iiii	d	Octa.Innoce.	21	23
v	e	Depo.of Edw.	21	12
vi	f	*Twelfe day.*	21	1
vii	g	Felix & Janu.	20	49
viii	A	Lucian priest.	20	37
ix	b	Joyce vir.	20	25
x	c	*Sunne in Aqua.*	20	12
xi	d	Atlas.	19	59
xii	e	Archarde.	19	46
xiii	f	Hylary bish.	19	32
xiiii	g	Felicia.	19	17
xv	A	Maurice.	19	3
xvi	b	Marcel.	18	47
xvii	c	Dep.of Anth.	18	32
xviii	d	Prisca virgin.	18	17
xix	e	Wolfrane Bi.	18	1
xx	f	Fabian & Seb.	17	5
xxi	g	Agnes Vir.	17	28
xxii	A	Vincent Mar.	17	11
xxiii	b		16	5
xxiiii	c	Timothie.	16	37
xxv	d	Conuer.Paul.	16	19
xxvi	e	Policar. mart.	16	1
xxvii	f	Joh.Chry.do.	15	12
xxviii	g	Valerii.bish.	15	23
xxix	A	Theodor.prie.	15	5
xxx	b	Matilde quene	14	46
xxxi	c	Satur. & Vic.	14	26

A necessary and perfect rule to
know the beginning and ending of
euery Terme, with their Returnes.

⁋ Hillary Terme beginneth the xxiii. day of Ianuary (if it be not Sunday) and endeth the xii. of February. Which Terme hath foure Returnes: *That is to say,*
Octavis Hilarii. Quind. Hilarii. Crast. Purific. Octav. Purific.

⁋ Easter Terme begynneth xvii. dayes after Easter, and endeth the Monday next after Ascension day. And it hath fiue Returnes: *That is to say,*
Quind. Paschæ. Tres Paschæ. Mense Paschæ. Quinq. Paschæ. Crastin. Ascension.

⁋ Trinitie Terme begynneth the Fryday next after Trinitie Sunday, and endeth the Wednesday fortnight after: And hath foure Returnes: *That is to say,*
Crastin. Trinitatis. Octav. Trinit. Quind. Trinit. Tres Trinit.

⁋ Michaelmas Terme begynneth the ix. of October (if it be not Sunday, as aforesayd) and endeth the xxviii. of Nouember: And hath eight Returnes: *That is to say.*
Octavis Michael. Quind. Micha. Tres Micha. Mense Micha. Crast. Anima. Crast. Martini. Octa. Martini. Quind. Martini.

⁋ Note also that the Exchequer openeth eyght dayes before any Terme begyn: except Trinitie Terme, in which it openeth but foure dayes before.

March hath xxxj.dayes.

First day Sun riseth xviii.min.after vi.set.xiii.mi.after v.
The x.day Sun riseth at vi.Setteth at vi.
The xvii.day Sun riseth xlvii.min.after v.set.xiii.mi.after vi.
The 24 day Sun riseth xxx.mi.after v.set.30.mi.after vi.

The declination of the Sunne.

i	d	David.	3	49
ii	e	Chadde.	3	26
iii	f	Maurice.	3	2
iiii	g	Adrian.	2	38
v	A	Focas & Euse.	2	14
vi	b	Vict. & Victo.	1	51
vii	c	Perpetu.	1	27
viii	d	Depo.of Fel.	1	3
ix	e	XL.martyrs.	0	39
x	f	Agapite.	0	16
xi	g	*Sunne in Aries.*	0	8
xii	A	Gregorie.	0	32
xiii	b	Theodore.	0	55
xiiii	c	Candide.	1	19
xv	d	Longine.	1	42
xvi	e	Hila & Ionace.	2	6
xvii	f	Gertrude.	2	29
xviii	g	Edward King.	2	53
xix	A	Josep.ma.hui.	3	17
xx	b	Cuthbert.	3	40
xxi	c	Benedic.	4	3
xxii	d	Affrodose.	4	26
xxiii	e	Theodore.	4	49
xxiiii	f	Agapite.Fast.	5	12
xxv	g	*Annun.of Mar.*	5	35
xxvi	A	Castor.	5	58
xxvii	b	Marciani.	6	21
xxviii	c	Rupert.	6	44
xxix	d	Victorine.	7	6
xxx	e	Quirine.	7	28
xxxi	f	Adeline.	7	0

ALMANACKE FOR X. YEERES, 1581

Februarie hath xxviij.daies.

The 2.day Sun riseth ix.min.after vii.setteth ii.min.after iiii.
The 8. day Sun riseth lviii.min.after vi.set.2.mi.after v.

The xvi.day Sun riseth xl.min.after vi.setteth xx.mi.after 5.
The xxiiii.day Sun riseth xxx.mi.after vi.set.xxx.mi.after v.

The declination of the Sunne.

i	d	Brigit. Fast.	14	7
ii	e	*Purifi.of.Mary.*	13	47
iii	f	Blase Mart.	13	26
iiii	g	Gilbert confes.	13	6
v	A	Agathe vir.	12	46
vi	b	Dorothe vir.	12	26
vii	c	Angule.	12	5
viii	d		11	44
ix	e	*Sunne in Pisces.*	11	22
x	f	Scolastica.	11	1
xi	g	Sother.	10	39
xii	A		10	18
xiii	b	Wolfran Bish.	9	56
xiiii	c	Valentine.	9	33
xv	d	Faustin.	9	11
xvi	e	Julian.	8	49
xvii	f	Germanici.	8	26
xviii	g	Hugh bishop.	8	4
xix	A	Simeon.	7	41
xx	b	Mildred virg.	7	19
xxi	c	Lxxix.martirs.	6	56
xxii	d	Peters chayre.	6	33
xxiii	e	Policarp.Fast.	6	10
xxiiii	f	Matth.Apostle.	5	46
xxv	g	Inuent.Paul.	5	23
xxvi	A	Alexander.	5.	0
xxvii	b	Augustine.	4	36
xxviii	c	Oswald Bish.	4	13

		May hath xxxj.dayes.		
		First day, Sun ryseth xxvi.mi.after iiii.set.xxxiiii.mi.after vii. The 8.day.Sun riseth xvi.mi.after iiii.Set.xiiii.mi.after 7.		
		The xvi.day Sun riseth vi.min.after iiii.set.liiii.mi.after vii. The xxiiii.day Sun riseth at iiii.Setteth at viii.		
			The declination of the Sunne.	
i	b	*Philip & Iacob.*	17	49
ii	c	Athanasius.	18	5
iii	d	Inuē. of yᵉ cros.	18	20
iiii	e	Christopher.	18	35
v	f	Goddard.	18	49
vi	g	John port lat.	19	4
vii	A	Ioh.of Beuer.	19	17
viii	b		19	31
ix	c	Trans.of.Nic.	19	44
x	d	Gordian.	19	57
xi	e	Anthony.	20	8
xii	f	*Sunne in Gem.*	20	21
xiii	g	Seruitius.	20	33
xiiii	A	Bonifact.	20	45
xv	b	Isidore.	20	56
xvi	c	Felix bishop.	21	6
xvii	d	Tran.of Ben.	21	17
xviii	e	Dioscor.mart.	21	27
xix	f	Dunstane.	21	37
xx	g	Bernardine.	21	46
xxi	A	Helene queene.	21	55
xxii	b	Transl.Barn.	22	3
xxiii	c	Desiderii.	22	12
xxiiii	d	Seruule.	22	19
xxv	e	Urbane	22	27
xxvi	f	Augustine.	22	33
xvii	g	Bede priest.	22	40
xviii	A	Germane.	22	47
xix	b	Corone Mar.	22	52
xxx	c	Felix.	22	57
xxxi	d	Petronil.	23	3

Aprill hath xxx.dayes.

First day Sun riseth xix.min.after v. Set. xli.min.after vi.
The viii.day Sun riseth vi.min.after v.Set. liiii.mi.after 6.

The xvi.day Sun riseth li.min.after iiii.Set.ix.min.after vii.
The 24.day Sun riseth 38.min.after iiii.Set 22.mi.after 7.

			The declination of the Sunne.	
i	g	Gildarde.	8	13
ii	A	Mary Egypt.	8	35
iii	b	Richard Bysh.	8	57
iiii	c	Ambrose.	9	19
v	d	Vincent.	9	41
vi	e	Sextus.	10	2
vii	f	Euphemie.	10	23
viii	g	Dionysius.	10	44
ix	A	Perpetuus.	11	6
x	b	Appoline.	11	25
xi	c	*Sunne in Taurus.*	11	45
xii	d		12	6
xiii	e	Julian.	12	26
xiiii	f	Tiburtii.	12	47
xv	g	Osmunde.	13	6
xvi	A	Isydore.	13	26
xvii	b	Anicete.	13	45
xviii	c	Clutherius.	14	4
xix	d	Alphege.	14	23
xx	e	Victor.	14	41
xxi	f	Simon.	15	0
xxii	g	Sother.	15	18
xxiii	A	*George Martyr.*	15	35
xxiiii	b	Wilfride.	15	53
xxv	c	*Marke Euan.*	16	11
xxvi	d	Clete.	16	29
xxvii	e	Anastasius.	16	45
xxviii	f	Vitalis.	17	2
xxix	g	Pet.of Mil.	17	18
xxx	A	Depo.of Erk.	17	34

Iuly hath xxxj. dayes.

First day Sun riseth lviii.min. after iii. Set.ii.minu.after viii.
The viii.day Sun riseth ii.mi.after iiii.set 58.mi.after.vii.
The xvi.day Sun riseth xvi.min.afteriiii.Set xliiii.mi.after vii.
The 24.day Sun riseth xxxi.mi.after iiii.Set xxx.mi.after 7.

The declination of the Sunne

i	g	Octa.of John.	22	13
ii	A	Visita.Marie.	22	5
iii	b	Transla.Tho.	21	56
iiii	c	Transl.Marti.	21	47
v	d	Zoe.Virgin.	21	36
vi	e	Martialis.	21	27
vii	f	*Dog daies begin.*	21	19
viii	g	Depo.of.Grim.	21	8
ix	A	Cyril Bishop.	20	57
x	b	Seuen breth.	20	47
xi	c	Trans.of Ben.	20	35
xii	d	Nabor & Felix.	20	24
xiii	e	*Sunne in Leo.*	20	12
xiiii	f	Reuell.	19	59
xv	g	Trans.Swith.	19	49
xvi	A	Tra.Osmond.	19	33
xvii	b	Kenelme.	19	19
xviii	c	Arnulph.	19	5
xix	d	Ruffine & Just.	18	56
xx	e	Margaret.	18	37
xxi	f	Praxede.	18	22
xxii	g	Mary Magd.	18	9
xxiii	A	Appolinaris.	17	23
xxiiii	b	Cristine. Fast.	17	37
xxv	c	*Iames Apostle.*	17	22
xxvi	d	An. moth.Mar.	17	5
xxvii	e	VII.Sleep.	16	49
xxviii	f	Sampson.	16	22
xxix	g	Martha.	16	7
xxx	A	Abdon & Sen.	15	59
xxxi	b	Germane.	15	41

Iune hath xxx.dayes.

First day. Sun riseth liiii.min. after iii. Set. vi.min. after 8.
The xi. day Sun riseth xv.mi. after iii. set. 15.mi. after viii.

The xvi. day Sun riseth 1.min. after iii. Set. x.mi. after viii.
The xxiiii. day Sun riseth liiii.mi. after iii. Set. vi.mi. after 8.

The declination of the Sunne.

i	e	Nichomede.	23	8
ii	f	Marcell.	23	12
iii	g	Erasmus.	23	15
iiii	A	Petroclus.	23	18
v	b	Boniface.	23	22
vi	c	Melon.	23	24
vii	d	Paule bish.	23	26
viii	e	Transt. Edm.	23	27
ix	f	Juan Confess.	23	27
x	g	Trans. Wolsto.	23	28
xi	A	Barnab. apost.	23	28
xii	b	*Sunne in Cancer.*	23	28
xiii	c	Anthonie	23	28
xiiii	d	Basill Bishop.	23	27
xv	e	Viti. & Mede.	23	26
xvi	f	Tran. of Rich.	23	25
xvii	g	Botulphe.	23	24
xviii	A	Mar. & Mar.	23	22
xix	b	Geruasius.	23	19
xx	c	Trans. of Ed.	23	15
xxi	d	Walburge.	23	12
xxii	e	Albane.	23	8
xxiii	f	Audrie. Fast.	23	3
xxiiii	g	*Iohn. Baptist.*	22	59
xxv	A	Amandi.	22	54
xxvi	b	John & Paul.	22	48
xxvii	f	Crescens.	22	42
xxviii	d	Leo. Fast.	22	35
xxix	e	*Peter. Apostle.*	22	29
xxx	f	Com. of Pau.	22	22

September hath xxx.dayes.

First day Sun riseth xxxvi.mi.after v.Set.xxiiii.mi.after vi.
The vii.day Sun riseth xlix.mi.after v.Set.xi.mi.after vi.

The xiii.day Sunne ryseth at vi.and setteth at vi.
The 24.day Sun riseth xxiii.min.after vi.set 37.mi.after 5.

The declination of the Sunne.

i	f	Gyles.	4	39
ii	g	Antho.Mar.	4	16
iii	A	Lupe Byshop.	3	53
iiii	b	Transl.Cuth.	3	31
v	c	Bertine.	3	7
vi	d	Eugenius.	2	44
vii	e	*Nati.Eliza.Reg.*	2	20
viii	f	Natiu.Marie.	1	58
ix	g	Gorgonii.	1	34
x	A	Sylvius Bish.	1	10
xi	b	Pro. and Jac.	0	48
xii	c	Martinian.	0	24
xiii	d	*Sunne in Libra.*	0	0
xiiii	e	Holy Crosse.	0	24
xv	f	Philetus.	0	47
xvi	g	Edith.	1	11
xvii	A	Lambert.	1	34
xviii	b	Vict. & Cor.	1	58
xix	c	Januar.mart.	2.	21
xx	d	Eustace. Fast.	2	44
xxi	e	*Matthew Apo.*	3	8
xxii	f	Mauricius.	3	32
xxiii	g	Tecla virgin.	3	55
xxiiii	A	Andochius.	4	18
xxv	b	Firmine.	4	41
xxvi	c	Cypri. & Just.	5	3
xxvii	d	Cosine & Da.	5	27
xxviii	e	Truyerius.	5	50
xxix	f	*Michael Archa.*	6	13
xxx	g	Hierome priest.	6	36

August hath xxxj.daies.

First day Sun ryseth xl.min.after iiii.Setteth xx.mi.after vii.
The viii.day Sun riseth li.min.after iiii.Set.ix.mi.after.7.
The xvi.day Sun riseth vi.mi.after v.setteth liiii.mi.after vi.
The 24.day Sun riseth xx.min.after v.set.30 mi. after vi.

The declination of the Sunne.

i	c	Lammas day.	15	23
ii	d	Steuen.	15	5
iii	e	Inuent.Step.	14	48
iiii	f	Justine.	14	30
v	g	*Festum Niuis.*	14	11
vi	A	Transla.Christ.	13	51
vii	b	Feast of Jesu.	13	33
viii	c	Cyriacke.	13	13
ix	d	Romane mar.	12	54
x	e	Laurence mar.	12	34
xi	f	Tiburt.	14	14
xii	g	Clare.	11	53
xiii	A	Hippolit.	11	33
xiiii	b	*Sunne in Virgo.*	11	14
xv	c	Assum.Mar.	10	54
xvi	d	Roche Mart.	10	32
xvii	e	*Dog dayes end.*	10	12
xviii	f	Octa.Laur.	9	50
xix	g	Lewes.	9	28
xx	A	Barnard.	9	7
xxi	b	Priuati.	8	46
xxii	c	Timothi.	8	24
xxiii	d	Fast.	8	2
xxiiii	e	*Bartholo.Apost.*	7	39
xxv	f	Lewes kyng.	7	18
xxvi	g	Seuerine.	6	55
xxvii	A	Rufuse mar.	6	33
xxviii	b	August.bish.	6	11
xxix	c	John behead.	5	47
xxx	d	Felix & Audac.	5	25
xxxi	e	Cuthbert.	5	2

Nouember hath xxx.daies.

First day Sun riseth xxx.min.after vii.setteth xxx.mi.after iiii.
The 8.day Sun riseth xlii.mi.after vii.sets 18.min.after 4.
The xvi.day, Sun riseth li.min.after vii.sets iiii.min.after iii.
The xxiiii.day Sun riseth at viii.sets at iiii.

The declination of the Sunne

i	d	*All Saintes.*	17	26
ii	e		17	43
iii	f	Wenefride.	17	59
iiii	g	Amantius.	18	15
v	A	Lete Priest.	18	31
vi	b	Leonard.	18	46
vii	c	Wilbrode.	19	1
viii	d	Foure crown.	19	16
ix	e	Theodore.	19	30
x	f	Benet.	19	44
xi	g	Martin Bish.	19	58
xii	A	Paterne.	20	10
xiii	b	*Sun in Sag.*	20	22
xiiii	c	Trans.Erken.	20	36
xv	d	Machute.	20	48
xvi	e	Depo. of Edm.	20	59
xvii	f	*Init.Reg.Eliz.*	21	10
xviii	g	Oct.of.Mart.	21	21
xix	A	Eliza.martyr	21	33
xx	b	Edmund king.	21	41
xxi	c	Presen.Mar.	21	51
xxii	d	Cicilie virg.	21	59
xxiii	e	Clement.	22	8
xxiiii	f	Grisogen.	22	17
xxv	g	Katherine.	22	25
xxvi	A	Line.	22	32
xxvii	b	Agricola.	22	39
xxviii	c		22	46
xxix	d	Saturn. Fast.	22	52
xxx	e	*Andrew Apo.*	22	57

October hath xxxj. dayes.

First day Sun riseth xxxvi.mi.after vi.Set.xxiiii.min.after v.
The viii.day Sun riseth 47 min.after vi.set.13.mi.after v.

The xvi.day Sun riseth iii.mi.after vii. sets lvii.min.after 4.
The 24.day Sun riseth xiv.mi.after vii.sets xli.mi.after 4.

The declination of the Sunne

i	A	Remigius.	6	59
ii	b	Leodegarii.	7	22
iii	c	Candide.	7	44
iiii	d	Fraunces.	8	6
v	e	Appoline.	8	39
vi	f	Fayth.	8	51
vii	g	Marci.	9	13
viii	A	Pelagius.	9	34
ix	b	Dionysius.	9	56
x	c	Gereon & Vict.	10	18
xi	d	Nicasius.	10	40
xii	e	Wilfride	11	1
xiii	f	Edward king.	11	23
xiiii	g	*Sunne in Scorpi.*	11	44
xv	A	Wolfran.	12	5
xvi	b	Mic.of yᵉ moūt.	12	26
xvii	c	Etheldred.	12	47
xviii	d	*Luke Euangelist.*	13	7
xix	e	Fredeswide.	13	27
xx	f	Austrebert.	13	47
xxi	g	xi.M.virgins.	14	7
xxii	A	Mary Salom.	14	26
xxiii	b	Romane.	14	45
xxiiii	c	Maglori.	15	4
xxv	d	Crispine.	15	23
xxvi	e	Ursula.	15	41
xxvii	f	Florence. Fast	16	0
xxviii	g	*Simon & Iude.*	16	17
xxix	A	Narcissus.	16	35
xxx	b	Germane.	16	52
xxxi	c	Quintin. Fast	17	6

Now in this Kalender going before, there is added vnto great purpose, more then is vsed in any Almanacke before this time: that is to say, the Sunnes declination for euery day of the Moneth for this yeere of our Lord 1581. Wherby you may know the latitude of any place, by the taking of the height of the Sunne vpon the Meridian, for to knowe the altitude of the Pole of the worlde, as I doe throughly teach in my booke called *The Regiment for the Sea*. And for that, I will not trouble you the Readers heereof with many tables of the Sunnes declination this yeere 1581. as the first yeere after the Bissextill, and for to know the true declination, when this yeere is expired, then note these few words following. the next yeere, being the ii. yeere after the Bissextill, that is to say, the yeere 1582. in Marche, when that the Sunne has swift declination. Then the x. day of March: Whilest that the Sun hath South declination, adde or put to vi. minutes more then is in the kalender: for the next day, being the xi. day of March, then beginning the North declination, then rebate vi minutes, from the which is set downe in the kalender, and that shalbe the true declination of the Sunne. And also that yeere, in September the xiii. day, then adde vi. minutes for the North declination and the xiiii. day, rebate vi. minutes for the South declination. And also for the iii. yeere of Bissextill, the x. day of Marche, then adde xii. minutes more to the South declination, and the xii. day, then the Sun shall have North declination, then rebate xii. minutes lesse. And also for the xiii. day of September, adde xii. minutes more for the North declination, and the xiiii. day rebate xii. minutes for the Sunnes South declination. And furthermore, for the yeere of Bissextill, that is, the yeere 1584. then the tenth day of Marche rebate vi. minutes from the Sunnes South declination, and the xi. day adde vi. minuts more vnto the Sunnes North declination. And then furthermore, for the xii. day of September, rebate vi. min. more from the Sunnes North declination, and the xiiii. of the moneth, adde vi. minutes more vnto the Sunnes South declination and so shall

December hath xxxj.daies.

First day Sun riseth vi.min.after viii.sets liiii.mi.after iii.
The viii.day Sun riseth x.mi.after viii.sets l.mi.after iii.

The xiii.day Sun riseth xv.min.after 8.sets 45.mi.after iii.
The xxiiii.day Sun riseth v.mi.after viii.sets lv.mi.after 3.

			The declination of the Sunne	
i	f	Elegius.	23	3
ii	g	Libane.	23	8
iii	A	Depo.of Osm.	23	12
iiii	b	Barbara.	23	15
v	c	Saba.	23	19
vi	d	Nicholas.	23	22
vii	e	Ambrose.	23	24
viii	f	Concep.Ma.	23	25
ix	g	Cyprian.	23	26
x	A	Eulalie.	23	27
xi	b	Damase.	23	28
xii	c	*Sunne in Capri.*	23	28
xiii	d	Luce Vir.	23	28
xiiii	e	Nicasi bishop.	23	27
xv	f	Valerius.	23	26
xvi	g	O sapientia.	23	25
xvii	A	Lazarus conf.	23	24
xviii	b	Gratian.	23	21
xix	c	Venesia.	23	18
xx	d	Julian. Fast.	23	14
xxi	e	*Thomas Apost.*	23	11
xxii	f	XXX.martyrs.	23	6
xxiii	g	Victor virgin.	23	1
xxiiii	A	Candida Fast	23	55
xxv	b	*Christmas day.*	22	5
xxvi	c	*S.Steuen.*	22	43
xxvii	d	*S.Iohn.*	22	36
xxviii	e	*Innocents.*	22	28
xxix	f		22	21
xxx	g	Tra.of James.	22	13
xxxi	A	Siluester.	22	4

The last quarter the xxvii. day at a xi. of the clocke at night, colde darke mistie wether.

February.

The new Moone the ii. day at iiii. a clocke at afternoone, temperate according vnto the time of the yeere.

The first quarter, the tenth day, xi. minutes at high noone, temperate.

The full Moone, the xviii. day, at iii. a clocke viii. minutes at afternoone, windy.

The last quarter, the xxvi. day, at xi. of the clocke ten min. at noone, temperate ayre, but windy.

Marche.

The newe Moone, the v. day, at one a clocke xliiii. minuts after midnight, temperate and moyst.

The first quarter, the xii. day at v. of the clocke in the morning, temperate.

The full Moone the xx. day at viii. of the clocke, xiii. minutes in the forenoone temperate, and iiii. or v. dayes after, winde.

The last quarter the xxvii. day, at ix. of the clocke at night, temperate.

Aprill.

The newe Moone the iii. day, at xi. of the clock, xlviii. minutes at high noone, warme.

The first quarter the tenth day, at xi. of the clocke, at night, cold and windy.

The full Moone, the xviii. day, at a xi. a clocke at night, like to be tempestuous wether.

The last quarter the xxvi. day at iii. of the clocke, v. minutes in the morning, thunder and raine.

May.

The newe Moone the ii. day, at ix. of the clocke xxxviii. minutes at night, temperate.

you haue the Sunnes true declination for that day. For the declination of the Sunne is most swiftest in March and September, therefore adde or diminish all the rest of the moneth, the like as is set downe both for May and June, and July, and also Nouember, December, and January: the declination as it is, wil serue well enough, but the rest of the monethes there is some errours, which may bee considered, by adding or rebating sometime v. minutes, or iiii. iii. or ii. minuts and you doe see as it doeth beare by proportion from the Equinoctiall, as in March and September, then the declination is most swiftest, in February, Aprill, August, and October meane, and in the rest of the Monethes, slowe . &c.

1581.
An Almanacke and Prognostication for the yeere of our Lorde 1581. being the first yeere after Bissextill.

The golden number, is   v
   The Epact, is   xiv.
   The Dominicall letter, is   A
The first Sunday in Lent, is the xii. day of Februarie.
Easter day is the xxvi. day of March.
Ascension day, is the fourth day of May.
Whitsunday, is the xiiii. day of May.
Betweene Newyeeres day and Shrouetide are five weekes iust.

Ianuarie. 1581.

The new Moone, the v. day at vi. of the clocke in morning, colde and frost.

The first quarter, the xi. day at ten of the clocke vi. minutes at night, temperate according to the time of the yeere.

The full Moone Eclipsed, the xix. day, at viii. of the clocke, xxvi. minutes at night, windy temperate ayre.

September.

The first quarter the vi. day, at v. a clocke in the morning winde and tempest.

The full Moone the xii. day, at vi. a clock xlviii. minuts at night, after two dayes winde.

The last quarter the ix. day, at vii a clocke at night, great winde to followe.

The newe Moone the xxvii. day, at ix. a clocke, ten minutes at night, temperate.

October.

The first quarter the v day at iii. a clocke in the afternoone cloudy wether.

The full Moone the xii. day, at v. a clocke xi. minutes in the morning, mizzeling.

The last quarter, the xix. day at noone, temperate.

The newe Moone, the xxvii. day, at ii. a clocke, x. minutes at afternoone, windie.

Nouember.

The first quarter, the iii. day at midnight, colde darke cloudy wether.

The full Moone, the x. day at iiii. a clocke xvii. min. temperate ayre, but windie.

The last quarter, the xviii. day, at viii. a clock in the forenoone temperate.

The newe Moone, the xxvi. day, at v. a clocke xxxviii. minuts in the morning, temperate.

December.

The first quarter, the iii. day, at vii. a clocke in the morning, temperate and mist.

The full Moone, the tenth day at v. a clocke, xxxiii minutes in the morning, temperate.

ALMANACKE FOR X. YEERES, 1581

The first quarter the x. day, at iiii. of the clocke at after noone, cloudy dark wether.

The full Moone the xviii. day at ten of the clocke, xxxi. min. in the forenoone, temperate according to the time.

The last quarter the xxv. day, at vii. of the clocke in the forenoone, moyst wether.

Iune.

The newe Moone the first day, at viii. a clocke, lv. min. in the forenoone, temperate warme.

The first quarter the ix. day, at ten a clocke in the forenoone, temperate and cloudy.

The full Moone the xvi. day, at vii. of the clocke, lvii. minutes at after noone, the wether variable.

The last quarter the xxiii. day at noone, muche winde and tempest.

The new Moone the last day at ix. of the clocke xlviii. minuts at night, moyst wether.

Iuly.

The first quarter the ix. day, at one of the clocke in the morning, temperate.

The full Moone Eclipsed, the xvi. day at iiii. a clocke xviii. minutes in the morning, warme.

The last quarter the xxii. day, at vii. a clocke in the afternoone temperate warme.

The new Moone the xxx. day, 29. mi. at high noone, warme.

August.

The first quarter the vii. day, at iiii. a clocke in the afternoone, cloudy wether to folowe.

The full Moone the xiiii. day at high noone temperate.

The last quarter the xxi. day at v. a clocke in the morning, windy.

The newe Moone, the xxix. day, at iiii. a clocke xxiii. minutes in the morning, temperate.

This quarter of the yeere is likely for to be drye and windy, in the beginning, and a quarter spent of Aprill, very muche raine, after that better wether.

The Sommer time beginneth the xi. day of June at vii. of the clocke at night, at what time the Sunne entreth the first point of *Cancer,* and doeth continue vnto the xiii. day of September. This quarter of the yeere is like to bee meane, according vnto the time, and about the xxiiii. day of June, windy.

Autum beginneth the xiii. day of September, at ix. a clocke in the morning, at what time the Sunne entreth the first point of *Libra,* and continueth to the xi. day of December. This quarter of the yeere is like to be indifferent wether, at the first, windy, and towardes the ende raynie and mistie wether.

1582.
An Almanacke and Prognostication for the
yeere of our Lorde 1582. being the seconde
yeere after the Bissextill.

The golden number, is   vi.
    The Epact, is   vi.
    The Sundayes letter, is   G.
The first Sunday of Lent, is the iiii. day of March.
Easter day, is the xv day of Aprill.
Ascention day, is the xxiiii. of May.
Whitsunday is the iiii. of Iune.
Betweene Newyeres day, and Shrouesunday, are vii. weekes and vi. dayes.

Ianuarie. 1582.

The first quarter, the first day at iii. of the clocke at afternoone, temperate.

    The full Moone, the viii. day at ix. of the clocke xxvi. minutes at night, great windes.

ALMANACKE FOR X. YEERES, 1581

The last quarter the xviii. day, at iiii. a clocke in the morning, winde and tempest.

The newe Moone, the xxv. day at vii. a clocke, iiii. minutes at night, colde raynie wether.

This yeere of our Lord 1581. there are ii. Eclipses of the Moone, the first Eclipse is the xix. day of Januarie, at viii. of the clocke, xxvi. minutes at night, within iii. degrees of the Dragons taile, and shalbe darkened xiiii. pointes xxxviii. minutes. The Moone shalbe begin to come vnder the shadowe of the earth heere with vs at London before vii. of the clocke: and shall continue from the beginning vnto the end, iii. houres. And this Eclipse shalbe seene in the South East parte of the worlde.

The second Eclipse shalbe the xvi. day of July, at iiii. of the clocke, xviii. minutes in the morning, within iiii. degrees and a halfe of the Dragons head, and shalbe darkened xiii. pointes xvi. minutes and the Moone shall begin to come vnder the shadow of the earth with vs heere at London before iii. of the clock, and shall continue from the beginning vnto the ende, more then two houres: and this Eclipse shall bee seene in the South West, and by West, at the Moones going downe vnder the Horizon.

The disposition of the iiii. quarters of the yeere, and according vnto the accustomable order that is vsed to begin at the winter part of the yeere, at what time the Sunne entreth the first point of *Capricorne*, in the yeere of our Lorde 1580. the xi. day of December, at vii. a clocke in the morning and doeth continue vnto the tenth day of March. This part of the yeere is likely to bee colde and windy, and about the ende of Januarie, colde, darke, cloudy wether, as Snowe and suche like, and the beginning of March rainy wether.

The Spring time beginneth the tenth day of March, at viii. a clocke in the morning, at what time the Sunne entreth into the first point of *Aries*, and doeth continue vnto the xi. day of June.

The first quarter, the xxix. day, at iii. a clocke in the afternoone temperate.

May.

The full Moone, the vii. day at v. a clocke xviii. minutes in the afternoone, temperate.

The last quarter, the xv. day, at v. a clock in the morning temperate.

The new Moone the xxi. day, at vii. of the clocke iiii. minuts in the after noone, warme wether.

The first quarter, the xxix. day, at vii. a clocke xxxvi. minuts in the morning, temperate.

Iune.

The full Moone, the vi. day, at vi. a clock xliiii. minutes in the morning, windy.

The last quarter, the xiii. day, at x. a clocke before noone, temperate.

The newe Moone, the xx. day, at v. a clocke xviii. minutes in the morning, moyst wether.

The first quarter, the xxvii. day, at xi. a clocke at night, moyst wether.

Iuly.

The full Moone, the v. day, at v. a clocke lii. minutes at after noone, temperate.

The last quarter, the xii. day, at iiii. a clock in the after noone, warme.

The newe Moone, the xix. day, at iiii. a clocke xxxii. minutes in the afternoone, warme wether.

The first quarter, the xxvii. day, at iiii. a clocke in the after noone, rayne and thunder.

August.

The full Moone, the iiii. day, at v. a clocke, v. minutes in the morning, warme.

The last quarter, the xvii. day, at one of the clocke in the morning, temperate.

The newe Moone, the xxvii. day, at vii. of the clocke xiiii. minutes in the morning winde and mist.

The first quarter, the xxx. day at xi. of the clocke l. minutes at night, frost.

February.

The full Moone, the vii. day at ii. of the clocke, xiv. minutes at after noone, winde and raine, tempestuous wether.

The last quarter the xv. day, at viii. of the clocke xxx. minutes at night, raine, and Snow and winde.

The newe Moone, the xxii. day, at vi. of the clocke x. minuts at night, raine or Snow.

Marche.

The first quarter, the first day, at ten a clocke in the forenoone, myst.

The full Moone, the ix. day, at ix. a clocke in the forenoone, rainy wether.

The last quarter, the xvii. day, at x. of the clocke before noone, raine and tempest.

The newe Moone, the xxiiii. day, at iii. a clocke in the morning, rayne, hayle, and tempest iiii. or v. dayes together.

The first quarter, the xxx. day, at midnight, whot and moyst wether.

Aprill.

The full Moone, the viii. day, at ii. a clocke in the morning tempestuous wether.

The last quarter, the xv. day, at x. of the clocke at night temperate.

The newe Moone, the xxii. day, v. minutes before high noone before the change ii. or iii. dayes raine, but after temperate.

The full Moone, the xxix. day, at iiii. a clocke liiii. minutes at after noone, windy.

December.

The last quarter, the vi. day at midnight, cold raynie weather.
The newe Moone, the xv. day, at ii. a clocke xvii. minutes in the morning, frost.
The first quarter, the xxii. day, at xi. a clocke x. minutes at noone, temperate.
The full Moone, the xxix. day, at viii a clocke, xxvi. minutes afore noone, temperate.

This yeere of our Lord 1582. there is an Eclipse of the Sunne the xx. day of June, at v. of the clocke xviii. minuts in the morning, within ii. degrees of the Dragons taile, and shalbe darkened iii. points, vii. minutes, this Eclipse shalbe but small, &c.

The disposition of the iiii. partes of the yeere, and first of winter, when that the Sunne entreth into the first point of *Capricorne*, and that is the 11. day of December, at one a clocke at noone in the yeere of our Lorde 1581. and shall continew vnto the x. day of March. This parte of the yeere, is likely to be moyst and windy, and about a quarter of January very much winde.

The Spring time beginneth the x. day of March at ii. a clocke xxvii. minutes in the afternoone, at what time the Sunne entreth the first point of *Aries*, and shal continue vnto the xi. day of June: This quarter of this yeere is likely to bee reasonable temperate, and about the xx. day of April, much rayne, and the beginning of May, windy, &c.

The Sommer part beginneth the xi. day of June, at one of the clocke ix. minutes in the morning, at what time the Sunne entreth the first point of *Cancer*, and continueth vnto the xiii. day of September, this quarter of the yeere is likely to bee tem-

ALMANACKE FOR X. YEERES, 1581

The last quarter, the x. day, at vii. a clocke in the afternoone, temperate.

The newe Moone, the xviii. day, at v. a clocke xlviii. minutes in the morning, warme and moyst.

The first quarter, the xxvi. day, at ix. a clocke in the morning, temperate ayre.

September.

The full Moone, the ii. day, at xii. a clocke, xlviii. minutes at high noone, temperate.

The last quarter, the ix. day, at iii. a clocke in the morning, temperate.

The newe Moone, the xvi. day at ix. a clocke xxvii. minutes at night, temperate.

The first quarter, the xxiiii. day at midnight, temperate wether.

October.

The full Moone, the first day, at ix. a clocke xxviii. minutes at night, temperate and moyst.

The last quarter, the viii. day, at iii. a clock in the after noone, raine and tempest, and sodainie windes.

The newe Moone, the xvi. day, at ii. a clocke liii. minutes after noone, moyst.

The first quarter, the xxiiii. day, at iii. a clocke at afternoone, winde and tempest.

The full Moone, the last day, at viii. a clocke xlv. minutes afore noone, raine and winde.

Nouember.

The last quarter, the vii. day, at v. a clocke xl. minutes in the morning, raine and tempest.

The newe Moone, the xv. day, at ix. a clocke xxv. minutes afore noone, temperate.

The first quarter the xxiii. day, at iii. a clocke in the morning, colde mizzeling wether.

February.

The last quarter, the iiii. day, at v. of the clocke viii. minutes at night, temperate according vnto the time.

The newe Moone, the xii. day at vi. of the clocke xxxviii. min. in the morning, great winde.

The first quarter, the xix. day, at iii. of the clocke vii. minutes in the morning stormy wether.

The full Moone, the xxvi. day, at x. of the clock xxiii. minutes before noone, colde, raine or snowe.

March.

The last quarter, the vi. day, at one of the clocke iiii. minutes at noone, rayne and windy.

The newe Moone, the xiii. day, at vii. a clocke xiiii. minutes at night, temperate and dry.

The first quarter, the xx. day, at x. a clocke before noone, raine and tempest.

The full Moone, the xxviii. day, at two a clocke xxvi. minutes in the morning, warme and moyst.

Aprill.

The last quarter, the v. day, at vi. a clocke xxxvi. minutes in the morning, temperate.

The new Moone, the xii. day at iiii. a clocke viii. minutes in the morning, temperate.

The first quarter, the xviii. day at viii. a clocke lvii. minutes at night, the wether variable and vnstedfast.

The full Moone, the xxvi. day, at vi. a clocke xliii. minutes at after noone, temperate, and inclined to moysture.

May.

The last quarter, the iiii. day, at viii. a clocke xxvi. minutes at afternoone, much rayne a long time together.

The newe Moone, the xi. day, at high noone temperate.

perate and windy, and not too whot in the beginning, and the ende of July, much winde, and the later part of August, cloudy and darke wether, enclined vnto moystures.

Autum, the latter part of the yeere begins the xiii. day of September, at ii. of the clocke iii. minutes in the morning, at what time the Sunne entreth the first point of *Libra*, and continueth vnto the xi. day of December. This quarter of the yeere is likely to be very colde and moyst, and towards the end of October, windy, &c.

An Almanacke and Prognostication for the
yeere of our Lorde 1583. being the thirde
yeere after the Bissextill.

The golden number, is   vii.
   The Epact, is   xvii.
   The Sundayes letter, is   F.

The first Sunday in Lent, is the xvii. day of February.
Easter day the last day of March.
Ascention day, the ix. day of May.
Whitsunday, the xix. day of May.
Betweene newyeeres day and Shrouesunday vi. weekes and v. dayes.

Ianuary 1583.

The last quarter, the v. day at ix. a clocke at night, raine and tempest.

The newe Moone, the xiii. day at ix. a clocke at night, raine and sodeine stormes of winde.

The first quarter, the xx. day, at vii. of the clocke at night, frost.

The full Moone, the xxvii. day, at vii. of the clocke at night temperate.

September.

The new Moone, the vi. day, at one a clocke xxxviii. minutes in the morning, cold, darke, cloudy, windy, & rainy wether.

The first quarter, the xiiii. day, at one a clocke xxviii. minutes in the morning, raine and tempest.

The full Moone, the xxi. day, at xii. a clocke ii. minutes at high noone, temperate.

The last quarter, the xxviii. day, at iiii. a clocke xx. minutes in the morning, moyst.

October.

The new Moone, the v. day, at iii. a clocke xxxvi. minutes at afternoone, temperate and somewhat windy.

The first quarter, the xiii. day at vii. a clocke xli. minutes at night, raine, &c.

The full Moone, the xx. day, at xi. a clocke at noone, raine, winde, and tempest.

The last quarter, the xxvii. day at one a clocke xxx. minutes at noone, temperate and moyst.

Nouember.

The newe Moone, the iiii. day at ix. a clocke in the forenoone, windy.

The first quarter, the xii. day, at high noone, windy & tempest.

The full Moone, the xix. day at ix. a clocke xiiii. minutes in the forenoone, temperate.

The last quarter, the xxvi. day, at ii. a clocke xx. minutes in the morning, dry and warme, according vnto the time of the yeere.

December.

The newe Moone, the iii. day at iiii. a clocke in the morning, windy.

The first quarter, the xii. day, at iii. a clocke xiiii. minutes in the morning, temperate.

The first quarter, the xviii. day at viii. a clock in the morning, temperate.

The full Moone, the xxvi. day, at x. a clocke, xxvi. minutes before noone, temperate.

Iune.

The last quarter, the iii. day, at vi a clocke in the morning, hot, likely to thunder.

The newe Moone, the ix. day, at vii. a clocke xvii. minutes at afternoone, winde and tempest.

The first quarter, the xvi. day, at x. of the clocke at night temperate.

The ful Moone, the xxiiii. day, at midnight, or somwhat past, raine and thunder.

Iuly.

The last quarter, the ii. day, at x. a clocke xxvi. minutes before noone, temperate.

The new Moone, the ix. day, at iii. a clocke xxvi min. in the morning, colde darke mistie wether for the time of yeere.

The first quarter, the xvi. day, at one a clocke xiv. minutes at noone, temperate.

The full Moone, the xxiiii. day, at ii. a clocke xxiiii. min. at noone, raine, haile, and thunder.

The last quarter, the last day, at v. a clock at after noone, raine lightning and thunder.

August.

The new Moone, the vii. day, at one a clocke at noone, warme.

The first quarter, the xv. day at vii. a clocke xi. minutes in the morning, temperate.

The full Moone, the xxiii. day, at ii. a clocke in the morning, temperate.

The last quarter, the xxix. day, at x. a clocke vi. minutes at night, the wether diuers.

tinueth vnto the xi. day of December. This part of the yeere is likely to be colde and moyst, and windy.

1584.
An Almanacke and Prognostication for the yeere of Christes incarnation, 1584. being the yeere of Bissextill.

The golden number, is   viii.
   The Epact.   xxviii.
   The Sundayes letter,   E & D.
The first Sunday in Lent the viii. day of March.
Easter day, the xix. day of Aprill.
Ascention day, the xxviii. day of May.
Whitsunday the vii. day of Iune.
Between newyeeres day, and Shrouesunday, viii. weeks and iiii. dayes.

Ianuary.

The newe Moone, the ii. day, at xi. a clocke viii. minutes at night, snow, sleete, and cold wether, iii. or iiii. dayes together, and winde to follow.

   The first quarter, the x. day at iii. a clocke v. minutes at after noone, raine, hayle, or sleete and notable change of wether.

   The full Moone, the xvii. day at vi. a clocke xvi. minutes in the morning, temperate.

   The last quarter, the xxiiii. day at two a clocke in the after noone, sodeine windes, and calmes betweene.

February.

The newe Moone, the first day, at iiii. a clocke xliii. minutes at after noone, fayre and windy.

   The first quarter, the viii. day at ten a clocke 47. minutes at night temperate.

The full Moone, the xviii. day, at vii. a clocke in the morning, temperate.

The last quarter, the xxv. day, at vi. a clocke xlviii. minutes at night, colde &c.

This yeere of our Lorde 1583. there is no Eclipse of the Sunne, nor of the Moone.

The disposition of the 4. quarters of he yeere 1583, and first of the Winter part, and that beginneth the xi. day of December, at vii. a clocke ten minutes at night in *Anno* 1582, at what time that the Sunne entreth the first point of *Capricorne*, and continueth vnto the tenth day of March. This part of the yere is likely to bee reasonable windy, and about the midst of February, windy, but towards the ende of the quarter, much raine or snowe.

The Spring time beginneth the x. day of March at viii. a clock xvii. minutes at night, at what time the Sunne entreth the first point of *Aries*, and continueth vnto the xi. day of June. This part of the yeere is likely to bee temperate and moyst, in the beginning: and about the beginning of May, by the meane of the coniunction of *Saturne* with *Iupiter*, in the signe of *Pisces*, and also furthered by the sextill Aspect of *Saturne* & the Sun, it is likely to be great abundāce of rain, wth ouerflowing of al lowe grounds, except Gods prouident power bee vnto the contrary, vnto the vtter destruction both of corne and hay that yere, except the hylly grounde doe helpe.

The Sommer part of the yeere beginneth the xii. day of June at vi. a clocke lix. minutes in the morning, at what time the Sunne entreth the first point of *Cancer*, and continueth vnto the xiii. day of September: This part of the yeere is likely to bee for the most part rayne, by the meanes of the late coniunction of *Saturne* and *Iupiter*, and oftentimes thunder & lightning.

Autum the latter part of the yeere, beginneth the xiii. day of September at ix. a clocke xiii. minutes at night, and con-

Iune.

The first quarter, the v. day, at iiii. a clocke xxiii. minutes in the morning, likely to thunder.

The full Moone, the xiii day, at two a clocke xxviii. minutes in the morning, windy.

The last quarter, the xii. day, at iii. a clocke in the morning, windy.

The newe Moone the 27. day, at vii. a clocke xl. minutes at after noone, temperate and moyst.

Iuly.

The first quarter, the iiii. day, at iii. a clock xv. minutes at after noone, temperate.

The full Moone, the xii. day, at v. a clocke xlii. minutes at after noone, temperate warme.

The last quarter, the xx. day, at high noone warme.

The newe Moone the xxvii. day, at iiii. a clocke 26 minuts in the morning, warme.

August.

The first quarter, the iii. day at v. a clocke viii. minutes in the morning, warme, like to thunder.

The full Moone, the xi. day, at viii. a clocke xiii. minutes in the forenoone, temperate.

The last quarter, the xviii. day, at vii. a clocke at afternoone, wyndy.

The newe Moone, the xxv. day at a xi. a clocke, xiii. minutes at noone, warme.

September.

The first quarter, the first day, at ten a clocke, xx. minutes at night, temperate.

The full Moone, the ix. day, at x. clocke xlii. minutes at night, temperate.

The full Moone, the 15 day, at v. a clocke xliii. minutes at after noone, temperate.

The last quarter, the 23. day at ix. a clocke 33. minuts before noone, colde.

March.

The newe Moone the second day, at vii. a clocke 24. minutes in the morning, temperate.

The first quarter, the ix. day at vi. a clocke xx. minutes in the forenoone, darke, colde rayny wether.

The full Moone, the xvi. day, at vi. a clocke 38. minutes beforenoone, temperate.

The last quarter, the 24. day at v. a clocke 14. minutes before noone, warme.

The newe Moone, the last day, at vii. a clocke xv. minutes at after noone, warme, and after, raine and tempest.

Aprill.

The first quarter, the vii. day 12. min. at high noone temperate.

The full Moone, the 14. day at 8. a clocke 34. minutes at night, temperate, the winde Westerly.

The last quarter, the 22. day, at xi. a clocke 13. minutes at night, windy.

The newe Moone, the last day, at 4. a clocke 34. minutes in the morning. very warme wether.

May.

The first quarter, the vi. day, at 7. a clocke 13 minutes at afternoone, temperate.

The full Moone, the 14. day, at xi. a clocke before noone, rayne.

The last quarter, the xxii. day, at two a clocke 22. minutes at afternoone, winde.

The newe Moone, the xxix. day, xxxvi. min. at high noone, winde and raine.

The first quarter the xxix. day, at ii. a clocke iii. minuts in the morning, frost.

This yeere of our Lorde 1584, there is an Eclipse of the Moone, the vii. day of Nouember, at xi. a clocke iv. minu. at midnight, the Moone being within two degrees of the Dragons tayle, and shalbe darkened xviii. points xiiii. min. and the Moone shall begin for to come vnder the shadow of the earth heere with vs at London, before xi. a clocke, and shall continue neere iii. houres from the beginning vnto the ende, and the Eclipse shall be seene due South upon the Meridian, when that it is at the greatest.

The disposition of the iiii. partes of the yeere, and first of winter, at what time the Sunne entreth the first point of *Capricorne*, the xii. day of December, in the yeere 1583. at one of the clocke in the morning, and doth continue vnto the ix. day of Marche. This part of the yeere is likely to be colde and moyst, and in Christmas much raine or snowe, but afterwarde better wether.

The Spring time beginneth the x. day of Marche, at what time the Sunne entreth the first point of *Aries*, at ii. of the clocke vii. min. in the morning, and continueth vnto the xi. day of June. This part of the yeere is likely to bee windy, and myst in the beginning, and about the midst of May much raine, and toward the end faire and warme.

The Sōmer time beginneth the xi. day of June, at what time the Sun entreth the first point of *Cancer*, at xii. a clock xlix. min. at high noone, & continueth vnto the xii. day of September. This part of the yeere is likely to be temperate warme, enclined to some moystnesse.

Autum, the latter part of the yeere beginneth the xiii. day of September, at what time the Sunne entreth the first minute of *Libra*, at ii. a clocke xxxii. minutes in the morning, and continueth vnto the x. day of December. This quarter of the yeere is likely to be temperate in the beginning, but towardes the end

The last quarter, the xvii. day, at ii. a clocke viii. minutes in the morning, colde darke cloudy wether.

The newe Moone, the xxiii. day, at ten a clocke xxii. minuts at night, moyst and windy.

October.

The first quarter, the first day, at v. a clocke viii. minutes at afternoone, winde and tempest.

The full Moone, the ix. day, iiii. minutes before high noone, colde and moyst

The last quarter, the xvi. day, at iii. a clocke xiii minutes at after noone, and vi. dayes before, much winde, and after temperat.

The newe Moone, the xxiii. day, xx. min. before high noone, hot, according vnto the time of the yeere.

The first quarter, the last day, at one a clocke ix. min. at after noone, moyst.

Nouember.

The full Moone, the vii. day, at xii. a clocke at midnight, temperate.

The last quarter the xiiii. day, at two a clocke viii. minutes at after noone, warme.

The newe Moone, the xxii. day, at iiii. a clocke in the morning, warme for the time.

The first quarter, the last day, at ix. a clocke before noone, warme for the time of the yeere.

December.

The full Moone, the vii. day at xi. a clocke xviii. minutes in the forenoone, windy.

The last quarter the xiiii. day, at two a clocke xxvi. minutes in the morning, cloudy wether.

The newe Moone, the xxi. day, at xi. a clocke at night, temperate.

The first quarter, the xvii. day, at iii. a clocke xiiii. minutes in the morning, temperate.

Marche.

The full Moone, the v. day, at v. a clocke xxix. minutes at after noone, temperate warme.

The last quarter, the xiii. day at ii. a clocke ix. minutes in the morning, temperate.

The newe Moone, the xxi. day at iiii. a clocke xiii. min. in the morning, cloudy weather.

The first quarter, the 28. day, at 10 of the clocke 12. minuts in the morning, temperat.

Aprill.

The full Moone, the iiii. day at iiii. a clocke xxii. minutes in the morning, temperate, the winde Northeast.

The last quarter, the xi. day, at viii. a clocke xxvii. minutes at night, temperate.

The newe Moone, the xix. day, at v. a clocke xxiii. minutes at afternoone, temperate.

The first quarter, the xxvi. day, at iii. a clocke 32. minutes at afternoone, windy.

May.

The full Moone, the iii. day, at iiii. a clocke v. minutes at after noone, winde, raine, and tempest.

The last quarter, the xi. day, at iii. a clock at afternoone, temperate.

The newe Moone, the xix. day, at iiii. a clocke in the morning, warme, like to raine and thunder.

The first quarter, the xxv. day, at viii. a clocke 35. minutes at after noone, temperate.

Iune.

The full Moone, the ii. day, at iiii. a clocke xl. minutes in the morning, raine.

too warme for the time of the yeere, for that the moyst part of the Planets is in a firy triplicitie.

1585.
An Almanacke and Prognostication for the yeere of our Lorde 1585. being the first yeere after the Bissextill.

The golden number, is	ix.
The Epact, is	ix.
The Sundayes letter, is	C.

The first Sunday in Lent, is the xviii. day of February.
Easter day, is the xi. day of Aprill.
Ascention day, is the xx. day of May.
Whitsunday, is the xxx. day of May.
Betweene newyeeres day, and Shrouesunday, are vii. weekes and ii. dayes.

Ianuary 1585.

The full Moone, the v. day, at ix. a clocke xiiii. minutes at night, much winde.

The last quarter, the xii. day, at iii. a clocke xiiii. minutes at afternoone, raine.

The newe Moone, the xx. day, at v. a clocke xxxiiii. minuts at night, temperate.

The first quarter, the xxviii. day, at iiii. a clocke xxvi. minutes at afternoone rain.

February.

The full Moone, the iiii. day, at vii. a clocke xl. minutes in the morning, temperate.

The last quarter, the xi. day, at vii. a clocke xl. minutes in the forenoone, windy.

The newe Moone, the xix. day, at xii. a clocke xxiii. minuts at noone, moyst.

The full Moone, the xxviii. day, at vi. a clocke xi. minutes in the euening, temperate.

October.

The last quarter, the vi. day, at v. a clocke, xxv. minutes in the morning, temperate and moyst.

The new Moone, the xii. day, at ix. a clocke 25. minutes at night, temperate.

The first quarter, the 20. day, at viii. a clocke lii. minutes in the forenoone, temperate.

The full Moone, the xxviii. day, at ix. a clocke xliiii. minutes before noone, moyst.

Nouember.

The last quarter, the iiii. day, at xii. a clock 1. minutes at noone faire and windy.

The newe Moone, the xi. day, at ix. a clocke 36. minutes in the morning, moyst.

The first quarter, the xix. day, at v. a clocke 38. minutes in the morning, great winde.

The full Moone, the 26. day, at xii. a clocke at midnight, mysty weather.

December.

The last quarter, the iii. day, at vii. a clocke lvi. min. at night, winde and raine.

The newe Moone, the x. day, at xii. a clocke, 34. minutes at night, temperate.

The first quarter, the 19. day, at ii. a clocke xxvi. minuts in the morning, temperate.

The full Moone, the 26. day, at xii. a clocke xlviii. minutes at noone, the weather very strange, sometime, faire, sometime, snowe, sleete, and sometime winde.

This yeere of our Lorde 1 5 8 5. there is no Eclipse of the Moone, nor of the Sunne.

ALMANACKE FOR X. YEERES, 1581

The last quarter, the tenth day, at vii. a clocke xiiii. minuts in the forenoone, temperate.

The newe Moone, the xvii. day, at xii. a clocke 27. minutes at noone, moyst.

The first quarter, the 24. day, at ii. a clocke 1. minutes in the morning, temperate.

Iuly.

The full Moone, the first day, at vi. a clocke xlvii. minutes at afternoone, temperate, and after winde to folow.

The last quarter, the ix. day at ten a clocke at night, thunder and tempest.

The new Moone, the xvi. day, at viii. a clocke at night temperate.

The first quarter, the 23. day, at xi. a clocke xiii. minuts in the forenoone, raine and thunder.

The full Moone, the last day, at ix. a clocke lv. minutes in the forenoone, warme.

August.

The last quarter, the viii. day, at ten a clocke, xl. minutes in the forenoone, raine.

The newe Moone, the xv. day, at iii. a clocke 30. minutes in the morning, warme and moyst.

The first quarter, the xxi. day, at xii. a clocke xv. minutes at midnight, warme.

The full Moone, the 30. day, at one a clock liii. minuts in the morning, temperate and moyst.

September.

The last quarter, the vi. day, at ix. a clock viii. minuts at night, temperate.

The newe Moone, the xiii. day, at xi. a clocke xliii. minutes at noone, temperate.

The first quarter, the xx. day, at iii. a clocke at afternoone, temperate.

ALMANACKE FOR X. YEERES, 1581

The disposition of the 4. quarters of the yeere 1585. and first of the Winter part, that is in 1584. the xi. of December, at vi. a clocke l. min. in the morning, at what time the Sunne entreth the first scruple of *Capricorne*, and continueth vnto the x. day of Marche. This season of the yeere is likely to bee very cold, and windy, with frost, and about the xii. day of January, much snow or raine, and towards the end better weather.

The Spring time beginneth the x. day of March, at what time the Sun entreth the first minute of *Aries*, at vii. a clocke, liiii. minutes in the forenoone, and continueth vnto the xi. day of June. This season of the yeere is likely to be windy, and cloudy, towards the end of April, much winde, and the end of the quarter, raine.

The Sommer season of the yeere beginneth the xi. day of June, at vi. a clocke xxxvi. minutes, at what time the Sunne entreth the first point of *Cancer* at after noone, and continueth vnto the xii. day of September. This season of the yeere, is like for to be reasonable cold for the time, and not too hot, nor to lack moysture.

Autum, the last part of the yeere, beginneth the xiii. day of September, at what time the Sunne entreth the Equinoctial of *Libra*, at viii. a clocke xxi. min. in the morning, and continueth vnto the xi. day of December. This season of the yeere is likely to be colde and moyst, and toward the end of Nouember, much winde.

1586.
An Almanacke and Prognostication for the
yeere of our Lorde 1586. being the seconde
yeere after the Bissextill.

The golden number, is	x.
The Epact, is	xi.
The Sundayes letter, is	B.

The first Sunday of Lent, is the xx. day of February.
Easter day, is the iii. day of Aprill.
Ascention day, is the xii. day of May.
Whitsunday, is the xxii. day of May.
Betweene Newyeeres day, and Shrouesunday, are vi. weekes and one day.

Ianuarie. 1586.

The last quarter, the ii. day, at iiii. a clocke xxiii. minutes in the morning, cold.
The newe Moone, the ix. day, at vi. a clocke xviii. minuts at night, frost.
The first quarter, the xvii. day, at ten a clocke at night, frost.
The full Moone, the 24. day at midnight, raine and snow.
The last quarter, the last day, at iii. a clocke at after noone, temperate.

February.

The newe Moone, the viii. day, xiiii. minutes at high noone winde.
The first quarter, the xvi. day, at iii. a clocke at afternoone, winde, raine, and tempest.
The full Moone, the xxiii. day, at ten a clocke before noone, winde and tempest.

Marche.

The last quarter, the ii. day, at iiii. a clock in the morning, raine, like to thunder, although that it be contrary to the time of yeere.
The newe Moone, the x. day, at vi. a clocke 27. minutes in the forenoone, temperate.
The first quarter, the xviii. day, at iiii. a clocke in the morning, winde.
The full Moone, the 24. day, at vi. a clocke 32. minutes at after noone, very warme.

The last quarter, the last day, at vii. a clocke at night temperate.

Aprill.

The newe Moone, the viii. day xi. a clocke xvii. min. at night, very warme.
The first quarter, the xvi. day, at one a clocke at noone, hot likely to thunder.
The full Moone, the xxiii. day, at iii. a clocke 30. minutes at afternoone, winde with moysture.
The last quarter, the last day, at vii. a clocke at night, temperate.

May.

The newe Moone, the viii. day, at one a clocke 32. minutes at noone, temperate.
The first quarter, the xv. day, at vii. a clocke at night, temperate.
The ful Moone, the xxii. day, at one a clocke at noone, warme.
The last quarter, the 30. day, at v. a clocke in the morning, temperate and moyst.

Iune.

The new Moone, the vii. day, at one a clocke 25. minutes at noone, & the day before, much winde, & after temperate.
The first quarter, the xiii day at midnight, much raine.
The full Moone, the xx. day, at xi. a clocke 32. minu. at night, temperate.
The last quarter, the xxviii. day, at x. a clocke xvi. minutes at night, temperate.

Iuly.

The newe Moone, the vi. day, at xi. a clocke xxviii. minutes before noone, thunder and tempest.

The first quarter, the xiii. day, at iiii. a clocke in the morning, tempest.

The full Moone, the xx. day, at high noone, raine, lightning, & thunder.

The last quarter, the xxviii. day, at iii. a clocke at after noone, winde, raine, and haile, a certaine time together.

August.

The new Moone, the iiii. day, at viii. a clocke xi. minutes at afternoone, warme.

The first quarter, the xi. day, at x. a clocke xxvi. minutes in the morning, temperate.

The full Moone, the xix. day, at ii. a clocke 31. mi. in the morning, colde, darke, cloudy weather.

The last quarter, the xxvii. day, at vi. a clocke ix. minutes in the morning, strange vntemperate weather.

September.

The newe Moone, the iii. day, at iiii. a clocke xxvi. minutes in the morning, temperate.

The first quarter, the ix. day, at viii. a clocke at night, temperate and warme.

The full Moone, the xvii. day, at vii. a clocke at night, temperate.

The last quarter, the xxv. day, at viii. a clocke vii. minutes at night, winde doeth followe.

October.

The newe Moone, the ii. day, at one a clocke at noone, winde, and small raine.

The first quarter, the ix. day, at ix. a clocke ix. minutes in the forenoone, temperate.

The full Moone, the 17. day, xx. minuts at noone, temperate.

The last quarter, the last day, at ten a clocke xxiii. minutes at night, colde and moyst.

ALMANACKE FOR X. YEERES, 1581

Nouember.

The first quarter, the viii. day, at two a clocke xvii. minutes in the morning, winde and moyst.

The full Moone, the xvi. day, at vi. a clocke iiii. minuts in the morning, temperate.

The last quarter, the xxiii. day, at v. a clocke at after noone, colde rayny weather.

The newe Moone, the last day, at ix. a clocke xl. minutes before noone, temperate and dry.

December.

The first quarter, the vii. day, at ten a clocke xv. min. at night, temperate.

The full Moone, the xv. day, at x. a clocke xlviii. minutes at night, winde and tempest.

The last quarter, the xxiii. day, at one a clocke in the morning, muche winde.

The newe Moone, the xxix. day, at ten a clocke l. minutes at night, frost.

This yeere of our Lorde 1586, there is no Eclipse neither of the Moone, nor of the Sunne.

The disposition of the iiii. partes of the yeere 1586. and first of the Winter quarter, and that beginneth in the yere 1585. the xi. day of December at xii. a clocke 39 min. at noone, at what time the Sunne entreth the first point of *Capricorne*, and continueth vnto the x. day of Marche. This season of the yeere is likely for to bee very windy, and about the ende of January, much raine, and towardes the end of the quarter, better weather.

The Spring time beginneth the x. day of Marche, at what time that the Sunne entreth the first minute of *Aries*, at one a clocke xiv. minutes at noone, and continueth vnto the xi. day of June. This season of the yeere is likely to bee resonable temperate, and towards the end windy.

The Sōmer quarter of the yeere beginneth the xi. day of June, at xii. a clocke xxvii min at midnight, at what time that the Sunne entreth the first scruple of *Cancer,* and continueth vnto the xiii. day of September. This part of the yeere is like to bee temperate and winde, sauing at the beginning much rain, but afterwardes reasonable weather.

Autum, the last part of the yeere, beginneth the xiii. day of September, when that the Sun entreth the Equinoctiall point of *Libra,* that is, at ii. a clocke x. min. at afternoone, & continueth vnto the xi. day of December. This quarter of the yeere is likely for to be cold and moyst, and sometimes windy.

1587.
An Almanacke and Prognostication for the
yeere of Christes incarnation, 1587. *being the*
iii. yeere after the Bissextill.

The golden number, is	xi.
The Epact, is	i.
The Sundayes letter, is	A.

The fitSunday in Lent the v. day of March.
Easteray, the xvi. day of Aprill.
Ascention day, the xxv. day of May.
Whitsunday, the iiii. day of June.
Betweene newyeeres day, & Shrouesunday, are viii. weekes iust.

Ianuary. 1587.

The first quarter, the vi. day, at vii. a clocke 25. minutes at night, cold darke, weather, like to snow.

The full Moone, the xiiii. day, at one a clocke viii. minutes at noone, temperate.

The last quarter, the xxi. day, at viii. a clocke xxiiii. min. before noone, colde.

The newe Moone, the 28. day at one a clocke xl. minutes at noone, temperate.

February.

The first quarter, the v. day, at iiii. a clocke v minutes at after noone, temperate.

The full Moone, the xiii. day, at one a clocke xv. min. in the morning, windy.

The last quarter, the xix. day, at iiii. a clocke 35. min. at after noone, temperate.

The newe Moone, the xxvii. day, at v. a clocke in the morning, moyst.

March.

The first quarter, the vii. day, at x. a clocke 32. minutes in the forenoone, winde and raine.

The full Moone, the xiiii. day at xi. a clocke xiii. min. at noone, temperate, and after ii. dayes, much winde.

The last quarter, the xxi. day at ii. a clocke xvi. minutes in the morning, temperate.

The newe Moone, the xxviii. day, at xi. a clocke xl. minutes at midnight, winde, and raine, and after faire weather.

Aprill.

The first quarter, the vi. day, at one a clock xl. min. in the morning, temperate and warme.

The full Moone, the xii. day, at vii. a clocke xl. min. at night, winde, raine, it may thunder.

The last quarter, the xix. day, at ii. a clocke at after noone, windy.

The newe Moone, the xxvii. day, at iiii. a clocke xxi. minutes at after noone, temperate.

May.

The first quarter, the v. day, at one a clocke vii. min. at noone, temperate.

The full Moone, the xii. day, at iii. a clocke, 32. minutes in the morning, temperate.

The last quarter, the xix. day, at iiii. a clocke 25. minuts in the morning, temperate and moyst. The new Moone, the xxvii. day, at vii. a clock 32. minuts before noone, warme, with some shewres.

Iune.

The first quarter, the iii. day, at viii. a clocke xl. minutes in the euening, temperate.

The full Moone, the x. day, at xi. a clock xviii. min. at noone, warme, like to thunder.

The last quarter, the xvii. day, at vii. a clocke 26. min. at after noone, warme with some Sewres.

The new Moone, the 25. day, at ix. a clocke in the euening, moyst.

Iuly.

The first quarter, the iii. day, at ii. a clocke 32. min. in the morning, temperate.

The full Moone, the ix. day, at viii. a clocke 27. min. at afternoone, greate winde.

The last quarter, the xvii. day, at xii. a clocke 26. min. at high noone, winde and raine.

The newe Moone, the xxiiii. day, at ix. a clocke before noone, warme.

August.

The first quarter, the first day, at vi. a clocke xii. minutes in the forenoone, darke, colde, mistie weather.

The full Moone, the viii. day, at vii. a clocke before noone, hot, with raine, lightning, and thunder.

The last quarter, the xvi. day, at vi. a clocke before noone, faire and windy.

The new Moone, the 23. day, at vii. a clocke xvi. min. at after noone, raine.

The first quarter, the xxv. day, at high noone, temperate, like to bee frost.

February.

The full Moone, the ii. day, iii. minuts at high noone, temperate.

The last quarter, the ix. day, at one a clocke xxvii. minuts at noone, temperate.

The newe Moone, the xvi. day, at xi. a clock 34. min. at noone, temperate.

The first quarter, the xxiiii. day, at viii. a clocke 32 minuts before noone, raine.

Marche.

The full Moone Eclipsed the iii. day, at one a clocke xx. min. in the morning, temperate.

The last quarter, the ix. day, at viii. a clocke at night, temperate.

The Moone changeth the xvii. day, at ii. a clocke in the morning, much winde.

The first quarter, the xxv. day, at iii. a clocke xlviii. minutes in the morning, temperate.

Aprill.

The full Moone, the first day, at high noone, winde & raine.

The last quarter, the viii. day, at ii. a clocke 34. minuts in the morning, temperate.

The new Moone, the xv. day, at v. a clocke iiii. minuts at after noone, winde.

The first quarter, the xxiii. day, at viii. a clocke xxvi. minutes at night, temperate.

The full Moone, the xxx. day, at viii. a clocke xxxii. mi. in the euening, temperate.

May.

The last quarter, the vii. day, at xi. a clocke xv. min. at noone, bee somewhat windy and moyst, and much raine about the ende of June, and the tenth day of July, much winde, and towardes the end oftentimes thunder.

Autum, the last quarter of the yeere, and that beginneth the xiii. day of September, a viii. a clocke at night, for then the Sunne entreth the first point of *Libra*, and continueth vnto the xi. day of December. This parte of the yeere is likely to be windy and moyst, and about the ende of October, very much foule weather, with raine and tempest, and to continue in manner at sundry times vnto the ende of the quarter, etc.

1588.
An Almanacke and Prognostication for the yeere of our Lorde 1588. being the yeere of Bissextill.

The golden number, is	xii.
The Epact, is	xii.
The Dominicall letters, are	G & F.

The first Sunday in Lent, is the xxv. day of Februarie.
Easter day, is the vii. day of Aprill.
Ascention day, is the xvi. day of May.
Whitsunday, is the xxvi. day of May.
Betweene Newyeeres day and Shrouetide are vi. weekes and vi. dayes.

Ianuarie. 1588.

The full Moone, the iii. day, at vii. a clock xlvi. minutes at night, temperate and moyst.

The last quarter, the xi. day, at vi. a clocke in the morning, temperate.

The newe Moone the xvii. day, at x. a clocke xiii. minutes at night, stormy weather.

The last quarter, the xii. day, at viii. a clocke at night, colde.

The newe Moone, the xix. day, at ten a clocke xiiii. min. before noone, the weather differeth.

The first quarter, the xxvi. day, at iii. a clocke xlv. min. at after noone, temperate.

This yeere of our Lorde 1587. there is an Eclipse of the Moone, the vi. day of September at viii. a clocke 36. minutes, it shalbe at the greatest darknes, and shall continue iii. houres, vi. minutes from the beginning vnto the ende: and the Moone shalbe darkened ix. pointes, and the Moone shall beginne to come vnder the shadowe of the earth heere with vs at London, at vii. a clocke 33. minutes, the Moone beeing within vii. degrees of the Dragons tayle. This Eclipse shalbe seene in the East South East.

The disposition of the iiii. quarters of the yeere 1587. and first of the Winter season of the yeere, and according vnto the order of the Astrologians, it beginneth the xi. day of December 1586. at vi. of the clocke xxviii. minutes at night, at what time that the Sunne entreth the first part of *Capricorne*, and continueth vnto the tenth day of Marche. This season of the yeere is likely for to bee temperate, and not too cold, and in the beginning windy, the rest temperate, considering the time of the yeere.

The Spring time beginneth the x. day of Marche at what time that the Sunne entreth the Equinoctial point of *Aries*, at vii. a clocke 35. minuts in the euening, and continueth vntil the xi. day of June. This quarter of the yeere is likely to bee windy and moyst, and in the beginning windy, but the rest of the time indifferent.

The Sommer part of the yeere beginneth the xii. day of June at vi. a clocke xvii. minutes in the morning, at what time that the Sunne is iust vpon the Solstick of *Cancer*, and continueth vnto the xiii. day of September. This season of the yeere is likely to

The first quarter, the 30. day, at xii. a clocke at high noone, raine, haile and thunder.

September.

The ful Moone, the vi. day, at viii. a clocke 36. min. at night, raine and tempest.

The last quarter, the xiiii. day, at xii. a clock midnight, temperate.

The newe Moone, the xxii. day, at v. a clocke 20. minu. in the morning, colde and mystie.

The first quarter, the xxviii. day, at viii. a clocke at night, vncertaine wether.

October.

The full Moone, the vi. day, at high noone past ten minutes, temperate.

The last quarter, the xiii. day, at iiii. a clocke ix. minutes at afternoone, winde and raine.

The newe Moone, the xxi. day, at ii. a clocke xliiii. minutes at after noone, foggy or mysty weather.

The first quarter, the xxviii. day, at vi. a clocke 36. minuts in the morning, stormy weather.

Nouember.

The full Moone, the v. day, at ix. a clocke before noone, the weather differeth, and not certaine.

The last quarter, the xiii. day, at vii. a clocke 35. min. before noone, frost.

The newe Moone, the xix. day, at midnight, temperate warme.

The first quarter, the xxvi. day, at vi. a clock xx. min. at night, windy.

December.

The full Moone, the v. day, at one a clocke xxx. minutes in the morning, temperate.

ii. or iii. dayes before the quarter, colde, darke raynie weather, but after that temperate.

The newe Moone the xv. day, at viii a clocke xxxiii. minuts before noone, temperate.

The first quarter, the xxiii. day, at x. a clocke xxv. minutes before noone, windy.

The ful Moone, the xxx. day, at iiii. a clocke in the morning, warme with shewres.

Iune.

The last quarter, the v. day, at x. a clocke iiii. minuts at night, temperate.

The new Moone, the xiii. day at midnight, windy and moyst.

The first quarter, the xxi. day, at viii. a clocke xxxii. minutes at after noone, windy.

The full Moone, the xxviii. day, at xi. a clocke at noone, temperate.

Iuly.

The last quarter, the v. day, at xi. a clocke 25. minuts at noone, raine.

The new Moone, the xiii. day, at ii. a clocke l. minuts at after noone, raine.

The first quarter, the xxi. day, at iiii. a clocke 25. minutes in the morning, winde and raine.

The full Moone, the xxvii. day, at vii. a clocke xv. min. at after noone, warme with shewres.

August.

The last quarter, the iiii. day, at iii. a clocke in the morning, temperate.

The Moone changeth, the xii. day, at iiii. a clocke xl. minu. in the morning, and ii. dayes before, muche winde, but afterwards temperate.

The first quarter, the xix. day, at ten a clocke before noone, temperate.

The full Moone Eclipsed, the xxvi. day at iiii. a clocke 27. mi. in the morning, temperate.

September.

The last quarter, the ii. day, at ix. a clocke at night, temperate.

The newe Moone, the tenth day, at v. a clocke 32. minuts at after noone, temperate.

The first quarter, the xvii. day, at iii. a clocke 27. min. at after noone, temperate.

The full Moone, the xxiiii. day, at iiii. a clocke 30. minutes at after noone, temperate.

October.

The last quarter, the ii. day, at iii. a clocke 33. minutes at after noone, the weather vncertaine.

The new Moone, the x. day, at v. a clocke vii. minutes in the morning, temperate and moyst.

The first quarter, the xvi. day, at ten a clocke at night, temperate.

The full Moone, the xxiiii. day, at vii. a clocke xiiii. minutes before noone, windy.

Nouember.

The last quarter, the first day, at xi. a clock v. minuts at noone, raine.

The newe Moone, the viii. day, at iiii. a clocke xvi. minutes at after noone, colde and moyst.

The first quarter, the xv. day, at vii. a clocke before noone, winde and raine.

The full Moone, the xxiii. day, at one a clocke in the morning, temperate.

December.

The last quarter, the first day, at v. a clocke xii. minutes in the morning, temperate.

The new Moone, the viii. day, at ii. a clocke l. minutes in the morning, stormie weather.

The first quarter, the xiiii. day, at viii. a clocke at night, colde and moyst.

The full Moone, the xxii. day, at viii. a clocke 37. minutes at night, temperate.

This yeere 1588. there are two Eclipses of the Moone, the first is the ii. day of March at one a clocke xx. minutes after midnight, within iii. degrees and xv. minutes of the Dragons head, and shalbe darkened xvii. points xv. minuts, and the Moone shal begin to come vnderneath the shadowe of the earth heere with vs at London at xi. a clocke xxxii. minutes and shall continue from the beginning vnto the end iii. houres, xxxvi. minutes, and the greatest of these Eclipses shalbe seene in the South, and by West quarters of the world.

The second Eclipse shalbe the xxvi. day of August at iiii. a clocke xxvii. minutes in the morning, within ii. degrees & xvi. minutes of the Dragons taile, & shalbe darkened 18. points xvii. minutes: and the Moone shal begin for to come vnderneath the shadowe of the earth heere with vs at London, at ii. a clocke xxxvi. minutes, and shal continue from the beginning vnto the end, iii. houres xlii. minutes: and this Eclipse shalbe seene in the South West, and by West quarters of the worlde.

The disposition of the iiii. partes of this yeere 1588. and first of the Winter season of the yeere, and according vnto the accustomable maner, that doth begin the xi. day of December, at xii. a clocke xviii. minutes at midnight, at that time that the Center of the Sunne toucheth the first point of *Capricorne*, and continueth vnto the x. day of Marche. This season of the yeere is like to be windy & moyst, with many cold stormes, and about iii. partes of January spent in much wind, and in February much winde, raine or snowe.

The Spring time, the second part of the yeere beginneth the x.

day of March, at one a clocke, xxiiii. minutes in the morning, for then the Sun entreth the Equinoctiall point of *Aries*, and continueth vnto the xi. day of June. This season of the yeere is like to be cold, mixed sometime with raine and winde, but toward the end better weather.

Sommer, the iii. part of the yeere, beginneth the xi. day of June at xii. a clocke vi. minutes at high noone, for then the Sunne entreth *Cancer*, and continueth vnto the xiii. day of September. This parte of the yeere is like to bee temperate and windy, and in July likely to raine, and August likely to bee faire, etc.

Autum, the last part of the yeere beginneth whē that the Sun entreth the Equinoctial of *Libra*, that is, the xiii. day of September, at one a clocke xlix. minutes in the morning, and continueth vnto the x. day of December. This part of the yeere is like to be very colde and misty.

1589.
An Almanake and Prognostication for the
yeere of our Lorde 1589. being the first
yeere after the Bissextill.

The golden number, is	xiii.
The Epact, is	xxiii.
The Sundayes letter, is	E

The first Sunday in Lent, is the xvi. day of February.
Easter day, is the xxx. day of Marche.
Ascension day, is the viii. day of May.
Whitsunday, is the xviii. day of May.
Betweene Newyeeresday, and Shrouesunday, are fiue weekes and iiii. dayes.

Ianuary. 1589.

The newe Moone, the vi. day, at ii. a clocke at after noone, colde, cloudy, darke weather.

The first quarter, the xiii. day, at one a clocke at noone, colde.

The full Moone, the xxi. day, at iiii. a clocke before noone, raine and tempest.

The last quarter, the xxix. day, at x. a clocke before noone, cold and frost.

February.

The newe Moone, the iiii. day at xi. a clocke 34. min at midnight, cloudy colde weather.

The first quarter, the xii. day, at v. a clocke iiii. minutes in the morning, colde, and moyst.

The full Moone, the xx. day at ix. a clocke before noone, wind.

The last quarter, the xxvii. day, at vi. a clocke in the euening, cloudy, likely to snowe.

Marche.

The newe Moone, the vi. day, at x. a clocke xxv. min. before noone, raine and tempest.

The first quarter, the xiii. day, at xii. a clocke xxv. min. at midnight, temperate.

The full Moone, the xxi. day, at xi. a clocke 31. minutes at night, raine and tempest.

The last quarter, the xxviii. day, at xii. a clocke at midnight, winde and raine.

Aprill.

The new Moone, the iiii. day, at ten a clocke xxv. min. at night, temperate.

The first quarter, the xii. day, at vii. a clocke xiii. minuts in the euening, warme with shewres.

The full Moone, the xx. day, at xi. a clocke xii. minu. at noone, moyst.

The last quarter, the xxvii. day, at v. a clocke xii. minu. in the morning, temperate.

May.

The newe Moone, the iiii. day, at xi. a clocke xiiii. min. at noone, winde and raine.

The first quarter, the xii. day, at one a clocke at noone, temperate and fayre.

The full Mooone, the xix. day, at viii. a clock xlvi. minu. in the euening, much winde.

The last quarter, the xxvi. day, at xi. a clocke xiiii. minutes at noone, moyst.

Iune.

The new Moone, the iii. day, at one a clocke in the morning, winde and tempest.

The first quarter, the xi. day, at iiii. a clocke x. min. in the morning, temperate.

The full Moone, the xviii. day, at iiii. a clocke xxv. minuts in the morning, moyst.

The last quarter, the 24. day, at vii. a clocke at night, winde and rayne.

Iuly.

The newe Moone, the ii. day, at iiii. a clocke at after noone, warme with moysture.

The first quarter, the x. day, at v. a clocke xliii. minuts at after noone, temperate.

The full Moone, the xviii. day, at xi. a clocke xxx. min. at noone warme.

The last quarter, the xxiiii. day, at v. a clocke xl. minutes in the morning, warme.

August.

The newe Moone, the first day, at iiii. a clocke xl. minu. in the morning, cloudy warme weather.

The first quarter, the ix. day, at iiii. a clocke in the morning, warme, and it may thunder.

ALMANACKE FOR X. YEERES, 1581

The full Moone, the xv. day, at vii. a clocke at afternoone, tempestuous weather.

The last quarter, the xxii. day, at vii. a clock 35. mi. in the euening, temperate.

The newe Moone, the xxx. day, at xi. a clocke at night, cloudy darke weather.

September.

The first quarter, the vii. day, at xii. a clocke xliiii. min. at high noone, warme.

The full Moone, the xiiii. day, at iii. a clocke l. minuts in the morning, the weather vnconstant.

The last quarter, the xxi. day, at xii. a clocke xl. min. at noone, temperate.

The newe Moone, the xxix. day, at ii. a clocke vii. min. at after noone, cloudy and windy weather.

October.

The first quarter, the vi. day, at vii. a clock xlviii. min. at night, windy and moyst.

The full Moone, the xiii. day, at ii. a clocke xxxii. min. at after noone, windy.

The last quarter, the xxi. day at viii. a clocke in the morning sodaine winde.

The newe Moone, the xxix. day at iiii. a clocke xl. min. in the morning, moyst weather.

Nouember.

The first quarter, the v. day, at ii. a clocke x. min. in the morning, winde and raine.

The full Moone, the xii. day, at iiii. a clocke in the morning, colde and moyst.

The last quarter, the xx. day, at iiii. a clocke xxvi. minu. in the morning, faire and windy.

The newe Moone, the xxvii. day, at v. a clocke xxiiii. minutes in the euening, winde and stormie weather.

December.

The first quarter, the iiii. day at x. a clocke xvi. min. before noone, tempestuous weather.

The full Moone, the xi. day, at viii. a clocke xxxiiii. minutes at night, temperate.

The last quarter, the xix. day, at xii. a clocke xxvii. minutes at midnight, temperate and colde.

The new Moone, the xxvii. day, at v. a clock in the morning, colde and windy.

This yeere of our Lorde 1589. there is an Eclipse of the Moone, the xv. day of August, at vii. a clocke iii. minuts in the euening, within x. degrees of the Dragons taile. This Eclipse shall bee but small, for it is darkened but iii. points l. minutes at the Moone rising being in the East, & by South quarters of the worlde.

The disposition of the iiii. quarters of the yeere, and first of the Winter quarter of the yeere, and that beginneth the xi. day of December, in the yeere 1588. at vi. a clocke vii. minutes in the morning, and continueth vnto the x. day of Marche. This season of the yeere is like to bee very colde according vnto the time, and towardes the ende of February, much winde and stormes, and towards the end or beginning of March, much raine, etc.

The Spring time being the second part of the yeere beginneth the x. day of Marche, at vii. a clocke xiii. minutes in the morning, at what time that the Sunne entreth the Equinoctiall point of *Aries*, and continueth vnto the ii. day of June. This season of the yeere is likely to bee faire and windy, sauing that the first part of May, may bee windy with raine.

Sommer, the iii. part of the yeere beginneth the xi. day of June, at v. a clocke liii. minutes at after noone, at what time that the Sunne entreth the first point of *Cancer*, and continueth vnto the xiii. day of September. This part of the yeere shalbe reasonable temperate Sommer, sauing about the beginning of the quarter rayne, and also the ende of July muche raine, and at the end of the quarter, great windes.

Autum, the last part of the yeere beginneth the xiii. day of September, at vii. a clocke xxvii. minutes in the morning, at what time that the Sunne entreth the Equinoctiall pointe of *Libra*, and continueth vnto the xi. day of December. This quarter, of the yeere is likely to bee colde and moyst, and towardes the ende windy, etc.

1590.
An Almanacke and Prognostication for the yeere of our Lord 1590. being the second yeere after the Bissextill.

The golden number, is   xiiii.
   The Epact, is   iiii.
   The Sundayes letter, is   D.

The first Sunday in Lent, is the viii. day of Marche.
Easter day, is the xix. day of Aprill.
Ascention day, is the xxviii. day of May.
Whitsunday, is the vii. day of June.
Betwene newyeres day, and Shrouesunday, are viii. weekes and iii. dayes.

Ianuary, 1590.

The first quarter, the second day, at viii. a clock at night, winde, raine, or snow.

   The full Moone, the x. day, at ii. a clocke xliii. min. at after noone, temperate.

   The last quarter, the xviii. day, at vi. a clocke xxxii. min. in the euening, colde and windy.

   The new Moone, the xxv. day, at iii. a clocke xxii. min. at after noone, windy.

February.

The first quarter, the first day, at viii. a clocke xxx. min. before noone, frost.

The full Moone, the viii. day at midnight, temperate.

The last quarter, the xvi. day, at ii. a clocke at after noone, colde.

The new Moone, the xxiiii. day, at one a clocke xiii. minuts in the morning, colde and moyst.

Marche.

The first quarter, the ii. day at midnight, temperate.

The full Moone, the xi. day, at iii. a clocke xliii. min. in the morning, temperate.

The last quarter, the xviii. day, at viii. a clocke in the euening, windy.

The new Moone, the xxv. day, at x. a clocke xvii. minutes before noone, temperate.

Aprill.

The first quarter, the first day, at high noone, temperate.

The full Moone, the ix. day, at vii. a clocke xx. minuts at after noone, temperate and warme.

The last quarter, the xvii. day, at iii. a clocke xvi. minuts in the morning, fayre and windy.

The newe Moone, the xxiii. day, at viii. a clocke xxvii. min. in the euening, faire and warme.

May.

The first quarter, the first day, at vii. a clocke before noone, warme.

The full Moone, the ix. day at viii. a clocke xxvii. min. before noone, temperate and moyst.

The last quarter, the xvi. day, at viii. a clocke xxvii. min. before noone, temperate.

The newe Moone, the xxiii. day, at vi. a clocke xli. min. before noone, temperate.

The first quarter, the last day, at iii. a clocke xiii. min. in the morning, temperate.

Iune.

The full Moone, the vii. day, at vi. a clocke li. minutes at after noone, warme.

The last quarter, the xiii. day, at xxvii. minuts at high noone, warme.

The new Moone, the xxi. day, at vi. a clocke xxx. min. at after noone, raine and thunder.

The first quarter, the xxix. day, at viii. a clocke x. min. at after noone, temperate and moyst.

Iuly.

The full Moone, the vii. day, at iiii. a clocke in the morning, faire and windy.

The last quarter, the xiii. day, at vi. a clocke xxvii. min. at after noone, temperate.

The new Moone, the xxi. day, at viii. a clocke xxiii. min. before noone, warme.

The first quarter, the xxix. day, at high noone, moyst and warme.

August.

The full Moone, the v. day, at high noone, warme.

The last quarter, the xii. day, at ii. a clocke xxx. min. in the morning, much raine.

The newe Moone, the xix. day, at xi. a clock xxx. min. at noone, temperate dry.

The first quarter, the xxviii. day, at ii. a clocke in the morning, warme.

September.

The full Moone, the iii. day, at vii. a clocke xlvii. minuts in the euening, moyst.

The last quarter, the x. day, at ii. a clocke x. minutes at after noone, temperate.

The new Moone, the xviii. day, at iiii. a clock at after noone, lightning, thunder, and tempest.

The first quarter, the xxvi. day, at one a clocke xxxiii. minutes at noone, temperate.

October.

The full Moone, the iii. day, at iiii. a clocke xxvi. minutes in the morning, winde and tempest.

The last quarter, the x. day, at v. a clocke xxxiii. min. in the morning, much winde.

The new Moone, the xviii. day, at ix. a clocke xxx. min. before noone, moyst.

The first quarter, the xxv. day, at xi. a clocke at night, temperate.

Nouember.

The full Moone, the first day, at ii. a clocke iiii. minuts at after noone, temperate.

The last quarter, the viii. day, at x. min. at midnight, cold rainie weather.

The new Moone, the xvii. day, at ii. a clocke xiii. min. in the morning, temperate.

The first quarter, the xxiiii. day at vii. a clocke viii. minuts in the morning, temperate.

December.

The full Moone, the first day, at ii. a clocke lii. min. in the morning, temperate.

The last quarter, the viii. day, at ix. a clock at night, cold cloudy weather.

The new Moone, the xvi. day, at v. a clocke viii. min. in the euening, frost.

The first quarter, the xxiii. day, at iii. a clocke at after noone, colde, and moyst.

Moone in the signe of *Sagittarie*, and the last quarter in the signe of *Pisces*. And from the xi. day of June vnto the xii. day of July the Sun is in the signe of *Cancer*, then the Moone changeth in the signe of *Cancer*, & the first quarter of the Moone in *Libra*, the ful Moone in *Capricorn*, the last quarter in *Aries*. And from the xii. day of July vnto the xiii. day of August, then the Sunne is in the signe of *Leo*, so that the Moone at her change is in the signe of *Leo*, and the first quarter in the signe of *Scorpio*, the ful Moone in the signe of *Aquarius*, and the last quarter in the signe of *Taurus*. And from the xii. day of August, vnto the xiii. day of September, the Sun is in the signe of *Virgo*, therefore the change of the Moone is in the signe of *Virgo*, and the first quarter in the signe of *Sagittarius*, the full Moone in the signe of *Pisces*, and the last quarter in the signe of *Gemini*. And also from the xiii. day of September vnto the xiii. day of October the Sunne is in the signe of *Libra*, and also the change of the Moone in *Libra*, the first quarter in the signe of *Capricorn*, the full Moone in *Aries*, and the last quarter in the signe of *Cancer*. And from the xiii. day of October vnto the xii. day of Nouember the Sun is in the signe of *Scorpio*, therefore the Moone changeth in *Scorpio*, the first quarter of the Moone in the signe of *Aquarius*, & the full Moone in the signe of *Taurus*, the last quarter in the signe of *Leo*. And from the xii. day of Nouember vnto the xi. day of December the Sun is in the signe of *Sagittarius*: so that the change of the Moone is in the signe of *Sagittarius*, and the first quarter in the signe of *Pisces*, the full Moone in the signe of *Gemini*, and the last quarter in *Virgo*. And from the xi. day of December vnto the x. day of January the Sunne is in the signe of *Capricorn*. Wherefore the Moone changeth in *Capricorne*, and the first quarter in the signe of *Aries*, the full Moone in *Cancer*, the last quarter in *Libra*, &c.

Now by these notes or remembrances you may knowe what signe the Moone is in for euer, as thus, looke howe many dayes there is passed from the entrance of the Sun into any of the signes, as is afore declared for euery moneth in the yeere, so

ALMANACKE FOR X. YEERES, 1581

An order and rule to knowe what signe and degree, that the Moone is in for euer, as heereafter followeth.

As thus, first from the x. day of January, vnto the ix. day of February, the Sunne is in the signe of *Aquarie*, and then the Moone changeth in the signe of *Aquarie*, then the Moone being in the coniunction with the Sunne, then the first quarter of the Moone is in the signe of *Taurus*, being iii. signes from the Sunne: and then the full Moone is in the signe of *Leo*, being opposite or right against the Sunne, that is iust vi. signes a sunder: and then the last quarter of the Moone shewes in the signe of *Scorpio*, iii. signes behinde the Sunne, that is vnto the Westwarde of the Sunnes rising and setting before the Sun, for that all the motions of the Planets, as the Sunne, and the Moone is to goe vnto the Eastwardes, as I doe further shewe in my booke called the *Regiment for the Sea*, and also from the ix. day of February, vnto the x. day of March, the Sun is in the signe of *Pisces*.

Then the change of the Moone is in the signe of *Pisces*, and the first quarter of the Moone is in the signe of *Gemini*, and the full Moone in the signe of *Virgo*, and the last quarter in the signe of *Sagittarius*.

And furthermore from the x. day of Merche, vnto the x. day of Aprill the Sunne is in *Aries*, then the change of the Moone is in the signe of *Aries*, the first quarter of the Moone is in the signe of *Cancer*, and the full Moone in the signe of *Libra*, the last quarter in the signe of *Capricorne*. And from the x. day of Aprill vnto the xi. day of May, the Sunne is in the signe of *Taurus*, then the change of the Moone is in the signe of *Taurus*, the first quarter in the signe of *Leo*, and the ful Moone in the signe of *Scorpio*, & the last quarter in the signe of *Aquar*. And from the xi. day of May vnto the xi. day of Iune, then the Sunne is in the signe of *Gemini*, then the Moone changeth in the signe of *Gemini*, the first quarter in the signe of *Virgo*, the full entreth the first point of *Cancer*, and continueth vnto the xiii. day of September. This season of the yeere is likely to be temperate warme Sommer, sauing about the midst of August muche raine, &c.

Autum, the last part of the yeere beginneth the xiii. day of September, at one a clocke xxvi. min. at after noone, for then the Sunne entreth *Libra*, and continueth vnto the xi. day of December. This part of the yeere is likely to bee reasonable temperate, sauing in October it may be very windy, and toward the end some what colde &c.

The full Moone, the xxx. day, at v. a clocke xxvi. minu. in the euening, colde.

This yeere of our Lorde 1590. there are two Eclipses, the one of the Sunne, and the other of the Moone. The first Eclipse is of the Sunne, the xxi. day of July, at viii. a clocke xxiii. minutes in the forenoone, within iiii. degrees of the Dragons head, and shalbe darkened ix. points xxiiii. minuts, and the Moone shall begin for to shadow the Sun to vs heere at London at vii. a clocke xx. minutes: and shalbe clearely voyded of the Sunnes obscuritie, at ix. a clocke xxvi. minutes, so that it shal continue from the beginning vnto the end ii. houres vi. minutes. And this Eclipse shalbe seene in the East, and by South, etc. The second Eclipse shalbe of the Moone, the xxx. day of December, at v. a clocke xxvi. minutes in the euening, within vi. degrees of the Dragons head, and the Moone shal be darkened viii. points x. minutes: and the Moone shall begin for to come vnder the shadow of the earth heere with vs at London before the Moones rising, so that the Moone shall rise Eclipsed in the East, NorthEast quarters of the worlde, and the Eclipse shalbe ended at vi. a clocke lvi. minutes, etc.

The disposition of the iiii. seasons of this yeere 1590. and first of the Winter part, and the beginning is the xi. day of December in *anno* 1589. at xi. a clocke iv. minutes at noone, at what time that the Sunne entreth the first point of *Capricorne*, and continueth vnto the x. day of Marche. This part of the yeere is likely to be very colde, and windy, with frost and snowe, etc.

The Spring time, the second season of the yeere beginneth the x. day of Marche, at one a clocke ii. min. at after noone, for then the Sun entreth the Equinoctiall of *Aries*, and continueth vnto the xii. day of June. This part of the yere is like to be reasonable temperate, but in the beginning winde and raine, but the rest reasonable weather.

Sommer, the thirde part of the yeere, beginneth the xi. day of June, at xi. a clocke xliii minutes at night, for then the Sun many degrees the Moone is in those signes mentioned, according vnto the change, full and quarter of the Moone, as before is rehearsed, as for example, thus, For this yeere 1581 the xii. day of March, the Moone was in her first quarter at v. a clocke in the morning, and the Sun that same day was in the ii. degree of *Aries*, for that the Sun entred *Aries* the x. day of Marche, which is ii. dayes after the entrance of the Sun in *Aries*: so that you may know that the Moone must needed be at the iust quarter of the Moone, ii. degrees in the signe of *Cancer*. And now in like maner for the full of the Moone insuing, and that is the xx. day of March at viii. a clock before noone, nowe reckon for euery day from the Sunne entrance into *Aries* one degree, so that the xx. day the Sun is x. degrees in the signe of *Aries*, therefore at the time of the Moones ful, the Moone was in x. degrees of *Libra*. And furthermore for the last quarter of the Moone, & that is the xxvii. day at ix. a clocke at night, so that there is xvii. daies since the Sunnes entrance into the signe of *Aries*: therefore the Moone is at the quarter in the xxii. degree of *Capri*. And furthermore for the change of the Moone, that is the iii. day of Aprill at noone, and now it is neere 24. degrees of *Aries*. For from the x. day of March vnto the iii. day of Aprill, there is 24. daies, so that you may conclude that the Moone changeth neere the 24. degree of *Aries*, and by this order you may knowe what signe that the Moone is in. And also how many degrees especially at the change, ful, and quarter of the Moone. And also this being wel noted, you may know for euery day what signe that the Moone is in, as you knowing at the change, ful, & quarter of the Moone, how many degrees that the Moone is in any signe, so adding xiii. or xiiii. degrees for euery 20 houres, so that the moone doth goe through a signe, in somewhat more then ii. daies for that euery figure doth containe iust xxx. degrees. So by these meanes you may perfectly know what signe that the Moone is in, for that you haue but ii. signes for to count vpon, & so considering frō the change vnto yᵉ first quarter, or frō the quarter vnto the ful, or frō the full vnto the last quarter, or from the last quarter vnto the change, you knowing what signe that the Moone is in, you may giue a neere gesse at the rest allowing as I haue saide, for euery day and night, xiii. or xiiii. degrees, for I cannot set it downe certaine, for that the Moone doeth goe sometimes faster, and sometimes slower, as I doe further shew in my booke called the *Regiment for the Sea*.

A briefe note for either the change of the Moone, quarter, or full of the Moone.

If that they happen in the midst of any Moneth, then it is the beginning, or first part of the signe, if the end of the Moneth the midst of the signe, if the beginning or first of the moneth the end of the signe.

For that the beginning of the yeere according vnto sundry purposes, that a number of persons do not know when that it ought to begin, I do think it necessary for to shewe the beginning of the yeere according vnto the true vse of the thing.

First, the yeere in generall, beginneth the first day of January, or Circumcision of Christ, commonly called Newyeeresday.

The ii. the yeere of the beginning, to wit, the yeere of our Lorde, according vnto the computation of the Church of England, beginneth on the day of the Annuntiation of our Lady, being the xxv. day of Marche.

3 The beginning of the yeere of *Bissextil*, commonly called Leape yeere, then they doe alter the Sundayes letter, that is at Saint Matthewes day, or the xxiiii. day of February.

4 The beginning of the yeere for the vse of the Prime, and Epact, whereby it is knowne in generall, the age or change of the moone, beginneth on S. Davids day, the first day of March.

5 The yeere beginneth according to Astronomie or Astrologie, when that the Sun entreth the first point of *Aries*, which according vnto the use of Astrologie, is the generall significator

what shall happen in the whole yeere, and that is about the x. day of March.

6 The yeere beginneth for to write the raigne of our Souereigne Lady the Queenes Maiestie, the 17. day of Nouember.

> For to iudge the weather by the colour
> *of the Skie, cloudes, circles, and other*
> *extraordinary tokens.*

And furthermore, as touching this how for to iudge what weather doeth follow by diuers significations, as of wind or raine, or faire weather, by diuers things, aswell by the cloudes, colour of the skie, circle in the ayre, very meet for them that shall trauell by Sea or by land &c. And first this is to be obserued, the shifting of the winde, and especially heere in this our Climate, if that the winde doeth shift or alter itselfe against the dayly motion, then winde and raine followeth, & no certaine weather, but if that the winde doth alter or shift itselfe with the course of the daily motion, then whersoeuer that the wind bloweth, that is generall fayre weather. For to know what I do cal the dayly motion, is this, If the winde bee at the East, and doth come vnto the South, or the wind blowing at South, and doth shift vnto the West, or the winde at West doeth shift vnto the North, or the winde at North, and doeth shift itselfe into the East, it is a signification of faire wether. But it the winde doth shift itself from the West vnto the South, or from the South vnto the East, or from the East vnto the North, or from the North to the West, then it is generall seene, that it will be foule weather both of winde and raine, and vnconstant weather, and this I doe call against the dayly motion, for that the winde doth shift itselfe against it. And also if that the skie aloft bee full of long streames like vnto Horses and Mares tayles, that is a token of great Southerly windes to followe, but if that the skie aloft bee kordy, or looke rocky, then Southerly windes and fayre weather. And also if that the Skie bee cleare aloft without cloudes at the setting or rising of the Sunne, and against the Sunne reddish or blewish in maner of a part of a circle by the horizon, then that signifieth East windes or North East windes, the redder the more wind. If the sky be very cleere at the setting of the Sunne without cloudes, and none of that signification, then Westerly or NorthWest winde is likely to folow. If at the setting of the Sunne, that there is thicke blacke cloudes to the Northwardes, and the cloudes risyng upwardes and not cleere at the horizon, it will raine at night, but if that, the Horizon be cleere vnder the cloudes, then faire weather. Also if that in the day time there bee any great quantitie of white cloudes like vnto great heapes of wooll, then raine followeth. Also if that vnto the North or NorthEast quarter, that there is seene ii. or iii. dayes together harde by the Horrizon in the Winter parte of the yeere, white cloudes like hilles, or towards them, snow shall followe. If vnto the South part the like signification be, then rain followeth. Also if before the Suns risyng at the breake of the day, that the Element be very redde, then winde and raine followeth, but if the euening be red, then a good signification of weather. If that the Sunne or Moone haue any circles about them, if it be cleere, and of little countenance, then it betokeneth good weather, but if that the circles be blackish and broken in partes, it betokeneth no good weather. And also if there bee any galles or peeces of circles neere the Sunne, it betokeneth no good weather: if that the Rainbowe be seene in the morning, it signifieth raine, if in the afternoone, fayre weather. Also if in the night, there appeares a Rainbow which is not commonly seene, that the Moone shal haue a circle opposite, then that signifieth stormy weather both winde & rain. Also if in the night that starres seeme to shoote and fall, it sheweth that the wind will be in that quarter that the starres shoot towardes. And also if any knowne starres to you doe seeme bigger then of custome, that in the Sommer sheweth wind, and sometime winde and raine, and in the Winter cold and frost. And furthermore if vnto the North part the moone, not being aboue the horizon, nor yet neere the place that it is very bright, as though that the day began to breake with white and light streames running to and fro, that sheweth very much cold to follow, but not presently vntill iiii. or v. daies be passed, the more lighter or brighter, the more cold to followe. And furthermore in all the East part of England, I doe meane from Barwike vnto Douer, if that vnto the Eastwardes or Seawardes, that anything doe come or shewe itselfe higher or bigger then of custome, then that signifieth Easterly windes, also if that the fome of the water do swim like heapes of fleeses of Wool very high, that in like maner sheweth Easterly windes, and also if long threedes like cobwebs doe flie in the ayre, that sheweth Easterly windes, & furthermore if at or after any of the quarters of the Moone that the winde bloweth at the South West, and very much winde, and so continueth vnto the ful, or change of the Moone, and then doth shift vnto the Northwest, that will make very high tydes & floods, much exceeding all other floods and so as oftentimes as the wind is at NorthWest, it wil make great floods, but as is before expressed, it will exceede meruellously, as well in the riuer of Thames, as in other places vpon this part of England, and also the winde Easterly doeth make short ebbes in the riuer of Thames, that is to say, that the flood shall come in Sommer by neere an houre, neither the water will not ebbe out so lowe by iii. or iiii. foote of water, as it doeth accustomably. And also the winde at South or at South West, doth make long ebbes in the riuer of Thames, that is to say that the ebbes shalbe longer then of custome by more then halfe an houre, and also the water shal fal lower by a yard then of custome, whether that it be in Spring tydes or Nepe tydes &c. And also heere is one speciall thing to be noted of al Seamen, that is generall in all places where it doth ebbe and flowe that the first halfe flood, that it shall hie more water, by double then that it shall doe the latter halfe flood, that is to say, where as it doth flow iii. fadome from the low water vnto the full Sea, that in the first halfe flood, that is iii. houres, it shall flow ii. fadome: and the later halfe flood, to a full Sea, but one fadome: and so in like maner in the first iii. houres it shal ebbe ii. fadome downe right, and the later halfe ebbe which is iii. houres, it shal ebbe but one fadome to a low water, &c.

A rule for the letting of blood, purging, bathing, *setting sowing, and planting.*

First, let not blood at anytime without great cause, for it bringeth weakenesse and many infirmities, if you do see that it be after good digestion and fasting in a faire temperate day, & beware of all maner of excesse, as labouring, watching, & carnall copulation, and so foorth, and after that vse some meates of light digestion, and abstaine from all the aforesaide vnto the fourth day. And these signes bee most vnmeete for letting of blood, the Moone being in *Taurus, Leo, Virgo,* and *Capricornus,* the last halfe of *Libra,* and the first halfe of *Scorpio,* the rest al good so that the Moone be not in the signe that gouerneth the member. Furthermore, let the flegmatike in the signe of *Aries & Sagittarius.* Melancholike persons in *Libra and Aquarius,* and for the cholericke persons, in *Cancer, Scorpio* and *Pisces*: & the sanguine people in *Aries, Cancer, Libra, Scorpio, Sagittarius, Aquarius & Pisces.* Furthermore, from the newe Moone to the first quarter, a meet time for to let young men blood, and from the first quarter to the full Moone, good for middle age, and from the full to the last quarter meete for aged folke, and from the last quarter to the change, best for old men.

Furthermore, there is to bee noted this, that you let not blood when *Mars* and *Saturne* haue any aspect the one to the other: neither the Moone to *Saturne* or *Mars,* neither any aspect of the Moone to the Sunne, nor the Moone to the tayle of the Dragon, and in the Spring time let blood in the right side, and in Haruest, on the left side.

Of purging.

The best time for to take Purgations, is neither when the time is too hot nor to cold, for by the rules of Astronomie, the best time is when the Moone is in colde and moyst signes, as in *Cancer*, *Scorpio*, *Pisces*, and *Gemini*, being comforted by any aspect of the good Planets, and the Moone in *Aries*, *Taurus*, *Leo*, *Virgo*, and *Capricorne*, be nought to purge, & the cause of the vomiting of the Purgation, is if the Moone haue aspect to any Planet retrograd.

The Moone in *Aries*, *Leo*, *Sagittarius*, *Cancer*, *Scorpio*, and *Pisces*, be very good to bath, and these following be euill to bath as *Taurus*, *Virgo*, and *Capricorne*.

Good to stoppe fluxes, rewmes, and Laxes, the Moone in *Taurus*, *Virgo*, and *Capricorne*.

Good to comfort the vertue Attractiue, the Moone in *Aries*, *Leo*, and *Sagittarius*.

The powers retentiue, the Moone in *Taurus*, *Virgo*, & *Capricorne*.

For the digestiue, the Moone in *Gemini*, *Libra*, and *Aquarius*.

For the expulsiue vertue, the Moone in *Gemini*, *Cancer*, *Scorpio*, and *Pisces*.

For setting, sowing, & planting.

Good to sow seedes, the Moone in *Taurus*, *Cancer*, *Virgo*, *Libra*, and *Capricornus*, in the increase of the Moone, and to plant or graft, the Moone in *Taurus* and *Aquarius*, in the increase of the Moone, being fixed signes, and being much better for planting, sowing, and grafting, the Moone hauing sextill or trine aspect with *Saturne*, it is good to do anything about digging or caring of grounde.

Nowe followeth the nature of the xij. signes with their properties.

Aries, is hot and dry, of the nature of fire, Cholerike, Masculine, of the daye, Orientall, of the house of *Mars*, and the exaltation of the Sunne, and the moueable signe, and of a bitter sauour and of the humane members keepeth the head and the face.

Taurus, is cold and dry, of the nature of the earth, Melancholike, Feminine, of the night, Meridional, a fixed signe, the house of *Venus*, the exaltation of the Moone, and of a sowre Sauour, and keepeth of man, the necke and gorge.

Gemini, is hot & moyst, of the nature of the ayre, Sanguine, Masculine, of the day, Occidentall, and common, the house of *Mercury*, of a sweete sauour, & keepeth of man the armes, shoulders and handes.

Cancer is cold and moyst, of the nature of water, Flegmatike, Feminine, of the night, Septentrionall, a moueable Signe, the house of the *Moone*, the exaltation of *Jupiter*, of a salt sauour and keepeth of man the brest and stomacke.

Leo is hot and dry, of the nature of fire, Cholerike, Masculine, of the day, Oriental and fixed, the house of the *Sun*, of a bitter sauour, and keepeth of man the heart, backe, and sides.

Virgo is colde and dry, of the nature of the earth, Melancholike, Feminine, of the night, Meridionall, & Common, the house of *Mercury*, and of a sowre sauour, and keepeth of man the belly, bowels, and inwarde partes.

Libra is hot and moyst, of the nature of the ayre, Sanguine, and Masculine, of the day, Occidental, and moueable, the house of *Venus*, the exaltation of *Saturne*, of a sweete sauour, and keepeth of man the nauell and lower partes of the belly, with the loynes.

Scorpio is colde and moyst, of the nature of the water, Flegmatike, Feminine, of the night, Septentrionall, and fixed, the house of *Mars*, of a salt sauour, & keepeth of man the priuie parts and the bladder.

Sagittarius is hot and dry, of the nature of fire, Cholerike, and Masculine, of the day, Orientall and Common, the house of *Iupiter*, of a bitter sauour, and keepeth of man the thighes.

Capricornus is cold and dry, of the nature of the earth,

Melancholike, Feminine, of the night, Meridionall, & Moueable, the house of *Saturne*, the exaltation of *Mars*, the sowre sauour, & keepeth of man the knees.

Aquarius, is hot and moyst, of the nature of the ayre, Sanguine, Masculine, of the day. Occidental, and fixed, the house of *Saturn*, and of a sweete sauour, and keepeth of man the shins and legs.

Pisces, is cold and moyst, of the nature of Water, Flegmatik, Feminine, of the night, Septentrional and Common, the house of *Iupiter*, and the exaltation of *Venus*, of a salt Sauour, and keepeth of man the feete.

The nature, course, and qualitie of the vii. lightes or Planets.

Saturne is highest of the vii. Planets, and slowest in his proper motion, being colde and dry of nature, malicious and enimie to nature, and destroyer of life and of the body, he gouerneth the right eare, the milt, the bladder, & of humours, the Melancholike, and part of flegme, his colour is like vnto leade requiring neere xxx. yeeres to fulfill his course, his metall is lead.

Iupiter is next vnto *Saturne*, temperate, faire and bright, being hot & moist, sanguine, louing hauing regard ouer the loungs, the sides, the gristles, and of the seede or natural humour of man, his metall is Tynne, requiring xii. yeeres to finish his course.

Mars is hot and dry, of nature cruell, and of the body is attributed to him the left eare, the veines, the genitories, and of humours, the cholores, and as some say, hee gouerneth the Liuer, being of a red colour, euill of nature, his mettal is Iron and Steele, and in two yeeres he endeth his course through the xii. signes in the zodiacke.

The *Sunne* is placed in the middest of all the Planets, most cleare and bright, the Well of pure light, hee is the principall Planet in the firmament, he is the cause of Winter and Sommer, of the day and night, being hot and dry, louing, giuing light & life vnto al things, hauing natural vertue, he ruleth the brain the marrowe, the sight, the sinewes, & generally he ruleth all the right part of the body. His metal is pure gold, going through the xii. signes in 365. dayes, 5. houres 55. min. 13. secondes.

Venus is colde and moyst, louing, flegmatike, and of the body she gouerneth the backe bone, the buttocks, the lower part of the belly, & the matrix, with the Moone, the fat, her colour is bright, yea brighter then *Iupiters*. her metall is coper, her course is like the Sunnes course, neuer aboue xlviii. degrees from the Sun, called the morning starre or Lucifer, when thet shee riseth before the Sunne, and setting after the Sunne, then shee is called the euening starre or *Vesper*.

Mercury is next vnto *Venus*, somewhat shining, but not very bright, hee is good with the good Planet, & euill with euill, when he is ioyned with them his mettall is quicke siluer, his course is like vnto the Sunnes course, neuer aboue xxix. degrees from the Sunne.

The *Moone* is the lowest of the Planets, being cold & moyst, louing, hauing dominion ouer the stomacke and belly, and of the mother of women, and generall ouer the members of the left side of the body, her mettall is siluer, running ouer the whole zodiacke, in xxvii. dayes, and viii. houres.

Furthermore you must note that *Iupiter* and *Venus* are called good & fortunate, but *Iupiter* is called the greater good fortune, and *Venus* the lesse. Now *Saturne* and *Mars* be called euill fortune, but *Saturne* is called the greater unfortunate, and *Mars* the lesser. the Sunne or Moone are called mean or betweene both, that is to say, neither fortunate, nor unfortunate, but indifferent, &c.

And according vnto some authours, as *Cyprianus, Leouitius*, and other, I haue thought good for to shewe what Countries, Cities or Townes are attributed vnder euery one of the xii. signes: for according vnto the iudgement Astrologicall, If that any obscuritie be either of the Sunne or Moone, as the Eclipses of either of them, if that it happeneth in such a signe, then it threatneth the countries, cities or townes, that are vnder the said signe, And also if that there bee any firy Meteor or Blasing starres, or Comets, so according vnto their appearing & walke and the place of their going out doeth threaten those places in like maner, &c.

Countries vnder Aries & Mars.

Basternia, Syria, Palestina, England, France, Germany, Burgandie, Svveueland, and of Cities with townes, *Naples, Aucona, Ferara, Florence, Verona, Capua, Lindauia, Cracouia. &c.*

Vnder Taurus & Venus.

Parthia, Media, Cyprus the lesser, *Asia,* landes named *Cyclades, Irelande, Heluetia* and of Cities and Townes, *Bouony, Tigure, Lucerna, Herbypolis, Lepsia, Posna, &c.*

Vnder Gemini and Mercurius.

Hyrcania, Armenia, Cyrene, Marmaria the lower *Egypt,* and part of *Lombardie,* and *Flanders, Brabant,* and of Cities and Townes, *London, Louen, Bridges, Mentz, Hasforde, Noremberge, &c.*

Vnder Cancer and the Moone.

Numidia, Africa, Bithinia, Carthage, Phrigia, Holland, Zeland, Scotland, the kingdome of *Granate,* and of Cities and Townes, *Constantinople, Venice, Pisa, Millan, Treuers, Yorke, S. Andrew, Lubeck.*

Vnder Leo & the Sunne.

Italy, Scicilie, Apuleia, Bohemia, Phœnicia, and part of *Turkie, Sabina,* and of Cities with townes *Damascus, Rome, Confluence, Rauenna, Cremona, Prage.*

Vnder Virgo & Mercurius.

Mesopotamia, Babylon, Assyria, Grece, Athaia, Crete, & of Cities and Townes, *Hierusalem, Corinth,* the *Rhodes, Papia, Tolose, Lions, Paris, Heydelberge, Basill. &c.*

Vnder Libra and Venus.

Bastriaua, Caspia, Thebaida, Aethiopia, Lyuonia, Austrige, Oasis, and of Cities and Townes, *Caieta, Lauda, Suessa, Placentia, Friburge, Argentine, Spiers, Frankford, &c.*

Vnder Scorpius & Mars.

Iudea, Capadocia, Getulia, Mauritana, Norvvay, Catholonia, and of Cities and Townes, *Valentia, Padua, Mesana, Aquileia, &c.*

Vnder Sagittarius and Libra.

Spaine, Arabia the happy, *Hungary, Sclauonia, Celtica, Misnia,* and of Cities and Townes, to wit, *Collen Narbona, Stutgardia, Rotenburge, Buda, &c.*

Vnder Capricornus and Saturne.

India, Arriana, Macedonia, Thracia, Grece, Saxonie, Hesia, Orchney Ilands, *Macheline, Oxforde, Brandenburge, Constantia, Fauentia, Augusta, Vendell, &c.*

Vnder Aquarius and Saturne.

Arabia desart, great *Tartaria, Denmarke, Sogdiana Sarmatia,* and of Cities *Hamburge, Brema, Salisburye, &c.*

Vnder Pisces and Iupiter.

Lydia, Pamphilia, Calabria, Normandy, Portugall, Cicilie, and of Cities and Townes, *Alexandria, Hispalis, Compostell, Ratisbone, Wormes, &c.*

A briefe note of such extraordinary lights or Comets Blasing starres, and fiery Meteors as haue appeared since the yeere of our Lorde 1572.

And first of that which appeared & happened the yeere of our Lorde 1572. about the 17. or 18. day of Nouember, being in the

May.

In the moneth of May you cannot see the vii. starres.

Iune.

The vii. starres rise the first day at ii. a clocke ii. minutes.
  The vii. starres rise the x. day at one a clocke xxii. minuts.
  The vii. starres rise the xx. day, at xii. a clocke xlii. minutes.

Iuly.

The vii. Starres rise, the first day at xii. a clocke ii. minutes.
  The vii. starres rise the x. day at xi. a clocke xxii. minutes.
  The vii. starres rise the xx. day at x. a clocke xlii. minutes.

August.

The vii. starres rise the first day at x. a clocke ii. minutes.
  The vii. starres rise the x. day at ix. a clocke xxii. minutes.
  The vii. stars rise the xx. day at viii. a clock xlii. min. & are in the noonestead or South at iiii. a clocke iii. min. in the morning.

September.

The vii. starres rise the first day, at viii. a clocke ii. minuts, and set at iiii. a clocke xii. min. in the morning.
  The vii. starres rise the x. day at vii. a clock xxii. and South at iii. a clocke xxxii. minutes.
  The vii. starres, rise the xx. day at vi. a clocke xlii minuts, & are South at ii. a clocke lii. minutes.

October.

The vii. starres rise the first day at vi. a clocke ii. minutes, and are South at ii. a clocke xii. minutes.
  The vii. starres rise the x. day at v. a clocke xxii. minutes, and are South at one a clocke xxxii. minutes.
  The vii. starres rise the xx. day at iiii. a clocke xlii. minuts, and are South at xii. a clocke lii. minutes, & set at ix. a clocke ii. min. in the morning.

ALMANACKE FOR X. YEERES, 1581

*Now followeth the rising noone-
steede or being South, and setting of the vij.
starres, as long as they giue light by the night being
calculated for the latitude of London, and will
continue these 100. yeeres without much error, and heere with vs they ryse neere the
North East, and set neere the NorthEast [sic], and
doe shine or abide aboue our Horizon 16.
houres, 20. minutes.*

Ianuarie.

The vii. Starres are South at viii. a clocke xii. minuts, and set at iiii. a clocke xxii. min. the first day.

The vii. starres are South at vii. a clocke xxxii. minuts, and set at iii. a clocke xiii. min. the x. day.

The vii. starres are South at vi. a clocke iii. min. and set at iii. a clocke ii. min. the xx. day.

February.

The vii. Starres are South at vi. a clocke xii. minutes, and set at ii. a clocke xxii. min. the first day.

The vii. starres are South at v. a clocke xxxii. min. and set at one a clocke xlii. min. the x. day.

The vii. starres set at xii. a clocke ii. minutes the xx. day.

Marche.

The vii. starres set at one of the clocke xxii. minutes the first day.

The vii. starres set at xi. a clocke xlii. min. the x. day.

The vii. starres set at xi. a clocke ii. minuts the xx. day.

Aprill.

The vii. Starres set at x. a clocke xxii. min. the i. day.

The vii. starres set at ix. a clocke xlii. minutes the x. day.

The vii. starres will not be seene a the latter end of Aprill.

Aquarius: and so vnto the longitude of *Capricorne*: and the beame or tayle did at the first stande or point vnto the East North Eastwardes, and his walke or motion was made vnto the Westwarde, going faster than the dayly motion. So that his walk or motion is contrary vnto al the direct motions of the lightes of the heauens, beginning vpon the North parte of the Equinoctiall. First going or passing very swiftly, & afterwardes more slowly, so that it hath passed by the signe or marke called the Dolphin, and so vnto the North part of the Eagle, going more Northerly then that it did at his first appearing. All this time the Comet was Occidentall, vntill the later part of Nouember, and in the signe of *Sagittarius*, there it had the longitude of the Sunne, and so it hath changed from the Occidentall part vnto the Orientall part, comming neerer the Equinoctiall againe, and hath passed through the signe or marke of the Serpent holder, and also since that it hath been Orientall, the beame or tayle doeth point vnto the North Westwardes. And thus it hath passed and doeth continue yet vntill this time. &c.

North partes in the Marke or bond of *Casopia*, which is within the compasse of the signe of *Taurus*: this Starre was rounde without any tayle, so that he cauld not bee knowe from other starres but only by his bignesse. And also that there hath neuer no such starre been seene in that place of the heauens, for that it did shewe itselfe to be as bigge as the Planet *Iupiter*, which is one of the biggest in sight in the heauens, except the Sunne and Moone, or *Venus*: and so it continued, shewing itselfe in the skie a whole yeere and iii. moneths, and so wasted away by litle & litle, till that it was cleane consumed.

This starre was very strange, for that it had no walke or motion but still remayned in one place from his first appearing, vntill that it was all wasted, and no more to bee seene, euen as a thing that had been let downe, from out of the heauens and so drawne vp agayne that way it came: which was a very rare thing as hath byn written, knowne, and heard of &c.

The second, was in the yeere of our Lord 1577. the x. day of Nouember. This was a Blazing Starre, notably seene and knowne with a very great tayle or beame, poynting or standing vnto the Eastwardes from the Starrewarde, and also the beame or tayle was somewhat crooked like a Bowe. This Comet did first appeare in the signe of *Sagittarius* and so passed directly the signes into *Capricornus* and *Aquarius*, and so into *Pisces*, and there went out not farre from *Pegasus* or the fliyng horse, so that the walke or motion of this Comet, did directly followe his tayle, and did continue vnto his first appearing vnto his goyng cleerely out and not too bee seene, the time was neere 3. Monethes from the first appearing vnto the end.

The third Comet or Blasing starre, did appeare this yeere 1580. the viii. or ix day of October, in the longitude of the signe of *Pisces*, but that it was vnto the North part of the Equinoctiall, and the walke or motion of this Comet is contrary vnto the motion of all other starres for y^t it cometh the retrograde way of al the wandering stars or Planets, so that it commeth from the longitude of *Pisces*, vnto the longitude of

APPENDIX A

meridian 339° 42′ 51″ from her original or starting meridian. The table represents Dr Dee's attempt to solve the problem of the plain chart which ignores the convergence of the meridians. The date at which it was compiled appears to have been 1558, and the reference to a diameter of 50 inches suggests the dimensions of the polar projection upon which he considered the rhumbs could best be plotted, failing a globe. This would, however, make a very unwieldy chart. The use of the 'paradoxall compass' or spiral rhumb drawn on a chart was taught by Dee to the brothers Borough when they were chief pilots of the Muscovy Company, and is described by John Davis in his *Seaman's Secrets*, 1595. The Canon here reproduced was no doubt one of the principal tables which Dee included in Volume II of his *General and Rare Memorials of the Perfect Arte of Navigation* hastily written in 1576. The long title of this volume (which was never actually printed) runs: *A great volume, in which are contained our Queen Elizabeth her Arithmeticall Tables Gubernatick: for Navigation by the Paradoxall Compass (by me invented anno 1557) and Navigation by Great circles; and for longitudes and latitudes, and the variation of the Compass, finding most easily and speedily etc.*[1]

The Ashmolean manuscript here reproduced is evidently a first draft, but the many figures struck out by the computer are not here reproduced. Neither is an extra column, which Dee included, obtained by deducting 360° from the longitude 'continuate' after the globe has once been encircled.

As author of *The Perfect Arte of Nauigation*, Dee had addressed himself to Sir Christopher Hatton in hope of his patronage, but it is hardly surprising that he did not get the necessary assistance, for as he himself wrote: 'The second Booke or Volume ... will be of more hundred pounds Charges to be prepared for the print (in respect of the Tables and Figures thereto requisite): than you would easily believe. This matter of charges so far

---

[1] Dee's writings on navigation are treated at some length in Taylor, *Tudor Geography*, chs. v–vii, and by Waters, *Art of Navigation*, Apps. 8A, 8B.

Appendix A

CANON GUBERNAUTICUS, by JOHN DEE (1558)

EDITOR'S NOTE

The set of Tables which Dee entitled *Canon Gubernauticus*, that is to say, *A Navigational Canon* or *Rule*, has the sub-title: *An Arithmeticall Resolution of the Paradoxall Compass*. On the title-page of the manuscript (Ashmolean MS 242) is written: 'The diameter 50 ynches'. Briefly, the 'paradoxall compass' was the curving line (not a great circle) which a wind-rhumb or fixed compass direction followed when traced on a globe or on the projection of a globe. The Table is a list of points fixed by latitudes and longitude by means of which the 'paradoxall' line could be plotted on a globe (or on a net-work of parallels and meridians) assuming that the course followed lay on some one of the seven standard rhumbs between north and south, and east and west. A ship sailing due north or south did not change longitude, while a ship sailing due east or west did not change latitude. The figures in the Tables are arranged so that for each one degree change of latitude that he observes, the pilot can read his change of longitude east or west, according to the course he is on. The first rhumb makes $11°\frac{1}{4}$ with the meridian, the second rhumb makes $22°\frac{1}{2}$ with the meridian, the third $33°\frac{3}{4}$, and so on up to the seventh which runs at an angle of $78°\frac{3}{4}$ with the meridian. The longitude figures are given in two ways 'continuate' and 'resolute'. In the first case the ship is supposed to sail continuously from latitude $0°$ (the equator) to latitude $80°$, without changing course, and the total easting or westing made is set down. If such a ship sailed from the equator on the 7th rhumb, she would pass spirally nearly twice round the whole circumference of the globe, making an easting or westing of $699° \ 42' \ 51''$, and so arriving in latitude $80°$ on

AN ALMANACK FOR XX YEERES, 1581

November.

The vii. Starres rise the first day at iiii. a clocke x. min. & set in the South at xii. a clocke xii. min. & set at viii. a clocke xxii. minutes in the morning.

The vii. starres rise the x. day at iii. a clocke xxii. minutes, & are South at xi. a clocke xxxii. min. and set at x. a clocke l. mi.

The vii. starres in the South the xxxday at ix. a clocke iii. mi. and set at vii. a clocke ii. min. in the morning.

December.

The vii. Starres rise the first day at ii. a clocke x. minutes, & set at vi. a clocke xxii. minutes.

The vii. stars are South at ix. a clocke xxxii. min. and set at v. a clocke xlii. minutes.

The vii. starres be in the Meridian or South the xxx. day at vii. a clocke iiii. minutes, and set at v. a clocke ii. min. in the morning.

FINIS.

Imprinted at London by
Richard Watkins and James
Roberts 1581.

Nouember.

The vii. Starres rise the first day at iiii. a clock ii. min. & are in the South at xii. a clock xii. min. & set at viii. a clock xxii. minutes in the morning.

 The vii. starres rise the x. day at iii. a clock xxii. minuts, & are South at xi. a clocke xxxii. min. and set at vii. a clocke xlii. min.

 The vii. starres in the South the xx. day at x. a clocke lii. mi. and set at vii. a clocke ii. min. in the morning.

December.

The vii. Starres rise the first day at x. a clocke xii. minutes, & set at vi. a clocke xxii. minutes.

 The vii. stars are South at ix. a clocke xxxii. min. and set at v. a clocke xlii. minutes.

 The vii. starres be in the Meridian or South the xx. day at viii. a clocke lii. minutes, and set at v. a clocke ii. minutes in the morning.

FINIS

Imprinted at London by
Richard Watkins, and Iames
Robertes. 1581.

passeth my slender hability, and, withall, is so dreadfull to the Printers, for feere of greate los thereby susteining (so rare and few men's Studies are in such matters employed), that delay on my part is rather that way Constrained.'

The manuscript has not survived save for the section here printed, but it appears to have contained much of the material of a sea manual.

the diameter 50 ynches

Canon
Gubernauticus

An
Arithmeticall
Resolution of the
Paradoxall
Compas

APPENDIX A

I

Latitude	11. D 15. M Longitude Continuate			11. D 15. M Longitude Resolute		
D	D	M	S	D	M	S
1	0	11	56	0	11	56
2	0	23	53	0	11	57
3	0	35	50	0	11	57
4	0	47	48	0	11	58
5	0	59	46	0	11	58
6	1	11	45	0	11	59
7	1	23	45	0	12	0
8	1	35	47	0	12	2
9	1	47	51	0	12	4
10	1	59	57	0	12	6
11	2	12	5	0	12	8
12	2	24	16	0	12	11
13	2	36	30	0	12	14
14	2	48	47	0	12	17
15	3	1	7	0	12	20
16	3	13	31	0	12	24
17	3	25	59	0	12	28
18	3	38	31	0	12	32
19	3	51	7	0	12	36
20	4	3	47	0	12	40
21	4	16	31	0	12	44

I

Latitude	11. D 15. M Longitude Continuate			11. D 15. M Longitude Resolute		
D	D	M	S	D	M	S
21	4	16	31	0	12	44
22	4	29	20	0	12	49
23	4	42	14	0	12	54
24	4	55	14	0	13	0
25	5	8	20	0	13	6
26	5	21	33	0	13	13
27	5	34	53	0	13	20
28	5	48	20	0	13	27
29	6	1	55	0	13	35
30	6	15	38	0	13	43
31	6	29	29	0	13	51
32	6	43	29	0	14	0
33	6	57	38	0	14	9
34	7	11	56	0	14	18
35	7	26	24	0	14	28
36	7	41	3	0	14	39
37	7	55	53	0	14	50
38	8	10	55	0	15	2
39	8	26	10	0	15	15
40	8	41	38	0	15	28
41	8	57	20	0	15	42

DEE'S *Canon Gubernauticus*, 1558

I. II. D 15. M

Latitude	Continuate			Resolute Longitude		
D	D	M	S	D	M	S
41	8	57	20	0	15	42
42	9	13	16	0	15	56
43	9	29	27	0	16	11
44	9	45	54	0	16	27
45	10	2	38	0	16	44
46	10	19	40	0	17	2
47	10	37	0	0	17	20
48	10	54	40	0	17	40
49	11	12	41	0	18	1
50	11	31	4	0	18	23
51	11	49	51	0	18	47
52	12	9	3	0	19	12
53	12	28	42	0	19	39
54	12	48	49	0	20	7
55	13	9	26	0	20	37
56	13	30	35	0	21	9
57	13	52	17	0	21	42
58	14	14	34	0	22	17
59	14	37	27	0	22	53
60	15	0	58	0	23	31
61	15	25	9	0	24	11

I. II. D 15. M

Latitude	Continuate			Resolute Longitude		
D	D	M	S	D	M	S
61	15	25	9	0	24	11
62	15	50	3	0	24	54
63	16	15	44	0	25	41
64	16	42	17	0	26	33
65	17	9	47	0	27	30
66	17	38	20	0	28	33
67	18	8	3	0	29	43
68	18	39	4	0	31	1
69	19	11	32	0	32	28
70	19	45	38	0	34	6
71	20	21	34	0	35	56
72	20	59	34	0	38	0
73	21	39	53	0	40	19
74	22	22	47	0	42	54
75	23	8	34	0	45	47
76	23	57	54	0	49	0
77	24	50	8	0	52	34
78	25	46	38	0	56	30
79	26	47	27	1	0	49
80	27	53	0	1	5	33

APPENDIX A

2

Latitude	22. D 30. M Longitude			
	Continuate		Resolute	
D	D M S		D M S	
1	0 24 47		0 24 47	
2	0 49 36		0 24 49	
3	1 14 27		0 24 51	
4	1 39 20		0 24 53	
5	2 4 15		0 24 55	
6	2 29 13		0 24 58	
7	2 54 14		0 25 1	
8	3 19 18		0 25 4	
9	3 44 26		0 25 8	
10	4 9 38		0 25 12	
11	4 34 55		0 25 17	
12	5 0 17		0 25 22	
13	5 25 45		0 25 28	
14	5 51 19		0 25 34	
15	6 17 0		0 25 41	
16	6 42 48		0 25 48	
17	7 8 44		0 25 56	
18	7 34 48		0 26 4	
19	8 1 1		0 26 13	
20	8 27 23		0 26 22	
21	8 53 55		0 26 32	

2

Latitude	22. D 30. M Longitude			
	Continuate		Resolute	
D	D M S		D M S	
21	8 53 55		0 26 32	
22	9 20 37		0 26 42	
23	9 47 30		0 26 53	
24	10 14 35		0 27 5	
25	10 41 53		0 27 18	
26	11 9 24		0 27 31	
27	11 37 9		0 27 45	
28	12 5 9		0 28 0	
29	12 33 25		0 28 16	
30	13 1 58		0 28 33	
31	13 30 49		0 28 51	
32	13 59 59		0 29 10	
33	14 29 29		0 29 30	
34	14 59 20		0 29 51	
35	15 29 33		0 30 13	
36	16 0 8		0 30 35	
37	16 31 6		0 30 58	
38	17 2 28		0 31 22	
39	17 34 5		0 31 47	
40	18 6 28		0 32 13	
41	18 39 9		0 32 41	

DEE's *Canon Gubernauticus*, 1558

Latitude	22. D 30. M Longitude					
	Continuate			Resolute		
D	D	M	S	D	M	S
61	32	6	3	0	50	28
62	32	58	7	0	52	4
63	33	51	55	0	53	48
64	34	47	36	0	55	41
65	35	45	19	0	57	43
66	36	45	14	0	59	55
67	37	47	33	1	2	19
68	38	52	30	1	4	57
69	40	0	20	1	7	50
70	41	11	20	1	11	0
71	42	25	49	1	14	29
72	43	44	10	1	18	21
73	45	13	50	1	22	40
74	46	34	22	1	27	32
75	48	7	25	1	33	3
76	49	46	47	1	39	22
77	51	33	26	1	46	39
78	53	28	32	1	55	6
79	55	33	29	2	4	57
80	57	49	58	2	16	29

Latitude	22. D 30. M Longitude					
	Continuate			Resolute		
D	D	M	S	D	M	S
41	18	39	9	0	32	41
42	19	12	19	0	33	10
43	19	46	0	0	33	41
44	20	20	14	0	34	14
45	20	55	3	0	34	49
46	21	30	29	0	35	26
47	22	6	34	0	36	5
48	22	43	20	0	36	46
49	23	20	50	0	37	30
50	23	59	6	0	38	16
51	24	38	11	0	39	5
52	25	18	8	0	39	57
53	25	59	0	0	40	52
54	25	40	50	0	41	50
55	27	23	41	0	42	51
56	28	7	37	0	43	56
57	28	52	42	0	45	5
58	29	39	0	0	46	18
59	30	26	36	0	47	36
60	31	15	35	0	48	59
61	32	6	3	0	50	28

APPENDIX A

3

Latitude	33. D 45. M Longitude					
	Continuate			Resolute		
D	D	M	S	D	M	S
1	0	40	6	0	40	6
2	1	20	14	0	40	8
3	2	0	24	0	40	10
4	2	40	37	0	40	13
5	3	20	53	0	40	16
6	4	1	13	0	40	20
7	4	41	37	0	40	24
8	5	22	5	0	40	28
9	6	2	38	0	40	33
10	6	43	17	0	40	39
11	7	24	3	0	40	46
12	8	4	57	0	40	54
13	8	46	0	0	41	3
14	9	27	13	0	41	13
15	10	8	37	0	41	24
16	10	50	13	0	41	36
17	11	32	02	0	41	49
18	12	14	05	0	42	3
19	12	56	22	0	42	17
20	13	38	54	0	42	32
21	14	21	42	0	42	48

3

Latitude	33. D 45. M Longitude					
	Continuate			Resolute		
D	D	M	S	D	M	S
21	14	21	42	0	42	48
22	15	4	47	0	43	5
23	15	48	10	0	43	23
24	16	31	52	0	43	42
25	17	15	54	0	44	2
26	18	00	18	0	44	24
27	18	45	05	0	44	47
28	19	30	16	0	45	11
29	20	15	53	0	45	37
30	21	01	57	0	46	4
31	21	48	29	0	46	32
32	22	35	31	0	47	2
33	23	23	04	0	47	33
34	24	11	10	0	48	6
35	24	59	50	0	48	40
36	25	49	06	0	49	16
37	26	39	00	0	49	54
38	27	29	33	0	50	33
39	28	20	47	0	51	14
40	29	12	45	0	51	58
41	30	5	29	0	52	44

APPENDIX A

56. D 15. M

Latitude	Longitude Continuate			Longitude Resolute		
D	D	M	S	D	M	S
1	1	29	48	1	29	48
2	2	59	39	1	29	51
3	4	29	34	1	29	55
4	5	59	33	1	29	59
5	7	29	38	1	30	5
6	8	59	51	1	30	13
7	10	30	14	1	30	23
8	12	00	49	1	30	35
9	13	31	37	1	30	48
10	15	2	40	1	31	3
11	16	34	0	1	31	20
12	18	5	39	1	31	39
13	19	37	38	1	31	59
14	21	9	59	1	32	21
15	22	42	44	1	32	45
16	24	15	55	1	33	11
17	25	49	34	1	33	39
18	27	23	43	1	34	9
19	28	58	24	1	34	41
20	30	33	40	1	35	16
21	32	9	33	1	35	53

56. D 15. M

Latitude	Longitude Continuate			Longitude Resolute		
D	D	M	S	D	M	S
21	32	9	33	1	35	53
22	33	46	5	1	36	32
23	35	23	18	1	37	13
24	37	1	14	1	37	56
25	38	39	55	1	38	41
26	40	19	24	1	39	29
27	41	59	44	1	40	20
28	43	40	58	1	41	14
29	45	23	9	1	42	11
30	47	6	20	1	43	11
31	48	50	34	1	44	14
32	50	35	54	1	45	20
33	52	22	23	1	46	29
34	54	10	5	1	47	42
35	55	59	3	1	48	58
36	57	49	21	1	50	18
37	59	41	3	1	51	42
38	61	34	14	1	53	11
39	63	28	59	1	54	45
40	65	25	22	1	56	23
41	67	23	28	1	58	6

DEE's *Canon Gubernauticus*, 1558

Latitude	45. D o. M Longitude					
	Continuate			Resolute		
D	D	M	S	D	M	S
61	77	29	41	2	1	52
62	79	35	27	2	5	46
63	81	45	25	2	9	58
64	83	59	55	2	14	30
65	86	19	20	2	19	25
66	88	44	06	2	24	46
67	91	14	42	2	30	36
68	93	51	39	2	36	57
69	96	35	31	2	43	52
70	99	26	55	2	51	24
71	102	26	37	2	59	42
72	105	35	34	3	8	57
73	108	54	55	3	19	21
74	112	26	04	3	31	9
75	116	10	42	3	44	38
76	120	10	49	4	0	7
77	124	28	46	4	17	57
78	129	7	17	4	38	31
79	134	9	30	5	2	13
80	139	39	00	5	29	30

Latitude	45. D o. M Longitude					
	Continuate			Resolute		
D	D	M	S	D	M	S
41	45	1	47	1	18	55
42	46	21	54	1	20	7
43	47	43	17	1	21	23
44	49	6	0	1	22	43
45	50	30	8	1	24	8
46	51	55	45	1	25	37
47	53	22	56	1	27	11
48	54	51	46	1	28	50
49	56	22	20	1	30	34
50	57	54	44	1	32	24
51	59	29	4	1	34	20
52	61	5	27	1	36	23
53	62	44	1	1	38	34
54	64	24	54	1	40	53
55	66	8	15	1	43	21
56	67	54	13	1	45	58
57	69	42	58	1	48	45
58	71	34	41	1	51	43
59	73	29	34	1	54	53
60	75	27	49	1	58	15
61	77	29	41	2	1	52

APPENDIX A

4 45. D o. M

Latitude	Longitude Continuate			Longitude Resolute		
D	D	M	S	D	M	S
1	1	0	0	1	0	0
2	2	0	1	1	0	1
3	3	0	4	1	0	3
4	4	0	10	1	0	6
5	5	0	21	1	0	11
6	6	0	37	1	0	16
7	7	1	0	1	0	23
8	8	1	31	1	0	31
9	9	2	11	1	0	40
10	10	3	1	1	0	50
11	11	4	2	1	1	1
12	12	5	16	1	1	14
13	13	6	44	1	1	28
14	14	8	27	1	1	43
15	15	10	26	1	1	59
16	16	12	43	1	2	17
17	17	15	19	1	2	36
18	18	18	15	1	2	56
19	19	21	32	1	3	17
20	20	25	11	1	3	39
21	21	29	14	1	4	3
22	22	33	43	1	4	29
23	23	38	39	1	4	56
24	24	44	4	1	5	25
25	25	50	0	1	5	56
26	26	56	29	1	6	29
27	28	3	32	1	7	3
28	29	11	11	1	7	39
29	30	19	28	1	8	17
30	31	28	25	1	8	57
31	32	38	4	1	9	39
32	33	48	27	1	10	23
33	34	59	36	1	11	9
34	36	11	34	1	11	58
35	37	24	23	1	12	49
36	38	38	6	1	13	43
37	39	52	46	1	14	40
38	41	8	25	1	15	39
39	42	25	6	1	16	41
40	43	42	52	1	17	46
41	45	1	47	1	18	55

DEE'S *Canon Gubernauticus*, 1558

3

33. D 45. M

Latitude	Continuate			Longitude Resolute		
D	D	M	S	D	M	S
61	51	46	33	1	21	29
62	53	10	39	1	24	6
63	54	37	33	1	26	54
64	56	7	27	1	29	54
65	57	40	36	1	33	9
66	59	17	17	1	36	41
67	60	57	50	1	40	33
68	62	42	37	1	44	47
69	64	32	02	1	49	25
70	66	26	23	1	54	31
71	68	26	42	2	0	9
72	70	33	06	2	6	24
73	72	46	28	2	13	22
74	75	07	40	2	21	12
75	77	37	46	2	30	6
76	80	18	04	2	40	18
77	83	10	08	2	52	4
78	86	15	50	3	5	42
79	89	36	25	3	21	35
80	93	16	35	3	40	10

3

33. D 45. M

Latitude	Continuate			Longitude Resolute		
D	D	M	S	D	M	S
41	30	5	29	0	52	44
42	30	59	02	0	53	33
43	31	53	26	0	54	24
44	32	48	43	0	55	17
45	33	44	56	0	56	13
46	34	42	08	0	57	12
47	35	40	23	0	58	15
48	36	39	44	0	59	21
49	37	40	14	1	0	31
50	38	41	58	1	1	44
51	39	44	59	1	3	1
52	40	49	21	1	4	22
53	41	53	09	1	5	48
54	43	2	29	1	7	20
55	44	11	27	1	8	58
56	45	22	10	1	10	43
57	46	34	45	1	12	35
58	47	49	20	1	14	35
59	49	6	03	1	16	43
60	50	25	04	1	19	1
61	51	46	33	1	21	29

APPENDIX A

7 · 78. D 45. M

Latitude	Continuate			Resolute		
D	D	M	S	D	M	S
21	108	1	26	5	22	4
22	113	25	40	5	24	14
23	118	52	12	5	26	32
24	124	21	9	5	28	57
25	129	52	39	5	31	30
26	135	26	52	5	34	13
27	141	3	57	5	37	5
28	146	44	3	5	40	6
29	152	27	19	5	43	16
30	158	13	55	5	46	36
31	164	4	2	5	50	7
32	169	57	51	5	53	49
33	175	55	33	5	57	42
34	181	57	20	6	1	47
35	188	3	23	6	6	3
36	194	13	54	6	10	31
37	200	29	7	6	15	13
38	206	49	18	6	20	11
39	213	14	44	6	25	26
40	219	45	42	6	30	58
41	226	22	29	6	36	47

7 · 73. D 45. M

Latitude	Continuate			Resolute		
D	D	M	S	D	M	S
1	5	1	39	5	1	39
2	10	3	24	5	1	45
3	15	5	20	5	1	56
4	20	7	32	5	2	12
5	25	10	7	5	2	35
6	30	13	10	5	3	3
7	35	16	46	5	3	36
8	40	21	1	5	4	15
9	45	26	1	5	5	0
10	50	31	52	5	5	51
11	55	38	40	5	6	48
12	60	46	31	5	7	51
13	65	55	31	5	9	0
14	71	5	46	5	10	15
15	76	17	21	5	11	35
16	81	30	23	5	13	2
17	86	44	59	5	14	36
18	92	1	16	5	16	17
19	97	19	21	5	18	5
20	102	39	22	5	20	1
21	108	1	26	5	22	4

DEE's *Canon Gubernauticus*, 1558

Latitude	67. D 30. M Longitude					
	Continuate			Resolute		
D	D	M	S	D	M	S
41	108	42	29	3	10	33
42	111	55	58	3	13	29
43	115	12	33	3	16	34
44	118	32	18	3	19	46
45	121	55	25	3	23	7
46	125	22	1	3	26	36
47	128	52	14	3	30	13
48	132	26	13	3	33	59
49	136	4	7	3	37	54
50	139	46	12	3	42	5
51	143	32	54	3	46	42
52	147	24	39	3	51	45
53	151	21	53	3	57	14
54	155	25	2	4	3	9
55	159	34	32	4	9	30
56	163	50	39	4	16	7
57	168	13	40	3	23	1
58	172	43	52	4	30	12
59	177	21	32	4	37	40
60	182	6	56	4	45	24
61	187	00	54	4	53	58

Latitude	67. D 30. M Longitude					
	Continuate			Resolute		
D	D	M	S	D	M	S
61	187	00	54	4	53	58
62	192	4	16	5	3	22
63	197	17	52	5	13	56
64	202	42	32	5	24	40
65	208	19	6	5	36	34
66	214	8	45	5	49	39
67	220	12	40	6	3	55
68	226	32	2	6	19	22
69	233	8	1	6	35	59
70	240	1	48	6	53	47
71	247	16	1	7	14	13
72	254	53	18	7	37	17
73	262	56	17	8	2	59
74	271	27	37	8	31	20
75	280	29	56	9	2	19
76	290	9	47	9	39	51
77	300	33	43	10	23	56
78	311	48	17	11	14	34
79	324	00	2	12	11	45
80	337	15	31	13	15	29

APPENDIX A

67. D 30. M

Latitude	Continuate Longitude			Resolute		
D	D	M	S	D	M	S
1	2	24	52	2	24	52
2	4	49	46	2	24	54
3	7	14	45	2	24	59
4	9	39	52	2	25	7
5	12	5	10	2	25	18
6	14	30	41	2	25	31
7	16	56	28	2	25	47
8	19	22	34	2	26	6
9	21	49	2	2	26	28
10	24	15	54	2	26	52
11	26	43	13	2	27	19
12	29	11	2	2	27	49
13	31	39	24	2	28	22
14	34	8	22	2	28	58
15	36	37	59	2	29	37
16	39	8	18	2	30	19
17	41	39	23	2	31	5
18	44	11	17	2	31	54
19	45	44	3	2	32	46
20	49	17	44	2	33	41
21	51	52	24	2	34	40

67. D 30. M

Latitude	Continuate Longitude			Resolute		
D	D	M	S	D	M	S
21	51	52	24	2	34	40
22	54	28	6	2	35	42
23	57	34	54	2	36	48
24	59	42	52	2	37	58
25	62	22	4	2	39	12
26	65	2	34	2	40	30
27	67	44	26	2	41	52
28	70	27	45	2	43	19
29	73	12	36	2	44	51
30	75	59	3	2	46	27
31	78	47	11	2	48	8
32	81	37	5	2	49	54
33	84	28	51	2	51	46
34	87	22	35	2	53	44
35	90	18	22	2	55	47
36	93	16	18	2	57	56
37	96	16	30	3	0	12
38	99	19	5	3	2	35
39	102	23	11	3	5	6
40	105	31	56	3	7	45
41	108	42	29	3	10	33

DEE'S *Canon Gubernauticus*, 1558

56. D 15. M

Latitude	Continuate			Longitude Resolute		
D	D	M	S	D	M	S
61	115	58	41	3	2	24
62	119	06	56	3	8	15
63	122	21	29	3	14	33
64	125	42	49	3	21	20
65	129	11	28	3	28	39
66	132	48	3	3	36	35
67	136	33	16	3	45	13
68	140	7	56	3	54	40
69	144	32	59	4	5	3
70	148	49	30	4	16	31
71	153	18	44	4	29	14
72	158	02	6	4	43	22
73	163	01	12	4	59	6
74	168	17	50	5	16	38
75	173	54	2	5	36	12
76	179	52	33	5	58	31
77	186	15	43	6	23	10
78	193	08	23	6	52	40
79	200	36	50	7	28	27
80	208	49	58	8	13	8

56. D 15. M

Latitude	Continuate			Longitude Resolute		
D	D	M	S	D	M	S
41	67	23	28	1	58	6
42	69	23	22	1	59	54
43	71	25	10	2	1	48
44	73	28	58	2	3	48
45	75	34	53	2	5	55
46	77	43	1	2	8	8
47	79	52	29	2	10	28
48	82	6	25	2	12	56
49	84	21	57	2	15	32
50	86	40	14	2	18	17
51	89	01	25	2	21	11
52	91	25	40	2	24	15
53	93	53	10	2	27	30
54	96	24	08	2	30	58
55	98	58	48	2	34	40
56	101	37	24	2	38	36
57	104	20	11	2	42	47
58	107	07	24	2	47	13
59	109	59	19	2	51	55
60	112	56	17	2	56	58
61	115	58	41	3	2	24

DEE's *Canon Gubernauticus*, 1558

7 · 78.D 45.M

Latitude	Longitude Continuate			Longitude Resolute		
D	D	M	S	D	M	S
61	389	35	7	10	12	53
62	400	7	47	10	32	40
63	411	1	40	10	53	53
64	422	18	16	11	16	36
65	433	59	08	11	40	52
66	446	6	04	12	6	56
67	458	41	20	12	35	16
68	471	47	53	13	6	33
69	485	29	32	13	41	39
70	499	51	11	14	21	39
71	514	57	20	15	6	9
72	530	52	30	15	55	10
73	547	41	12	16	48	42
74	565	27	57	17	46	45
75	584	17	16	18	49	19
76	604	24	09	20	6	53
77	625	11	23	20	47	14
78	647	36	38	22	25	15
79	672	6	20	24	29	42
80	699	42	51	27	36	31

7 · 78.D 45.M

Latitude	Longitude Continuate			Longitude Resolute		
D	D	M	S	D	M	S
41	226	22	29	6	36	47
42	233	5	21	6	42	52
43	239	54	35	6	49	14
44	246	50	30	6	55	55
45	253	53	28	7	2	58
46	261	3	52	7	10	24
47	268	22	07	7	18	15
48	275	48	39	7	26	32
49	283	23	56	7	35	17
50	291	8	28	7	44	32
51	299	2	47	7	54	19
52	307	7	27	8	4	40
53	315	23	05	8	15	38
54	323	50	20	8	27	15
55	332	29	53	8	39	33
56	341	22	30	8	52	37
57	350	29	02	9	6	32
58	359	50	26	9	21	24
59	369	27	46	9	37	20
60	379	22	14	9	54	28
61	389	35	07	10	12	53

Appendix B

THE WILLS OF WILLIAM BOURNE (1573), AND DOROTHY BOURNE (1582)

EDITOR'S NOTE

The Wills of William Bourne and his wife Dorothy (formerly Mistress Beare) are preserved in the Kent County Archives at Maidstone. They are here transcribed from photostat copies of the originals.

Probate of William's Will was granted to Richard Walker on behalf of his Executrix (his widow) on 6 July 1582, which puts the year of his death beyond doubt. His widow died in December of the same year, and her Will was proved in January 1583. In both cases probate was granted by or on behalf of William Lewyn, Doctor of Law. Mistress Bourne left her four handsome rings to her sons by her first marriage, which suggests that they had been given to her by her first husband. She was unable to write her name, and affixed her mark to her Will, but this would be usual for the middle-class woman of her day. Her daughter Marie was to be 'put forth to learning', which may only refer to apprenticeship. The four younger boys were not to receive their share of the house property until they came respectively to twenty-four years of age, an age at which some apprenticeships terminated. Edward Darbishere, whom she appointed overseer of the Will, was portreeve of Gravesend at the time of her death.

WILLIAM BOURNE'S WILL

In the name of God Amen The Seconde day of Februarie 1573 *Item* ffirste I bequeathe my Sowle to all myghtie god hoping to be saved by the deathe and pretious bloodsheading of Jesus Christe etc. I bequeath my Bodye to the will and pleesare of god etc. I do geve and bequeathe unto my iiij Sonnes (that is to saye George Bourne, Richard Bourne, William Bourne and Daniell Bourne) everie one of them twentie poundes a pece to be paide unto them at the age of XXI^{tie} yeres and everie one of them to be heyre one unto an other of them. I doe geve unto George Bourne my halfe tyde that William Clegent & I are partner in to him and his heyres. And I do geve unto Daniell Bourne my other half tyde that Richard Warde and I are partner in to him and his heyres. I do geve unto my Sonne William Bourne my howse at west malling to him and his heyres. I do geve unto my mother my lease of the howses at the Townes eand to be good unto my children at her discretion. And yf that anie of my two children that have Tides do die wthout heyres, Then I will that my Sonne Richard sholde have the tyde. I do make my wife Dorothye my Executrix. And also I do geve to everie one of my iiij Sonnes as much plate as shalbe worth iij li. vis. viiid. my howses and Tenements according unto my fathers will. And Dorothie my wife to have the profittes of my houses and Tenements to bring up my children in the feare of god and to set them to Schol whereby that they may have some facultie to live

by me   Wylliam Bourne

APPENDIX B

DOROTHY BOURNE'S WILL

In the name of God Amen for Dorothie Borne of Gravesende in the Countie of Kent wedowe made and declared the viijth day of december 1582. Imprimes beyng sicke of bodye, but of perfecte memorie thankes be geven to my Lorde and Saviour Jesus Christe I commend my Sowle to the comicion of my sayde Savioure Jesus Christe by whose blessed passion I hope only to have remission of Sinnes, and to attaine to that everlasting Joye which he therby most derely hathe purchased for me and all miserable Sinners. Also I comite this my bodye to the earthe, there to be buried according to the discretion of my Executor and Overseer hereunder appointed, And now in consideration and recompense of the summe of fowre-score powndes geven by my late husband Borne to his and my fowre Sonnes, George Borne Richard Borne Willm Borne and Daniell Borne by his last will and Testament I geve and bequeathe to my sayd fowre Sonnes all that my Interest and terme of yeres wch I have yet to come of and in all those Messuages, Tenements and gardens scituat lying and beyng at the higher eands of the strete of Milton next Gravisend in the Countie of Kente, upon this Condicion not wthstanding (that is to saye that my sayd fowre Sonnes theire Executors Administrators or Assignes do paie or cause to be paide to my dawghter Marie Borne yerelie during her naturall life if the saide Terme of yeres shall so longe continue the full Summe of five powndes of Lawfull money of England at the now mansion howse of Eduard Darbyshire gent. scituat in Gravisend a foresayde. Also yf it shall fortune anie of my sayde Sonnes or ther Executors or Assignes to make defaulte of payment of his or theire porcion of money contrarie to the true intente and meaning hereof, That then my mynde is that my sayde dawghter shall enter into have and enjoye his and theire part and portion of the sayd Interest and terms of yeres of and in the premisses so makeing defaulte of payment.

anie thinge herein mentioned to the contrarie notw^{th}standing. Or if all or any of my sayd fowre Sonnes shall refuse the benefit of this my Leagacie, Then I will and my intente is, that my sayde dawghter shall solie receave and have his and theire parte and portion of the sayde interest and terme of yeres of and in the premisses so refusing. Also I geve and bequeathe to my sayde dawghter Marie thes parcelles of howsholde goodes and howseholde stuffe following, that is to say all the furniture and stuffe in the Sonne Chamber as there is now remaynethe videlicit a joyned bedsted wth iij silke curteins, a newe featherbed a new mattris, a strawe bed, ij bolsters, ij pillowes of downe, ij blankettes the best coverlett the trundle bedsted there wth all the furniture thereof, a joyned Table wth a frame, vj joyned stoles a Corte cupbord a chest, the hanginges wth the Stories, also a bed of downe in the parlor, also one paire of fine shetes. Also three other paire of the best shetes, ij of the best pillowcotes, ij of the best Towells, ij of the best Table clothes, ij dozen of the best napkins, also my churchyng kercher, Also my best saltseller of silver and gilte, also my best silver bowle parcell gilte, also my silver Canne parcell gilte, also halfe a dozen of Silver spones. Also the greatest brass potte, one chafer and skillet the best kettle, vj of the best platters vj pewter dishes, of the best sorte. Also, one dozen of plate Trenchers. Item I geve to my Sonne Samuell Bere my great rynge wth a seale also my best rynge wth the Cattay Stone, and my husbands gowne faced with beare. Also I geve unto John Beare my Sonne my golde rynge with a Rube, the cloke lyned with Beare and a Jerkin with satten Sleves. Also I geve to James Bere my Sonne my rynge with a red stone, and my husbandes best gowne garded wth velvet. Also I give to Samuell Beres wife John Beres wife and James Beres wife all my wearing Apparrell of Lynnen and wollen equallie to be devided betwene them by the discretion of my Sonne John and Edward Darbishire. Also I geve to everie of my poorest ffarmers xij^d. Also to evrie of my Maides Ten shillinges. Also I geve to Thomas ffortie vjs viij^d. Also my will and mynde is that my Sonne John Beare shall have the custodie of my daughter Marie by him to be put forthe to learning. And also I will that my saide John Bere shall have the receipte and custodie of all suche summes of money and parcells of goodes and howseholde stuffe & plate as before is bequeathed to my sayde daughter Marie untill she be maried or come to her full age of xxj^{tie} yeres wch shall firste happen. Also my will is that my Sonne John Bere shall receave to the use of my foure youngest Sonnes all the yerely Rentes and profittes coming & arising of the sayde Messuage and gardens in Milton aforesaid untill there shall come to theire severall ages of xxiiij^{tie} yeres. And I make and constitute my saide Sonne John Bere my full and whole Executor of this my Testament. And the sayde Edwarde Darbishere Supervisor of the same to which sayd Edward Darbishire I geve xs for his paines in this behalfe. In testimonie whereof I the wthin written Dorothie Borne have published this my present Testament, and for more confirmation therof have set my marke the daye and yere forthe wthin written.

Witness unto this my present will and Testament as followeth Henrie Browne Curat of Gravisend, by me Thomas ffortie. William Lucas marke

Appendix C

THE WRITINGS OF WILLIAM BOURNE,
c. 1565–1581: A BIBLIOGRAPHY

By D. W. Waters and R. A. Skelton

This includes all known or recorded manuscripts and printed editions. It will be noted that none of Bourne's published works was reprinted between 1643 and 1962.

The following abridged forms are used for bibliographical reference:

Arber: E. Arber, *A Transcript of the Registers of the Company of Stationers of London 1554–1646* (1873–7).

Bosanquet: E. F. Bosanquet, *English Printed Almanacks and Prognostications to 1600* (1917).

Greg & Boswell, *Records*: W. W. Greg and E. Boswell, *Records of the Court of the Stationers' Company, 1576 to 1602* (1930).

Jackson, *Records*: W. A. Jackson, *Records of the Court of the Stationers' Company, 1602 to 1640* (1957).

McKerrow: R. B. McKerrow, *Printers' and Publishers' Devices, 1485–1640* (1913).

McKerrow & Ferguson: R. B. McKerrow and F. S. Ferguson, *Title-Page Borders, 1485–1640* (1932).

S.T.C.: Pollard and Redgrave, *Short-Title Catalogue 1475–1640* (1926).

Wing: D. T. Wing, *Short-Title Catalogue 1640–1700* (1945–51).

Abbreviations used in the location lists are:

L.   Library.   P.L.   Public Library
C.L. College Library.   U.L.   University Library.

Private collections are cited under their owner's name: Earl

APPENDIX C

of Crawford (Haigh Hall, Wigan), E. R. Crone (Amsterdam), W. A. Engelbrecht (Rotterdam), Harrison D. Horblit (New York), Paul Mellon (Washington, D.C.), Boies Penrose (Devon, Pennsylvania), Henry C. Taylor (New York).

(1) *Manuscripts and editions published in Bourne's lifetime*

[c. 1565] ['Treatise of the nature and quality of water as touch-inge ye sinckinge or swymminge of thinges'.]
    MS; now lost. A 'written Booke' presented to Sir William Cecil. See above, p. xxv.

[c. 1566] ['A litle Boke of Statick'.]
    MS; now lost. On the measurement of the mould of a ship; claimed by Bourne to have proved helpful to seamen and shipwrights. This was presumably incorporated in Bk. IV of Bourne's *Treasure for traueilers*, printed in 1578. See above, p. xxv.

[1567] [An Almanacke and pronostication for iij. yeres with serten Rules of nauigation. London, printed by Thomas Purfoot, 1567.]
    Printed almanac for the years 1567-9. No copy is known; the title above is transcribed from the entry to Thomas Purfoot in the Stationers' Register, 1566/7 (Arber, I, 336). The edition of 1571 was substantially a reissue (see below). Bosanquet's reasons for supposing that the 1567 edition included the Rules only, without the Almanac, are unconvincing (Bosanquet, 80). An earlier printing project, suggested by the licence of 'an allmanacke and pronostication of maister Browne [sic]' to Henry Denham in 1565/6 (Arber, I, 302), explains the use of a Kalendar for 1564.

[1571] An Almanac- / ke and Prognostication / for three yeares that is / to saye for the yeare of oure / Lord. 1571. and 1572. & 1573. / nowe newlye added vnto

440

APPENDIX C

S.T.C. 3423 is a 'ghost', represented only by the imperfect B.M. copy of S.T.C. 3424.)

An unauthorized verbatim reprint of the 1574 edition (see above, p. 118), with the same declination tables. On 8 January 1577 Thomas Hacket had assigned the copy of the *Regiment* to John Wight (Greg & Boswell, *Records*, 1).

[1578] [The Arte of shootinge in greate ordonaunce. London, Henry Bynneman, 1578.]

No copy is known; the title above is transcribed from the entry to H. Bynneman in the Stationers' Register, 22 July 1578 (Arber, II, 333). The work is also listed, as in print, in Bourne's *Almanacke and Prognostication for x. yeeres*, fol. A6ᵛ (1581)

Later editions: 1587, 1643.

1578 A booke called the / Treasure for traueilers, deuided / into fiue Bookes or partes, con- / taynyng very necessary matters, for / all sortes of Trauailers, eyther by / Sea or by Lande, written by / William Bourne. / (.·.) / [ornament] / ¶ Imprinted at London for Thomas / Woodcocke, dwelling in Paules / Churchyarde, at the sygne of the / blacke Beare. / 1578.

4°. 132 leaves: *⁴ **⁴ ***⁴ A–Ff⁴ Gg² Aaa–Eeee⁴ Ffff² Aaaaa² Bbbbb–Eeeee⁴. Between sigs. G and H is a leaf, also signed H1 and bearing a woodcut of triangulation; between sigs. H and J is another (conjugate?) leaf, unsigned. Each of the five books has its own foliation: I, 1–32 (29 occurring twice, on the two leaves signed H1); II, 1–25; III, 1–22; IV, 1–21; V, [1]–16. Printed by T. Dawson. The verso of the title-page has a woodcut of the arms, crest and motto of Sir William Winter. Dedication (*2ʳ) to Sir William Winter, Master of the Queen's Ordnance at Sea. The colophon (Eeee 4ᵛ) repeats the wording of the imprint.

bridge (Pepys); Paris, Bib. Nat.; Lib. of Congress, Huntington L.; Turnbull Lib., Wellington, New Zealand. *Here reprinted*, pp. 135-281.

The manual is an expansion of the 'Rulles of Nauigation' in Bourne's *Almanacke* of 1567 and 1571. The tables of the sun's declination are for the years 1573-76. The evidence for date of publication is Bourne's reference, in the dedication (dated 6 December 1580) of his *Almanacke* of 1581, to his *Regiment for the Sea* printed 'less than vii. yeeres past'. Later editions: 1577, 1580, 1584, 1587, 1592, 1596, 1601, 1606 (?), 1611, 1617 (?), 1620, 1631. Dutch editions (trans. from London edition of 1592): 1594, 1599, 1609. Spanish edition (from part of 1580 edition): 1585.

1577 ¶ A Regiment for the Sea: Contey- / *nyng most profitable Rules, Mathe-* / matical experiences, and perfect knowledge / of Nauigation, for all Coastes and Coun- / treys: most needful and necessary for al Sea- / faryng men and Trauellers, as Pilotes, / *Mariners, Marchaunts, &c.* / Exactly deuised and made, / by William Bourne, / [woodcut of flagship] / ¶ Imprinted at London, nigh vnto the three / Cranes in the Vintree, by Thomas Dawson, / *and Thomas Gardyner, for Iohn Wight.*

[colophon, Q4ᵛ:] ¶ Imprinted at London nigh vnto the three / Cranes in the Vintree, by Thomas Dawson, and / *Thomas Gardiner, for Iohn Wyght, dwelling* / *at the North doore of Paules.* / *Anno Domini, 1577.*

4°. 76 leaves: A–C⁴ A–Q⁴. The woodcut of the flagship is now printed on the title-page, in place of the sea-astrolabe.

S.T.C. 3424. *Location:* B.M. (C.55.d.26, wanting Q4), Bodleian, National Maritime Museum (wanting Q4), St. Andrews U.L., Aberdeen U.L., Glasgow P.L.; E. R. Crone; Boston P.L. (Note that

APPENDIX C

The MS is in three parts: (1) 'Of certayne principall matters belonging vnto great Ordnance'; (2) 'Certayne conclusions of the skale of the backside of the Astrolobe' — on surveying; (3) 'A litle briefe note howe for to measure plattformes and bodyes and so foorth'. It contains the substance of Bourne's *Arte of shooting in great Ordnaunce* and *Treasure for traueilers*, both first printed in 1578.

1573 [Will of William Bourne, 2 February 1573.]
Kent Record Office, Maidstone. *Here printed*, p. 435.

[1574] ¶ A REGIMENT / for the Sea: / conteyning most profitable Rules, / *Mathematical experiences, and perfect / knowledge of Nauigation, for all Coastes and / Countreys: most needefull and necessarie for all Seafaring / men and Trauellers, as Pilotes, Mariners, / Marchants,* &c. Exactly deuised and / made by William / Bourne. / [woodcut of 'A Sea astorolob or ring'] / ¶ Imprinted at London by Thomas Hacket, and / are to be solde at his shop in the Royall Exchange, / at the Signe of the Greene Dragon.

4°. 76 leaves: A–C⁴ A–Q⁴. Sigs. A1–Q3 [second series] are foliated 1–63; ff. 25, 55, 56, 64 are unnumbered, and ff. 38, 40 are misnumbered 41, 43. The title is framed in a woodcut border (see Fig. 1 herewith). The verso of the title-page (A1ᵛ) has a woodcut representing the flagship of the Lord High Admiral *(reproduced here,* Fig. 9). Dedication (A2ʳ) to Lord Clinton and Saye, Earl of Lincoln, Lord High Admiral. No colophon.

In a variant issue (Paris, Bib. Nat.) the imprint on the title-page reads: 'Imprinted at London for Thomas Hacket...'

S.T.C. 3422. *Location:* London, R. Inst. Naval Architects (Scott Coll.), Magdalene Coll. Cammy / late Rulles of Nauiga- / tion, y^t was printed / iiij. yeres past. / [rule] / ⁋ Practised at Grausend for the Me- / ridian of London by William / Bourne student of the Ma- / thematicall science. / (. ⋮ .) / [rule] / ⁋ *Imprinted at London in* / Paules Churchyarde, at the / signe of the *Lucrece*, by / Thomas Purfoote. / (. ⋮ .)

[*colophon*, G7^v:] ⁋ Imprinted at Londō in Paules / churcheyarde, at the signe of the Lucrece / by Thomas Purfoote, / 1567.

8°. 56 leaves: A–G⁸.

Substantially a reissue of the (lost) *Almanacke* of 1567, with a new title-page and the new Almanac of the Moon. In the 'sixt Rule' slips of paper bearing dates 1571–72–73 were pasted over 1567–68–69 where the latter dates occurred.

S.T.C. 417. Bosanquet CLXXVI. *Location:* C.C.C. Oxford, Bodleian (wanting all after G.5). Here reprinted, pp. 23–114.

[*c.* 1572] 'The Property or Qualytyes of Glaces / Acordyng vnto ye seuerall mackyng / pollychynge & Gryndyng of them'.

MS, 7 leaves, undated. B.M., Lansdowne MS 121, art. 13 (Burghley papers). Dedicated to Lord Burghley, Lord Treasurer (hence after September 1572), following a conference with him. See above, pp. xxiv–xxv.

Printed by J. O. Halliwell, *Rara Mathematica* (1839), 32–47; reprinted 1841.

[*c.* 1573] [Treatise on gunnery, survey, surveying instruments, mensuration of superficies and solids, and other mathematical practices.]

MS, 107 leaves, without title and undated. B.M., Sloane MS 3651. Dedicated to Lord Burghley and apparently intended for printing, with many careful drawings and diagrams. See above, pp. xxv–xxvi.

APPENDIX C

uamente, / Por Guillelmo Bourne y Impresso en Londres / Año de M.D. LXXX.

This Spanish translation of the 'Hidrographicall discourse to goe vnto Cattay, fiue seuerall wayes' forms part (sigs. R1^r–6^v, ff. [129]–134) of the following work: HYDROGRAFIA / LA MAS CVRIOSA QVE HASTA AQVI / ha salido a luz, en que de mas de vn derrotero general, se en- / seña la nauegacion por altura y derrota, y la del Este Oeste: / con la Graduacion delos puertos, y la nauegacion / al Catayo por cinco vias diferentes. / *Compriesto por el Licenciado Andres de Poça natural de la ciudad de Orduña abogado enel muy noble y muy leal Señorio de Vizcaya.* / [device] / Impresso con priuilegio Real en Bilbao por Mathias / Mares, Año de 1585.

Location: B.M. (533.f.19).

1587 [head-piece ornament] / The Arte of shooting in great / *Ordnaunce.* / Contayning very necessary matters for all sortes of / Seruitoures eyther by Sea or by Lande. / *Written by* William Bourne. / (.·.) / [device of Thomas Woodcock, McKerrow no. 247] / Imprinted at London for / Thomas Woodcocke. / 1587.

[*colophon*, N4^v:] AT LONDON, / *Imprinted by* Thomas Dawson / for Thomas Woodcocke. / An. Dom. 1587.

4°. 54 leaves: A⁶B–N⁴. Sigs. B1^r–N3^v are paginated 1–94. Dedication (A2^r) by Bourne to Ambrose Dudley, Earl of Warwick, 'Generall *of the Queenes Maiesties Ordnaunce*'.

S.T.C. 3420. *Location:* B.M. (C.122.b.6), Royal Artillery Inst., Magdalene Coll. Cambridge (Pepys); Paris, Bib. Nat.; Lib. of Congress (wanting A1).

Presumably a reprint of the lost 1578 edition (see above). T. Woodcock had evidently acquired the copy on the death of H. Bynneman.

S.T.C. 418. Bosanquet CLXXXII. *Location:* C.C.C. Oxford. *Here reprinted,* pp. 321–413.

The Epistle to the Reader is signed (A.6ʳ): 'From the Queenes house called Vpnor Castle in Kent, the sixt of December. 1580. Thy friende W.B.' On A6ᵛ is 'A note of such bookes as haue beene written by the Author William Bourne, that are extant in Print' (four in all, being the printed editions entered here under 1578 and 1580).

(2) *Editions published after Bourne's death*

1584 ¶ A: REGIMENT: FOR: THE / SEA, CONTAIN-ING. VERY. NECESSARY MAT- / ters for all sorts of Sea-men and Trauailers, as Masters / of ships, Pilots, Marriners, and Marchants. / NEWLY CORRECTED AND / amended y [*sic*] the Author. / Wherevnto is added a Hidrographicall discourse /to goe vnto Cattay, fiue seuerall wayes, / written by William Bourne. / [woodcut of flagship] / IMPRINTED AT LONDON BY T.ESTE / for Iohn Wight.

[*colophon,* V4ʳ, *within Wight's device:*] 1584 / ¶ Imprinted at London by / T.East for Iohn Wight.

4°. 92 leaves: ¶1⁴ ¶A–¶C⁴A–V⁴. Sigs. B1–T4 are foliated 1–76 (ff. 37, 57–60 misnumbered 30, 97–100); sigs. V1–4 are foliated 70, 70, [blank], 53.

Not in S.T.C. *Location:* Edinburgh P.L.; Harvard U.L. (imp.), Yale U.L. (H. C. Taylor).

A reprint of the edition of 1580, with the same declination tables.

1585 DISCVRSO / HYDROGRAFICO / SOBRE LA NAVEGACION DEL CA- / tayo en que se platica assi delos dos camonis ya ma- / nifiestos y notorios, como de otros tres que se- / gun buen discurso y conjectura podria / auer, sacado de vn libro Ingles Ilamado Regimiento del Mar, / compriesto nue- /

seene and augmented by the foresaid Author, / William Bourne...

[*colophon*, X1ᵛ, *within woodcut printer's device of John Wight, McKerrow no. 205:*] 1580. / Imprinted at London by / T.East, for Iohn Wight.

4°. 94 leaves: ¶A–¶C⁴ A–V⁴X². (X2 blank and missing in Bodleian copy.) Sigs. A1–V4 are foliated 1–80.

S.T.C. 3425. *Location:* Bodleian, John Rylands L.; Harvard U.L., Princeton U.L. (G. Kane). *Additions here reprinted*, pp. 292–314.

This is the third edition, although only the second authorized by Bourne, who has added a second Address to the Reader, some passages in the text, and the Discourse of the Passage to Cathay; see above, pp. 283–91. The declination tables are for the years 1577–80.

1581 An Almanacke and Progno- / stication for x. yeeres, beginning / at the yeere of our Lorde 1581. and / ending the yeere 1590. being cal- / culated for the Meridian of London. / Wherein is set downe the change, quarters, / and fulles of the Moone, with the Eclipses / that doe happen in the said x. yeeres: / And also, according vnto the accustomable man- / ner, *the iudgement of the weather, and the moueable* / partes, with diuers other necessary matters, / before this time in no Almanacke / *and Prognostication.* / Written by *William Bourne*, Student and Practi- / *cioner in the Mathematicall sciences.* / [rule] / [woodcut of the earth and heavens] / [rule] / Imprinted at London by Richard Wat- / kins and Iames Robertes. 1581 / Cum Priuilegio.

[*colophon*, G2ʳ:] Imprinted at London by / Richard Watkins, and Iames / Robertes. 1581.

8°. 50 leaves: A–F⁸G². Dedication (A3ʳ) to the Earl of Lincoln, Lord High Admiral.

S.T.C. 3432. *Location:* B.M. (G.2934, wanting A4, B3; 303.c.10, wanting Fff4 and Aaaaa 1–Eeeee 4, i.e. all Bk. v), Bodleian, National Maritime Museum, Earl of Crawford, London U.L., John Rylands L., Sheffield U.L. (wanting ★1), Glasgow U.L., St Andrews U.L.; Lib. of Congress, New York P.L., Folger L., Yale U.L. (H. C. Taylor), Wisconsin U.L., Huntington L., Watkinson Lib. (Hartford, Cal.), H. D. Horblit, P. Mellon, B. Penrose; State Library of Victoria, Melbourne, Australia. Later edition: 1641.

[1578?] [Inuentions or Deuises. Very necessary for all Generalles and Captaines, or Leaders of men, as wel by Sea as by Land: Written by William Bourne. An. 1578.]

This edition, no copy of which is known, must have been printed before 6 December 1580, when Bourne listed it among his works 'extant in Print' in his *Almanacke and Prognostication for x. yeeres* (1581), fol. A6ᵛ.

The title here given is taken from the edition of *c.* 1590.

1580 'A dyscourse as tochynge yᵉ Q. majisties Shippes'.

MS. 2 leaves. B.M., Lansdowne MS 29, art. 20 (Burghley papers). Endorsed: '2 March 1579. by Willm. Bourne'. (The date is old style.)

1580 ¶ A REGIMENT FOR THE / SEA, CONTEIN-ING VERY NECESSARY MAT- / ters, for all sorts of Sea-men and Trauailers, as / Masters of ships, Pilots, Mariners & Marchaunts, / NEWLY COR-RECTED AND AMEN- / ded by the Author. / Where-vnto is added a Hidrographicall discourse / to goe vnto Cattay, fiue seuerall wayes. / Written by *William Bourne.* / [woodcut of flagship] / IMPRINTED AT LONDON BY *T.EAST.* / for Iohn Wight.

[*end,* X 1ʳ:] Thus endeth the Regimēt for the Sea, now the / third time imprinted, 1580, being exactly ouer /

1587 ¶ A Regiment for the Sea; / *Containing very necessarie matters for* / all sorts of Sea-men and trauailers, as Masters of / Ships, Pilots, Marriners, and Marchants. Newly / corrected and amended by the Author. / Where- / unto is added a Hidrographical discourse / to goe vnto Cattay, fiue seuerall wayes: Written / by William Bourne. / [woodcut of flagship] / ¶ Imprinted at London by T.East, for Iohn Wight.

[*colophon*, V4^v, *within Wight's device*:] 1587. ¶ *Imprinted at London by* / T.East, for Iohn Wight.

4°. 92 leaves: A–C⁴ A–V⁴. Sigs. A1–V2 are foliated 1–70 [*sic* for 78]; ff. 77, 78 are misnumbered 70, 70.

S.T.C. 3426. *Location:* B.M. (G.2322), C.C.C. Oxford.

A reprint of the edition of 1584, with the same declination tables.

[*c.* 1590?] Inuentions / or Deuises. / Very necessary for all Ge- / neralles and Captaines, or Lea- / ders of men, as wel by Sea as / by Land: Written by / *William Bourne.* / *An. 1578.* / [ornament] / At LONDON / Printed for *Thomas Woodcock.* / dwelling in Paules Churchyard, / at the signe of the black / Bear.

4°. 62 leaves: ¶4*4 A–N⁴O². Sigs. B1^r–O2^v are paginated 1–98. The title is framed in a woodcut border (McKerrow & Ferguson, no. 117 and p. 104; the date of printing being inferred by them from the state of wear of the woodblock). Dedication by Bourne (¶2^r) to Lord Howard of Effingham. No colophon. It was printed by T. Orwin.

S.T.C. 3421. *Location:* B.M. (C.71.cc.16), Patent Office, War Office, Emmanuel Coll. Cambridge, Peterborough Cath., Nat. Lib. of Scotland; Paris, Bib. Nat.; New York P.L., Folger L., Huntington L., H. D. Horblit.

APPENDIX C

The book was in print by 1581 (above, pp. 445, 447). No later edition. Woodcock's copyrights were transferred by his widow, after his death in 1594, to Paul Linley (Arber, III, 58), and the *Inventions* was entered to John Flasket on 26 June 1600 (Arber, III, 164–5); but it was never reprinted.

1592 A Regiment for the Sea, / Containing verie necessarie matters for all / sorts of men and trauailers; wherevnto / is added an Hydrographicall discourse / touching the fiue seuerall passa- / ges to Cattay; written by / William Borne. / Newlie corrected and amended by Thomas Hood; who / hath added a new *Regiment*, / and Table / of declination. / [woodcut of flagship] ¶ Imprinted at London by T.Est, for Thomas Wight. 4°. 92 leaves: A² ¶ B–¶ C⁴ A–V⁴X². Sigs. A1–V3 are foliated 1–79. Dedication (A2ʳ) by Thomas Hood to the Earl of Cumberland, for 'the inclination of your mynde to marine causes'. No colophon. S.T.C. 3427. *Location:* B.M. (C.60.f.8; Gabriel Harvey's copy), Magdalene Coll. (Pepys), Norwich P.L., Peterborough Cath. (see below, 1596); Folger L., New York P.L., Williams Coll. Mass.

Evidence for date: the B.M. copy is in a contemporary vellum binding with Hood's *The Marriners guide*, 1592, which has a separate title-page and separate signatures. John Wight had died in 1589, and his business was continued by his son Thomas. This is the first edition edited by Hood, who added his own dedication and address to the reader and revised the declination tables to run 1593–96.

1594 De Const der Zee-vaerdt, / begrypende seer nootwendighe saecken / voor allerhande Zee-vaerders, als Schippers, Stuerlieden, / Piloten, Bootsvolck ende Coop-lieden. / Van nieus door den Authoor oversien ende verbetert, midsgaders een bequaem / Hydro-

graphical discours, om door 5. verscheyden wegen na Cathaia eñ / China te seylen; Beschreven door den seer ervarenen / Willem Bourne, Engelsman. / [woodcut of a ship] / t'Amstelredam, by Cornelis Claesz. op't Water, in't Schrijf-boeck. A°. 1594.
4°. 60 leaves: *⋆*4 A–O⁴. Sigs. A2–O3 are foliated 2–55. No colophon.
Location: Nederlandsch Historisch Scheepvaart Museum, Amsterdam.

For Bourne's two prefaces, following the dedicatory letter, is substituted the Dutch printer's address to the reader (*⋆* 3), beginning: 'Den Drucker tot den Leser / door L.T. / Den goetwillighen Leser sal verstaen / dat wy tot dienst van de lofwaerdighe Zee-vaert / door oversettinghe uyt den Engelsche in onse Nederlandtsche sprake in druck ende aenden dagh ghebrocht hebben / dit nuttelijck boecxken / ghenoemt de Cunst der Zee-vaert . . .'. This is a free Dutch translation from the 1592 edition of *A Regiment for the Sea*, with declination tables for the years 1593–96. Mr G. A. Cox, Director of the Nederlandsch Historisch Scheepvaart Museum, who kindly supplied a description of this edition, conjectures the translator to have been Lucas Jansz. Waghenaer, as suggested by the following interpolation in Chapter 15 (f. 35): 'Omdat ghy daerom nu te beter weten moecht / soo heb ick in mijn tweede Boeck / ghenoemt het Tresoor der Zeevaert, uytghetoghen sekere principael plaetsen door de gheheele werelt / . . .'. The *Thresoor der Zeevaert*, Waghenaer's second book, had been published at Leyden in 1592, and was reprinted by Claesz. in 1596. 'L.T.', who signs the printer's address, is perhaps Leonard Terwoort of Antwerp, who in 1574–6 had engraved five maps for Saxton

APPENDIX C

and in 1591 engraved a plate of a sector for Thomas Hood, published in Hood's *The making and vse of the Geometricall Instrument called a Sector* (1598). (See A. M. Hind, *Engraving in England in the Sixteenth and Seventeenth Centuries*, 1 (1952), 98.) We owe this suggestion to Mlle. G. de la Roncière and M. Roger Hervé, of the Bibliothèque Nationale, Paris, who kindly supplied information on the edition of 1609.

1596 A Regiment for the Sea, containing / verie necessarie matters for all sorts of men and / trauailers, whervnto is added an Hidrographicall discourse / touching the fiue seuerall passages into Cattay, written by / William Borne / Newly corrected and amended by Thomas Hood, D. in Phisicke, who hath ad- / ded a new Regiment, and Table of declination / Wherevnto is also adioyned the Mariners guide, with a perfect / Sea Carde by the said Thomas Hood. / [woodcut of flagship] ¶ Imprinted at London by T.Este, for Thomas Wight. 1596.

4°. 92 leaves: A² ¶ B-¶ C⁴ A-V⁴X². Sigs. A1-V3 are foliated 1-79; fol. 38 is misnumbered 18. No colophon.

S.T.C. 3428. *Location:* B.M. (G.7311 (1)), National Maritime Museum, Magdalene Coll. Cambridge (Pepys); Folger L., New York P.L., Haverford C.L., Minnesota U.L. (Bell).

A reprint of the edition of 1592, with the same declination tables, and with the addition of Hood's *The Mariners Guide, with a perfect Sea Carde*; this has separate title-page and signatures. The only known copy complete with chart is that of New York P.L., but Peterborough Cath. has *The Mariners Guide* (with chart) bound up with the 1592 *Regiment*, and an impression of the chart alone is in the Pepysian Library (here reproduced, Fig. 12).

1599 De Const der Zee-vaerdt, / begrypende seer noot-wendighe saecken voor aller- / hande Zee-vaerders, als Schippers, Stuerlieden, Piloten, / Boots-volck ende Coop-lieden. / Van nieus door den Authoor oversien eñ verbetert, midsgaders een bequaem / Hydrographical discours, om door 5. verscheyden wegen na Cathaia eñ / China te seylen; Beschreven door den seer ervarenen / Willem Bourne, Enghelsman. / [woodcut of a ship, as 1594 edn] / t'Amstelredam, by Cornelis Claesz. op't Water, in't Schrijf-boeck. An. 1599.

4°. 60 leaves: ★★★4A–O4. Sigs. A2–O3 are foliated 2–55. No colophon.

Location: B.M. (C.125.c.35).

A reprint of the edition of 1594, with the same declination tables.

1601 A / Regiment / for the Sea. / *Contayning very necessarie matters* / for all sorts of men and trauailers: / Whereunto is added an Hydrographicall / *discourse touching the fiue seuerall* / passages into Cattay. / Written by William Borne. / Newly corrected and amended by Tho.Hood, / *D. in Physicke, who hath added a new Regiment* / for the yeare 1600. and three years following, / and a Table of declination. / Whereunto is also adioyned the *Mariners guide*, with / a perfect Sea Carde by the said / Thomas Hood. / AT LONDON, / Printed by T. Wight. / 1601.

4°. 106 leaves: ¶A2 ¶B C4 A–V4Y4Aa4. No colophon. The signatures are continuous throughout, those of *The Mariners Guide* being V2ᵛ–Aa4ᵛ.

The title is enclosed in a woodcut border showing navigation instruments and ships (McKerrow & Ferguson no. 265).

Not in S.T.C. *Location:* E. R. Crone; Yale U.L. (H. C. Taylor).

A reprint of the edition of 1596, with new declina-

APPENDIX C

tion tables for 1600–03. In this edition Hood promises shortly 'a booke called the Mariners ease' (fol. 19). Information on this edition was kindly supplied by Mr Taylor.

This seems to be the last edition put out by Hood, the date of whose death is given as 1598 by *D.N.B.* and by Venn, *Alumni Cantabrigienses*.

[1606?] [A Regiment for the Sea. London, Edmund Weaver, 1606?]

This edition, of which no copy is known to exist, is cited by Anthony Linton, *Newes of the Complement of the Arte of Navigation* (London, 1609), fol. 24: 'The Regiment of the Sea, printed at *London, Anno* 1606.'

The *Regiment* was entered to Edmund Weaver, with the assent of T. Wight, on 6 May 1605 and 2 March 1607 (Arber, III, 288–9, 342). The copy still belonged to Wight, who was a draper and not a member of the Stationers' Company.

1609 De Conste der Zee-vaert, / begrypende seer nootwendighe saecken voor alder- / hande Zeevaerders, als Schippers, Stuerlieden, / Piloten, Bootsvolck ende / Cooplieden. / Van nieus door den Autheur oversien ende verbetert, midts / gaders een bequaem Hydrographical discours, om door vijf ver- / scheydenē weghen naer Cathaia ende China te seylen; / beschreven door den seer ervarenen Willem / Bourne, Enghels-man. / [woodcut of shipping, including galleys and galleons] / 't Amsterdam, by Cornelis Claesz. op't Water int / Schrijf-boeck. Anno 1609.

4°. 60 leaves: ★★★⁴A–O⁴. Sigs. A2–O3 are foliated 2–55. No colophon.

Location: Paris, Bib. Nat.

A reprint of the edition of 1599, with the same declination tables.

1611 A / Regiment / for the Sea. / *Containing very necessarie matters* / to all sorts of men and trauailers: / whereunto is added an Hydrographicall / *discourse touching the fiue seuerall* / *passages into Cattay*: / Written by *William Borne*. / Corrected and amended by *Thomas Hood, D.* / *in Phisicke, who hath added a new Regiment* / and a Table of declination with the Mariners guide, and a perfect Sea Card there- / unto belonging. / AT LONDON: / Printed by *Thomas Snodham*, for / *Edmund Weaver*. / 1611.

4°. 86 leaves: A–N⁸. Sigs. B3–N8 are foliated 1–95. The title is enclosed in the same woodcut border as in the edition of 1601. No colophon.

S.T.C. 3429. *Location:* B.M. (51.c.3), London U.L.; W. A. Engelbrecht.

On 7 November 1608 Thomas Snodham became a master printer in place of Thomas East deceased, whose business he had bought from the widow (Jackson, *Records*, 36). Thomas Wight had died in 1608; see note under edition of [1606?].

A reprint, with declination tables for 1609–12.

[1617?] [A Regiment for the Sea. London, E. Weaver, 1617?].

A lost edition, conjectured from the facts that the tables in the 1620 edition commence from 1617 and that the examples of their use are for 1617.

1620 A / Regiment / for the Sea: / *Containing very necessary matters* / for all sorts of men and trauailers: / whereunto is added an Hydrographicall / *discourse, touching the fiue seuerall* / *passages into Cattay.* / Written by *William Borne.* / Whereunto is added a new Regiment, A Table / *of Declination, the Mariners guide, with a per-* / fect Sea Card thereunto belonging, by / *Thomas Hood, D. in Physicke.* / Newly corrected this yeere 1620. / AT LONDON / Printed by *W.I.* for *Edmund* / *Weauer*. 1620.

4°. 106 leaves: ¶² A–N⁸. Sigs. B1–N8 are foliated

APPENDIX C

1–96. The title is enclosed in the same woodcut border as in the editions of 1601 and 1611. No colophon. The printer was William Jones.
S.T.C. 3430. *Location:* B.M. (1395.g.32), Glasgow U.L., Lincoln Cath.
With declination tables for 1617–20.

1631 A / REGIMENT / for the Sea: / *Containing very necessary matters* / for all sorts of men and travailers: / Whereunto is added an Hydrographicall / discourse, touching the fiue severall / *Passages into Cattay.* / Written by *William Borne.* / [rule] / Whereunto is added a new Regiment, a Ta- / ble of *Declination*, the *Mariners Guide*, with a / perfect Sea *Card* thereto belonging, / by *Thomas Hood* D. in Phisicke. / Newly corrected this yeare 1631. / [rule] / AT LONDON / Printed by *W.I.* for *Thomas Weauer*, / and are to be sold at his shop at / the great North Dore / of Paules. 1631.

4°. 106 leaves: Π² A–M⁸ N–O⁴. Sigs. B1–D4 are foliated 1–20; D5–E2 unnumbered; E3–O2 foliated 29–96. No colophon.
S.T.C. 3431. *Location:* Bodleian; Harvard U.L.
Although Edmund Weaver lived until 1638, his rights in the *Regiment* seem by 1631 to have been transferred to his son Thomas.
A reprint of the edition of 1620, with declination tables for 1633–36. The address to the reader is signed 'Thomas Hood, 1633'.

1641 A MATE FOR / MARINERS, / And a Treasure for / TRAVELLERS. / [rule] Wherein is shewed the taking of Heigth's / and Distances, and plotting of Countries. / The Longitude and Latitude of the most notable / Places of the World, their Bearing and Distance / from LONDON. / *The measuring of all Superficies and Sollides.* / Building of Ships by proportion and how to molde / them that they may be good Saylors and well qualified. / To find their Weight swimming, with their Lading and / Tackling, and to weigh such as are Sunke. / [rule] LIKEWISE, / *Tables of the Sunnes Declination and right Ascention, and* / the Declination of the principall fixed Starres, / for finding the Latitude. / And also, certaine Tables for the more easie and exact / casting up of any *Traverse*, and resolving of any / *Proposition* in plaine Sayling. / [rule] LONDON, / Printed by *B. Alsop* and *T. Fawcet*, for WILLIAM LUGGER, and / are to be sold at his Shop on *Tower*-Hill, neere the *Posterne*- / Gate, 1641.

[*colophon*, Ee4^r:] LONDON, / Printed by B. ALSOP and THO: FAWCET, for / WILLIAM LUGGER, and are to be sold at his Shop / on *Tower*-Hill, neere the *Posterne*- / Gate, 1641.

4°. 114 leaves: A²a⁴B–Z⁴ Aa–Ee⁴. Sigs. BI^r–Aa⁴^v are paginated 1–184.

Not in Wing. *Location:* Marsh's L. Dublin (wanting sigs. A, Dd, Ee); H. D. Horblit.

This contains Bks. I–IV of *The Treasure for traueilers*, reprinted from the edition of 1578, the separate tables of contents for each book being now brought together in the preliminaries, and the dedication omitted. In place of Bk. V, this edition has 16 leaves Bb1–Ee4) with declination tables for 1640–43, 'Questions of Navigation', and tables of diff. of latitude and departure.

The rights in *The Treasure for traueilers*, having passed from T. Woodcock's widow to Paul Linley (9 February 1596; Arber, III, 58) and from him to J. Flasket (26 June 1600), 'evidently became derelict and were granted to W. Lugger on 7 December 1640' (Jackson, *Records*, 338, 489).

1643 THE / ARTE / OF / SHOOTING / IN GREAT /

APPENDIX C

ORDNANCE. / CONTAINING VERY / NECESSARY MATTERS / for all sorts of Servitours either / by Sea or by Land. / *Written by* William Bourne. / [ornament and rules] / LONDON, / Printed in the yeare, 1643.

[*sig.* K1^r:] THE / GUNNERS / DIALOGUE / WITH THE ART OF / Great *Artillery*. / BY / ROBERT NORTON / Enginier and Gunner. / [ornament and rules] / LONDON / Printed in the year, 1643.

4°. 51 leaves: A^{3}B–N^4. Sigs. B3^r–N1^v are paginated 5–92; the last three leaves are folding diagrams. No colophon.

Wing 3859. *Location:* B.M. (57.b.25 (2, 3)), Bodleian, Aberdeen U.L.; Harvard U.L., Yale U.L.

Bound up, in the B.M. copy, with two other tracts on gunnery, which have on their respective title-pages printer's devices at this date in the possession of E. Griffin (McKerrow no. 306) and R. Bishop (McKerrow no. 292).

The previous edition (1587) was printed by T. Woodcock. After his death in 1594 his copyrights were assigned by his widow to Paul Linley (Arber, III, 58); on 26 June 1600 that of *The Arte of Shooting* was entered to John Flasket (Arber, III, 164–5), and on 20 December 1619 it was assigned by Valentine Simms to E. Griffin.

1839 A Treatise / on the properties and qualities of glasses / for optical purposes, / according to the making, polishing and grinding of them. / By William Bourne / From MS. Lansd. Mus. Brit. 121.

Pp. [32]–47 in J. O. Halliwell, *Rara Mathematica* (London, 1839; reprinted 1841).

The original MS is entered above, [*c.* 1572].

1962 A REGIMENT FOR THE SEA / *and other writings on navigation* / by / WILLIAM BOURNE / *of Gravesend, a*

458

Fig. 16. Tail-piece from John Wight's edition of
A Regiment for the Sea (1580)

gunner / (c. 1535–1582) / Edited by / E. G. R. TAYLOR / *Emeritus Professor of Geography in the University of London* / CAMBRIDGE / *Published for the Hakluyt Society* / AT THE UNIVERSITY PRESS / 1963

The present edition.

NOTE TO THE BIBLIOGRAPHY

ALL editions of *A Regiment for the Sea*, from 1574 to 1631, contain tables of the sun's declination (above, pp. 187–205), calculated for each day of a four-year (or leap-year) cycle, the years being numbered 1, 2, 3 and *bissextilis*. These tables are preceded by a twenty-year cyclic table (above, p. 189), enabling the declination tables to be used for four further leap-year cycles, i.e. for twenty years in all: '... these foure yeres being expired, you must after the year of Bissextilis, beginne agayne at the yere one.' In the *Regiment* of 1620 only this cyclic table embraces five further leap-year cycles, i.e. twenty-four years in all.

In the Bibliography, the declination tables of editions of the *Regiment* have been described as for the four-year period.

INDEX

advertisements, 317, 328
almanac, xxiii, xxiv, 2; of the moon, 10–12; (1571–3) 37–49; (1581–90) 345–94
altitude, 83–7, 166
Antarctic Circle, 162; Polar Circle, 163
Apian, Peter, xv
Arab navigators, 12, 18
Arctic Circle, 119, 161; Polar Circle, 163
astrolabe, 15, 83–5, 122, 206–8
astrology, 12, 325
auge, 120, 168
Averall, William, 316

Bacon, Nicolas, xxiii
Baker, Humfrey, xxiii n
Baker, William, xxxiv
Barking Creek, 294
Barlow, Richard, 5, 122, 286
Barlow, William, 317
Beare, Dorothy, see Bourne, Dorothy
Beare, James, xx, xxi n, 8, 284, 287, 290, 437
Beare, John, xx, xxi, 437–8
Beare, Samuel, xx, 437
Besson, Jacques, xxvii
Best, George, 287, 290
Billingsgate Stairs, xvii
Billingsley, Henry, xxviii
Borough, John a, 6
Borough, Stephen, xviii, xix, xxix, 6, 7, 416
Borough, William, xviii, xix, xxix, 6, 288, 416
Bourne, Dorothy, xx, 435–6
Bourne, George, 435–6
Bourne, John, xx
Bourne, Marie, xxi, 434–6
Bourne, Samuel, 435–6
Bourne, William, as citizen, xx; his death, xxiv; and Dr Dee, xxxii, 290, 313; at Gravesend, xv–xix; a gunner, xix, xxxii, 115; an innkeeper, xiii, xxii; his instruments, xxix, xxx, 13, 109, 111, 131; a mathematical practitioner, xxii, 9, 321; parentage and private life, xx–xxiv; his reading, xvi, xxvii–xxix, 326; his surveying, xxix, xxxi; gunner at Upnor Castle, xxxii, 313; his Will, 434–5; his writings, xiii, xiv, xxiv–xxvii, xxxii, 440–59
Bourne, William (the younger), 435–436
Browne, Henry, 438
Bulwarks, Gravesend and Tilbury, xix
Burghley, Lord, xxiv–xxvi, 117

Cabot, Sebastian, xviii, xxviii n, 6, 7, 290
Calais, xv, 6
Calicut, 288
Canary Islands, 94, 97, 238–9
Cartier, Jacques, 5
Cathay, 6, 285, 286, 301–14
Chancellor, Nicholas, xxii
Chancellor, Richard, xviii, 6
charts, 4, 5, 19, 107, 130, 131, 231, 294
Christopher Inn, xviii
Clinton, Lord, xxvii, xxxiii, 115, 116, 319
coastal survey, 233–7
Cole, Humfrey, xxvii, xxxiv, 14
colures, 163
comets, 318, 409, 410
compass, magnetic, 3; points of, 59, 60, 172–4; as time-piece, 20; variation of, 5, 85, 86, 211, 212, 273–7
Continental Shelf, 1

INDEX

Copernicus, 11
Copland, Robert, 2
Cortes, Martin, his *Art of Navigation*, 7, 8, 9, 16, 20, 89, 91, 109, 117, 125, 132, 188, 230, 266, 273, 276, 384
course made good, 125
cross-staff, 8, 15, 87–9, 122, 126, 206, 209, 237
Cuningham, William, xv n, 123 n, 285
currents, ocean, 284, 288, 306–7

'dangers', 1, 2
Darbishere, Edward, xxi, 434, 436–8
Davis, John, 268, 416
day, length of, 226–9
declination, 14, 15, 167, 187; how to handle, 211–24; *see also* tables
Dee, John, xxiii, xxv, 7, 122, 124, 285, 286, 290, 313, 316; his *Preface*, xxviii, xxix, 121; his *Tables*, 20, 415–34
degree, 166; great, 16; of latitude, 16; of longitude, 16, 95–6; raising a, 16, 89–91, 125
dial, *see* sandglass
dial, equinoctial, 13, 109, 110, 131
Dieppe, 5, 6
Digges, Leonard, xv, xvi, xxiii
Digges, Thomas, xxii–xxiv, xxv, xxix, xxxii, xxxiii, 15
dip (magnetic), 15
distance and departure, 16, 89–91, 125, 231—3
Dragon's head and tail, 168
Drake, Francis, 3, 132, 315
Dudley, John, xxiii

ecliptic, 163
Eden, Richard, xxvii, xxvii n, 7, 133, 284
engineers, military, 1
epact, 60–2, 174; *see also* tables
ephemerides, 11
equinoctial circle, 160
establishment of the port, 2, 13
excentric, 120, 296

Feild, John, 11
Fenton, Edward, xxii
Fernelius, Johannes, xxviii n
Finaeus, Orontius, xv
fixed stars, 99–111; navigation by, 254–5; tables of, 256–64
Frobisher's Voyages, 284, 285
Frozen Sea, 224

Gemini, Thomas, xvi, xvii
Gemma Frisius (Jewafritius), xv, 107
Gilbert, Humfrey, 224, 286
globe, sailing by the, 107–10, 246–9
golden number, *see* prime
Grand Bankes, 3, 5
Gravesend, xvi–xix, 3 n, 434, 438; latitude, 85; tides, 67, 183
Greenwich Palace, xvi, xix
guard stars, 8

Hacket, Thomas, 115, 118
Hakluyt, Richard, xviii, 3 n, 133, 286, 288
Hariot, Thomas, 15, 122, 131
Harvey, Gabriel, xxxiv, 115
Hatton, Christopher, 416
Hawkins, John, 132
Henry VIII, 1, 5, 6, 17
Hester, John, xxxiv
Honter, Johann, 285
Hood, Thomas, 131, 319
Hore, Richard, 3
horizon circle, 159
Howard, Lord Charles, xxvii n, xxxiii, 319
Hudson's Strait, 290

Ibn-Majid, 121
instruments, *see* astrolabe, compass, cross-staff, equinoctial dial

Jewafritius, *see* Gemma Frisius
Jugge, Richard, 8, 9, 15, 109, 124, 266 n, 284
kalendar, 9, 10, 11, 12; (of 1564) 25–36; (of 1574) 146–51; (of 1581) 332–43

INDEX

landmarks, 2
latitude (in England), 96–9, 243–5; by a fixed star, 17–18; navigation by, 415; by sun and star, 14, 15, 167
Law Terms, 157, 331
lead & line, 3; *see also* soundings
Leicester, Earl of, xv n
Leovitius, Cyprianus, 11, 318, 406
Lisle, Viscount, 6
Lisle, Lord, 6
Lloyd, Humfrey, 12
log, English, 126–8, 237, 238, 297–9
log, mechanical, xxvii
Lok, Michael, 285
Long, Ferry, xvii, xxi
longitude, 238, 239; in England, 96–99, 243–5; degree of, 16, 17, 128–130; and time, 17, 96–9; by eclipses, 94
Lord Admiral, Lord High Admiral, *see* Clinton; *see also* Lisle
Lucar, Cyprian, 286
Lucar, Emanuel, 286
Lumley, Lord, 11, 12, 319
lunar distance, 17, 239
lunar kalendar, 2; *see also* almanac

Madox, Richard, xxii, 17
Marco Polo, xxxii, 290
mariner, *see* navigator
mariner's compass, 3, 59–60, 172–4, 211, 212
mathematical books, xiv; instruments, xv, 4; practitioners, xxiii, xxxiv; tables, xv, 4
mathematics, applied, xiv–xvi
Medway, River, xvi, xxxiii n
Mellis, John, xxiii n
Mercator, Gerard, 19, 130, 287
meridian, how to find, 86, 209, 210
meridian circle, 159
minute of measure, 166; of time, 166
Moon, age of the, 2, 60–2, 174–6; motions of, 68–72, 120, 296; rising and setting of, 183–7; and the Zodiac, 395–8; *see also* lunar kalendar, almanac

Morris, William, xxii
Mortlake, xxxii, 313
Muscovy Company, xiii, 7, 124

'Navigation, the New', 1, 3, 4, 5, 6, 18; Rules of, 12; Use of, 169; by the Fixed Stars, 99–111
'navigator, a good', 12, 56–8, 121, 170
New Year, dates of, 318, 398
nocturnal, 18
Norman, Robert, xxxiv, 14, 18, 132
North-East Passage, 225, 288, 293, 309
North Parts, 299, 300, 310–16
North Star, Regiment of, 230; *see also* Pole Star
North-West Passage, 225, 293, 308
Nova Zemla, 225, 288
Nunes, Pedro, 15, 122, 130

Orontius Finaeus, 19, 107
Ortelius, Abraham, 124, 288

Palissy, Bernard, xxxv
paradoxall compass, 415, 416
parallax, 120, 121, 122, 239
Paramantia, Cape, 124, 125
Peele, James, xxii n
perspective glasses, xxiv, xxv
pilots, 2, 3, 4, 7, 12
planets, nature of the, 53, 54, 405–8
Pleiades, tables of the, 20, 110–12, 411–13
Plutarch, xxviii, 326
Pointers, the, 8
Polar Route, 5, 310–14
Pole, raising the, 15, 16; raising the Pole Star, 8, 13, 14, 87–9
Poles of the World, 164; of the Zodiac, 164
Popinjay, Richard, xxxiii
Portsmouth, xxxiii
precession of the equinoxes, 15, 18
prime, 60–2; *see also* tables
Ptolemy, 3, 94
Purfoot, Thomas, 8, 9, 114

INDEX

Rastall, John, xiv
Rathborne, Aaron, 317
Recorde, Robert, xiv, xv, 19, 107
Regiment of the North Star, 125, 230
Reinhold, Erasmus, 12
rhumbs, 13
Ribault, Jean, 6
Rotz, Jean, 5, 6, 17
rules to know the (Law) Terms, 159; for letting of blood, etc., 50, 402–405; of navigation, 12, 55–112
Rutter of the Sea, 2

Sacrobosco, Johannes de, 18, 107
sandglass, 3, 18, 119
sea manual, 2, 18, 19
sea mile, 16
Seven Stars, *see* Pleiades
Shepherds' Kalendar, 10, 11
ships: *Anne Francis*, 290; *Edward Bonaventure*, xix, 7, 115 n; *Foresight*, 115 n, 116 n; *Revenge*, 116 n; *Searchthrift*, xviii
Sidney, Sir Henry, 6
solar declination, 3, 5, 14, 15, 122, 211–24, 331–44; *see also* tables
soundings, 1, 3, 16; in the Channel, 91, 92, 131, 270, 271
Star, New, in Cassiopeia, 315, 316, 408, 409
stars, fixed, *see* fixed stars
Stationers' Company, 8, 118 n
Sun, altitude of, 83–7; declination, 3, 5, 14, 15, 122, 211–24, 331–44; motions of, 68, 69

tables: Dee's, 20, 415–34; declination, 14, 15, 122, 190–205, 211–24, 331–44; fixed stars, 18, 100, 102–5, 256, 264; Pleiades, 20, 110–12, 411–13; prime and epact, 61, 117, 152, 175; prime, Sunday letter, leap year and moveable feasts, 152; reign of Kings, 156; tides, 65, 67, 181, 183
Taisnier, Jean, 284
Tartaglia, Nicholas, xv, xxvii
Thames floods, 401
theodolite, xxix
Thorne, Robert, 5, 286
tide barges, xvii; computer, 14 n
Tilbury, xvii, xix
trans-polar route, 310–14
transit, 14
triangulation, xix
Trinity House, xviii
Tropic Circles, 161

Upnor Castle, xvi, xxxii, 313

variation, of the needle, 14, 85, 86, 132; *see also* compass
vernacular texts, xiv–xvi
Vespucci, Amerigo, 17

Ward, Luke, xxii
Warwick, Earl of, xxvii
weather, signs of the, 399–402
Werner, Johann, 15 n
Wight, John, 118
Willes, Richard, 286
Winter, John, 288
Winter, Sir William, xix, xxvii, 284 n
Wright, Edward, 130
writing masters, xxii, xxiii

year, first day of the, 398

zenith, 165
Zodiac, 162; motions of the Sun and Moon through, 68–73, 318; Poles of the, 164; signs of the, 52, 403–5, 407–8